general editor John M. MacKenzie

When the 'Studies in Imperialism' series was founded more than twenty years ago, emphasis was laid upon the conviction that 'imperialism as a cultural phenomenon had as significant an effect on the dominant as on the subordinate societies'. With more than fifty books published, this remains the prime concern of the series. Cross-disciplinary work has indeed appeared covering the full spectrum of cultural phenomena, as well as examining aspects of gender and sex, frontiers and law, science and the environment, language and literature, migration and patriotic societies, and much else. Moreover, the series has always wished to present comparative work on European and American imperialism, and particularly welcomes the submission of books in these areas. The fascination with imperialism, in all its aspects, shows no sign of abating, and this series will continue to lead the way in encouraging the widest possible range of studies in the field. 'Studies in Imperialism' is fully organic in its development, always seeking to be at the cutting edge, responding to the latest interests of scholars and the needs of this ever-expanding area of scholarship.

Scotland, the Caribbean and the Atlantic world, 1750–1820

Manchester University Press

Scotland, the Caribbean and the Atlantic world 1750–1820

Douglas J. Hamilton

MANCHESTER
UNIVERSITY PRESS
Manchester and New York

distributed exclusively in the USA
by PALGRAVE

Copyright © Douglas J. Hamilton 2005

The right of Douglas J. Hamilton to be identified as the author of this work has been asserted by him in accordance with the Copyright, Designs and Patents Act 1988.

Published by Manchester University Press
Oxford Road, Manchester M13 9NR, UK
and Room 400, 175 Fifth Avenue, New York, NY 10010, USA
www.manchesteruniversitypress.co.uk

Distributed in the United States exclusively by
Palgrave Macmillan, 175 Fifth Avenue,
New York, NY 10010, USA

Distributed in Canada exclusively by
UBC Press, University of British Columbia, 2029 West Mall,
Vancouver, BC, Canada V6T 1Z2

British Library Cataloguing-in-Publication Data is available

Library of Congress Cataloging-in-Publication Data is available

ISBN 978 0 7190 7183 6 paperback

First published by Manchester University Press in hardback 2005

This paperback edition first published 2010

The publisher has no responsibility for the persistence or accuracy of URLs for any external or third-party internet websites referred to in this book, and does not guarantee that any content on such websites is, or will remain, accurate or appropriate.

Printed by Lightning Source

For Mum and Dad

CONTENTS

List of tables — viii
General editor's introduction — ix
List of abbreviations — xi
Note on currency — xii
Acknowledgements — xiii
Map of eighteenth-century Scotland — xiv
Map of the Windward archipelago and the
eighteenth-century Caribbean — xv

	Introduction	*page* 1
1	Scotland in the eighteenth century	11
2	The eighteenth-century West Indies	32
3	Scots on the plantations	55
4	Mercantile connections	84
5	Scots doctors in the West Indies	112
6	Scots in West Indian politics	140
7	Scots, the Caribbean and British imperial politics	169
8	Repatriation from the West Indies	195
	Conclusion	221

Bibliography — 224
Index — 245

LIST OF TABLES

1.1	Scottish migration to the West Indies, 1750–99	*page* 23
2.1	Plantation settlement in Tobago, 1770	43
3.1	The enslaved population on Hampden estate, Jamaica, 1771–80	77
4.1	Sugar prices at Glasgow, autumn 1777	97
6.1	Scots in the Windward Island legislatures, c. 1766–96	145

GENERAL EDITOR'S INTRODUCTION

On Friday 8 April 1831, Sir Walter Scott recorded in his journal that he had been taking his leave of his friend Major John Scott, who 'being afflicted with a distressing asthma has resolved upon selling his house of Ravenswood which he had dressed up with much neatness and going abroad to Jamaica'. This intriguing entry looks both backwards and forwards. On the one hand, the West Indies were far from being unknown territory for the Scots over the previous century and a half. On the other, going there for one's health would have seemed bizarre in that earlier period, when the Caribbean vied with India for unhealthiness. Seeking a superior, health-giving climate was to become much more a characteristic of the later nineteenth and twentieth centuries.

When Robert Burns was famously saved from heading for Jamaica by the success of his Kilmarnock edition in 1786, he had already written a song, 'Will ye go to the Indies, my Mary?', in which he invited Mary Campbell 'to leave auld Scotia's shore' and join him. 'But a' the charms o' the Indies', he wrote, 'Can never equal thine'. In 1792, another of his amours, Nancy Craig McLehose, sailed for Kingston to join her husband, only to find that he had taken a black mistress. These literary references indicate that, if the Indies had its charms, it also had its Scots population.

Yet the role of Scots in the Caribbean has never featured strongly in the historical literature. When we think of the Scots overseas, we have tended to concentrate on North America, or India, or perhaps New Zealand. We often imagine that the Scots were attracted by terrain and climates which they found fairly familiar, like Nova Scotia or Otago. In the past, the literature has also focused primarily on the 'long nineteenth century', the era from the time of the Clearances to the wave of migration that preceded the First World War. Douglas Hamilton sets out to show us how far the Scots were also active in the West Indies in the eighteenth century.

Using a wide range of records in the Caribbean, the United States and the United Kingdom, he examines the Scottish social and economic contexts from which they departed, the conditions, charming or not, in which they found themselves in the West Indies and the various ways in which they participated in the life of the islands in that period. They were already following a considerable tradition of Scots migration within the Atlantic world, reflecting the growing power of Glasgow and other Scots towns in the trades of North America and the Caribbean. Their education and their traditional specialisms gave them a considerable role in plantation management, in merchant activity, in the military and in professions like the medical. They became active in local politics, interacted with the slave population and with other colonists, and also repatriated cash to oil activities at home, in developing estates, expanding mercantile companies, funding education and paying their way into metropolitan politics.

GENERAL EDITOR'S INTRODUCTION

It is an important story which contributes greatly to an understanding of the richness and diversity, as well as the infamy, of the undertakings of the Scots overseas, including their involvement in slavery and the slave trade. It contributes to an understanding of their astonishing role in the Atlantic economy, as well as to their search for the 'main chance' when they returned to Britain. This book also contributes to an understanding of white ethnicity, of the manner in which Scots often held on to ethnic and cultural forms that rendered them distinctive, sometimes emphasising their Scottishness, while also seeking to blend into their environment when it suited them. In all of these respects, Hamilton's work will stand as a landmark in the developing understanding of Scots in contexts, like the Caribbean, which have so far been little studied.

John M. MacKenzie

LIST OF ABBREVIATIONS

ACA	Aberdeen City Archives
APS	American Philosophical Society, Philadelphia
BUL	Bristol University Library
CSP	*Calendar of state papers, colonial series, America and the West Indies*
GCA	Glasgow City Archives
HCA	Highland Council Archives, Inverness
HSP	Historical Society of Pennsylvania, Philadelphia
IHR	Institute of Historical Research, London
InvM	Inverness Museum
IRA	Inverness Royal Academy
JMA	Jamaica Archives, Spanish Town
NAS	National Archives of Scotland, Edinburgh
NLJ	National Library of Jamaica, Kingston
NLS	National Library of Scotland, Edinburgh
NMM	National Maritime Museum, Greenwich
OSA	Sir John Sinclair, *The statistical account of Scotland, 1791–1799*, ed. D. J. Withrington and I. R. Grant, Wakefield, 1975–83
PRO	The National Archives, Public Record Office, Kew
UASCA	University of Aberdeen, Special Collections and Archives

NOTE ON CURRENCY

In the text the terms '£ sterling' and '£ currency' have been used. The former refers to British currency, the latter to the currencies of the individual Caribbean colonies.

ACKNOWLEDGEMENTS

This book has been a long time coming. It began as a doctoral thesis at the University of Aberdeen and along the way I have accumulated a huge range of debts to friends, family and colleagues. It gives me great pleasure to record my thanks to them all. At Aberdeen, Allan Macinnes and Marjory Harper supervised my thesis, while Andrew Mackillop and Tom Devine have both added to my understanding in their usual robust ways. The postgraduate community at Aberdeen added enormously to this work, and it is an especial pleasure to thank Drs Robert Blyth, Alison Cathcart, Fiona Downie, John Frame, Steve Murdoch and Joyce Walker. I would also like to thank former colleagues at the McNeil Center for Early American Studies in Philadelphia, and particularly the then director, Richard S. Dunn, and Roderick McDonald, Kariann Yokota and Carolyn Eastman. At the University of York, Jim Walvin and Liz Buettner provided inspiration and wise counsel. David Alston, Bernard Bailyn, Ned Landsman, P. J. Marshall and Andrew O'Shaughnessy all offered valuable suggestions and insights. John MacKenzie, as my thesis examiner and general editor, has been a constant source of advice and encouragement, for which I am very grateful. I would like to thank the archivists and librarians who dealt so professionally and graciously with my stream of requests for manuscripts and books. Mr Archibald Stirling of Keir generously gave permission to quote from his family's papers. Lastly, I would like to thank my family. I'm certain they often wondered what on earth I was doing, or where it was all leading, but it was their support that enabled me to carry on doing it. I hope they will see this book as some kind of explanation.

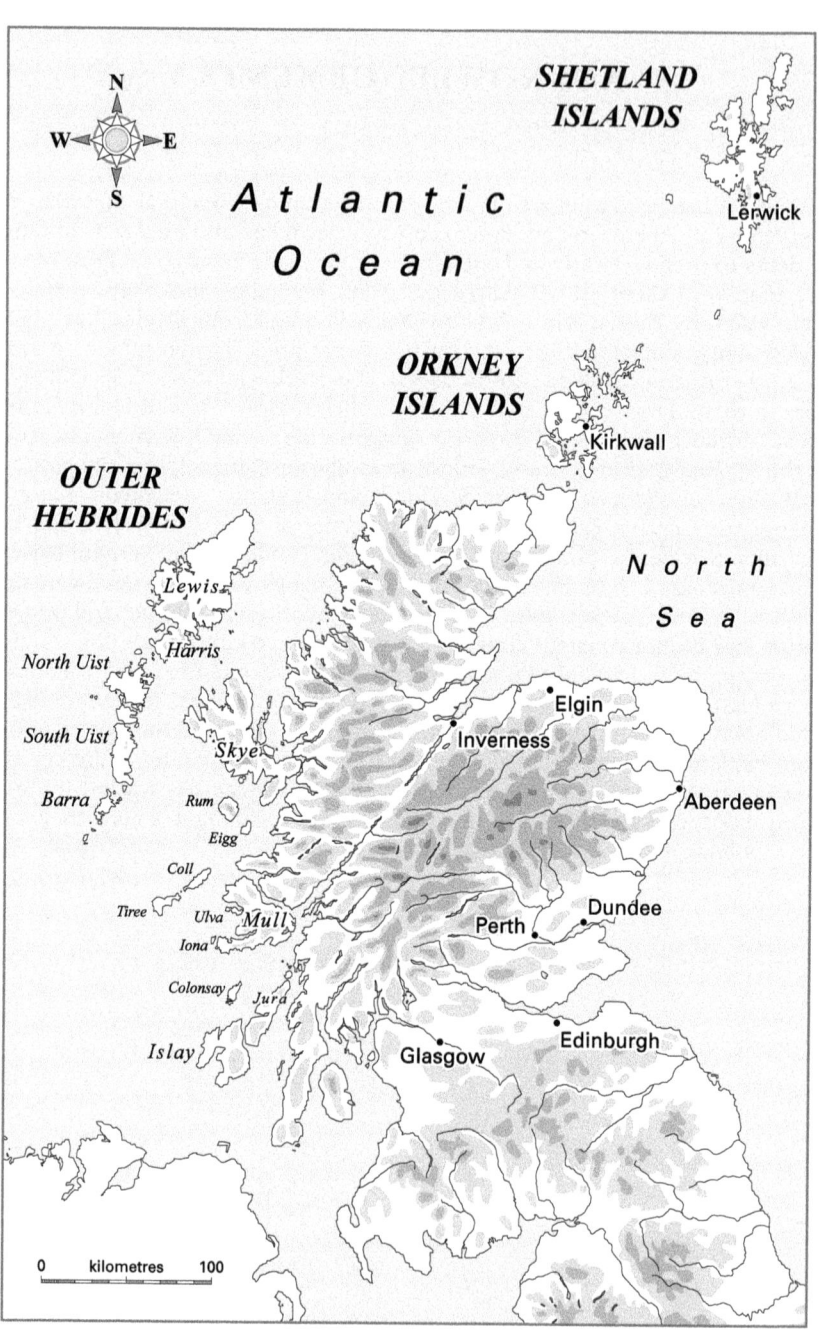

Eighteenth-century Scotland

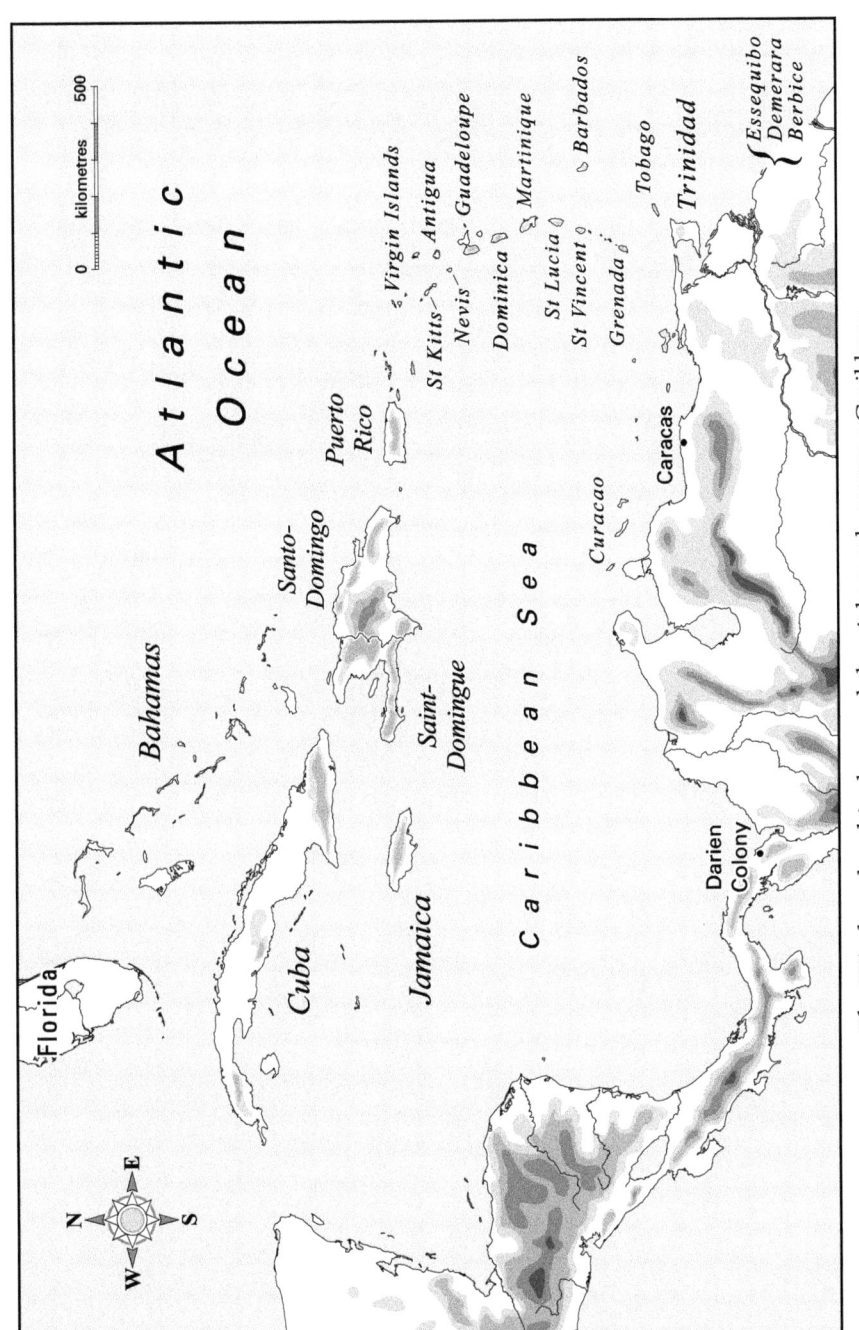

The Windward archipelago and the eighteenth-century Caribbean

INTRODUCTION

In 1786, an Ayrshire man prepared to leave Scotland to take up the post of book-keeper on Charles Duncan's plantation near Port Antonio in north-east Jamaica. The man was an aspiring poet, and he wrote of his misgivings about venturing 'across th' Atlantic's roar' in the weeks before his departure. In the end, his poetry saved him. As he waited for his ship at Greenock, word came that the first edition of his work, published in Kilmarnock, had been greeted with acclaim in Edinburgh, and that a second edition was to be commissioned. Jamaica was thus denied a book-keeper as Robert Burns went on to become a key figure in Scottish literature.[1]

Although Burns's later experiences were not typical of those of most Scots in this period, many others did consider careers in the Caribbean, and, as this book shows, thousands actually went. There were a number of reasons why they did so: Burns, for example, wrote odes of farewell to Mary Campbell and at least two other women. More prosaic explanations were outlined forcefully by James Baillie from Inverness, who became an influential West India merchant, planter and politician: 'I am astonished that any Person can think of Injuring there children so much Who are not born to Independant fortunes, as to keep them after their Education in so compleat and in such a miserable country when they have such a Country as Grenada, St Vincent or the other West India islands to send them to, or what do you think of the East Indies for a change?'[2]

Baillie wrote in the context of the expansion of the British Empire in 1763, but the limitations of the Scottish economy he alluded to had led Scots to seek advancement abroad since the middle ages. Whether merchants in a Scottish community in Danzig, Vere or Brugge, or soldiers and officers in the service of foreign monarchs, notably in France and Scandinavia, Scots had a well-established tradition of overseas employment. From the sixteenth century, Scots also began to look to the Atlantic, trading to Iberia and the Azores.[3]

Early in the seventeenth century Scottish adventurers began to develop more distinctly imperial ventures in the Atlantic, beyond the plantation of Ulster. Short-lived and ultimately unsuccessful attempts were made to establish a New Scotland colony, or Nova Scotia, on the North American seaboard throughout the 1620s and then, in the 1630s, Scots imperialists turned their attention to Africa. In 1634 Charles I granted a thirty-one year charter to the Scottish Guinea

Company to trade with, and explore further, the African coast from the Senegal River to the Cape of Good Hope.[4] The enterprise was wound up around 1639, and its failure, following on the heels of the hand-over of New Scotland, along with the Cromwellian interregnum between 1649 and 1660, caused Scottish imperial ambitions in the Atlantic to atrophy for thirty years. During this period, Scottish involvement in the Caribbean was largely restricted to the involuntary transportation of captured Scottish soldiers to Barbados and Jamaica.

The restoration of the Stuart monarchy in 1660 saw renewed attempts by Scots to establish their own colonies. Charles II received representations for the settlement of Scots colonies in Barbados and St Lucia, and he offered the island of Dominica to Scotland in 1671. There were further proposals in 1678 for the settlement of St Vincent by Scots.[5] While these plans came to naught, there was increasing Scottish involvement in the English Caribbean in the period immediately after the Restoration. In 1667, Lord Willoughby, governor of Barbados, wrote to the Lords of Trade in London requesting the free transfer of Scots to that island: 'If your Lopps. shall open a trade in Scotland, for the transportation of the people of that Nation hither, and prevent any accesse of Irish in the future, it will accommodate all the ends propounded and abundantly gratify his Matys. good subjects here.'[6]

The numerical strength of the Barbadian militia had declined from the 1650s, and Willoughby's determination to bolster it with three or four thousand Scots was, to a considerable degree, based on a fear of a revolt by the 'Creolised generation' of enslaved Africans.[7] In the context of the second Anglo-Dutch War, which drew in the French in the Caribbean theatre, it was also predicated on their Protestantism. As Willoughby put it, 'I am for the down right Scott who I am certain will fight without a crucifix about his neck'.[8] The demand for Scottish 'servants' continued into the early eighteenth century. In 1701, George MacKenzie petitioned the Barbados council for payment for 'several Scotch servants' brought to the island. This desire for Scots was equally apparent in North America. Indeed, demand was so great between 1665 and 1685 that the English Privy Council granted over twenty-six special warrants to allow ships to carry Scottish indentured servants to the English colonies.[9]

Yet it would be a mistake to assume that all Scots in the Caribbean before the Act of Union were either exiles or indentured servants. Several, despite the difficulties of being Scottish in an English colony (and therefore foreign nationals), were able to enter the islands' elites. In the last years of the seventeenth century, Thomas Maxwell was repeatedly elected speaker of the Barbados assembly, and he was later appointed a member of the council. His perceived Scottishness was challenged: when Governor Grey recommended him to the Council of Trade and Plantations in January 1700, he noted that Maxwell was 'of a Scotch name, but English born: of admirable parts and a considerable estate'. But Maxwell did maintain Scottish links, notably with his distant relation Sir James Maxwell of Pollok.[10] Scottish nationality could also be conveniently ignored. In 1699, a patent was issued allowing Alexander Skene to take the influential post of island secretary in Barbados, 'provided he proved his qualifications, it being objected that he is not a native-born subject of England, Ireland or the Plantations'.[11] It is clear from this that while Scots were sometimes able to get ahead, their status as foreigners, despite sharing a monarch, could be an effective barrier to them. They remained reliant on English concessions.

In addition to those Scots in Barbados, it has been estimated that there were over 200 Scots on the islands of Nevis, Montserrat and Antigua in 1678. Others were to be found living in or trading with Dutch colonies. Robert Milne, from Auchlie near Aberdeen, for example, went to Holland about 1696, and then travelled to Curaçao with Captain Grieve in 1698. In total, perhaps 4,500 Scots went to the Caribbean in the second half of the seventeenth century, that is, before the Act of Union.[12]

This increasing involvement in the empires of other countries did not diminish Scots' efforts to establish colonies of their own in this period. The most successful and long-standing Scottish settlement was founded on the American mainland, at East New Jersey from 1683. Contemporaneously with the East New Jersey settlement, a group largely composed of landowners and merchants from south-west Scotland planted a short-lived colony in Carolina between 1684 and 1686.[13] The least successful ventures, in terms of the losses sustained, were the endeavours of the Company of Scotland Trading to Africa and the Indies to establish a colony at Darien on the Isthmus of Panama. The attempts to found settlements at New Edinburgh and Fort St Andrew between 1698 and 1700 were the most ambitious of all the seventeenth-century Scottish schemes, and aimed to establish a settled Scottish entrepot between the two great trading oceans of the Pacific and the Atlantic. Their failure, so devastating in loss of life and capital, had serious economic and political implications for Scotland, and also had the effect of increasing the population of Jamaica, whence some of the survivors fled.[14]

It is clear that in Scotland the idea of imperial engagement was not just an eighteenth-century phenomenon. Significantly, these early imperial undertakings were conceived and led by members of the Scottish gentry and nobility, along with those from mercantile and professional backgrounds. It is equally apparent that Scots from other social ranks were involved (as indentured servants) in imperial ventures. An emerging tradition of transatlantic migration and enterprise predated the Act of Union of 1707 and existed, albeit in a relatively minor way, alongside the more substantial migrations to north and east Europe, Scandinavia and the Baltic.

After 1707, the balance between European and Atlantic involvement swung decisively to the west. Access to the English empire after 1707 created new opportunities that were seized upon by Scots. The first acquisition of new land in the Caribbean after the Act of Union, in St Kitts in 1713, offered the chance for Scots to obtain land in the new British empire. The second decade of the eighteenth century saw two Scotsmen as governors of St Kitts, Walter Douglas and Walter Hamilton. During this period, Scots were prominent among the grantees receiving estates of over 100 acres.[15] The beleaguered refugees from Darien swelled Scottish numbers in Jamaica, and formed the basis of a considerable Argyll community of the western part of the island.

In the North American colonies, the Scottish presence grew similarly in the first half of the eighteenth century, perhaps most notably in the Chesapeake, where Glasgow merchants played an increasingly important role in the tobacco trade from the 1740s. In 1735, a Highland community had been established at New Inverness, later Darien, in Georgia. This was followed by Highland settlements in New York in 1738 and at Cape Fear, North Carolina, in 1739.[16]

In the context of this tradition of Scottish imperial activity, the upsurge in Caribbean enterprise and settlement after the acquisition of the Windward Islands in 1763 appears as part of an important upward trend in imperial involvement, not as a stunning new departure for Scottish people and their capital. Nonetheless, the volume of migration to the Caribbean, and its significance for Scotland and the West Indies, was considerable. The book argues that Scots like James Baillie were disproportionately numerous in the Caribbean, and that they were extremely successful across a range of activities including planting, trading, medicine and politics.

Contemporary observers were certainly aware of a Scottish presence. A resident on Rhimesbury plantation in Jamaica believed that 'of the Europeans the Scotch are most numerous, as well in Kingston as all over the island'. Janet Schaw, a Scottish 'lady of quality', found a 'whole company of Scotch people, our language, our manners, our circle of friends and connections, all the same' during a visit to Antigua in 1775. Edward Long, the cantankerous Jamaican planter-historian, remarked, 'This hospitable alacrity to assist and befriend their countrymen, in a place where they might otherwise become destitute of support, and sick of life, produces likewise an event very favourable to the colony, by inviting into it frequent recruits of very able hands, who add not a little to its population and strength.'[17]

This notion, which contemporary observers liked to call 'clannishness', was central to the Scottish experience in the eighteenth-century Caribbean. For those writers, it was an aspect of Scottish social organisation to be admired because it redounded to the advantage of the islands. 'Clannishness' underpinned the networks that Scots employed to organise themselves in the islands. For Scots, the real significance of the networks lies not so much in 'clannishness', but in their relationship to clan*ship*. The bonds were an adaptation of the long-standing forms of social relations based on regional and familial connections outlined in Chapter One. Their groupings evinced a flexible notion of kinship that allowed pragmatic alliances to sit alongside more traditional biological bonds. The fluidity of these social relations enabled Scots to accommodate non-Scots within their Caribbean networks. This challenges the perception sometimes advanced by historians that Scottish networks represented a display of (sometimes invented) ethnic solidarity in the face of an alien culture.[18] That these social forms were being adapted to an imperial setting at the same time as they were under attack in Scotland adds a particular resonance.

The idea of the 'network' is often used by historians as a convenient short-hand for groups of people bound together by a range of interests; they were, as Zoë Laidlaw puts it, 'mechanisms which were consciously utilised by their members to benefit themselves or others'.[19] In the pre-industrial world, these mechanisms took different forms and had different purposes. There were professional connections: Laidlaw highlights three different networks arising from common military service, humanitarianism, and the scientific community. Pearson's and Richardson's examination of groups of investors in fire insurance in Liverpool, Manchester and western England between 1776 and 1824 emphasises that it was 'practical experience of working together in a business environment which highlighted common interests and facilitated resource pooling'. Previous contacts in slave trading in Liverpool, or in manufacturing in Leeds and Manchester, led to co-operation in insurance. Networks could also be based on other bonds. As Charles Tilly argues, the 'most effective units of migration' were 'sets of people linked by acquaintance, kinship and work experience'.

Peter Mathias reminds us that the 'family matrix was so often central to the operations of business', not least as a means of reducing risk of various kinds. The importance of family ties in business is reinforced by scholarly studies of merchant communities in both northern and southern Europe, notably Ida Bull's essay on immigrant merchants in Trondheim. Meanwhile, J. C. Sola-Carbacho's work on Madrid merchants has emphasised the importance of *paisanaje*, or sense of community based on local association, among migrant groups in the Spanish capital.[20] It is clear that many groups of people employed networks based on ties of kinship, local association or profession to raise capital, facilitate communication and recruit employees across a range of functional areas, most notably in business, and so in a sense Scots were not unique. But they were distinctive.

This study shows not only that did Scottish networks exist throughout eighteenth-century West Indies, and especially in the period after the Seven Years War, but that the cohesion within these groupings was not based simply on Scottishness. Although the networks were, at their hearts, based on a local or familial link with Scotland, they were by no means exclusive. Scottish involvement in the Caribbean empire played a crucial role in forging a unity among Britons during the eighteenth century. This book also argues, following Long's assertion of the value of Scots in Jamaica, that the networks were critical to the success of Scots in the islands. The networks provided opportunities, for employment, for investment and for advancement; and they provided security for those taking their chances, in two ways. At one level, the welcoming embrace of friends or family in the Caribbean was, as we will see, of great importance for Scots stepping off the boat in Kingston, St George's or Scarborough. They also provided economic security, through the availability of capital backed up by heritable Scottish security or Scots partnership law. This was not just a tale of success, however. Making money in the Caribbean was risky: high mortality, the threat of indebtedness and the difficulties of repatriating money all meant that not all Scots fulfilled their ambitions in the islands. This book explores these themes through a study of Scottish involvement in planting, trade, medicine and politics.

Although it is a study in Atlantic world history, this book draws on a number of (often distinct) historiographical traditions. Since the 1960s, the explosion of scholarly interest in Scottish history has promoted a sophisticated understanding of Scotland's past. An increasingly important part of this literature has assessed the role of Scots and Scotland abroad. This includes localised and specialised studies of aspects of Scottish emigration and enterprise around the world,

INTRODUCTION

some of it written by historians of Scotland, some by other historians working in Scotland, and some by historians of the countries in which Scots settled.[21] The general interest in Scottish overseas expansion, however, has tended to focus on North America, the antipodes or Africa. The tropical empires of the eighteenth century, and the Caribbean in particular, have received far less scholarly attention.[22]

This outward-looking Scottish history fits with a general shift in British historiography that leans away from purely anglocentric approaches in three senses. The first is that as a shared enterprise, empire helped to integrate the peoples of Britain. Not only did the pursuit of imperial gain bind the interests of the Scots and the English together, but the mobility required of them forced them to live side by side, in the colonies, in the port cities and in the corridors of power. Secondly, it suggests that in looking for centres of imperial power, the search ought not to stop at London. From what follows, it is clear that Glasgow and the English outports all witnessed the rise of local elites whose business relied on empire. For medical education, Scotland, and especially Edinburgh, was the hub of the empire. Thirdly, the implication behind J. G. A. Pocock's assertion that British history in the eighteenth century 'must be thought of as the history of four realms' is that the Atlantic, far from being a barrier between Britain and its colonies, was actually a link.[23]

The Atlantic world has been subject to considerable scholarly attention, taking its cues from the work of Bernard Bailyn, D. W. Meinig, Ian K. Steele and others. Taken collectively, important work from the mid-1990s has helped to focus Bailyn's 'view from the moon', and this study aims to clarify it still further by arguing that Scots and their overseas interests can tell us a great deal about the way in which the Atlantic world was created.[24] It seeks to understand the relationship between an integral and important part of an imperial power and a colonial sphere. This relationship was about exchanges of people, goods and ideas, and it impacted right across both regions to transform the social, economic, political and physical landscapes. A study of Scottish–Caribbean connections suggests that they were among the key bonds forging a transnational maritime world of exchange. In short, it argues that these connections, and the Atlantic world of which they were part, existed, and changed the lives of the people who experienced them. It does this by assessing the role of Scots on the plantations and as merchants, doctors and politicians in the islands. The final chapter considers the repatriation of people and capital from the Caribbean, and their impact on developments in Scotland. But the book begins, as did the eighteenth-century adventurers to the Caribbean, in Scotland.

Notes

1 J. Mackay, *RB: A biography of Robert Burns* (Edinburgh: Mainstream Publishing, 1992), p. 200; R. B. Sheridan, 'The role of Scots in the economy and society of the West Indies', in V. Rubin and A. Tuden (eds), *Comparative perspectives on slavery in New World plantations* (New York: New York Academy of Sciences, 1977), p. 97. The line comes from 'Will ye go to the Indies, my Mary?'
2 NLS, MS5515(161–2), Liston papers, James Baillie to Mrs Ramage, 24 July 1775.
3 G. G. Simpson (ed.), *Scotland and Scandinavia, 800–1800* (Edinburgh: John Donald, 1990); Simpson (ed.), *The Scottish soldier abroad, 1247–1967* (Edinburgh: John Donald, 1992); Simpson (ed.), *Scotland and the Low Countries, 1124–1994* (East Linton: Tuckwell Press, 1996); T. C. Smout et al., 'Scottish migration in the seventeenth and eighteenth centuries', in N. Canny (ed.), *Europeans on the move: Studies in European migration 1500–1800* (Oxford: Clarendon Press, 1994), pp. 76–112; S. W. Murdoch, *Britain, Denmark-Norway and the House of Stuart, 1603–60* (East Linton: Tuckwell Press, 2000); R. Law, 'The first Scottish Guinea company, 1634–39', *Scottish Historical Review*, 76, 2 (1997), 189; J. L. Israel, 'A conflict of empires: Spain and the Netherlands, 1618–1648', *Past and Present*, 76 (1977), 48–9, 51–4.
4 N. E. S. Griffiths and J. G. Reid, 'New evidence on New Scotland, 1629', *William and Mary Quarterly*, 49, 3 (1992), 492–508; Law, 'The first Scottish Guinea company'.
5 NAS, GD205/40/13/3, Ogilvy of Inverquharity papers, warrant from Charles II to Sir John Nisbet, 10 July 1671; GD205/40/13/4, Duke of Lauderdale to Sir John Nisbet, 22 July 1671. I am grateful to Allan I. Macinnes for these references. See also NAS, GD103/2/4/42, Society of Antiquities; D. Dobson, *Scottish emigration to colonial America, 1607–1785* (Athens, GA: University of Georgia Press, 1994), pp. 74, 76.
6 G. P. Insh, *Scottish colonial schemes, 1620–1686* (Glasgow: Maclehose, Jackson & Co., 1922), appendix D, Barbados correspondence, p. 231.
7 R. S. Dunn, *Sugar and slaves: The rise of the planter class in the English West Indies, 1624–1713* (Chapel Hill: University of North Carolina Press, 1972), pp. 75, 87, 124, 257.
8 Insh, *Scottish colonial schemes*, appendix D, p. 230; A. P. Thornton, *West India policy under the Restoration* (Oxford: Clarendon Press, 1956), p. 130.
9 *CSP*, vol. 19, p. 737, minutes of the council in assembly of Barbados, 2 September 1701; I. C. C. Graham, *Colonists from Scotland: Emigration to North America, 1707–1783* (Ithaca: Cornell University Press, 1956), p. 9
10 W. Fraser, *Memoirs of the Maxwells of Pollok* (Edinburgh: 1863), vol. 1, pp. 370–2. On Maxwell see *CSP*, vol. 15, p. 296; vol. 16, p. 110; vol. 18, p. 44.
11 See *CSP*, vol. 18, p. 31.
12 ACA, Baillie Court: propinquity books, vol. 1, pp. 586–9, 19 January 1722. I am grateful to Marjory Harper for this reference. See also Smout et al., 'Scottish migration', p. 87.
13 N. C. Landsman, *Scotland and its first American colony, 1683–1765* (Princeton: Princeton University Press, 1985), pp. 103, 275–8; L. G. Fryer, 'Robert Barclay of Ury and East New Jersey', *Northern Scotland*, 15 (1995), 1–17.
14 D. Armitage, 'The Scottish vision of empire: Intellectual origins of the Darien venture', in J. Robertson (ed.), *A union for empire: Political thought and the Union of 1707* (Cambridge: Cambridge University Press, 1995), pp. 97–117.
15 R. B. Sheridan, *Sugar and slavery: An economic history of the British West Indies, 1623–1775* (Barbados: Caribbean Universities Press, 1974), p. 158.
16 Landsman, *Scotland and its first American colony*, p. 11; J. M. Price, 'The rise of Glasgow in the Chesapeake tobacco trade, 1707–1775', *William and Mary Quarterly*, 11 (1954), 179–99; T. M. Devine, *The tobacco lords: A study of the tobacco merchants of Glasgow and their trading activities, c. 1740–1790* (Edinburgh: John Donald, 1975); A. W. Parker, *Scottish Highlanders in colonial Georgia: The recruit-

INTRODUCTION

    ment, emigration, and settlement at Darien, 1735–1748 (Athens, GA: University of Georgia Press, 1997).

17 Anon., *An account of the island of Jamaica, with reflections on the treatment, occupation and provisions of the slaves* (Newcastle: S. Hodgson, 1788) p. 7; J. Schaw, *Journal of a lady of quality, being the narrative of a journey from Scotland to the West Indies, North Carolina, and Portugal in the years 1774 to 1776*, ed. E. W. Andrews and C. M. Andrews (New Haven: Yale University Press, 1923) p. 81; E. Long, *The history of Jamaica, or general survey of the antient and modern state of that island* (1774; London: Frank Cass, 1970), vol. 2, p. 286.

18 A. L. Karras, *Sojourners in the sun: Scottish migrants in Jamaica and the Chesapeake, 1740–1800* (Ithaca: Cornell University Press, 1992), pp. 120–1; Landsman, *Scotland and its first American colony*, pp. 141–62.

19 Z. Laidlaw, 'Networks, patronage and information in governance: Britain, New South Wales and the Cape Colony, 1826–1843', DPhil thesis, University of Oxford, 2001, p. 48.

20 Laidlaw, 'Networks, patronage and information', pp. 48–86; R. Pearson and D. Richardson, 'Business networking in the industrial revolution', *Economic History Review*, 54, 4 (2001), 657–79; C. Tilly, 'Transplanted networks', in V. Yans-McLaughlin (ed.), *Immigration reconsidered: History, sociology and politics* (New York and Oxford: Oxford University Press, 1990), pp. 79–95; P. Mathias, 'Risk, credit and kinship in early modern enterprise', in J. J. McCusker and K. Morgan (eds), *The early modern Atlantic economy* (Cambridge: Cambridge University Press, 2001), p. 16; I. Bull, 'Merchant households and their networks in eighteenth-century Trondheim', *Continuity and Change*, 17, 2 (2002), 213–31; J. C. Sola-Corbacho, 'Family, *paisanaje*, and migration among Madrid's merchants (1750–1800)', *Journal of Family History*, 27, 1 (2002) 3–24.

21 The range includes: G. Donaldson, *The Scots overseas* (London: Robert Hale, 1966); D. S. MacMillan, *Scotland and Australia 1788–1850: Emigration, commerce and investment* (Oxford: Clarendon Press, 1967); J. D. Hargreaves, *Aberdeenshire to Africa: Northeast Scots and British overseas expansion* (Aberdeen: Aberdeen University Press, 1981); J. M. MacKenzie, 'Essay and reflection: On Scotland and the empire', *International History Review*, 15 (1993), 714–39; McKenzie, 'Empire and national identities: The case of Scotland', *Transactions of the Royal Historical Society*, 6th series, 8 (1998), 215–31; N. C. Landsman (ed.), *Nation and province in the first British empire: Scotland and the Americas, 1600–1800* (Lewisburg, PA: Bucknell University Press, 2001); M. Fry, *Scottish empire* (East Linton: Tuckwell Press, 2001); A. I. Macinnes et al. (eds), *Scotland and the Americas: A documentary source book* (Edinburgh: Scottish History Society, 2002); E. Buettner, 'Haggis in the Raj: Private and public celebrations of Scottishness in late imperial India', *Scottish Historical Review*, 81, 2 (2002), 212–39; A. Mackillop and S. Murdoch (eds), *Military governors and imperial frontiers c. 1600–1800: A study of Scotland and empires* (Leiden: Brill, 2003); T. M. Devine, *Scotland's empire, 1600–1815* (London: Allen Lane, 2003).

22 R. B. Sheridan, 'The rise of a colonial gentry: A case study of Antigua, 1730–1775', *Economic History Review*, 13, 3 (1961), 342–57; Sheridan, 'The role of Scots'; A. L. Karras, 'The world of Alexander Johnston: The creolization of ambition, 1762–1787', *Historical Journal*, 30, 1 (1987) 53–76; Karras, *Sojourners in the sun*; R. A. McDonald (ed.), *Between Slavery and Freedom: Special Magistrate John Anderson's journal of St Vincent during the apprenticeship* (Kingston: University of the West Indies Press; Philadelphia: University of Pennsylvania Press, 2001). This lacuna has been only partly filled by M. Quintanilla, 'The world of Alexander Campbell: An eighteenth-century Grenadian planter', *Albion*, 35, 2 (2003), 229–56.

23 L. Colley, *Britons: Forging the nation, 1707–1837* (London: Pimlico, 1994); K. Wilson, *The sense of the people: Politics, culture and imperialism in England, 1715–1785* (Cambridge: Cambridge University Press, 1995); A. Murdoch, *British history 1660–1832: National identity and local culture* (Basingstoke: Macmillan, 1998); K. Morgan, *Bristol and the Atlantic trade in the eighteenth century* (Cam-

bridge: Cambridge University Press, 1993); D. H. Akenson, *If the Irish ran the world: Montserrat, 1630–1730* (Liverpool: Liverpool University Press, 1997); C. A. Bayly, *Imperial meridian: The British Empire and the world, 1780–1830* (London: Longman, 1989), p. 15; P. J. Marshall, 'A nation defined by empire, 1755–1776', in A. Grant and K. J. Stringer (eds), *Uniting the Kingdom? The making of British history* (London: Routledge, 1995), pp. 208–22; J. G. A. Pocock, 'The limits and divisions of British history: In search of the unknown subject', *American Historical Review*, 87, 2 (1982), 330.

24 B. Bailyn, *Voyagers to the west: A passage in the peopling of America on the eve of the revolution* (London: I. B. Tauris, 1987); B. Bailyn, 'The idea of Atlantic history', *Itinerario*, 20 (1996), 19–44; D. W. Meinig, *The shaping of America*, vol. 1: *Atlantic America* (New Haven: Yale University Press, 1986); I. K. Steele, *The English Atlantic 1675–1740: An exploration of communication and community* (New York and Oxford: Oxford University Press, 1986); important studies include: D. Armitage and M. Braddick (eds), *The British Atlantic world, 1500–1800* (Basingstoke: Palgrave, 2002); A. Games, *Migration and the origins of the English Atlantic world* (Cambridge, MA: Harvard University Press, 1999); D. Hancock, *Citizens of the world: The Integration of the British Atlantic community, 1735–1785* (Cambridge: Cambridge University Press, 1995); E. H. Gould, *The persistence of empire: British political culture in the era of the American Revolution* (Chapel Hill: University of North Carolina Press for the OIEAHC, 2000).

CHAPTER ONE

Scotland in the eighteenth century

During the eighteenth century, Scotland experienced a series of profound economic, social, cultural and political changes. Industry and agriculture were transformed, moving Scotland from a relative economic backwater (in European terms) to a country that witnessed innovations in agricultural and industrial production able to rival those anywhere on the globe. Fostered by financial developments at home, Scotland began to play a key role in the vast commercial complex of the Atlantic, the profits of which in turn fired further growth, and set Glasgow on track to become the second city of the British Empire. The Enlightenment illuminated Scottish culture and society from philosophy to farming. More broadly it confirmed the place of Scottish intellectuals at the forefront of European thought, and had explicit ramifications in the world beyond Europe. Politically, too, Scotland underwent wholesale changes during the eighteenth century. In 1700, Scotland had been an independent political entity nursing the wounds inflicted on its Exchequer by the failure of the Darien scheme. By 1800, it was an integral part of a Great Britain that was locked in combat with Scotland's former ally, France.

Yet this picture of the blossoming of Scotland in the space of 100 years is somewhat problematic. Despite the eulogies of the 1790s that gloried in the advances made in Scotland, these transformations did not follow a pattern of untrammelled progress, but brought traumatic dislocations for many of Scotland's citizens.[1] The upheavals in patterns of landholding and manufacturing produced dramatic demographic changes that had fundamental implications for society as a whole. The path towards a politically integrated Britain was strewn with obstacles. The continuance of distinct Scottish traditions in law, education and religion ensured that complete integration was unattainable. But even more modest pretensions of unity were undermined at times by Jacobite rebellions, Scottish resistance, the uneven implementation of the rights of Britons and Wilkesite English resentment of Scottish success.

Scots were drawn to the Caribbean in disproportionately high numbers during this period, and especially after 1763. This chapter considers the manner in which social, economic and political developments in Scotland in the second half of the eighteenth century affected the ways in which Scots engaged with the Caribbean. It assesses the society from which these adventurers to the West Indies came and asks which Scots, in terms of their social backgrounds, were drawn to the Caribbean, rather than other parts of the empire. Finally, it considers how far their Scottish backgrounds affected the manner of their participation in the Caribbean.

Economy: changes on the land

Scotland was an overwhelmingly rural society in the eighteenth century. Despite the beginnings of industrialisation, more than two-thirds of the Scottish population were rural inhabitants in 1820.[2] Yet this did represent a decline in the countryside population and is symbolic of the shift towards more urban areas that began in the second half of the eighteenth century. This shift, along with other changes in rural society, had profound implications for the scale and nature of Scottish imperial activity.

Across Scotland, to a greater or lesser extent, agricultural practices were fundamentally re-ordered. It is also clear that some of the basic processes of change were substantially the same in the Highlands and the Lowlands. Since the 1980s, the mythologised image of traditional, backward Highland society being shunted into economic progress by clearance and capitalism in the aftermath of the Jacobite Rebellion of 1745 has been effectively undermined. It is now apparent that the process of clearance and moves towards more commercialised agriculture were begun by the Highland chiefs themselves before the Forty-Five.[3] This change was marked by a series of characteristics. Firstly, it was predicated on a shift in the nature of landholding from land held by chiefs in trust for the clan towards the introduction of legal title. This enabled clan chiefs to reinvent themselves as proprietors and as landed gentry. It also allowed them to impose commercially led imperatives on the land that involved the restructuring of patterns of settlement. Before the process of 'improvement' was inaugurated, communities tended to reside in *bàile* (traditional townships), which comprised a number of tenants farming communally under the direction of a tacksman. The phasing out of tacksmen, who acted as a kind of lesser gentry operating between the clan elite and its followers, and the transformation of communal farms into single tenancies, allowed landlords to develop large farms for the raising of black cattle or sheep. They also ushered in greater primary reliance on the payment of money rents to increase the revenue of the estates. As multiple tenancies were phased out, improving landlords introduced innovations that one authority has viewed as being as significant as the creation of sheep or cattle ranches. The establishment of crofting communities and planned villages allowed estates to branch out into activities more properly denoted as industrial rather than agricultural. These new communities exploited quarries and fishing grounds, and specialised in the production of kelp.[4]

In the Lowlands, where estates were usually more geared towards arable farming than their Highland counterparts, similar transformations took place. The process of change began during the seventeenth century, and took place over a longer time than in the Highlands. There was a general shift towards more commercially driven agriculture along with greater emphasis on money rent.[5] Although multiple-tenant farms never completely predominated in the Lowlands, the process of consolidating land into larger single-tenant units advanced in the later eighteenth century.[6] The ferm-touns and cot-touns, previously important centres of rural life in the Lowlands, were, like the *bàile* in the Highlands, swept away to make room for single tenancies. Social stratification was an important result of the greater significance attached to individual landholding as property. Although these tenancies and land held by owner-occupiers might form only very small farms, the emphasis on individual landholding relegated cottars (who leased land largely in return for labour) and landless labourers to a rank below even sub-tenants, who were distinguished in law by their payment of money rent. As in the Highlands, in the Lowlands there was an increase in planned villages built by major landowners from the 1770s. They, too, were sites for industries like fishing, spinning, weaving and distilling. The planned villages proffered further advantages for the landlords by providing a pool of casual labour and by allowing them to garner revenue from the collection of feu duties.[7]

Often the transformations in agriculture have been attributed to the large landowners who displayed enlightened and improving tendencies. It is certainly apparent that there was a particular linkage between the changes sponsored by some notable improvers and the Enlightenment.[8] Connections between the agriculture and the scientific interests of the Enlightenment were exemplified by the founding of specialist societies. It has been asserted, however, that this concentration on the great landowners has diverted proper attention from the activities of the tenantry, many of whom were in the vanguard of innovation, in the absence of their landlords. It has been argued further that although there was a general cultural shift towards 'improvement', the process was fuelled by more practical considerations, such as increasing demand from expanding urban centres and money wages increasing the level of disposable income.[9]

Indeed, some of the significance of the landlords lies in their responses to the fashionable ideas of the Enlightenment. Changes in estate landscapes were not always intended to bring about profit maximisation. The construction of new country houses and the laying out of gardens around them are indicative of a group of landowners determined to coalesce with a polite, mannered and enlightened British elite. Landowners' increasing mobility within British society gave them access to methods employed in England, and, as a result, the landowners provided the means through which many of the most important innovations were communicated to Scotland. Thus, while not all landowners were as practically progressive as a Grant of Monymusk or a Cockburn of Ormiston, they created an environment, arising from their southern contacts, their societies and their publications, in which agricultural transformation could be facilitated.

The Caribbean is significant here for two major reasons. In the first place, all these changes, whether designed to maximise profits or to beautify an estate, cost money. Domestic opportunities to raise revenue for 'improvement' were limited. As a result, a number of landed families looked to imperial enterprises in the Caribbean as a means of raising capital, as Chapter Eight explores. The second area of importance lies in the ambitions of younger sons of landed families, or those who were born without land, but aspired to it. While those with land could use West Indian wealth to promote changes, those without might generate sufficient capital to acquire it.

Urban and industrial change

The transformation of rural Scotland was mirrored by, and connected with, the increasing importance of the industrial sector of the economy and the growth of urban areas. In many ways the demographic shift towards urban centres beginning in the second half of the eighteenth century was predicated upon the revolution in agriculture. Without the changes on the land, and the attendant improvement in agricultural productivity, insufficient food would have been produced for consumption by the urban populace, which, without agrarian change, would have grown far more slowly.[10] But while urban growth relied on agrarian efficiency, it was also fired by advances in commercial enterprise and manufacturing industry.

The clearest examples of industrial activity were to be found in central Scotland, especially around Glasgow, although they were not confined to this region. The enormous expansion of Atlantic mercantile activity through the Clyde ports over the course of the eighteenth century brought an increase in ancillary services and the development of a commercial infrastructure. The rise of the Glasgow tobacco trade to a position of prominence by mid-century was augmented by the Caribbean sugar and cotton trades. The demands of these businesses for storage and merchandising facilities in port increased the need for staff. As a result, the urban centres around the Clyde were the fastest-growing in the country. Greenock, for example, witnessed a demographic explosion in which the population increased from 2,000 in 1700 to 17,500 in 1801.[11]

While commercial success was an important factor in the expansion of some towns, one of the main causes of the shift from country to town was the development of industry. In turn, industry was linked to the fortunes of the empire. Commerce was often geared specifically to the shipment and merchandising of colonial commodities and to the supplying of overseas markets with Scottish manufactures. Indeed those seeking to promote industrial development often did so in the context of colonial commerce. In 1774, the commentator John Campbell sought to encourage Moray Firth fishing as a source of herring for the Caribbean, and to promote the expansion of Inverness harbour and the construction of a canal to the Atlantic specifically to 'enable the active and assiduous Merchant to transport the Returns of his Trade with the West Indies to the East side of the Island'.[12] By the 1790s, one of the key imperial commodities, cotton, imported from the Caribbean and the American South, supplied the cotton manufacturing industry in the west of Scotland and allowed it grow with 'unparalleled speed from virtually nothing to become by far the greatest industry' by the 1790s.[13]

Cotton manufacturing witnessed a most spectacular expansion in the final quarter of the century, but it was not the only textile industry to undergo changes. The linen industry, promoted by the British Linen Company in Edinburgh, benefited from access to the protected colonial markets in the Americas, and demonstrates a key connection between burgeoning Scottish industrial output and imperial demand. Between 1765 and 1795, there was a ten-fold increase in Scottish linen exports to Jamaica, largely to meet the demand for coarse Osnaburg cloth for slave garments. By 1796, over 62 per cent of Scottish linen exports went to Jamaica. About three-quarters of these exports were actually produced in Scotland, and were designed to meet particular colonial specifications in terms of cloth colour and quality.[14]

The expansion of the textile industries also fostered advances in other industries in the same period. The demands for chemicals as bleaching and colouring agents redounded initially to the benefit of Highland kelp producers. The introduction of sulphuric acid from the Netherlands in the 1740s, and the construction of Prestonpans Vitriol Company in 1749, largely ended the use of sour milk as the acid in the bleaching process, and speeded it up enormously. Other chemical works producing sulphuric acid and chlorine grew up, and were informed by the work of scientists in the Scottish universities. Innovations, such as the patenting of dry bleaching powder in 1799 and developments in the field of colour dyeing, were promoted in Scotland. The production of the vegetable dye cudbear, in particular, provided employment for Gaelic-speaking Highlanders in Glasgow after 1777.[15] These concerns, more important in Scotland than the iron industry, promoted large-scale industrialisation, and provided a significant source of male employment for transplanted rural workers, to complement the role of women as spinners.

Away from textiles, other industries flourished. In Aberdeen, the quarrying and polishing of granite, both for use in the city and for export southwards, increased in the later part of the century. Coal, as a fuel to fire steam-driven machinery and for use in iron furnaces across Scotland, was extracted in increasing quantities, while the production of iron, though not taking off until the 1830s, nevertheless grew to meet the technological demands of industry and agriculture.[16]

These developments in industry pulled migrants into the cities and larger towns across Scotland, just as the re-ordering of the countryside pushed rural dwellers to the urban centres. Although there were high levels of internal migration, in general towns attracted new residents from their hinterlands: most people did not move to far-distant towns. Indeed, Scots were as likely to cross the Atlantic as to venture far in Scotland.[17] These processes, allied to the beginnings of growth in Irish migration to the west of Scotland, resulted in a general redistribution of the population from northern Scotland to the central belt between the 1750s and the 1820s. Strikingly, this internal migration relied heavily on kinship networks, which were employed to ease the entry of new arrivals in the city.[18] As we shall see, this pattern was followed by Scots practising long-range migration to the Caribbean.

Society: an expanding population

This geographically mobile Scottish population continued to grow during the second half of the eighteenth century, despite the clearances and increasing emigration to the Americas. In 1755, Scotland's population stood at under 1.3 million, but by 1801 it had passed 1.5 million, and it continued to grow thereafter. There are a number of explanations for this growth.

The eighteenth century saw a series of changes in the Scottish diet, partly as a result of changes in agricultural practice and partly as a consequence of British imperial activity. While less meat was consumed in Scotland in the eighteenth century than had been the case in the middle ages, Scots often benefited from a relatively nourishing diet.[19] In the Lowlands in particular, there was a greater availability of green vegetables, fruit and root vegetables. Imperial engagement in the east and west brought into Scotland increasing quantities of tea and sugar, both of which became available to ordinary Scots during the century. The growth of sugar consumption introduced a new source of calories into the Scottish diet. For England, it has been estimated that the fall in prices meant that West Indian sugar provided almost as much calorific value per penny as meat or beer.[20] Commenting on the consumption of tea and sugar in Britain, a Scottish writer in 1812 noted how global imperial connections had important effects on the lives of ordinary people: 'we are so situated in our commercial and financial system, that tea brought from the eastern extremity of the world, and sugar brought from the West Indies and both loaded with the expense of freight and insurance ... compose a drink cheaper than beer.'[21]

The introduction of the potato as a staple from the middle of the eighteenth century had a profound effect on the Scottish diet. Previous reliance on the oat crop to feed the Scottish people held them in thrall to the vicissitudes of a harvest that was known to fail frequently. Oats failed seven times in the second half of the eighteenth century, creating the circumstances under which famine might otherwise have occurred. Consequently, in 1794, one commentator remarked that the introduction of the potato was 'the greatest blessing that modern times could have bestowed on the country'.[22] The potato also supplied additional nutrition that complemented other food sources. This generally more varied diet had an impact on the Scottish population by fostering a greater resistance to disease, and thus increasing their chances of survival. Not only was disease confronted by a more resistant population, but it also came under attack from advances in medicine.

By the second half of the century some of the worst killers of Scots had declined or been eradicated. Of those that remained, smallpox was probably the most deadly, especially among children, meaning that the measures undertaken successfully to curb it in this period allowed an increase in the population.[23] Inoculation against smallpox, although apparently in use in the Highlands from the early part of the century, was not tried in parts of the south until the 1730, and was not widely employed before the 1760s. In the Highlands and the south-west, inoculation significantly cut down the outbreaks. In the Lowlands, however, inoculation was considered hazardous and was rarely employed. Thus Scotland lagged behind the Caribbean, where smallpox inoculation was first used in the 1720s, and widely used by Scottish doctors there from the 1750s. It was not until the Jenner's discovery of a vaccine in 1796, and its rapid acceptance as a safe means of combating the disease, that there was a dramatic decline in smallpox deaths in the central belt.

The improvements in diet and disease prevention, allied to an expansion of medical provision in urban hospitals, fostered a healthier and more populous nation. They were also matched by developments in medical education. Between 1497 and 1722, five chairs of medicine were established in Scotland, although it was not until the foundation of the medical school at Edinburgh in 1726 that Scottish medicine came to be highly regarded throughout Europe and beyond. By the second half of the eighteenth century, Scottish universities displayed a remarkable dominance in British medicine. It has been estimated that between 1751 and 1800, over 85 per cent of medical graduates in Britain came from one of the Scottish universities.[24] The increase in the number of medics came to be an important factor in encouraging Scottish doctors to venture to the Caribbean in search of patients. For not only did the number with medical training grow, but the cost of medicine limited the number of Scots (who may well have been experiencing better health in any case) who could call on their services.

Education

As the expansion of medical training suggests, a key factor in determining whether migration to the Caribbean was a viable option was educational attainment. By the eighteenth century, the presence of an enormous enslaved population limited opportunities for white artisans and unskilled labourers. As a result most Scots were essentially managers rather than labourers, and the positions they entered, whether planter, clerk, book-keeper, manager, attorney or physician, required them to have had access to at least rudimentary education.

In recruiting employees for work in the Caribbean, employers emphasised literacy and numeracy. Advertisements in Scottish newspapers for job vacancies in the Caribbean stipulated that candidates be suitably qualified as well as having a good recommendation. Those people writing the recommendations often stressed the educational attainments of the candidates. In trying to assist the family of William McDougall, who had gone bankrupt, Henry Dundas asked an acquaintance to find an apprenticeship for McDougall's thirteen-year-old son to a Jamaica trader. In doing so, Dundas specifically remarked, 'he is very well educated for his age'. Furthermore, he added, '[t]he boy is an excellent writer and can keep accounts.'[25]

The long-standing notion of Scotland as an especially well-educated nation has not gone unchallenged, however.[26] Even so, it is apparent that among those Scots most likely to go to the Caribbean, literacy was extremely high. In all parts of Scotland, and across all social groups, men were more likely to be literate than women. Among the landed class and the ranks of the professions, illiteracy was rare, at around 1 or 2 per cent. Merchants, too, were overwhelmingly literate.[27] All these groups benefited from gaining access to the universities and to the new academies, whose fees took them beyond the reach of the lower orders. As will be shown, it was from precisely these groups, with literacy levels at about 98 per cent, that venturers to the Caribbean were likely to be drawn. Thus while the famed 'lad o'pairts' was unlikely to be found at university in Scotland, 'the really splendid education which became available to the middle class for professional and commercial training'[28] ensured that young Scots were especially well qualified for employment in the Caribbean.

Scots in British politics

Following the Act of Union in 1707, some overseas opportunities were linked to political developments at home, while the distribution of political patronage in Scotland was often linked to the acquiescence of the government in London. From 1725, the management of Scottish politics and, as a consequence, the control of patronage, lay in the hands of the Second Duke of Argyll and his younger brother, the Earl of Ilay. Their accommodation with Robert Walpole provided his government with a cadre of obedient Scottish parliamentarians in return for the Campbells' control over Scottish appointments. Thus, Scottish affairs tended to be conducted by Scots with relatively little interference, or interest, from London. This control of Scottish politics, especially in the aftermath of the Jacobite risings, elevated Ilay Campbell to the status of Whig grandee. Although the Duke of Argyll broke with Walpole in 1737, Ilay remained with him, and survived Walpole's fall from office. Ilay became the Third Duke of Argyll in 1743 and attached himself to Henry Pelham, ensuring his continued control of politics north of the border.[29] The Campbells were also able to use their powerful position in Scotland to take advantage of Walpole's reliance on them and to assume control over some East India Company patronage.[30]

The period of the Seven Years War, and its aftermath, signalled the dawning of a new era in Scottish politics. At least in part, the military contributions of the newly raised Highland regiments heightened the perception of this as a war that had been fought by and for Britons. Moreover, the controversy surrounding the 1757 Militia Act served to indicate a changing emphasis in Scottish politics. The Act excluded Scotland, much to the displeasure of many in the country. While the older generation of politicians, including the Duke of Argyll, sought a solution from seventeenth-century Scotland in raising fencibles, a younger group insisted on the extension of the English legislation to Scotland. Campaigns to that effect were waged in 1760 and 1762, and drew on the fears of a French invasion to add weight to their claims. The continuing failure of the London ministry to apply the legislation to Scotland was seen by many Scots among the political class and the enlightened literati as discrimination against them, and as a divisive force that undermined the Union. In doing so, they demonstrated their desire for a close integration between Scotland and England, and an extension of the rights of Britons.[31]

After the Third Duke of Argyll's death in 1761 the mantle of Scotland's most senior politician passed to his nephew, John Stuart, Third Earl of Bute. Bute was one of a new generation of Scots. Educated at Eton, he had spent very little of his life in Scotland, but as a consequence of his connections to the Argyll family he remained a key figure in Scottish politics and was the natural, if reluctant, successor to his uncles. Bute's influence, as the former tutor to the recently crowned King George III, served to enhance his position and ensured that he also became an important figure in British politics.[32] He was Secretary of State for the Northern Department from 1761 to 1762 and, thereafter, first lord of the Treasury until 1763, the first Scotsman to hold the highest office in Britain. His influence came to have a profound effect on the rise of Scottophobia, and also for the governance of some Caribbean colonies.

There is little doubt that, by the 1760s, some Scots had begun to emerge as considerable players in London-based politics, much to the chagrin of some English observers. The rampant Scottophobia of John Wilkes, perhaps most clearly exemplified by the forty-fifth issue of *North Briton*, which led to his arrest in 1763, was a reflection of an expanding satirical commentary on the exploitation of patronage by Scots. Satirical work cast its net more widely than Scotland, taking in the 'degeneracy' of the period, or the French, or rival satirists. But Scots and Scotland were frequently seen as suitable targets. Even William

Hogarth, a staunch supporter of Bute, had earlier depicted the Scottish Jacobite as a scrawny, tartan-clad beggar at the gates of Calais.[33]

In the early 1760s, much of the satire was directed at the most notable dispenser of patronage to Scots: the Earl of Bute. Usually represented as a jack boot, Bute was on the receiving end of such a volume of satirical comment that there was reputedly enough to 'tapestry Westminster Hall'.[34] One of the recurring themes in the prints from the early 1760s was the extent to which Scots benefited from Bute's holding high office. In 'The Jack-boot kicked down, or English will triumphant', for example, the boot (Bute) is kicked over by William, Duke of Cumberland, while five kilted Scots are driven out by an English at bayonet point. Cumberland's presence, in a none-too-subtle allusion to the Jacobite defeat at Culloden, reinforced the accusations of Jacobitism levelled at Bute.[35] Satirical doggerel reinforced, in the strongest possible terms, this iconographic vilification of Bute. As one satirist wrote,

> Friend and favourite of France-a,
> Ev'ry day may you advance-a,
> And ven dead by tomb be writ on,
> 'Here lies von whom all may sh_t on,
> Oh, the Great, the Great North Briton![36]

Despite these calumnies, however, Scots continued to enter the political and mercantile elites in London and the outports of Bristol and Liverpool, to an extent that points more towards their acceptance in England than towards their denigration.

Scots were able to operate at all levels of government in Britain and in the West Indies, a fact that was a function of their ever-increasing number in the House of Commons. Between 1761 and 1767 twenty-eight MPs from the forty-five Scottish constituencies held state offices. Only nine of those were civilian posts in Scotland, and the figure of twenty-eight does not include those Scots who represented seats in England.[37] This latter group became more and more numerous as the century progressed. This upward trend in representation meant that by the 1790s the number of Scottish MPs had reached seventy, although there had been no increase in the number of constituencies north of the border.[38] It was bolstered by a number of Scots with West Indian connections, some of whom who were returnees from the islands and who became an integral part of West India lobbying. This group, in particular, seem to have centred its political activity around the major trading ports and financial centres, most notably London and Bristol. More generally, the increase in the number of Scots MPs allowed Scottish networks greater access to Parliament and to political patronage. The presence of an increasing number of Scots in the corridors of power in London coincided with the expansion and consolidation of power in the West Indies. And while this expansion was by no means constantly maintained, the confluence of these key factors affected significantly the chances of Scots, whose networks had ties with the metropolitan authority, of acquiring government jobs in the colonies. As a result, West India Scots found that their involvement of that enterprise they shared with the English, the empire, helped promote the integration of the kingdom.

Relocation to the Caribbean

Despite the apparent benefits of the changes wrought in Scotland in this period, the desire to seek abroad riches and opportunities perceived to be unavailable to them at home and a growing political influence in Britain were strong motivating factors in sending Scots to the Americas. Many thousands left Scotland in the final third of the century, and the flight of impecunious Highland Scots to the colonies to escape rent rises, social dislocation and unemployment has emerged as a common image. Bernard Bailyn's study of the 'Register of emigrants' for 1773 to 1776 has shown that virtually all Scotland saw emigration, with the Highland counties being most affected. Of the 3,872 Scots listed, 3,589 went to the Thirteen Colonies in North America.[39] Outside this very narrow but well-documented period, it is clear that large-scale migration from Scotland was directed to North America and later to settler colonies in the southern hemisphere.[40]

The 'Register of emigrants' records only 119 Scots out of 495 people travelling to the Caribbean during this three-year period. As Bailyn was aware, these figures are probably serious underestimates because often only emigrants in steerage were registered, and it is probable that even some of them went unnoted. More importantly, travellers who went to the Caribbean tended to go as cabin passengers and often went unrecorded. For example, the *Jamaica Packet*, which registered twenty-two steerage emigrants at Kirkcaldy in October 1774, also carried nine cabin passengers who were not listed.[41]

Directly applying the figures for 1773 to 1776 to cover the second half of the century suggests a migration of fewer than 2,000 Scots. In the context of contemporary observations in Jamaica of Scots comprising a third of the white population, and landholding in the Windward Islands of up to 50 per cent, this figure appears far too low.[42] The shortcomings of the 'Register of emigrants' as a source give an indication of the difficulty of determining with any accuracy the numbers of Scots emigrating to the Caribbean. It is, nevertheless, worth speculating as to the scale of Scottish migration.

Alan Karras's estimate of up to 6,000 Scots leaving for Jamaica between 1750 and 1799 is probably closer to the mark. He counted the ships leaving the ports of Greenock, Port Glasgow, Leith and Aberdeen, multiplied them by five to give the likely number of passengers, and added 5.6 per cent for Scots leaving through English ports.[43] While this is the best estimate available for Scots in Jamaica, it is still unreliable. Ships bound for the West Indies left ports other than those mentioned. There is also simply no way of knowing how many passengers went on each ship, and whether they reached Jamaica, let alone stayed there. Contemporary accounts by Lady Liston, Maria Riddell, Janet Schaw and William Jones suggest that nine was the usual number of passengers, rather than five.[44] If this was the norm, then the figure for Scottish emigration to Jamaica jumps to over 10,000, not including any who went in steerage. On the other hand, some ships might have been empty. Therefore, while Karras provides a useful estimate, it must be viewed with some caution.

Assuming that the proportion of different West Indian destinations provided by Bailyn for 1773–76 is representative, and allying them with the figures for Scots in Jamaica, it is possible to estimate Scottish migration to other islands, and to move towards more general figures for all British migrants that concur with other findings.[45] These are shown in Table 1.1.

The figures in italics are the starting points for the calculations. The first column is taken from Karras, and the second is based on applying nine migrants per ship, rather than five, to Karras's method. The third figure is derived from Trevor Burnard's estimate of 736 annual

Table 1.1 Scottish migration to the West Indies, 1750–99

	Karras (5 per ship)	9 per ship	Burnard
All to Caribbean	48,710	86,300	70,906
All to Jamaica	25,000	44,800	36,800
All to Windwards	12,456	22,300	18,336
Scots to Jamaica	*6,000*	*10,800*	*8,868*
Scots to Windwards	3,000–4,980	5,374–8,920	4,426–7,334
Jamaica and Windwards	9,000–10,980	16,174–19,720	13,294–16,202
Scots to the Caribbean	11,600	20,800	17,090

Sources: Karras, *Sojourners in the sun*, pp. 43–5; Burnard, 'European migration to Jamaica'; Bailyn, *Voyagers to the west*, pp. 209, 216, Table 6.4.

migrants to Jamaica, based on his analysis of the volume of migration required to sustain the white population in the face of high mortality.[46] Using Karras's method, Burnard's estimate would have required an average of 7.30 passengers to travel in each ship: a not implausible number. The figures for the Windwards must be viewed very cautiously, partly because the islands were not acquired until 1763. Two estimates for Scottish emigration to the Windwards are provided. The first is based on Bailyn's assertion that 24 per cent of British migrants were Scots. But the Windwards probably had a higher proportion of Scots, and the upper figure is based on Scots forming 40 per cent of the white population across those islands. While these estimates must remain tentative, it is evident that Scottish migration to the West Indies was considerable and probably amounted to about 17,000 departures. It is also clear that while emigrants to North America tended to be composed of family groups, the nature of the Caribbean environment and society meant that emigration there was more likely to involve an individual shot at wealth or advancement. Precisely this distinction is apparent from the records of Scots leaving in the 1770s.

The passengers leaving Greenock on the *Commerce* for New York in February 1774 included many family groups. All were labourers or artisans, and all gave their reason for leaving as 'Poverty and to get Bread'. Typical among those who left Caithness and Sutherland for Wilmington, North Carolina, in April 1774 was John McBeath of Kildonan in Sutherland. He 'left his own Country because Crops failed, he lost his Cattle, the Rent of his possession was raised, and bread had been long dear.' Worse still, he was unemployed. His decision to emigrate was heavily influenced by news from friends in America who assured him 'he would procure comfortable Subsistence in that Country for his Wife and Children.'[47]

The picture of the travellers to the Caribbean is rather different. In general, with the exception of a group of three married couples from Shetland who went to Antigua in 1774, the records suggest two major differences from the patterns of migration to the mainland colonies. Firstly, Caribbean travellers were young single males rather than family groups. The ship *Diana* left Greenock in September 1774 for Wilmington carrying thirty-six passengers, of whom fifteen were female. Ten were children and ten more were over thirty-five years old. They were accompanied by ten passengers going on to Jamaica. They were all male, and all aged between fifteen and twenty. Secondly, it is apparent that the Caribbean venturers were more affluent than the emigrants to the northern colonies. Of the group of thirty-six bound for Wilmington, nine were farmers, four were tailors, and one was a clerk. By contrast, of the twenty-seven travelling to Jamaica from Greenock in July 1775, there were two planters, twelve merchants, a doctor, a surveyor, two clerks, a tailor, two wrights and a blacksmith. Rather than citing penury as a motivation for leaving, these people went to 'follow' their employment, not to seek it. Or they went to live on their property, or to visit friends.[48] It seems from this that agricultural change in Scotland had a very profound impact on migration to North America, but the implications for movement to the Caribbean were rather more complex.

Most of these thousands of young Scots travelling to the Caribbean were not, strictly speaking, emigrants, because they intended to return home. Nor were they necessarily trying to escape the changes being wrought at home. The transformation of title and the management of estates, their more commercial focus and the more 'mannered' lifestyles of their owners required capital. For the landowners, rather than the tenants, the Caribbean, through either mercantile or proprietorial investments, offered a means of raising revenue to finance the changes in their estates and lifestyles.

For other Scots drawn from the mercantile and professional ranks, too, the Caribbean was an important destination. Some Scots from mercantile families went to the Caribbean as a means of acquiring an understanding of the running of the company, before being unleashed on the decision-making process at home. Like the migration of members of the gentry, their migration was not driven by hardship. Other Scots began to trade and plant once they arrived in the Caribbean, and used planting and mercantile activity as a means of making the fortunes that they would later re-invest in Scottish land and industry. This further fuelled the processes of change in Scotland.

The Scottish basis for Caribbean networks

The transformations in land use and management, and moves towards industrialisation and urbanisation, clearly resulted in a fundamental re-ordering of social relations in all parts of Scotland. But the older forms of relations continued to influence the way Scots organised their affairs in the Caribbean.

In the Highlands, the traditional pattern of landholding had involved title being granted by the Crown to the clan elite, who held it in trust for the clans. Clansmen were regarded, and regarded themselves, as part of an extended family headed by the clan chief. The extended family included not only members of the clan itself, but also those of other, associated clans. In return for the protection and patronage of a clan chief, the satellite clan would provide loyal support in time of conflict.[49] This social function of clanship helps to explain the functioning of the networks in the Caribbean: in family and locally based networks the sense of support and protection as well as promotion is palpable.

The structure of the kinship/friendship networks was not only complex, but flexible and responsive to changing local conditions. Different-sized clans were forced to evolve in different ways. Large, powerful clans were able to spread their influence and landholding by means of a 'canopy network' based on 'downward genealogical emplacement'.[50] This involved controlling large areas of land by placing kinsmen, all of whom were loyal to the chief, in charge of different parts of it. An alternative strategy, usually employed by the chiefs of lesser clans who lacked the means simply to acquire lands, was to gradually consolidate smaller holdings. Often this was done by marriage. This strategy brought new members and new lands to the kinship unit by sons marrying exogamously into other landed families. As far as possible, daughters were to remain within the existing unit, and to marry endogamously, to prevent the loss of control over land already held by the clan.[51]

The notion of 'kinship' as a bond needs to be complicated further. Clanship was based not merely on direct blood ties, but upon both the practicalities of geographical proximity and upon more pragmatic alliances of common interest. The geographical factor had the dual effects of differentiating between physically close an distant bloodkin, and of drawing those proximate, but non-biological, 'kin' into the clan's embrace. Often the latter aspect was reinforced, or even initiated, by a sense of common purpose. Large, powerful clans, for example, were able to lease land granted to them to lesser clans, and thereby establish and secure the lesser clan's loyalty. While the small clan was not bound to the larger one in a biological sense, notions of fealty and of shared interests linked the two in a form of fictive or imagined kinship. These pragmatic connections, it has been argued, bound unrelated groups into a 'nexus of shared interests and behaviour, which, at the margins or *in the right circumstances*, could cut across kinship ties, acknowledging putative as well as real ties of kinship.'[52] These forms of fictive kinship, created in response to local conditions by employing the device of marriage or invoking commonality of interest, were hugely important, and not just in the *Gaidhealtachd*. As will be shown, this kind of fluidity within social relations enabled Scottish networks in the Caribbean to encompass within them notions of blood-kinship and local identification, alongside more practical considerations of fictive or imagined kinship. In this manner, Scots were able to employ networks to manage the imperial interplay of kin and local, Scottish, British and transatlantic dimensions.

As these traditional structures in the Highlands were increasingly undermined by the shift from trusteeship to legal title, and by moves from customary to commercial relationships, the role of the chief was fundamentally recast as proprietor rather than protector.[53] But even as the structure of the *Gaidhealtachd* was transformed, the nature of the 'clannish' relationships was replicated and adapted to a Caribbean setting. As the following chapters will show, the founding principles upon which the Scottish networks in the Caribbean were constituted related to the importance of kinship and local associations and to the idea of a mutually beneficial arrangement. These factors, and their responsiveness to particular socio-economic circumstances, suggest that these apparently archaic forms of social relations were being adapted to a modern imperial context at precisely the same time as they came under attack in the Highlands.

Many Scots interested in the Caribbean came not from the Highlands, but from the Lowlands. But the strong cultural association between clanship and the Highlands should not obscure the fact that kinship bonds were also of profound importance in the Lowlands. Bonds of manrent, joining lords and men in mutual agreements under which lords protected men in return for their military service, had been important elements in establishing fictive kinship in Lowland society.[54] Into the late eighteenth century, heads of noble and gentry families could be designated as sources of patronage for the rest of the kin group. By this time, however, the process of 'modernisation' in the Lowlands was further advanced than in the Highlands and differences had become apparent. But it is also clear that family connections connected to underpin social relations in the Lowlands. The marriage alliances entered into by the Glasgow tobacco lords, for example, show patterns similar to the gendered matrimonial arrangements of clan society.[55]

It is apparent that the manner in which Scots employed connections among their families and friends to buttress their imperial activities was heavily influenced by customary social relations at home. One of the most striking features of the Caribbean networks was the way in which they developed fictive bonds to complement the more conventional biological aspects of kinship. As will be shown, the application of these pragmatic considerations of self-interest allowed the Scottish networks to be especially responsive to local Caribbean circumstances.

Conclusion

Across eighteenth-century Scotland great transformations were inaugurated, albeit in a more gradual fashion than terms like 'agricultural revolution' or 'industrial revolution' might imply. These processes of change were intertwined as alterations in land use impacted demographically by encouraging a shift to urban areas. The towns in turn would have been unable to accommodate the increasing demands for food had it not been for the improvements in agricultural productivity that supported the growing number of people no longer producing foodstuffs. There had also been a sea-change in the way people (and especially the elite and professional classes) regarded land use and industrial development. The commercialising of land and industry, perceived as indications of modernity, swept aside customary practices and relationships. Advances in education generated a highly qualified professional populace, particularly in medicine. All these developments were of profound importance to Scotland, but they also had impacts on the Caribbean. The Act of Union of 1707 cleared the way for Scots to the British Empire and allowed a resurgence of long-standing Scottish imperial ambitions. The commercialisation of land and industry required investment capital: one solution was to seek Caribbean employment or enterprise as a means of generating revenue. It is also striking that, while clearance drove thousands of Scots to the colonies, very few of them went to the West Indies. Those Scots venturing to the Caribbean came from quite distinctive social and gender groups. The reasons for this lie largely in the nature of Caribbean society. It is to this that the next chapter turns.

Notes

1 See the commentary from *OSA* quoted by T. C. Smout, *A history of the Scottish people 1560–1830* (London: Collins, 1969), p. 252.
2 *Ibid.*, p. 260.
3 A. I. Macinnes, 'Scottish Gaeldom: The first phase of clearance', in T. M. Devine and R. Mitchison (eds), *People and society in Scotland*, vol. 1: *1760–1830* (Edinburgh: John Donald, 1988), pp. 70–90.
4 *Ibid.*, p. 71; W. Ferguson, *Scotland, 1689 to the present* (Edinburgh: Mercat Press, 1994), p. 177.
5 T. M. Devine, *The transformation of rural Scotland: Social change and the agrarian economy, 1600–1815* (Edinburgh: Edinburgh University Press, 1994), pp. 23–4, 45–7.
6 R. A. Dodgshon, *Land and society in early Scotland* (Oxford: Clarendon Press, 1981), p. 212; Devine, *The transformation of rural Scotland*, p. 25.
7 Devine, *The transformation of rural Scotland*, pp. 11–15; Dodgshon, *Land and society*, pp. 285–7; M. Gray, 'The social impact of agrarian change in the rural lowlands', in Devine and Mitchison (eds), *People and society in Scotland*, vol. 1, pp. 54–8, 66–7.

8 C. W. J. Withers, 'Improvement and Enlightenment: Agriculture and natural history in the work of the Rev. John Walker (1731–1803)', in P. Jones (ed.), *Philosophy and science in the Scottish Enlightenment* (Edinburgh: John Donald, 1988), pp. 102–16; B. Lenman, *An economic history of modern Scotland 1660–1976* (London: Batsford, 1977), pp. 80–1, 97; Ferguson, *Scotland, 1689 to the present*, pp. 169–71.
9 Devine, 'The making of a farming elite? Lowland Scotland, 1750–1850', in T. M. Devine (ed.), *Scottish elites* (Edinburgh: John Donald, 1994), p. 65.
10 T. M. Devine, 'Urbanisation', in Devine and Mitchison (eds), *People and society in Scotland*, vol. 1, p. 32.
11 *Ibid.*, pp. 34–5.
12 J. Campbell, *A political survey of Britain, being a series of reflections on the situation, lands, inhabitants, revenues, colonies, and commerce of this island* (London: no imprint, 1774), vol. 1, pp. 213–15.
13 Smout, *History of the Scottish people*, p. 248.
14 A. J. Durie, *The Scottish linen industry* (Edinburgh: John Donald, 1979), pp. 88, 152–3; Lenman, *An economic history of modern Scotland*, pp. 96, 108–9, 111.
15 *Ibid.*, pp. 124–9.
16 *Ibid.*, pp. 109, 130–4.
17 Devine, 'Urbanisation', pp. 41–2.
18 In 1755, 51 per cent of Scots lived in the north, compared with 37 per cent in the central belt. By 1821, the former figure had declined to 41 per cent, while the latter had increased to 47 per cent. See Smout, *History of the Scottish people*, pp. 260–1; Lenman, *An economic history of modern Scotland*, p. 106; Devine, 'Urbanisation', p. 44.
19 A. Gibson and T. C. Smout, 'Scottish food and Scottish history', in R. A. Houston and I. D. Whyte (eds), *Scottish society, 1500–1800* (Cambridge: Cambridge University Press, 1989), pp. 68–9, 73.
20 C. Shammas, 'Changes in English and Anglo-American consumption from 1500–1800', in J. Brewer and R. Porter (eds), *Consumption and the world of goods* (London: Routledge, 1993), pp. 177–205. See also R. B. Sheridan, *Sugar and slavery: An economic history of the British West Indies, 1623–1775* (Barbados: Caribbean Universities Press, 1974), pp. 20–32.
21 David MacPherson, 'The history of European commerce with India' (1812), quoted in S. W. Mintz, 'The changing roles of food in the study of consumption', in Brewer and Porter (eds), *Consumption and the world of goods*, p. 264.
22 Smout, *History of the Scottish people*, pp. 269–70; Gibson and Smout, 'Scottish food', p. 72.
23 Macinnes, 'Scottish Gaeldom: The first phase of clearance', p. 80; Smout, *History of the Scottish people*, p. 271.
24 L. R. C. Agnew, 'Scottish medical education', in C. D. O'Malley (ed.), *The history of medical education* (Los Angeles: University of California Press, 1970), table 3, p. 260. Of the 3,024 graduates in this period, 2,594 were from Scottish institutions.
25 NLS, MS14828(38), Melville papers, letter from Henry Dundas to Samuel Long, 16 October 1796.
26 For the debate over literacy levels in Scotland see D. J. Withrington, 'Schooling, literacy and society', in Devine and Mitchison (eds), *People and society in Scotland*, vol. 1, and R. A. Houston, 'The literacy myth? Illiteracy in Scotland 1630–1760', *Past and Present*, 96 (1982), 81–102.
27 Houston, 'The literacy myth?', 90–2.
28 Smout, *History of the Scottish people*, p. 479.
29 *Ibid.*, pp. 218–19; J. M. Simpson, 'Who steered the gravy train, 1707–1766?', in N. T. Phillipson and R. Mitchison (eds), *Scotland in the age of improvement* (Edinburgh: Edinburgh University Press, 1970), pp. 47–72; A. Murdoch, *The people above: Politics and administration in mid-eighteenth-century Scotland* (Edinburgh: John Donald, 1980), pp. 4–9.

30 J. M. MacKenzie, 'Essay and reflection: On Scotland and the empire', *International History Review*, 15, 4 (1993), 717. On Scots in India see G. J. Bryant, 'Scots in India in the eighteenth century', *Scottish Historical Review*, 64, 1 (1985), 22–41.

31 J. Robertson, *The Scottish Enlightenment and the militia issue* (Edinburgh: John Donald, 1985); Murdoch, *The people above*, pp. 89, 103.

32 A. Murdoch, 'Lord Bute, James Stuart MacKenzie and the government of Scotland', in K. Schweizer (ed.), *Lord Bute: Essays in re-interpretation* (Leicester: Leicester University Press, 1988), pp. 117–46.

33 See Hogarth's 'Calais gate, or the roast beef of old England' (1749).

34 Horace Walpole, quoted in D. Donald, *The age of caricature: Satirical prints in the reign of George III* (New Haven: Yale University Press, 1996), p. 50.

35 'The jack-boot kicked down', in E. Sumpter, *The British antidote to the Caledonian poison, consisting of the most humorous satirical prints for the year 1762–3* (London: no imprint, 1762–63), plate 2.

36 'A new song' (1762), reprinted *ibid.*, pp. 3–4.

37 L. Colley, *Britons: Forging the nation, 1707–1837* (London: Pimlico, 1994), p. 125.

38 While it was only a trend, the numbers of Scots at Westminster increased steadily from somewhere in the low fifties in the 1760s to a figure in the middle to high sixties in the 1780s, and by the 1790s the figure was over seventy. See L. Namier and J. Brooke (eds), *The History of Parliament: The House of Commons, 1754–1790* (London, History of Parliament Trust, 1964), vols 2, 3; R. G. Thorne (ed.), *The History of Parliament: The House of Commons, 1790–1820* (London: History of Parliament Trust, 1986), vols 3, 4, 5.

39 B. Bailyn, *Voyagers to the west: A passage in the peopling of America on the eve of the revolution* (London: I. B. Tauris, 1987), pp. 92–3, 110–12, 132–3.

40 J. M. Bumsted, *The people's clearance: Highland emigration to British North America, 1770–1815* (Edinburgh and Winnipeg: Edinburgh University Press and the University of Manitoba Press, 1982); M. Harper, *Emigration from north-east Scotland*, vol. 1: *Willing exiles* (Aberdeen: Aberdeen University Press, 1988).

41 Bailyn, *Voyagers to the west*, pp. 78–81; Janet Schaw, *Journal of a lady of quality, being the narrative of a journey from Scotland to the West Indies, North Carolina and Portugal in the years 1774 to 1776* (ed.) E. W. Andrews and C. M. Andrews (New Haven: Yale University Press, 1923), p. 3; 'A list of persons who have taken their passage for Antigua on board the Jamaica packet', in V. R. Cameron, *Emigrants from Scotland to America, 1774–1775* (Baltimore: Genealogical Publishing Company, 1965), p. 53.

42 E. Long, *The history of Jamaica, or the general survey of the antient and modern state of that island* (1774; London: Frank Cass, 1970), vol. 2, p. 287. Long's estimate would suggest that 6,000 Scots, or people of Scots descent, lived in Jamaica.

43 A. L. Karras, *Sojourners in the sun: Scottish migrants in Jamaica and the Chesapeake, 1740–1800* (Ithaca: Cornell University Press, 1992), pp. 29, 31, 43–5.

44 NLS, MS5704(7), Liston papers, Lady Liston's journal from the United States to the West Indies; M. Riddell, *Voyages to the Madeira, and Leeward Caribbean islands* (Edinburgh and London: Peter Hill and T. Cadell, 1792), p. 3; Schaw, *Journal of a lady*, p. 4; O. F. Christie (ed.), *The diary of William Jones, 1777–1821* (London: Bretano's, 1929), p. 10.

45 Bailyn, *Voyagers to the west*, p. 209. According to Bailyn, of the 495 voyagers to the Caribbean, 29 went to Antigua, 25 to Barbados, 31 to Dominica, 75 to Grenada, 257 to Jamaica, 1 to Montserrat, 9 to Nevis, 28 to St Kitts, 14 to Tortola, 9 to St Vincent, 13 to Tobago and 4 to the Moskito Coast.

46 T. Burnard, 'European migration to Jamaica, 1655–1780', *William and Mary Quarterly*, 53, 4 (1996), 769–96.

47 'List of passengers from 3d Feby. excle. to the 10th of February 1774 inclusive', 'Report of the examination of the emigrants from the counties of Caithness and Sutherland on board the ship bachelor of Leith bound to Wilmington in North Carolina, 15 April 1774', in Cameron, *Emigrants from Scotland*, pp. 1–5, 10–11.

48 'List of passengers from this port [Greenock] from the 8th of September 1774 inclusive to the 15th September 1774 exclusive', 'List of passengers from this port [Greenock] from 7th July 1775 inclusive to the 14th July exclusive', in Cameron, *Emigrants from Scotland*, pp. 45–6, 80.
49 A. I. Macinnes, *Clanship, commerce and the House of Stuart, 1603–1788* (East Linton: Tuckwell Press, 1996), pp. 3–12.
50 R. A. Dodgshon, ' "Pretense of Blude" and "Place of thair Duelling": The nature of Scottish clans, 1500–1745', in Houston and Whyte (eds), *Scottish society*, pp. 173–5. Much of the following discussion of clan structures is drawn from Dr Dodgshon's essay.
51 Ibid., p. 176.
52 Ibid., pp. 184–6 (my emphasis). See also A. Cathcart, 'Patterns of kinship and clanship: The MacIntoshes of clan Chattan, 1291–1609', PhD thesis, University of Aberdeen, 2001.
53 Macinnes, 'Scottish Gaeldom: The first phase of clearance', p. 70.
54 T. M. Devine, *Clanship to crofters' war: The social transformation of the Scottish Highlands* (Manchester: Manchester University Press, 1994), p. 5; Dodgshon, ' "Pretense of Blude" ', p. 169, n. 2.
55 T. M. Devine, *The Tobacco lords: A study of the tobacco merchants of Glasgow and their trading activities, c. 1740–1790* (Edinburgh: John Donald, 1975), p. 12.

CHAPTER TWO

The eighteenth-century West Indies

Just as Scotland experienced great challenges and stresses in the second half of the eighteenth century so too did the West Indies. The most profound disjunctions lay between the free white residents and the communities of enslaved blacks and free people of colour. For Europeans, this manifested itself in the maintenance of a colour bar that determined the rights that were enjoyed or denied and the kind of employment that was undertaken. It also played a crucial role in their sense of self-awareness as being different from the 'Other' surrounding them. Throughout the eighteenth century, the fear of the Other was reinforced by frequent risings and rebellions by the enslaved, native Caribs and Maroons, all of which had profound effects on the European population in terms of loss of life and property. Despite the over-arching identity forged among whites in contradistinction to the Other, divisions within white society remained. When the social activities of Scots in the islands and the people with whom they associated in clubs, dinner groups, drinking establishments and theatres are considered, the nature of the divisions become clear.

There were also white women in the Caribbean, although their male counterparts heavily outnumbered them. Observations contained in a number of contemporary travelogues written by women allow their place in Caribbean society to be investigated. While white women were a minority within a minority group, black women were very much more numerous. This large, unfree group held attractions for the young single white men in the Caribbean. Although it is virtually impossible to assess quantitatively the scale of Scottish involvement in miscegenation, it is less difficult to determine the ways in which Scots reacted to fathering illegitimate mixed-race children.

THE EIGHTEENTH-CENTURY WEST INDIES

The location

The term 'West Indies' implies a coherence and uniformity among a number of British-owned islands located in the Caribbean Sea. The islands were geographically scattered, however, and the islands in the eastern Caribbean were over 1,000 miles from Jamaica. The conditions on the islands could be very different. The Windward Islands, and especially Tobago, were closer to the Equator and, consequently, hotter than Jamaica. Some islands had higher annual rainfalls, which was an important factor in the production of sugar and, as a result, helped to determine where people would settle. The *Scots Magazine* reported that 'Many people have tired of dry-weather estates [in Antigua] and have purchased in the new islands.'[1] Jamaica, with large mountains forming a spine down the middle, was split into the low-lying, warmer and less healthy southern region and the more temperate northern mountain region. St Vincent was divided into two zones, the one more wooded and mountainous, the other more fertile. This had an important bearing on relations among the island's inhabitants. Soil conditions, so critical to agricultural production, also varied. By the 1760s, when the 'new islands' in the Windwards were being touted as being blessed with wonderful soil and growing conditions, there was already an awareness of problems of soil erosion and degradation in Barbados, and this was soon to be apparent in Jamaica, St Kitts and Nevis.[2]

The islands were also composed of different populations. The islands principally under consideration here (Jamaica, Dominica, Grenada, St Vincent and Tobago) were all British territories by 1763. The latter four had a higher proportion of Scots than Jamaica, which may be accounted for by the fact that much of Jamaica was settled before Scots were legally allowed access to the empire. Dominica, Grenada and St Vincent also had large French populations, and this particular diversity caused considerable problems in the islands. The enslaved communities throughout the Caribbean heavily outnumbered the white populations. In Jamaica in the 1770s and 1780s, the enslaved outnumbered whites by eleven or twelve to one. In Tobago and Grenada the ratio was more like twenty-two to one, as new planters promoted the rapid transformation of the islands to sugar colonies.[3] In some islands, remnants of indigenous groups also survived, and in St Vincent, the presence of a hostile Carib population became highly problematic for the British authorities.

All this social diversity took place against a backdrop of profound instability. During this period the islands found the Seven Years War (1756–63), the American War of Independence (1776–83), and the French Revolutionary and Napoleonic wars (1793–1815) raging around them. As well as slave revolts, some of which coincided with the periods of war, the islands experienced the fallout from the revolutions on mainland America in 1776 and in France in 1789. The closing years of the century saw the problems of the British West Indies exacerbated by these international conflicts. Residents of Jamaica frequently expressed concern for themselves, their estates and their trade in letters home. In October 1778, George Baird, a Scottish merchant in Kingston, expressed the hope that a large fleet would be sent to Jamaica because French entry into the American War seemed imminent.[4] Throughout the war the residents were in a state of high alert. Jamaican trade was curtailed during the American War, not least in the loss of its trade with the Thirteen Colonies, but the island was never involved in the fighting itself. The authorities in Kingston took no chances, however, and seized Dutch vessels in the harbour in the wake of the declaration of war.[5] The same fears re-emerged in 1805 when Villeneuve led the French fleet across the Atlantic, pursued by Nelson, towards the Caribbean. Lady Nugent, the wife of the lieutenant-governor of Jamaica, wrote, 'To describe the state of my mind is quite impossible, and now I tremble so much, I can hardly hold my pen'.[6]

As troubling and as damaging to trade as the wars of the late eighteenth century were for Jamaica, the island was spared the fate of the Windward Islands. For the Windwards, colonised by Britain as the result of wartime gains, the trauma of warfare was a recurring theme in the years between their cession and the end of enslavement. In 1791, shortly before the outbreak of further hostilities between Britain and France, Thomas Atwood's *History of the island of Dominica* laid considerable emphasis on the effects of the previous war on the island. Roseau, the main town, had been a flourishing free port that was widely used by traders of many countries, including a substantial number of Scots. Atwood described an island that he considered to have great potential but which had not yet recovered from the trauma of war. Estates abandoned at the time of French occupation still lay empty.[7] Tobago remained in French hands until 1793, when it was recaptured by British forces at the beginning of the French Revolutionary War. For all the external difficulties of Caribbean islands, though, some of the main problems in the West Indies were internal.

Economy

The islands of the Caribbean were the central piece of the eighteenth-century Atlantic trading system. While the Atlantic system was much more complex than a simple triangular trade based on Europe, Africa and the Americas, and the Caribbean economies could be diverse and complex, the production of sugar by enslaved Africans and its sale in the rapidly expanding European markets formed the fulcrum about which the Atlantic economy turned.[8]

There was a perception among some who went to the Caribbean that fortunes were relatively easily acquired, and although it was never quite so straightforward, there were a number of ways of making money. The production of tropical staples, especially sugar and its derivatives, but also coffee, cotton, indigo, ginger and cocao, allowed profits to be made from planting and trade. Although the islands developed internal economies, the plantations were reliant on stores and supplies sent from Britain and North America, which presented opportunities for entrepreneurship. Few of these transactions involved cash and most were done on credit. As a result, financing Caribbean enterprises became yet another means of making money.[9] Men employed as plantation managers, lawyers, doctors and book-keepers, merchants' clerks, ships' captains and crews were all employed in this plantation complex, as were those producers and manufacturers in Europe and North America who supplied the plantations.

The performance of the island economies was by no means stable. Fluctuations in sugar yields and prices were caused by weather conditions, soil quality, war, revolt and market demand. The availability of credit varied with war and peace, and was subject to market confidence which could, as happened in 1772 and 1793, quickly evaporate. As later chapters indicate, these fluctuations presented Scots, like others in the Caribbean, with very considerable difficulties. At the heart of all this were the enslaved. Not only was there money to be made from enslaving Africans and forcing them to endure the desperate conditions of the middle passage, but the labour of the enslaved built the Caribbean economies. It was the enslaved who planted, tended, cut and processed the sugar cane on the proto-industrial unit of the sugar plantation.[10]

The alignment of social rank and colour became increasingly clear as the plantations of the West Indies became more and more reliant on the enslavement of Africans as the suppliers of labour. By the eighteenth century, the sight of multi-racial gangs of labourers, once a common feature in seventeenth-century Barbados, was unthinkable. Those whites who did venture to the West Indies as indentured servants in the eighteenth century went out as book-keepers or clerks: often they were literate or numerate Scots. Not only were these young men free, but they were also waged and were bound to serve their employers only for the duration of their indenture.[11]

The highly racialised work patterns in the islands ensured that, in the first instance, social status in the West Indies was conferred on the grounds of colour. In this way, whites were automatically members of the privileged elite and the enslaved were always at the bottom, while free people of colour occupied an uncomfortable middle ground. Gradations of colour were highly structured and widely understood.[12]

The colour divisions amounted to a *de jure* and *de facto* apartheid that manifested itself in a number of ways. In the labour market, those non-whites who were paid for their work received considerably less than their white counterparts. In Grenada in 1794, for example, the Scottish-owned firm of Anderson & Sutor charged its customers two and a half times as much for the labour of white masons as for black masons. Their general account for 12 October 1794 shows the rate for a white mason at 15s per day, and at 6s for a black mason. An unskilled black labourer was valued still lower, at 3s 9d per day.[13]

The power wielded by the free, ruling, white elite over the unfree black slaves was often abused. During the seventeenth century, some overseers had been accused of valuing the lives of horses more highly than those of the enslaved, and of administering savage punishments for minor offences. By the eighteenth century little had changed. Thomas Thistlewood, while overseeing the Egypt and Paradise estates in Jamaica, for example, subjected the enslaved in his charge to the most grotesque punishments.[14] There are relatively few accounts of Scots inflicting punishment beatings. Those that do exist suggest that Scots were just as culpable as anyone else. In Demerara in the 1760s, for example, a dispute arose on Admiral Sir James Douglas's Weilburg plantation between the attorney, William Brisbane, and the manager, Thomas Grant. Grant believed that Brisbane's lenient treatment of the enslaved 'has effectually put it out of my power to be any reall service to the Estate'. Brisbane on the other hand reported that he had merely prevented Grant from killing someone. His description of the beating is chilling: 'he flogged him till he lay without sense or motion then pour'd high [wines] on the back & set on fire the fellow brought to Live by pain run into ye river was saved with difficulty a mortification ensued & now allmost 2 years ago since it happen'd he can crawl'.[15]

Rebellion

Not surprisingly a number of groups in the islands reacted badly to the schemes and brutality of the British plantocracy. From the final third of the seventeenth century, whites found themselves confronted by periodic risings, insurrections and conspiracies fomented by Maroons, Black Caribs and the enslaved. The unstinting self-righteousness of the planters and their legislative bodies blinded them to the fact that these conflicts were largely the results of non-whites reacting against the inhumane or expansionary actions of the British.

In Jamaica in the 1730s, great efforts were undertaken to control the Maroon population. The Maroons were almost entirely composed of runaway slaves and their descendants, who formed two communities in 'cockpit country' in central Jamaica. After eight years of guerilla warfare, a landmark treaty that reserved land for the Maroons, providing that they pledged loyalty to the Crown, was signed between Cudjoe, the Maroon leader, and the Jamaican governor. The treaty ushered in a period of peace between the communities, with the Maroons even acting with British forces to put down slave insurrections. By the time of the French revolutionary crisis in the mid-1790s, however, the threat of an internal 'Other' resulted in a relatively minor confrontation escalating into all-out war between British troops and the Maroons. Led by the governor, Lord Balcarres, British forces prevailed, and a number of Maroons were exiled.

When St Vincent was controlled by France before 1763, an agreement between the French authorities and the Black Carib population (so called because of miscegenation between Caribs and runaways) resulted in the latter controlling the more fertile half of the island. In the 1760s, despite being warned by the London government not even to survey Black Carib land, the new local Land Commission granted 4,000 acres to white planters. Attempts by teams to survey the Carib lands were forcibly resisted, however. In 1768, Caribs forced the 32nd Infantry Regiment, which was supposed to provide protection for the survey teams, to retreat to Kingstown. British planters appealed to London for assistance in 1769, and by 1771 the increasingly 'daring insolence of the Caribbees' was reported in the British press.[16] Sir William Young, the Scottish governor of Dominica, was dispatched to St Vincent in 1772 to deal with the problem. In January 1773, despite calls from the planters for the Caribs to be removed from the island, he concluded a treaty that granted a large tract of land to them, in return for their acknowledgement of the sovereignty of the British king.[17] The planters' aim of banishing the Caribs was not fulfilled until the 1790s, following a major insurrection in 1795.

The greatest fear for whites, however, was a rising by the enslaved population who vastly outnumbered them. This fear was far from unfounded: the treatment of the enslaved ensured that revolts, as well as day-to-day acts of resistance, were frequent. All the Caribbean islands experienced slave insurrections. Tobago had almost annual revolts between 1770 and 1776. In Jamaica Tacky's Rebellion wreaked havoc from Westmoreland to St Thomas in the East between April and June 1760. In 1766, James Stirling on Hampden estate described 'a most dangerous rebellion... amongst the Corromantee Negroes belonging to sundry plantns'. The rising was quashed, but not before damage had been done to a number of plantations. Strikingly, Stirling wrote of the precariousness of the whites' situation, and used it to explain his desire to return home.[18] While none of the British islands experienced revolutions like that led by Toussaint Louverture in St Domingue, probably the most significant uprising took place in Grenada.

Fedon's Rebellion exploded on 2 March 1795. The Scottish lieutenant-governor, Ninian Home, Alexander Campbell and Mr Farquhar were captured by the rebels after their sloop had been outrun by a canoe crewed by 'mulattoes'. With the loss of the governor, the whites established an emergency council. It consisted of seven men, probably four of whom were Scots. Thomas Campbell, Andrew Farquharson and Alexander Frazer joined the president of the council, Kenneth Francis MacKenzie. None of the four were planters in Grenada, nor were two of the other councillors. Indeed, only one, Samuel Mitchell, had a Grenadian estate, a fact which troubled a contemporary observer. The question of absenteeism in general vexed him considerably, as did the presence of planters of French origin.[19] At least a part of the anxiety about the presence of French inhabitants was a fear that their fragile acceptance of British rule would disintegrate in time of conflict. In the context of an insurrection that had been encouraged by representatives of the revolutionary regime in France, Britons on the island found themselves confronted by an alliance of the French and the enslaved.[20] The insurgents continued to rampage across the island, taking hostages and destroying the estates.

When reinforcements arrived, the new Scottish commanding officer, General Colin Lindsay, sought planters to organise loyal slaves into fighting units, but he ran into the problem of absenteeism. There were very few planters on the island, and his efforts were thwarted. In the meantime, the rebels had killed hostages as reprisals for the hanging of insurgents. Important hostages like Ninian Home were reprieved. Dr Hay was spared to provide medical care, and Mr Ker, who had married into a French family, was also allowed to live. At least until 8 April 1795. On that day, as the insurgents' camp was attacked by British forces led by Augustus Campbell, forty-one hostages were murdered, including Home, Alexander Campbell, James Farquhar, William Muir, William Gilchrist, John Livingston and Duncan McDougall. For a time, at the beginning of 1796, the town of St George's was the only part of the island under European control, meaning that 'to all intents and purposes... Grenada was a black republic under arms', and it was not until July 1796 that full control was regained.[21] The author of the *Brief enquiry* estimated that the insurrection had cost the proprietors about £4.5 million currency.

A number of points emerge from these revolts. Firstly, while the position in which the planters found themselves was a result of their own slave-holding or land hunger, it is clear that they had good reason to be afraid. Secondly, the attacks and conspiracies on plantations adversely affected many Scots. A number lost their lives; many others lost estates and income. And thirdly, the frequency with which Scots were involved at the highest levels in dealing with these crises is striking.

Divisions in white society

The fears of being over-run or rebelled against played into other factors that together helped provide the cohesion in white society. The shock of being surrounded by people who looked different made the commonality of skin colour a key factor in the identity of the immigrant European. Surely the diarist William Jones was not alone in being 'amaz'd at the sight of such herds of tawny, sooty Beings, who crowded every street, their bodies little less than naked.'[22]

This entrenched fear resulted in a greater cohesion among whites in colonial society than might be found at home: 'The poorest White person here seems to consider himself nearly on a level with the richest, and emboldened by this idea, approaches his employer with extended hand, and a freedom, which, in the countries of Europe, is seldom displayed by men in the lower orders of life towards their superiors.' Bryan Edwards's remark on the apparent social equality among the white populations of the British West Indies echoes Janet Schaw's comments on society in Antigua on her arrival there in December 1774: 'Every Body in town is on a level as to station, and all are intimately acquainted, which may easily account for the general hospitality.' Writing in the early 1830s, another commentator noted that during the later part of the eighteenth century 'the only distinction in ranks consisted in white, coloured and negro persons. Tradesmen of every description, *if white*, were admitted and invited to the best society.'[23] Despite such observations, however, there were divisions in white society, one of which is implicit in Edwards's comment. The 'poorest White person' did not consider himself to be at the same level as the richest, only 'nearly'. While employees may have viewed themselves in this way, it is not at all clear that their employers would have perceived them as such. The increasing number of absentee landlords allowed their managers and attorneys the opportunity to be drawn into the upper echelons of white society, through the ownership of slaves and the holding of public offices and because they occupied the next rung on the social ladder, but the levelling of white society did not remove all distinctions. Some whites were barred from the elite because of their religious affiliation. In Jamaica, the community of Portuguese Jews in Kingston was excluded. In the Windwards, particular problems arose over the admission of French Catholics to the Grenada legislature.[24]

The most pronounced division in British white colonial society was based on wealth. As a consequence, book-keepers, clerks and overseers tended to be seen as a different group. Book-keepers were among the lowest-paid groups in society, earning perhaps £30 or £40 a year by the latter part of the century.[25] As one Scottish absentee wrote, 'it is better to make them look to a future reward for their good behaviour than to rise their wages – which never fails to spoil them completely.'[26]

In the meantime, the wages of book-keepers and overseers limited the extent of their social lives. When George Inglis of Inverness wrote to his manager in Demerara, he expressed concern about the behaviour of the book-keepers on his Bellfield estate, mentioning particularly their consumption of alcohol: 'I hope none of them have that accursed habit of Grogg drinking, so fatal to the lower class of people with you – when you write me mention how the young men do – and how they behave.'[27] Book-keepers spent much of their free time either drinking or sleeping with enslaved women, or both. Heavy drinking was certainly widespread. During a tour of the Caribbean as early as 1631, Sir Henry Colt found that his normal alcohol intake increased fifteen-fold. Despite the wishes of paternalistic landowners like George Inglis, many slipped into 'drunkenness and debauchery', often under pressure from their colleagues, who branded newcomers as 'greenhorns' or 'novices'.[28] This lifestyle often had a damaging effect on health. A Scottish doctor in Dominica, Jonathon Troup, noted in 1789 that 'affections of the liver [are] very common'. Troup himself, although warning against the perils of heavy drinking, was nonetheless guilty of overindulgence.[29] The danger came not just from the heavy consumption of alcohol in a hot climate, but from the risk of lead poisoning from the stills in which the rum was distilled.[30] The cumulative effect on the white population was damaging. Annual white mortality rates ran at about 10–12 per cent in the eighteenth century.[31]

For those who survived the noxious climate, low wages and heavy work-loads, there were opportunities for advancement. The mortality rate among whites in the islands led to a high turnover of employees and the chance for promotion to the next rung of plantation management and higher wages. With promotions came in an increase in status, allowing those who acquired money to rise in society and be accepted. An *arriviste* was not treated with the same kind of disdain in the West Indies as in Britain.

Bad behaviour was not just confined to the lower orders, however, and was explained or excused by their surroundings. James Baillie, a prominent planter and merchant in the islands, and later agent for Grenada and MP for Horsham, wrote: 'if you could only figure the Multiplicity of Provocations we meet with, with a parcel of wretches that are always doing something wrong, And other accidents & disappointments that are daily happening in this part of the world ... you woud Evenly Excuse a certain degree above those people that have no such temptations in their way.'[32]

Although people like Baillie might engage in bouts of drinking or womanising, few from the lower orders would necessarily have moved comfortably in more 'refined' circles. Social activity among the wealthy planter class that remained in the West Indies took various forms. In some islands a social highlight was a visit to the theatre, such as that experienced by Lady Liston in December 1800. During her visit to her home island of Antigua, she and her husband, Robert Liston (who was British ambassador to the United States), saw an adaptation of *Macbeth* in a small theatre in St John's. Lady Liston was less enamoured of the distractions on offer in some of the other West Indian islands, noting with a hint of pride during a stopover in Dominica, 'upon the whole I found that in point of society my native island, Antigua, has much the advantage of the other British islands.'[33] Dominica, one of the war-torn Windward Islands, was home to a much smaller and less settled white population, so the absence of genteel pursuits should not surprise. Jamaica, though, rivalled Antigua as the social centre of the British West Indies. A permanent theatre had been established in Spanish Town by 1776, along with libraries, social clubs and professional societies. Spanish Town had its own clearly demarcated social season between October and December when the island assembly was in session. By the end of the century, two more of Jamaica's towns had permanent theatres.[34] By the 1790s, more cultural entertainments had arrived in the Windward Islands. Grenada had an opera which in 1790 played host a troupe of French and Italian players.[35]

Social activites, whether for the lower orders or the elite, cut across the national groups comprising the British population. Scots were to be found in all groups throughout the eighteenth century. The most appreciable division was of social rank, but even this was a gulf that could be transcended by the acquisition of wealth. Clearly, the lifestyles of the wealthy groups were quite different from those of the lower orders. One commentator made a distinction between their lifestyles, describing that of the lower orders as allowing 'little time to devote to indolence and the luxuries of table', while 'among the merchants and planters, are many as fat and portly figures as well-fed aldermen.'[36]

Divisions in white society were made particularly apparent in the sphere of education. The lack of schools in the islands left many children untaught and was seen by Edward Long as 'one of the principal impediments' to the effectual settlement of Jamaica.[37] For those wealthy whites who remained in the islands long enough to raise families, the problem of education was solved either by bringing out a tutor from Britain or by dispatching their children back there to school. While these children had access to a higher quality of education, the practice of sending them away to school had a deleterious effect on the West Indies. In 1774, Long bemoaned the fact that a British education was not specifically geared to life in the tropics. He believed that children should study useful subjects like French, Spanish, botany and surveying, in addition to reading, writing and arithmetic. As Chapter Eight shows, Scottish schools began to rise to this challenge. In many cases, children sent away did not return to the islands as residents, preferring instead to remain in Britain, thereby depriving the colonies of young, educated and acclimatised individuals. Moreover, observers argued that this situation benefited the children not at all. Long was especially scathing. The schoolboy, he wrote, 'too often comes from the feet of Gamaliel ignorant, vicious, idle, and prodigal; a disgrace to his friends and a nuisance to his country. If suffered to remain in England, under the notion of finishing his manners, we find him, in the other view, in general rolling on the wheels of money into every species of town debauchery ... the constant dupe of artifice; the sure gudgeon of every knave and imposter.'[38] Long's hyperbole did not disguise his awareness that many parents felt they had little alternative to the impoverished state of education in the island. That is not to say that there were no schools in Jamaica. By 1770, four were operational: Wolmer's (founded 1736), Manning's (1738), Vere (1740) and Beckford's (1744). Further attempts were made in the last quarter of the century to remedy the education crisis. In the mid-1770s, the assembly granted monies for the establishment of new schools at Lucea in Hanover in 1777 and at Titchfield, Portland, which opened in 1785.[39]

Contemporary observers were almost unanimous in believing that distancing children with large allowances from their parents was detrimental to their upbringing. It encouraged absenteeism that resulted in estates being abandoned to the management of attorneys and overseers, while the owners indulged themselves in excess in Britain. Access to education represented a gulf of opportunity in white society, where the children of poorer families received little if any formal education. But Scots were among those who could afford to send their children home, which suggests again that they were to be found across the ranks of white society.

White women

In one notable group of white society Scots were under-represented. The institution of enslavement, as well as having profound effects on labour relations, had great significance for personal relationships in the eighteenth-century West Indies. The ease with which enslaved women could be compelled underpinned the proliferation of inter-racial relationships in the islands, as did the scarcity of white women in the Caribbean. White society in the Windward Islands was dominated by men. Of all the plantations allotments in Dominica, St Vincent and Tobago in 1767, none were to women.[40] By 1770 there were still parishes in Tobago with plantations on which there lived no white women. As Table 2.1 shows, fewer than one in eight plantation residents in Tobago were female, a statistic that is higher than for Scots-owned estates. Plantations owned by non-Scots were three times more likely to have women residents than those owned by Scots.

A similar picture emerges for Jamaica. In the late 1770s, a commentator was told of a parish with no married men and another where there were only two married couples. In Dominica, Jonathon Troup recorded in his journal that there were 'very few white women' in the island. In the Dutch island of St Eustatius, at the time of its seizure by British forces in 1781, only one in seven Scots in the island

Table 2.1 Plantation settlement in Tobago, 1770

	Scots-owned	non-Scots-owned	Total
Number of plantations	31	46	77
Number of white people resident	103	135	238
Number of white men resident	97	112	209
Number of white women resident	6	23	29
Percentage of women	5.8	17	12.2

Source: PRO, CO101/14(127), Grenada, original correspondence: secretary of state, 1769–70. Present state of plantations now settling in Tobago, 1770.

was married.[41] Clearly, Scots tended to travel to the West Indies alone. These were not lands in which they intended to make new lives for themselves and their families, if they had dependents at all. This was certainly the perception in Scotland. The entry for Kiltarlity in northern Scotland in the *Statistical account of Scotland* noted the decline in the male population as a result of young men leaving and young women staying. One of the destinations identified was the Caribbean.[42]

Despite the relative scarcity of white women in the West Indies, there is clear evidence that at least some women played a much more active role in colonial society than their numbers suggest. Dr Alexander Johnston provided medical care to a number of women, at least two of whom owned plantations. Indeed, one, Ann Tucker, owned one of the largest estates in the Jamaican parish of St Ann's.[43] Though a rarity, Tucker was not exceptional. The list of Jamaican landowners drawn up in 1754 indicates that there may have been as many as eleven Scots women who owned land in the island, although it is unclear whether they were residents. Of those eleven, one owned only one acre in the parish of St Ann's, but four were in possession of more than 500 acres.[44] At the turn of the century, a similar number were in possession of land in Jamaica. Scottish women landowners accounted for approximately one-fifth of the fifty-two women holding land in the island in the late 1790s. It is most likely that these women inherited their land from deceased male relatives, often fathers or husbands, who were apparently more prone to early death than women.[45]

Other women engaged in commercial activity. Mrs Tudhope ran a boutique in St John's in Antigua. Her shop, which maintained a stock of the latest fashions from London, was described as being as elegant as any boutique in the imperial capital. Moreover, far from being looked down upon as a working woman, Mrs Tudhope was 'generally esteemed'.[46] In fact, she performed an important function in the island by assisting the white elite to emulate the fashionable standards of metropolitan society. Colonials, no more than Scots, wanted to be regarded as provincial.[47] She was not the only woman to engage in some commercial venture in the islands. Although no women bought plantation land in Dominica in the 1760s, there were cases of their buying town lots which could be used as shops or taverns. In May 1767, twenty-one town lots were sold in Roseau, and among the purchasers were four women. Of those four, two may well have been Scottish. Jean Brown, from Aberdeen, ran a 'publick house and punch house' in Barbados in the 1750s, before moving to around 1759 the Danish island of St Croix, where she opened another punch house.[48]

As well as having to deal with the rigours of running a plantation or a business in the West Indies, women had to deal with their obstructive male colleagues. In 1756, Frances, the daughter of Gibson Dalzell, took responsibility for running her late father's Lucky Hill estate in Jamaica. She obtained a letter of administration so that she could act against her father's trustees, whom she wanted to have struck from control of the will. In the face of considerable prejudice, she had to make a particular effort to demonstrate her competence in a way that would not have been required of a male. As a result, although she was an absentee, she insisted that her manager keep her informed of all developments on the estate and keep very careful accounts for every transaction to ensure that 'my brother may give us no trouble, for I shall not permitt any of the trustees in England to interfere, as they have treated me since ye decease of my father very ill.'[49]

Single women also found themselves to be targets for ambitious men seeking either to consolidate their existing possessions or to begin their careers as landowners. Across the West Indies, there were incidents of young Scotsmen acquiring land through judicious marriages to heirs and widows. In St Kitts, both James Milliken and William McDowall acquired their first land through marriage. As a result of their West Indian connections, Messrs Milliken and McDowall returned to Scotland, where they founded a trading concern that became Alexander Houstoun & Co. of Glasgow. Richard Oswald, long before he became sufficiently influential to act as British negotiator with the Americans in 1783, acquired Jamaican land and influence by marrying Mary Ramsey.[50] In many ways it was probably the easiest way for men to acquire land, a point that was not lost on women at the time. Maria Nugent's comment, when visiting the Money Musk estate of Mrs Sympson, is worth quoting at length: 'Mrs. Sympson is a widow for a second time, and has an estate of ten or twelve thousand a year, which she manages entirely by herself. They say she is an excellent planter, and understands the making of sugar, &c. to perfection. She has many proposals, but finding all her admirers 'interested', she has wisely declined taking a third husband'.[51]

While it is important that the picture of women as industrious planters or shop-owners is presented, it does not, however, convey a wholly accurate impression of their role in the West Indies. These individuals were able to operate in the male sphere of a male-dominated world. Most white women remained at home, taking charge of the house and bringing up the children with the assistance of legions of domestic servants. Although few records of the lives of these women have survived, the accounts of contemporary commentators frequently make mention of them. Edward Long described the women of

Jamaica as 'lively, of good natural genius, frank, affable, polite, generous, humane, and charitable; cleanly in the persons even to excess; insomuch that they frequently bring on dangerous complaints by the too free use of bathing at improper periods.' Janet Schaw, like Long, wrote in favourable terms, describing women in the islands as 'the most amiable creatures in the world', while Thomas Atwood noted their high moral standards and their 'lovely' appearance. Despite the high praise, though, the effect of living in the islands appeared to many of the commentators to have had deleterious consequences for the women. William Jones was particularly scathing in his criticism of white women, and especially of those who had spent their whole lives in the island of Jamaica: 'All the breeding these seem to have is affected. As untaught, & almost as indelicate as those helpless Negroes they imagine themselves born to trample on, Not possessed of the least desire or attention to please; but on the contrary, pettish, insolent & proud. Domestic Oeconomy, one would suppose, had in it something which scared them.' Both Long and Schaw were concerned that some women were 'listless' and 'indolent'. Mrs Carmichael found, in the 1820s, that 'in society, the ladies are too generally found distinguished for their listlessness, and meagreness of conversation, which arise from the uninformed mind.'[52]

Many white women often wore considerable amounts of powder on their faces to ensure a pallid complexion, or masks to prevent any tanning. This was a conscious attempt to mark themselves out as being physically different from enslaved and free-coloured women. For them, whiteness symbolised superiority. This was taken to such an extent that the Scotswoman Janet Schaw was conscious of being one of the few white women who had a tanned face. Indeed, it is highly unlikely that many white women in the Caribbean would have agreed with her when she wrote, 'I have always set my face to the weather, wherever I have been. I hope you will have no quarrel at brown beauty.'[53] This aversion to women with dark skin was certainly not shared by white men in the islands.

Miscegenation

Inter-racial relationships, whether consensual or otherwise, took place throughout the islands. For planters, the possession of the enslaved implied ownership, not just of their labour, but of their bodies. The position of the slave-holder as owner of rights to their bodies was enshrined in colonial law that did not consider rape of the enslaved to be a legal offence.[54] It is more difficult to ascertain how many of these affairs took place; nor is it possible to determine how many Scots behaved in this way, but it is clear that the practice was not just confined to planters. The Scottish overseer of the Hope plantation near Kingston, Jamaica, was one who kept coloured mistresses and fathered their children, despite being described as 'about fifty, clumsy, ill made and dirty'.[55]

On the Mesopotamia estate in Westmoreland parish in Jamaica, one of the Scottish book-keepers, Andrew McAlpine, became the father of a boy named Robert in 1793, as the result of his liaison with a slave woman called Sarah Affir. In St Kitts, Janet Schaw found her old friend Lady Isabella Hamilton keeping an orientally dressed five-year-old mulatto girl as a 'pet' in 1775, implying, perhaps, that the girl was the illegitimate daughter of her husband. In 1789, Dr Jonathon Troup from Aberdeen arrived in Roseau in Dominica, where he found that two of his medical colleagues, Dr Fillan and Dr Carson, had six mulatto children each. Troup wasted little time in taking mistresses himself. In this he was far from unusual.[56]

Some of the effects of these affairs became the responsibility of the doctors, either in attending to pregnant women or, frequently, in providing treatments for sexually transmitted diseases. Over the months of his sojourn in Dominica, Troup was often called upon to alleviate the ailments of men whose escapades returned to haunt them. Indeed, Troup himself had to wait less than a month before he was similarly afflicted, in his case 'from Negroe wench of Dr. C'. Neither the resulting weeks of discomfort and inconvenience, nor his witnessing the distress of patients suffering from 'virulent gonnorhea', however, deterred him from continuing to 'make love to a number of Girls in [his] drunkenness'.[57]

The mothers of Fillan's and Carson's children, mulattos themselves, bore the doctors' names.[58] They, like others, were prepared to take responsibility for their actions. More importantly still, some were willing to acknowledge these relationships back in Scotland. Between November 1786 and April 1789, James Robertson of Tobago spent £178 7s 4d on the upkeep of his two mulatto children in Scotland, Charles and Daniel Robertson. In Jamaica, David Cooper, originally from Edzell in Angus, had followed his uncle to Montego Bay, where he married 'a black or brown woman' and had a family with her.[59] In other cases, Scots made provisions for their children in their wills. There were problems in bequeathing legacies to non-white beneficiaries because colonial law allowed only free-born whites to inherit. The only way for children of mixed race to inherit was to side-step the law, and have a private act passed by the island legislature and ratified in London. Such acts, which allowed these children to be treated equally in the eyes of the law were passed with some frequency by the Jamaica assembly.[60] In 1782, Alexander Johnston, a Scottish doctor and planter in St Ann's, Jamaica, purchased the freedom of two coloured children identified as Jemmy and Jenny Johnstone for £100. Similarly, Alexander Gordon of Tobago bequeathed a £40 annuity and freedom to a mulatto called May, who was married to John Gordon, a carpenter in Tobago. Perhaps the most generous bequest was that of John Shand of Jamaica, who, on his death in 1825, left around £5,000 to each of his ten coloured children.[61] That said, however, not all Scots bothered to meet their obligations. Probably the vast majority were like Troup, who at the end of March 1790 noted that 'Nancy felt the effects of Love . . . she told me she is with Child.' He left Dominica that same day.[62]

National divisions

Evidence suggests that when Scots crossed the Atlantic to the mainland colonies, they tended to form clearly defined groups. Throughout North America, there was a profusion of institutional 'ethnic anchors' for Scots. Church of Scotland and Episcopalian ministries and ministers existed in many mainland colonies, as did societies that were formed to assist emigrant Scots and provide an arena for networking and the maintenance (or perhaps the construction) of a Scottish consciousness.[63] In 1749, the St Andrew's Society of Philadelphia was established by twenty-six Scots, and attracted members who came from all parts of Scotland. It was founded ostensibly to provide charity to poor and destitute compatriots. Each member paid 20s as a joining fee, and a quarterly subscription of at least 5s.[64] In January 1749, Jane MacKenzie from Glasgow, 'being sick & having neither friend nor Relation in this place', humbly craved 'some relief of those Gentlemen of my Country'. She was awarded 40s.[65]

The society provided relief to many Scots, the majority of whom were women, but this was only one facet of its existence. It also provided a meeting place for influential Scots in the community of Philadelphia and its region. William Smith, principal of the College of Philadelphia, was a member, as was John Witherspoon from the College of New Jersey. Within a decade, the membership had swollen to seventy-nine. Later, as the rules were relaxed, honorary members in Scotland were admitted, as were corresponding members in Grenada (William Brown) and Jamaica (David White).[66] It was a similar story in New York, where 260 Scots joined the St Andrew's Society between 1756 and 1774, and there were similar groups in Nova Scotia, Charleston, South Carolina and Savannah, Georgia. But there were none in the British Caribbean.

In some ways this seems surprising, given the numbers of Scots in the islands, the experiences of Scots on the mainland and Janet Schaw's remarks about the presence of Scottish groups in Antigua: 'here was a whole company of Scotch people, our language, our manners, our circle of friends and connections, all the same'.[67] Schaw, a Presbyterian, was forced to attend a church 'which performs the English service' during her stay in Antigua. And although she felt herself to be 'no bigoted Presbyterian', she found in undertaking the Anglican 'ceremonies' 'the force of habit, too strong, I fear, to be removed'. In St Kitts, she heard a Scot give the sermon, but again in an Anglican church, and she lamented that 'tho' the whole Island is divided into regular parishes, and each has a handsome church, yet there is not the semblance of presbytery'.[68] Antigua did not acquire a Church of Scotland ministry until 1842.

In fact, the Church of Scotland showed very little interest in the Caribbean. Its first missionary, who lasted only three months before succumbing to disease, arrived in Jamaica in 1799. Not until 1819 was a kirk built in Jamaica. The real emergence in the islands coincided with the coming of abolition: churches opened in Grenada in 1833, in Tobago in 1837 and in St Vincent in 1841.[69] From Scots in the islands there was no demand for churches as indications of their religiosity or their nationality. For the vast majority, the practice of religion was relatively unimportant, and their identification with it was highlighted only in contradistinction to non-Protestants, as in Grenada in the 1760s. Proclaiming Presbyterianism as an alternative to Anglicanism was not an issue.

It is also striking that there were no Scottish societies in the islands, despite their proliferation on the mainland. There were no Caribbean equivalents of the St Andrew's Society of Philadelphia. There were masonic lodges practising the Scottish rite, as well as societies like the Grenada branch of the Beggar's Bennison. This latter group originated in Fife and specialised in a remarkable range of lewd activities, and was transferred to Grenada by the Scottish governor, Robert Melville. There were Scottish masonic lodges in St Kitts and Jamaica, and probably also in Grenada, and although they and other groups could be important meeting points, they were never exclusively Scottish as the St Andrew's societies to the north were.[70]

There are reasons why Scots in the Caribbean organised themselves differently from those in North America. At a practical level, the societies were not needed in the islands. As was shown in Chapter One, the image of the impecunious Scottish migrant applied less to the West Indies than to the mainland. The need for charitable organisations was very much diminished. Meanwhile, the strong networks tended to provide this kind of support if required, as well as acting as conduits for the disbursement of patronage. Another explanation lay in the intentions of the migrants when they left Scotland. Those who ventured to the West Indies tended to be young, educated, male and single, with plans to endure the Caribbean only for as long as it took to secure their fortune. They did not intend to settle permanently in the same way as their compatriots to the north. This factor, and their continuing correspondence with people in Scotland, meant that they were never required to try to recreate Scottishness abroad. This point may be taken further. Not only did they not need to recreate Scottish communities, but it is unlikely that they wanted to. These people were certainly Scots, but their identification with 'home' tended to be more closely focused on the locality from which they came, and from which their networks originated.

Their notion of identity was also flexible and multi-layered. In their Atlantic world, a willingness to be British was important. To succeed in the empire, and to make their way in England on their return, Scots had to be British. By the second half of the century many could do this comfortably. They shared with their southern neighbours a belief in Protestantism, in empire, in the Crown, in liberty and in commerce.[71] For Scots in the Caribbean to portray themselves as Britons was one thing; it was something else again for them to be accepted as such. But the institution of enslavement, and the perceptions of colour differences, helped to blur divisions in white society.

Notes

1 *Scots Magazine*, 33 (June 1771), 317.
2 *Scots Magazine*, 26 (May 1764), 283; 27 (April 1765), 216; 28 (August 1766), 443; R. H. Grove, *Green imperialism: Colonial expansion, tropical island edens and the origins of environmentalism, 1600–1800* (Cambridge: Cambridge University Press, 1995), pp. 275–8, 294.
3 L. J. Ragatz, *The fall of the planter class in the British Caribbean, 1763–1833* (1928; New York: Octagon Books, 1981), p. 30; R. M. Martin, *History of the West Indies, comprizing Jamaica, Honduras, Trinidad, Tobago, Grenada, the Bahamas and the Virgin Isles* (London: Whittaker & Co., 1836), vol. 1, pp. 267–8.
4 UASCA, MS3175, bundle 64, Duff House papers, George Baird to the Earl of Fife, 9 October 1778.
5 NLS, MS10924/9-10, Graham of Airth papers, letter from Alexander Clark to William Graham, 10 February 1781.
6 F. Cundall (ed.), *Lady Nugent's journal* (London: West India Committee for the Institute of Jamaica, 1939), pp. 298–9.
7 T. Atwood, *The history of the island of Dominica* (London: J. Johnson, 1791), pp. 104–37.
8 On the Atlantic economy see J. J. McCusker and K. Morgan (eds), *The early modern Atlantic Economy* (Cambridge: Cambridge University Press, 2001); D. Hancock, *Citizens of the world: London merchants and the integration of the British Atlantic community, 1735–1785* (Cambridge: Cambridge University Press, 1995); P. W.

Hunter, *Purchasing identity in the Atlantic world: Massachusetts merchants 1670–1780* (Ithaca and London: Cornell University Press, 2001). For non-sugar economies see V. A. Shepherd, 'Pens and pen-keepers in a plantation society: Aspects of Jamaican economic and social history, 1740–1845', PhD thesis, University of Cambridge, 1988; V. A. Shepherd (ed.), *Slavery without sugar: Diversity in Caribbean society and economy since the seventeenth century* (Gainesville, FL: University of Florida Press, 2002).

9 S. D. Smith, '*Merchants and planters* revisited', *Economic History Review*, 15, 3 (2002), 434–65.

10 There is an enormous literature on the slave trade and enslavement in the Caribbean. By way of introduction see D. Eltis, *The rise of African slavery in the Americas* (Cambridge: Cambridge University Press, 2000); D. Eltis et al., *The trans-Atlantic slave trade: A database on CD-ROM* (Cambridge: Cambridge University Press, 1999); R. Blackburn, *The making of new world slavery: From the Baroque to the modern 1492–1800* (London: Verso, 1997); J. Walvin, *Black ivory: A history of British slavery* (London: Harper Collins, 1992).

11 H. Beckles, '"Black men in white skins": The formation of a white proletariat in West Indian society', *Journal of Imperial and Commonwealth History*, 15, 1 (1986), 9; E. V. Goveia, *Slave society in the British Leeward Islands at the end of the eighteenth century* (New Haven: Yale University Press, 1965), pp. 206–7; E. Long, *The history of Jamaica, or general survey of the antient and modern state of that island* (1774; London: Frank Cass, 1970), vol. 2, p. 292.

12 The denomination of colours ran: white–quinteron–quateron–terceron–mulatto–negro. See Long, *History of Jamaica*, vol. 2, p. 260. For a similar structure, see B. Edwards, *The history, civil and commercial, of the British colonies in the West Indies* (London: John Stockdale, 1801, 3rd edition), vol. 2, p. 18.

13 NAS, CS96/4484(7), Court of Session, unextracted processes, day books of Anderson & Sutor.

14 J. P. Greene, 'Changing identity in the British Caribbean: Barbados as a case study', in N. Canny and A. Pagden (eds), *Colonial identity in the Atlantic world, 1500–1800* (Princeton: Princeton University Press, 1987), pp. 236–7; for graphic descriptions of Thistlewood's abuses, in his own words, see D. Hall (ed.), *In miserable slavery: Thomas Thistlewood in Jamaica, 1750–1786* (London: Macmillan, 1989), pp. 71–3.

15 NMM, DOU/6, Papers of Admiral Sir James Douglas, Thomas Grant to Sir James Douglas, 7 March 1766; William Brisbane to Douglas, 2 June 1766.

16 PRO, CO263/1 (no fol.), St Vincent, sessional papers, address by the council, 24 May 1769; *Scots Magazine*, 34 (January 1772), 46; M. Craton, *Testing the chains: Resistance to slavery in the British West Indies* (Ithaca: Cornell University Press, 1982), pp. 145–53; M. Craton, 'The Black Caribs of St Vincent: A re-evaluation', in R. L. Pacquette and S. L. Engerman (eds), *The Lesser Antilles in the age of European expansion* (Gainesville, FL: University of Florida Press, 1996), pp. 71–85; Grove, *Green imperialism*, pp. 288–9.

17 PRO, CO72/3 (no fol.), Dominica, entry books: letters to the Secretary of State, Sir William Young to Lord Dartmouth, 28 July 1772; Craton, *Testing the chains*, pp. 150–3. The 1773 treaty was printed in full in *Scots Magazine*, 35 (April 1773), 175–6.

18 GCA, T-SK22/2, Stirling of Keir papers, James Stirling to Archibald Stirling, 8 July 1766; Craton, *Testing the chains*, pp. 125–39, 153, 172–4; Hall (ed.), *In miserable slavery*, pp. 96–110.

19 E. L. Cox, 'Fedon's Rebellion 1795–96: Causes and consequences', *Journal of Negro History*, 67, 1 (1982), 7–19; Anon., *A brief enquiry into the causes of, and conduct pursued by the colonial government, for quelling the insurrection in Grenada* (London: R. Faulder, 1796), pp. 13–14, 18, 21–2.

20 Victor Hugues, having led rebellions in Guadeloupe and St Lucia, set his sights on Grenada. For examples of Hugues's proclamations on the Grenada insurrection, see Anon., *Brief enquiry*, appendix 7.

21 Craton, *Testing the chains*, p. 189.
22 O. F. Christie (ed.), *The diary of William Jones, 1777–1821* (London: Bretano's, 1929) p. 11.
23 Edwards, *History of the West Indies*, vol. 2, pp. 6–7; J. Schaw, *Journal of a lady of quality, being the narrative of a journey from Scotland to the West Indies, North Carolina and Portugal in the years 1774 to 1776*, ed. E. W. Andrews and C. M. Andrews (New Haven: Yale University Press, 1923), p. 85; A. C. Carmichael, *Domestic manners and social conditions of the white, coloured, and negro populations of the West Indies* (London: Whittaker, Treacher & Co., 1833). See also Goveia, *Slave society*, pp. 212–14.
24 E. Brathwaite, *The development of Creole society in Jamaica, 1770–1820* (Oxford: Clarendon Press, 1971), p. 105. The conflicts between Protestants and Catholics in Grenada are explored in Chapter six below.
25 In 1759, the book-keeper on the Lucky Hill estate in Jamaica earned £25, while Robert Burns was engaged at £30 per annum in 1786: UASCA, MS3175/B2(56)1/2, Duff House papers, current account of Lucky Hill estate with Thomas Bontein; J. MacKay, *RB: A biography of Robert Burns* (Edinburgh: Mainstream Publishing, 1992), p. 200.
26 InvM, Letterbook of George Inglis, 1801–03, pp. 81–3, George Inglis to Hugh Inglis, 19 April 1801.
27 Ibid., pp. 149–50, George Inglis to Hugh Inglis, 1 October 1801.
28 R. S. Dunn, *Sugar and slaves: The rise of the planter class in the English West Indies, 1624–1713* (Chapel Hill: University of North Carolina Press, 1972), p. 6; Christie (ed.), *Diary of William Jones*, p. 44.
29 UASCA, MS2070, Journal of Jonathon Troup, fol. 12v, 16 May 1789, fol. 40v, 9 August 1789.
30 J. Quier, 'Fifth letter from Mr. Quier', in J. Quier et al., *Letters and essays on the small pox and inoculation* (London and Edinburgh: J. Murray and C. Elliot, 1778), pp. 152–3; R. B. Sheridan, *Doctors and slaves: A medical and demographic history of slavery in the British West Indies, 1680–1834* (Cambridge: Cambridge University Press, 1985).
31 T. Burnard, 'European migration to Jamaica, 1655–1780', *William and Mary Quarterly*, 53, 4 (1996), 775–80.
32 NLS, MS5513(187–8), Liston papers, James Baillie to Mrs Ramage, 10 May 1770.
33 NLS, MS5704, Liston papers, Lady Liston's journal from the United States to the West Indies, December 1800–April 1801, p. 27.
34 M. Craton, 'Reluctant Creoles: The planters' world in the British West Indies', in B. Bailyn and P. D. Morgan (eds), *Strangers within the realm: Cultural margins of the first British Empire* (Chapel Hill: University of North Carolina Press, 1991), p. 353; Brathwaite, *The development of Creole society*, pp. 51, 128.
35 *St. George's Chronicle and New Grenada Gazette*, 15 October 1790.
36 George Pinckard, *Notes on the West Indies* (1806) quoted in Goveia, *Slave society*, p. 205.
37 Long, *History of Jamaica*, vol. 2, p. 246.
38 Ibid., p. 247; Schaw, *Journal of a lady*, p. 92.
39 Brathwaite, *The development of Creole society*, pp. 116, 128, 168–9.
40 PRO, CO106/9(246–53), Grenada, miscellanea: account sales of plantation allotments in the islands of Tobago, Dominica and St Vincent, March to May 1767.
41 Christie (ed.), *Diary of William Jones*, p. 23; UASCA, MS2070, Journal of Jonathon Troup, fol. 12v, 16 May 1789; PRO, CO318/8(61–108), West Indies, original correspondence: secretary of state, list of burghers resident in St Eustatius, 20 February 1781.
42 'Inverness-shire, Ross and Cromarty', *OSA*, vol. 17, p. 184.
43 A. L. Karras, 'The world of Alexander Johnston: The creolization of ambition, 1762–1787' *Historical Journal*, 30, 1 (1987), 65.
44 PRO, CO142/31 Jamaica, miscellanea: list of landholders in the island of Jamaica, 1754.

45 NLS Map Library, EMAM.s.5–7: J. Robertson, 'Map of the counties of Surrey, Middlesex and Cornwall in the island of Jamaica', 1804; Cundall (ed.), *Lady Nugent's journal*, p. 81.
46 Schaw, *Journal of a lady*, p. 115.
47 Greene, 'Changing identity in the British Caribbean', p. 231.
48 PRO, CO106/9(251), Grenada, miscellanea: account sales of town lots in Roseau town, Dominica, 14 May 1767; ACA, Baillie Court: propinquity books, 1637–1797, vol. 3, pp. 1,355–7. I am indebted to Dr Marjory Harper for the latter reference.
49 UASCA, MS3175/z/214, Duff House papers, Frances Duff to Mr Price, 6 July 1756, Frances Duff to Mr Howatt, 7 July 1756.
50 V. L. Oliver (ed.), *Caribbeana, being miscellaneous papers relating to the history, genealogy, topography and antiquities of the British West Indies* (London: Mitchell, Hughes and Clarke, 1909–19), vol. 6, p. 15; Hancock, *Citizens of the world*, pp. 51, 64–5.
51 Cundall (ed.), *Lady Nugent's journal*, pp. 80–1.
52 Long, *History of Jamaica*, vol. 2, p. 280; Schaw, *Journal of a lady*, pp. 81, 113; Atwood, *History of Dominica*, pp. 211–13; Christie (ed.), *Diary of William Jones*, p. 31; Carmichael, *Domestic manners*, p. 39.
53 Schaw, *Journal of a lady*, p. 115; B. Bush, 'White "ladies", coloured "favourites" and black "wenches": Some consideration on sex, race and class factors in social relations in white Creole society in the British Caribbean', *Slavery and Abolition*, 2 (1981), 249, 257.
54 H. M. Beckles, 'Property rights in pleasure: The marketing of slave women's sexuality in the West Indies', in, R. A. McDonald (ed.), *West Indies accounts: Essays on the history of the British Caribbean and the Atlantic economy in honour of Richard B. Sheridan* (Barbados: Press of the University of the West Indies, 1996), pp. 169–70.
55 Cundall (ed.), *Lady Nugent's journal*, p. 40.
56 R. S. Dunn, 'The story of two Jamaican slaves: Sarah Affir and Robert McAlpine of Mesopotamia estate', in McDonald (ed.), *West Indies accounts*, pp. 188–210; Schaw, *Journal of a lady*, pp. 123–4; Hall (ed.), *In miserable slavery*, pp. 62–3; UASCA, MS2070, Journal of Jonathon Troup, fols 11, 17.
57 Hall (ed.), *In miserable slavery*, p. 32; UASCA, MS2070, Journal of Jonathon Troup, fols 17, 19, 40v.
58 *Ibid.*, fol. 11.
59 NAS, CS96/1526, Court of Session, unextracted processes, journal of a Glasgow merchant, entries, 91, 96, 113, 115, 120, 123, 144, 153, 165; J. C. Cooper, *A Cooper family from north east Angus* (Elmvale: privately published, 1992), p. 24.
60 There are a number of cases in W. A. Feurtado, *Official and other personages of Jamaica from 1655 to 1790* (Kingston: W. A. Feurtado's Sons, 1896); for an example of an act see UASCA, MS3175/z198(1), Duff House papers.
61 Karras, 'The world of Alexander Johnston', 73; NAS, GD44/34/46/2(3), Gordon Castle muniments, wills of Alexander Gordon, 1800, 1801; Brathwaite, *The development of Creole society*, p. 41.
62 UASCA, MS3027, Journal of Jonathon Troup (no fols), late March, 17 May 1790.
63 N. C. Landsman, *Scotland and its first American colony, 1683–1765* (Princeton: Princeton University Press, 1985); N. C. Landsman, *From colonials to provincials: American thought and culture, 1680–1760* (New York: Twayne Publishers, 1998); D. Dobson, *Scottish emigration to colonial America, 1607–1785* (Athens, GA: University of Georgia Press, 1994), pp. 89, 104, 138, 145.
64 APS, APS361 Sa2, records of the St Andrew's Society of Philadelphia, rules for the society.
65 *Ibid.*, minutes of the society, 10 January 1749.
66 *Ibid.*, minutes of the society.
67 Schaw, *Journal of a lady*, p. 81.
68 *Ibid.*, pp. 93, 129–30.

69 H. Scott (ed.), *Fasti ecclesiae Scoticanae* (Edinburgh: Oliver & Boyd, 1928), vol. 7, pp. 660, 668–71.
70 NAS, GD126/30, GD126/28/2/1(7), Balfour–Melville papers; D. L. Matheson, 'Freemasonry in St. Christopher's island 1739–1983', *Year Book of the Grand Lodge of Antient Free and Accepted Masons of Scotland* (1984), pp. 78–9; F. Seal Coon, 'Scottish freemasonry in Jamaica', *Year Book of the Grand Lodge of Antient Free and Accepted Masons of Scotland* (1982), pp. 100–3, at p. 101.
71 See, among others, L. Colley, *Britons: Forging the nation, 1707–1837* (London: Pimlico, 1994); K. Wilson, *The sense of the people: Politics, culture and imperialism in England, 1715–1785* (Cambridge: Cambridge University Press, 1995); A. Murdoch, *British history 1660–1832: National identity and local culture* (Basingstoke: Macmillan, 1998).

CHAPTER THREE

Scots on the plantations

Scots arriving in the West Indies for the first time were assailed by the profound differences between their home country and their new stations. The immediate shock of the new was often allayed by the welcoming embrace of friends or relations, as Archibald Cameron from Lochaber noted: 'I happened luckly to se Archy Torcastle & John Cameron a brother of Stronse upon my Arraivel. John desaired me to make his House my home. I verry thankfully Accept his offer. Mr Gair the Gentleman I was recommended to by Doctor Gair was vastly keind to me Used all his Endeavours to get me provided, There being no prospect of a Birth in Town, I went up the Country with Archy to Mount Cameron.'[1] As well as pointing to a support network that welcomed newcomers, Cameron's remarks allude to the role played by the networks as vehicles for recruitment. As such they were of profound importance in the manning and maintenance of Scottish-owned plantations throughout the West Indies. The practice of employing relatives or associates from the same part of Scotland as overseers or managers was widespread throughout the later part of the century. It was done in a manner that suggests the adaptation of some traditional forms of clan trusteeship to a more entrepreneurial imperial setting.

Not only were Scots employed by planters, but many were landowners themselves, and they acted as magnets for employment applications. If they returned to Britain as absentees, their need to employ reliable attorneys and managers became all the greater if they were to continue to enjoy profits from their estates.

Jamaica and the Leeward Islands

After the failure of the Darien scheme to establish an independent Scottish Caribbean empire, a few survivors drifted across to Jamaica. One of the more prominent members of this small, wearied band was

Colonel John Campbell. He arrived in Jamaica in 1700 and settled in the parish of St Elizabeth in the west of the island. He was one of the first Campbells in Jamaica; many others were to be born in the island, or to follow from Argyll in western Scotland. Before his death in 1740, Campbell rose to be a prominent figure as a member of both the Jamaica assembly and council.[2] Importantly, Campbell began the establishment of an enormous network in Jamaica, based largely on people from Argyll, and consequently 'through his extreme generosity and assistance, many are now possessed of opulent fortunes.'[3] While it is difficult to be certain how closely related the various Campbells in Jamaica were, it is reasonable to suppose the existence of a Campbell network in the western part of the island. Indeed, the planter-historian Edward Long made a specific reference to this particular group in 1774, having heard 'a computation made of no fewer than one hundred of the name Campbel only actually resident in it [Jamaica] all claiming alliance with the Argyle family.'[4]

Instrumental in the increase of the Campbell colony in Jamaica (as in the case of colonies elsewhere in the Americas) were the attractions of potential wealth and the results of the fundamental changes taking place in the Scottish Highlands from the 1730s. Population growth, allied to the process of clearance, impelled many clansmen overseas. In Argyll in particular, the process of 'commercialising customary relations' through the elimination of *bàile* after 1737 by John Campbell, Second Duke of Argyll, created a pool of migrants, many of whom settled in North America but some of whom ventured to the Caribbean.[5] In many ways, the development of the Argyll community in western Jamaica demonstrates the successful operation of a network based on kinship and local association, and one that retained echoes of the very traditions under attack in Scotland.

There were Campbells all across Jamaica, but the heaviest concentration was in the county of Cornwall, particularly in the parishes of Hanover and Westmoreland. James Robertson's 1804 map of Jamaica noted eleven tracts of land in these two parishes, in addition to other named plantations like Salt Spring and Williamsfield, which were owned by Campbells. Four Malcolms, whose family had long-standing connections with the Campbells in Argyll, were also listed as owning land in the vicinity. Other estates in the area had names derived from places in western Scotland, including Campleton and Argyle in Hanover parish, and Glen Islay in Westmoreland.[6] This geographical proximity suggests that a distinctive feature of Scottish clanship – the 'basis of local affinity' – appeared in western Jamaica.[7]

During the eighteenth century, Jamaica witnessed the immigration and settlement of people not only from the west of Scotland but from virtually the whole country. Around 1727, a young man from the north-east set sail for Jamaica to join his brother. Like many Scots in the Caribbean, James Barclay came from a landed family. His brother in Jamaica, George, was heir to the estate of Cairness. James Barclay, after moving around the island for a couple of years, settled in Kingston and was employed as a book-keeper for a merchant. His earnings of £120 he described as 'not much more than bare Subsistence, if one go neat and handsome as those in my Station are obliged to do'. It is likely that he described his earnings in Scots currency, and that his income was a more probable £10 sterling. The 'bare Subsistence' would hardly have been alleviated by Barclay's attempts to save money to send to his mother.[8]

The subsequent career of James Barclay shows that there were opportunities for advancement in the colonies. By 1739, he had become acting patentee of the receiver-general's office and, according to his brother George, was doing the job most satisfactorily. James's rise in the Jamaican government continued, and by 1762 he had become auditor-general of the revenues at the same time as his compatriot Robert Graham was receiver-general.[9] James was not solely concerned with his own advancement, however. When his brother died in Scotland in 1756, James assumed the responsibility for his Jamaican estate, as well as inheriting the family lands at Cairness. His sister's husband, John Gordon of Buthlaw, informed him of his brother's death. The year before, he had told Gordon of his own brother's demise in Jamaica.[10] This relationship between the Barclays and the Gordons arose from a marriage connection between the two gentry families in the north-east of Scotland. James Barclay's two sisters had both married into the Gordons: one had married John, sixth laird of Buthlaw, and the other had married Thomas. In turn, both Gordons succeeded to the Cairness estate after James Barclay died in 1765. Thomas Gordon's son, Charles, followed his uncle to Jamaica, where he resided as a landowner for some years, before succeeding to the Buthlaw and then the Cairness estates in 1775 and 1776. The Gordons were also closely intertwined with one of the principal networks in eighteenth-century Jamaica, that of the estate manager and attorney Francis Grant.[11] Through him, the network expanded in a number of directions, and particularly through Grant kinship connections.

A number of branches of the Grant family had interests throughout the British Caribbean. Alexander Grant (later Third Baronet of Dalvey) founded his Atlantic trading empire on his plantation in Jamaica, while the Monymusk branch, headed by Sir Archibald Grant, was extensively involved in Jamaica and in ambitious projects for East Florida, notably during James Grant of Ballindalloch's tenure as governor there.[12] While there was mobility between the networks of the different branches, Francis Grant's was most closely associated with the Grants of Castle Grant. Francis's brother, John, was the chief justice of Jamaica during the 1770s. Like Francis, he was enmeshed in the familial network, and engaged in correspondence that linked this group with its 'home' locality. The continued association with their roots was a distinctive feature of Scottish networks on the plantations, as indeed across the range of their Caribbean enterprises. Lewis Grant of the Magoty estate in Hanover parish conducted a regular correspondence with Sir James Grant of Grant in Scotland, who was, in turn, frequently in contact with John Grant in Spanish Town.[13] As might be expected of a man in so powerful a position, John Grant was often called upon to act as attorney for deceased or absentee compatriots, and often for those with connections to north-east Scotland. While acting for Charles Gordon of Buthlaw, Grant settled accounts with the estate of George Richard, and purchased the Georgia estate in Trelawney for £26,000 currency. This estate, he wrote to Gordon, 'will become yours or mine at your option'.[14]

The other principal means of expanding the network came by overlapping with other similarly structured groups. In Jamaica, Francis Grant was a friend of Charles Stirling, the owner of Ardoch Pen in St Ann's. Through marriage, Stirling was related to the Graham family of Airth in Stirlingshire, and increasingly he provided younger Grahams with employment opportunities in the island. Not only did the family connection supply the Grahams with initial openings; it also provided them with a support mechanism and a means by which to create additional opportunities.

In the early 1780s James Graham left Scotland for Jamaica. On his arrival, he worked at the By Brooke estate in St Thomas in the Vale. He fell ill after two months, and went to Charles Stirling's Ardoch Pen to recuperate, after Stirling advised him that the northern part of the island was cooler and healthier. Following this advice, Graham stayed in the north, but moved away from Ardoch Pen. Instead he went to the Hampden estate in St James, which was owned by Thomas Stirling. After a short spell there, in spring 1785 he moved again, this time to the Content estate, at the request of Francis Grant, attorney for that plantation. In two years Graham had worked in three different parishes, on four different estates, but all within a network to which he was tied by a matrimonial link.[15]

As complex and expansive as these networks were, they did not draw in the whole of the Scottish population in the island, which was estimated in 1774 to be about one-third of the white population, or around 6,000 people.[16] Different groups of Scots formed alternative networks, some of which overlapped. Importantly, it is unlikely that any influential Scots were entirely dissociated from these groupings. One of the other groups was based in St Elizabeth parish. David Fyffe of Black River estate arrived in Jamaica from Dundee in the middle of the century, and went 'into the planting way'. By 1761, he leased a 1,600-acre pen with around 300 head of cattle in order 'to get a handsome competency to go home, and live amongst [my] friends'.[17] Fyffe's foray into estate management was not altogether successful. He encountered considerable financial difficulties brought on by the cost of the lease and the deaths of many of the enslaved labourers on the estate.

By 1769, he was still in business, but continuing to struggle under a financial burden. To ease his plight he borrowed money in London and Glasgow to pay off his loans in the West Indies. Relocating his debt in this way allowed him to repay the loan in Britain at a lower rate of interest than in Jamaica and left him free to return home, which he clearly wanted to do: he had 'natural inclinations to leave this island'. In seeking the loans, and the security for them, Fyffe drew heavily on his network of friends and family. His appeal to correspondents at home was successful, bringing him £1,000 from two investors shortly before he returned home. John Wedderburn, a landowner in St Elizabeth, provided the security for these advances for Fyffe. Wedderburn had fled Scotland shortly after the Jacobite defeat at Culloden, but later he too returned, in his case as Sir John Wedderburn of Balindean.[18] The ability of Fyffe to draw upon these resources was of profound importance. In itself, his network could not guarantee that his Caribbean adventure would bring him great wealth, but it did provide him with a far greater chance of success than might otherwise have been the case.

These were not the only members of the group, however. Fyffe sent news home of Dr McGlashan of Kingston, and reported that 'All Dundee folks here well'. Some of these folks lived in the neighbouring parish of Westmoreland, where John Wedderburn and Thomas Fotheringham (who hailed from Angus) leased out their Moor Park and Three Mile River estates in August 1788. John Kerr, who was Fotheringham's father-in-law, had owned these estates, along with the Dundee plantation and property in Savannah-la-Mar.[19]

Yet even this network, which seems in many respects to have been separate from the 'realm of Francis Grant', touched on it. Dr McGlashan, of whom David Fyffe wrote, practised medicine in Kingston in partnership with Dr William Elphinstone. Among Elphinstone's patients was Charles Gordon of Buthlaw, a key figure in Grant's network. Additionally, Elphinstone was a member of the Jamaica assembly in 1775 and in 1780 was an assistant judge at the Jamaica Supreme Court, where he could hardly have failed to encounter Justice John Grant. Both men were granted powers of attorney to act for the affairs of Charles Gordon.

Connections between people from north-east Scotland stretched across Jamaica to the south-eastern corner. After the death of George Forbes of Aberdeen and St Thomas in the East, Drs Charles Irvine and George Alexander, of that parish, and Cosmo Gordon (Forbes's brother-in-law) in St Ann's became executors of his will. Cosmo Gordon also retained strong links with people from Aberdeenshire in his own parish. In partnership with Mr Anderson at Huntly, St Ann's, Gordon maintained a correspondence with Dr Alexander Johnston, also from Aberdeenshire.[20]

Clearly groups of Scots in Jamaica developed systems of patronage networks that were designed to facilitate living and working in unfamiliar surroundings in the tropics. The networks evolved and intertwined as their community in the island grew. Yet it was not simply the size of the community that determined the complexity of the network. Other islands in the Leewards were home to much smaller, though often no less intricate and wide-ranging, networks.

Before 1707 English and Irish families were the most influential members of Antiguan society, but after 1707 Scotland became the most prominent of the sending nations. In Antigua alone, thirteen Scottish dynasties were established during the first three-quarters of the eighteenth century.[21] The example of Dr Walter Tullideph was used to illustrate how Scots seized the opportunities of the West Indies. Tullideph arrived in Antigua around 1726 and joined his brother, who was a merchant there. Employed as a factor by his brother, he also practised medicine in the island, and within ten years had acquired his first plantation through marriage. By 1757, he owned land in Antigua worth around £30,000, and the Baldovan estate in Angus, which he purchased for £10,000.[22] Both his daughters married well, with dowries of £5,000. Mary married the Hon. Colonel William Leslie, and Charlotte married Sir John Ogilvy of Inverquharity in 1754. Both these men owned estates in Antigua, and were near neighbours of the Tullidephs, while Ogilvy was the scion of a landed family in Angus. These matrimonial connections expanded Tullideph's network in the island, which had previously been limited to his brother David, his cousin Walter Sydserf (another doctor-planter) and his uncle, William Dunbar, a London merchant. Dunbar also had another nephew, John Halliday, who had been born in Antigua but whose family came originally from Galloway. Halliday became one of the island's most important residents, owning seven plantations and holding the office of collector of customs.[23]

The experiences of these Scots in Jamaica and Antigua are indicative of the operation of networks based on ties of kinship or local association. In a number of cases, there were clear examples of Scots using links developed at home to structure their enterprises overseas. This was done in a quite conscious fashion. James Barclay, who had utilised his familial and local connection during his residency in Jamaica, was approached by his brother-in-law to assist a young man soon to arrive in the island: 'This letter if it finds the ship at Greenock, will be delivered to you by Mr. Sutherland a young man of a reputable family in the North who has been bred in the merchant way at Glasgow. I know some of his relations here. I have been easily prevailed upon to recommend him (tho a stranger to myself) to the common offices due to a countryman at his arrival.'[24]

The real significance of this type of patronage can be seen in the plight of those who did not receive it. Lewis Grant, of the Magoty estate in Hanover, Jamaica, found himself repeatedly passed over for vacancies in favour of other men who received (as he saw it) preferential treatment. In a moment of desperation, he pleaded with Sir James Grant of Grant firstly to provide him with £500 'to begin the world with', and then to employ his influence to secure an appointment: 'You have it also, through the interest you have with many of your acquaintances who have Estates in this Country, much in your powr to serve me now[.] I have served a tedious apprenticeship to the planting business wherein I have had such opportunitys of being acquainted with Plantation management as must enable me to do the greatest justice to any property I may be entrusted to.'[25] The failure, or reluctance, of networks to provide assistance could leave those outside the circle at a considerable disadvantage. But such instances were rare, and although many Scots suffered financial crises, and were beset by problems of health and disease that were frequently relayed to people at home, there was a steady stream of Scots who sought opportunities in the Caribbean.

By the later part of the eighteenth century, the opportunities for developing a career in Jamaica or Antigua were more limited than they had been for Campbell, Barclay, Tullideph or Fyffe. Overseers or doctors arriving later in the century had fewer chances to buy up land and establish themselves as planters. And even those with access to patrons could find it difficult to find gainful employment. Justice John Grant, who had assisted many countrymen in his time, remarked to Sir James Grant of Grant, 'The folly young men flocking from Scotland to this country is to me unaccountable, very few of them get forward – many of them want bread, and in that number not a few of your clan.'[26]

Although some opportunities became scarcer, they did not dry up altogether. The limited life expectancy in the islands and the transience of the population meant that there was always a demand for book-keepers, overseers, managers and, increasingly as absenteeism became more prevalent, attorneys. And for those Scots who were determined to go to the Caribbean, the acquisition of Dominica, Grenada, St Vincent and Tobago in 1763 opened up a raft of new opportunities.

The Windward Islands

Unlike the older English possessions in the Leewards, colonised before Scots were legally entitled to access to the empire in 1707, the Ceded (or Windward) Islands were opened for occupation by all Britons at the same time, and Scots were particularly swift in seizing the new opportunities.

There were already some settlers of French descent in the islands. Those in Grenada found their lands safeguarded under the terms binding the island's capture by British forces in 1762, but those on St Vincent and Dominica received no such guarantees. The latter islands had been subject to a neutrality agreement between Britain and France since 1748; consequently, the French settlers were deemed to have acted in breach of the agreement and, as a result, retained no rights to the land.

The London government wanted to ensure the orderly sale of the newly available land, and to deter land speculation by requiring payments from the purchasers. The Scottish governor, Robert Melville, was told to forbid land sales until surveys had been completed. This bought the government time to appoint a Land Commission in 1764 and to decide how best to dispose of the land. Plots in Dominica were to be auctioned off in parcels of no more than 300 acres, with a maximum of 500 acres in the other three islands. Payments were to be made in instalments, and purchasers were required to have at least one white man and two white women for every forty acres within three months. This particular stipulation was designed to deter land speculation and to generate a sustainable white British population in the islands. To encourage settlement, provision was made for 'poor settlers'. This device was also intended to provide personnel for the local militias: peace may have broken out in Paris in 1763, but neither the British government nor the settlers were yet prepared to assume it was permanent.[27]

Scots moved quickly to buy up land in the Windward Islands, and purchased considerable tracts of land in plantation allotments and in town and pasture lots. In Tobago, Scots acquired over half the land put up for sale in the late 1760s. Of the seventy-seven plantations settling in the island in 1770, thirty-three of them were owned by Scots, accounting for 15,517 of the 30,440 acres made available. About one-fifth of this land was 'cleared' (i.e. ready for cultivation), and Scots tended to buy proportionately slightly more of the much cheaper uncleared land. This should not, however, imply that Scots were especially impecunious, because plantation allotments had both cleared and uncleared land within their boundaries, and in some parishes Scots actually bought more cleared land.[28]

In both Dominica and St Vincent the situations were similar. In St Vincent in 1765, over a third of the allotments (fourteen of thirty-eight) covering over a third of the land (2,707 of 7,340 acres) were acquired by Scots. Taken together, Scots in St Vincent, as in Tobago, bought more uncleared than cleared land, though the ratio varied across the parishes, and the difference between the amounts of uncleared and cleared land being bought was too small for one to argue that Scots were generally poorer than other settlers.[29] This is borne out by the situation in Dominica, where Scots bought marginally more cleared land than uncleared, even though cleared land was four or five times more expensive than uncleared land in rural Dominica. Even those Scots who qualified for a grant of a thirty-acre 'Poor Settler's Lot' were not so poor as to be unable to purchase other land. Duncan McIntosh was granted 100 acres of uncleared land in St Andrew parish, costing £1 6s an acre, on the same day as he was awarded a poor settler's lot in St George's. Another 'poor settler', Alexander Auchterlony, bought a ninety-four-acre estate only nine months after receiving his award.[30] Once again, the ratios between cleared and uncleared land varied between the parishes, and bore no relation to the number of Scottish-owned plantations in the locality. Importantly, though, the level of this early Scottish landownership was very high in Dominica, as it was in St Vincent and Tobago. More than half the lots and just under half the land made available in the six 'quarters' of the island in 1765 went to Scots.[31]

In addition to the plantation land offered for sale, the Crown made lots available in and around the principal towns in the islands. Here homes could be built, merchants could base their operations, doctors could establish practices, and taverns and theatres could be constructed for the entertainment of the citizenry. And just as Scots snapped up large swathes of plantation land, they were similarly prominent in purchasing town lots.

The two main settlements in Dominica witnessed a considerable Caledonian influx. In Roseau, the principal town in the island, the level of Scottish purchases stood at around 30 per cent between 1765 and 1767, while in Portsmouth, which was smaller, the level rose from just over a third of all lots in 1765 to half in 1767.[32] In 1765 St Vincent's largest settlement, Kingstown, had fifty-five available town and pasture lots, twenty-four of which went to Scots.[33] While there was no direct correlation between Scottish landownership and Scottish residence in the Windwards, the case of Jamaica suggests that the resident population was proportionately more Scottish than the ranks of the landowners. The difference in Jamaica was explained by the function of the networks in bringing other Scots to the island. This kind of group performed similarly in the Windwards, bringing more Scots with blood or fictive kinship bonds to the Caribbean.

The size of individual plots was restricted by the Land Commission regulation that 'no person will be permitted to purchase of the Crown in his own name, or in the name of others, in trust for him' more than 300 acres.[34] But by 1769 Governor-General Robert Melville had acquired over 1,000 acres in the parish of St Andrew in Dominica, in addition to land in Grenada and Tobago. The Dominica estate was held in five contiguous plots, none of which exceeded the 300-acre limit, and apparently without breaching the regulation. By 1769, it was valued at £33,190 currency, or about £20,115 sterling, including the enslaved population of 128, stock and crops.[35]

Melville's acquisition of land suggests something of the operation of networks in Dominica. All the land he bought had originally been granted to someone else. In all probability he purchased it from other Scots who in the late 1760s were part of his political cadre. John Weir, deputy provost marshal in Dominica, was granted a number of plots of land, including in February 1768 one of 230 acres in St Andrews that appeared in the appraisement of Melvill Hall estate in May 1769. A further 300 acres were granted to Alexander Sympson in February 1768, and transferred to Melville in July that year, while still more indentures passed land from Dr John Melvill to Robert Melville.[36] Another member of Melville's clique also owned land in the island. Walter Pringle, council president, was granted 151 acres in St Paul's, only seventeen days after Thomas Pringle was awarded 191 acres in the same parish.[37]

By the latter part of the century there was a network in Tobago based on a group of people with a specific geographical connection. The area formed a triangle between the towns of Elgin, Huntly and Banff in north-east Scotland, and the complex web of connections can be illustrated by the protracted negotiations surrounding a frequent occurrence in the West Indies: the administration of legacies.

In the late summer of 1790, William Russel, a Tobago planter, died. His estate was left in the capable hands of James Donaldson, Alexander Elder and Dr Alexander Gordon. His nephew, Alexander Tulloch of Port Louis, Tobago (but originally from Elgin), was to receive the sum of £500. But neither Donaldson nor his co-executors were willing to take on the responsibility. Helpfully, he offered the services of two other Tobago residents, Dr James Laing (from Elgin) and Mr John Robertson (from Fochabers). Alexander Tulloch in turn held a power of attorney for Alexander Gordon of Belmont plantation on the island. Gordon's brother, Charles, was a landowner in Scotland, and one of his tenants at Fochabers was William Logie, brother-in-law of the late William Russel and a correspondent of Alexander Tulloch.[38]

In time, Alexander Tulloch also passed away, and, as Elder informed Logie, he died intestate. At the same time, Elder also indicated his profound reluctance to have anything whatever to do with untangling the claims on the estate. In so doing he offered something of a contrast to other Scots in the islands. Yet his reluctance sprang from a weariness with frequent demands on his time, rather than from a lack of responsibility to his grouping. He wrote, 'Folks north of the Tweed think every person that dies in the West Indies must be worth a fortune and those who take the trouble to serve you without any recompense defraud you – I have had so much trouble and so little thanks for doing offices of this kind to my own countrymen that I have determined never to take anything of this sort in hand again.'[39]

Once more, John Robertson was prevailed upon to take over. Back in Scotland, the Logies found this all rather disconcerting. Tulloch's death meant that they had no direct connection in Tobago to look after their interests in the island, particularly as Alexander Gordon was in London and had handed the power of attorney to the now-deceased Tulloch. In the meantime, John McKachan had also died on the island, and his family in Keith were keen to recover his money. To these two ends, the Logies and McKachans applied to John Menzies, who was employed by the Gordon family at Gordon Castle, to get Charles Gordon and Baron Gordon in Scotland to prevail upon Alexander Gordon (then in London) to attend to matters in Tobago.[40]

This was not the only time when Alexander Gordon was involved in handling the affairs of a bereaved family. In the four years before his own death, he attempted to recover debts owed to the estate of Robert Stewart, formerly president of the Tobago council. Stewart's family was from Perthshire, and was acquainted with the Gordons, both in Scotland and in Tobago. Gordon's principal headache was recovering the money owed by the Youngs of Delaford plantation. Originally owned by Sir William Young, First Baronet of Delaford, former chairman of the Land Commission and former lieutenant-governor of Dominica, it, and its debts, had passed to his son, William, Second Baronet. The Stewart family had Gordon acting for them in Tobago, and Neil Fergusson acting for them in Scotland, in alliance with their solicitor in London.[41]

The situation was further complicated by the fact that Young was an absentee landlord. Sir William Young was MP for St Mawes between 1796 and 1804 (as well as agent for St Vincent between 1795 and 1802), and as such divided his time between London and his seat at Delaford Park in Buckinghamshire. By 1798, the Stewarts were no closer to recovering their money, which caused Elizabeth Stewart no little distress. She did not live to see her money, and by 1800 her son Neil planned to visit London to settle personally with Young, a plan that was singularly unsuccessful. Almost a year later Neil Fergusson wrote to Young to demand payment of the original bond of £900 along with the outstanding interest arrears.[42] Young, in waiting for the Delaford plantation to pay off its own debts, probably caused part of the delay in repayment. Although it had been poorly run in the past, Young was informed that it was one of the finest estates in the Caribbean. In any event, Alexander Gordon's own death in 1801 released him from the dispute, and it is noteworthy that his own affairs were left carefully ordered.[43]

This network of Scots whose members shared a common link with a part of north-east Scotland expanded in two ways: within Britain, to include individuals in other parts of Scotland and in London; and in Tobago through personal contacts between residents. The shambles surrounding these legacies also demonstrates that while it was possible to make money in the Caribbean, the repatriation of that wealth could be a long and frustrating process.

Grenada, as the largest and most important island in the Windward archipelago, attracted many Scots. Here too they established a new locus for networks based originally on kinship connections and subsequently expanded to include others. James and Alexander Baillie of Inverness purchased the Hermitage plantation, in the parish of St Patrick, in 1765. The brothers had worked together in a mercantile partnership in St Kitts before seizing the opportunities of the post-war Windwards. Alexander remained in St Kitts, while James moved south to manage their new estates. A key feature of his management, in common with that of many of his contemporaries, was his provision of employment for relatives from his home area, where his family owned the Dochfour estate. Yet, like other Scots, he found himself so inundated with requests for jobs that it became a source of frustration for him. He wrote, 'I wish the Rest of the ffamily well provided for, I woud willingly have been all the service I coud for any of them, but places are so seldom to be got, & Mr. Baillie had filled my hands so full of Relations, that I have found great difficulty to provide for two of them ...'.[44] Such sentiments echo those of John Grant of Spanish Town and of Mr Elder in Tobago, and were a common and perfectly understandable grievance among people in the West Indies. While they were aware of their obligations (and their indebtedness) to their networks and families, a number felt that too much was being asked of them. Alexander Johnston of Jamaica, who had provided for a number of people to whom he had a kinship or local bond, was not alone in venting his frustration when he commanded his brother, 'do not be plaguing me with recommendations'.[45]

When James Baillie returned to Britain to run his merchant company from London, he entrusted his affairs to Ninian Home, one of the principal figures in the island. In assuming the management of the estate, Home, despite his status, was required to keep Baillie informed of mundane plantation affairs: in 1787 he wrote to Baillie of the repairs required to the buildings at Hermitage.[46] Home, like Baillie, was a Scot, though from the Borders rather than the Highlands. Both men had been in Grenada since the mid-1760s, and had been involved in island politics since that time. Home's friendship with Baillie's brother Evan, formerly resident in the Caribbean, and by the 1780s a merchant in Bristol, cemented the connection between them as members of the island elite. Some years later, Evan Baillie recalled 'the polite and hospitable attentions' he had received from Home. Some of Home's communications to James Baillie went via Evan.[47] This kind of connection forged in the islands indicates while that networks were based on ties of local association and blood kinship, they could develop around the more circumstantial bonds of common interest discernible in fictive kinship.

After James Baillie's death in February 1793 and the murder of Ninian Home at the hands of insurgents in 1795, Hermitage remained in the hands of the Baillie family into the nineteenth century. Towards the end of the 1790s, the estate was in the care of Alexander Fraser, who was described as a 'planter of experience' and was probably a member of the Grenada council. His connections with the Baillies, and with Inverness, were strong: he had married Evan Baillie's niece 'some years ago', and organised Grenadian contributions towards the founding of the Northern Infirmary in Inverness.[48]

Hermitage bordered plantations in St Patrick parish and the adjacent parish of St Andrew owned by Alexander Campbell (Tivoli estate), John Aitchison (Belmont) and Peter Gordon.[49] These neighbourly connections were reinforced by the members' places in the island's political elite and by other bonds. Ninian Home and Alexander Campbell had been friends in Scotland, and had first travelled to Grenada together. It was a journey Campbell would probably not have made without Home's encouragement, and it is even less likely that he would have stayed had it not been for Home. Campbell's portrait continued to hang in the library of the Homes' family house in Scotland until at least the middle of the nineteenth century.[50] At the heart of this network were the ties of kinship and local association that were common to so many Scottish networks in the islands. The Baillies and Home and Campbell went to Grenada with pre-existing connections. Their proximity to each other in the island, their place in the Grenadian elite and perhaps their common nationality drew them together as a larger and more powerful group.

Following the murders of Home and Campbell in 1795, Home's Grenadian estates of Waltham and Paraclete were left in the hands of members of the network. In 1799, Alexander Fraser prepared to restock the Waltham estate on behalf of George Home, and in 1806 he was charged with unravelling the annuities attached to the estate of Alexander Campbell for which George Home had become liable.[51] These annuities related to the Paraclete estate, formerly owned by Ninian Home and Alexander Campbell. Paraclete was encumbered with debt at the time of its owners' deaths. The shambolic handling of the estate's affairs by Campbell's brother James resulted in George Home advancing money for the payment of the annuities. By 1806, Home was advised by Evan Baillie to vest Alexander Fraser with a power of attorney to try to recover the advances and other debts from Paraclete itself, although he remained pessimistic about the prospects. He believed that if the necessary legal documentation had been prepared by the Campbells, then the 'fatal incorrectness which reached all of their private concerns, woud, I very much fear, extend to this business.' To prevent further delays, Baillie advised Home to grant Richard Landreth power of attorney: 'Mr. Landreth is married to Mr. Fraser's sister and in his absence conducts all his business, and all others committed to his case'.[52]

These networks within the Windward Islands, though less extensive than some of those in Jamaica, nevertheless displayed considerable similarities. Their basic underpinning remained in the kinship or local associations that had developed in Scotland, before radiating outwards to draw in neighbouring planters and their acquaintances. Notably, as is particularly apparent in the Baillie–Campbell–Home network in Grenada, the networks were not restricted to one island: they operated in a transatlantic British nexus between members in

Grenada, Scotland, London and Bristol. And not only did the networks facilitate a transatlantic dialogue; they formed the basis for relationships between the colonies themselves.

Trans-colonial networks

Scottish contacts stretched across the Caribbean region from the Latin American settlements in Demerara and Berbice in the south to Florida in the north. The Young family's involvement in the West Indies began in Antigua, before being expanded by William Young (the elder) to include Dominica, St Vincent and Tobago. He also owned estates on the smaller islands of Bequia and Carriacou.[53] His was by no means the only family to own land in more than one colony.

James Brebner (later Gordon), chief justice of the Ceded Islands from 1765, pursued his landed interest in these islands, after consolidating his position in Antigua. Brebner also had property in St Kitts, after inheriting from his uncle James Gordon, who had been chief justice there between 1735 and 1741. Furthermore, of the eighteen Scots who bought land in St Vincent and Dominica in early 1765, only half are listed with places of origin. Of those nine, seven gave their place of origin as one of the 'older' islands.[54] One of the reasons for moving to the new islands, as well as the chance to expand, was a perception that conditions in the older islands were deteriorating. The *Scots Magazine* reported that increasingly frequent droughts were the motivation for people leaving Antigua.[55]

Some networks extended further than the islands of the Caribbean. The Grants of Monymusk, in addition to interests in Antigua, Jamaica and the Windwards, saw new opportunities in East Florida, which was also ceded to Britain in 1763. As in the Windward Islands, limits were applied to the size and number of land grants in East Florida. In order to circumvent these inconvenient regulations, the Grants of Monymusk and of Dalvey planned to use different family members to purchase land in the new colony.[56] One of those to whom they turned was their kinsman James Grant of Ballindalloch, who just happened to be the governor of the colony from 1763 to 1771. James Grant, as well as acting in an official capacity in East Florida, acquired land there, which he retained after returning to Britain. His indigo plantation turned a considerable profit during the early 1770s, without which revenue, he wrote, 'I should miss the Income of a Florida Governor', which amounted to £1,200 sterling *per annum*.[57]

The growing tension between colonists in North America and the London government depressed indigo prices and provoked the irascible Grant into a typically belligerent opinion: 'Accommodation wont do, Hostilities must commence to draw Order out of Confusion'. The development of a large colony was hindered not by the American War itself, because East Florida became a focal point for loyalists (a relatively high proportion of whom were Scots), but rather because the outcome of the war ended any plans for the area to remain a British colony outside the new United States. The Treaty of Versailles returned Florida to Spain in return for Britain's retention of Gibraltar. As a result many Scots were among the estimated 14,000 to 17,000 loyalists who moved south to the British West Indies after American independence.[58]

To the south, there was a considerable Scottish community in Demerara, despite its not being formally ceded to Britain until after the Napoleonic Wars. Among the estates owned was Weilburg, the property of Admiral James Douglas. Weilburg was a sugar estate acquired by Douglas towards the end of the Seven Years War while he was a naval commander in the Caribbean. Initially, Thomas Grant, with Lachlan MacLean as attorney, managed the plantation. Maclean was an important figure in the colony, and headed one faction in a deeply divided white population.[59] In summer 1765, Douglas dispatched his brother-in-law, William Brisbane of Ayr, to Demerara to act as attorney. This proved to be highly unsuccessful, for despite Douglas's request to Brisbane, 'for God's sake Willy don't run me into any more expenses than is absolutely necessary', the costs of the estate continued to mount, as he ordered stores from Dutch territories despite having ordered sufficient from Britain. A number of these expenses were drawn on de Bruin of Middelburg, to which port Weilburg's sugars were dispatched, while others were drawn on Gedney Clarke, an Anglo-American Barbados merchant and Demerara planter. Although the estate was owned and managed by Scots, it continued to operate within the Dutch sphere. Brisbane's failure to limit expenses was blamed on his wife. As Brisbane's replacement, Robert Milne, explained in 1767 while in Barbados en route to Demerara, 'Mr. Brisbane is infirm himself so everything is done under the instruction of his wife & that she carried herself so haughty to every person that presumed to advise her husband.' More worrying to Milne was the news that there had been 'a great feast in commemoration of the Pretender's birth day', and while he did not want to blacken Brisbane's reputation he felt it 'incumbent on me to give you all information concerning your intrest'.[60] Milne was aware of much bad blood between some of the managers in Demerara, and by the time he reached Demerara he found that the reports were false, and that the Weilburg estate could, with some investment in Africans, cattle and another mill, be the best plantation on the Demerara River.[61]

A group of Scots with particular connections to Inverness and its environs developed in Demerara towards the end of the eighteenth century, and maintained strong ties through the network to the Caribbean islands, Grenada in particular. Thomas Cumming of Inneshouse near Elgin owned the large sugar plantations of Kelty and Garden of Eden. He had extensive connections with Evan Baillie. Towards the end of the century, Cumming had returned to Scotland, leaving his estates in the care of Thomas Newburn, but had decided to get out of the planting business by selling the estates.[62] One of Newburn's correspondents was George Inglis, an Inverness merchant and owner of the Bellefield cotton plantation in Demerara. Inglis also corresponded with Thomas Cumming, and both were in regular contact with Evan Baillie in Bristol.[63]

Among a coterie of Invernessians in the colony who were related to Inglis or Baillie, was Inglis's 'intimate friend and near relation' Dr Colin Chisholm, to whom Inglis's cousin Hugh was directed for advice regarding the management of Bellefield estate. Chisholm, along with the Baillie connection (James Baillie owned the Northbrook plantation in Demerara), tied this network to Grenada, where Chisholm was a practising physician.[64] Chisholm was not the only doctor who practised in Grenada and owned land in Demerara. Andrew Farquharson, a surgeon in the island and member of the council, also owned land in Latin America, as did two other Scottish councillors, Thomas Campbell and Kenneth Francis MacKenzie.[65] These links indicate extensive networks not only within each colony, and between the colonies and the metropole, but also between colonies. That the Baillie brothers began their Caribbean enterprises in St Kitts, before even reaching the Windward Islands, further underscores this point.

James Baillie, as well as being a landowner in Demerara, Grenada and St Vincent, was involved in trade from the Dutch island of St Eustatius in the 1760s. There had been a Scottish presence there since at least the 1750s, no doubt attracted by opportunities for trade from the Dutch entrepot. By 1781, there were probably thirty-four Scotsmen on the island, five of whom were married, with ten children.[66] In the Danish island of St Croix, the McFarlane brothers dealt with Alexander Houstoun & Co. of Glasgow to trade with Glasgow and Copenhagen, while there was also a Highland community on the French island of Martinique at the turn of the century that raised almost £150 to contribute to the establishment of a hospital in Inverness. Alexander Rose of Inverness found 'several Clachnacuddin & north Country gentlemen' during a stop at St Lucia while en route for Jamaica in 1782.[67] This peripatetic tendency on the part of Scots ensured that there were networks throughout the Caribbean. The plantation networks, particularly in their trans-colonial and transatlantic modes, became especially important when a further variable was introduced to planter society.

Absenteeism

The key motivation for venturing to the Caribbean was the promise of wealth. For those who successfully amassed a great fortune, the instinct was, in general, to return to Britain in triumph and to enjoy their wealth far away from the rigours of the tropics. The fortunes accumulated by the more successful planters made them conspicuous additions to the fashionable elite in Britain, attracting even the attention of the king.[68] Some landowners who acquired Caribbean estates by inheritance or as investment never travelled to the West Indies, preferring instead to watch over their ledgers from Britain. But while the notion of following a fashionable cosmopolitan lifestyle supported by the profits from a far-distant plantation was undoubtedly attractive, it was nevertheless problematic. Those remaining in the Caribbean often viewed the absentees with distaste. They criticised them for following political agendas that were often contrary to the interests of the islands. When, in 1773, wealthy planters 'whose overgrown fortunes enable them to live [in Britain] in splendour' opposed a bill to allow foreign investment in British islands, they were attacked by those on a less secure footing. One pamphleteer, ostensibly directing his remarks to Lord North, expressed his hope that 'the labours of the honest and industrious planter, who lives on the spot which owns, will not be sacrificed to please and gratify the rich who live [in Britain].'[69]

In the Windward Islands, the question of British absenteeism had a particular resonance because French inhabitants, whose loyalty to the Crown was considered by British residents to be questionable, owned several major estates. Moreover, it was a matter of grave concern that absenteeism resulted in legislatures being composed of people without a major landed investment in the islands. Grenada, where a number of councillors spent time in Demerara as well as in Britain, found its legislature rather short-staffed. In the midst of a crisis over the role of Catholics in government in Grenada in 1771, Governor Leybourne found he could not quickly solve the problem because he had 'infinite difficulty in finding proper persons to make a Council ... such numbers of Principal Inhabitants being gone this year to England, the island is so thoroughly deserted.'[70]

For the plantation owners themselves, absenteeism presented a series of challenges. Whether the individuals were returnees or relatives who had inherited estates and their legacies, they were forced to rely on other people to manage their West Indian affairs. Managers who were paid a fixed salary, as well as receiving incentives and perquisites, ran estates. Unfortunately for the absentees, some managers abused their positions and diverted plantation expenses and resources for their own ends, to the extent that to be a manager 'was frequently better than enjoying title to the land'.[71] The absentees' selections of managers, then, carried an element of risk. On Gibson Dalzell's Lucky Hill estate in Jamaica, changes in personnel were not uncommon in the early 1750s, changes that were not caused, in the usual Caribbean fashion, by death. In October 1751, Peter Furnell informed Dalzell that Dr William Aikenhead (who also acted for Dalzell) had sacked the overseer. By January 1753, Furnell had been fired. That elicited a barbed response: 'As to your ordering another Agent to transact the Business of your Estate you have, no doubt, a Right to; but if you take the affair into Mature Consideration, it's a Query if you will find any other that wou'd have what I did, or that will be more Service to your Estate than I have been.'[72]

Precisely what Furnell had done wrong is unclear, although he certainly thought his position was defensible. Others were simply considered incompetent, as Francis Grant remarked of Charles Gordon's overseer: 'I see dayly too many instances of Carelessness & bad management in your Overseer, he is by no means the man [we] took him for.'[73] Given these very real problems, absentee planters relied on their networks to appoint, and then supervise, employees for their estates. Charles Gordon's problem with his overseer, for example, was to be dealt with by his attorney Francis Grant, in consultation with John Grant, the chief justice. The employment of attorneys to oversee the managers, and to deal with the legal affairs of the estates, was an important aspect of the management of absentee-owned estates and constituted a further extension of the role of the networks.

Not all managers, of course, were hugely incompetent, nor of 'low station and little learning'.[74] Many ran the estates efficiently, and engaged in frequent correspondence with their employers. For many Scots in the Caribbean, the management of an estate was more than simply a job: they were invested in the enterprise as family members as well as employees, and, as a result, failure was burdened with a much greater penalty than for those with no emotional attachment to their employers. Nor were all absentees just lavish spenders of colonial profits. Many of them kept a close eye on their investments. George Inglis placed great value on his income from the Bellefield estate in Demerara, and sent a constant barrage of letters to his manager and cousin, Hugh Inglis, regarding insurance, cotton production and the placing of Invernessians in the colony. As well as issuing instructions from afar, George had an almost insatiable appetite for news of the estate. In April 1801, he wrote to his cousin demanding 'an exact list of all the shipments you made from the beginning of last crop to the present date'. In May, he returned to his favourite theme of enjoining Hugh to write more fully and more frequently:

> I wrote you on the 29th Apl. and have since got your letter of 14th March, which is very satisfactory, but would have been still more so if you had told me what shipment you expect to make by the April fleet – You tell me that you have wrote me the day after you got the carpenter from Dr. Chisholm ... but as I have not got your letter does not this really convince you how necessary it is to send Copies of your letters if you wish me to receive them?[75]

The importance of having reliable representatives in the islands was brought home to two prominent Scottish families whose long-established estates in Grenada were destroyed in the insurrection that began in March 1795. In December 1766, Lieutenant-Colonel Alexander Johnstone bought the Baccaye plantation in St David's parish for £23,500. Johnstone was the second son of Sir James Johnstone, Third Baronet of Westerhall near Dumfries. All four of his brothers became MPs; one of them, George, was also governor of West Florida from 1763 to 1767, while another, William, married into the Pulteney family, whose name he took in 1767.[76] Alexander renamed his plantation Westerhall, and developed it very rapidly, so that by 1770 it ranged over 1,000 acres and was valued at £95,017 currency (or about £54,295 sterling). It continued to be an extremely valuable estate and was reckoned to be 'one of the best properties in the Islands', annually producing crops worth £10,000 in the years before 1795.[77]

Ninian Home's Waltham estate in St Mark's, purchased in 1776 for £34,000, had also been a profitable estate until shortly before the insurrection. After it, the prognosis was gloomy: 'The house at Waltham remains, but the works are burnt ... and of course the estate cannot again be cultivated in sugar but at some distance of time and after greater expence in re-establishing and replanting it.' Waltham incurred losses estimated at £41,693 currency (£23,489 sterling), a figure that included the value of buildings destroyed, enslaved workers and stock killed or missing and the projected value of crops for 1795–97, based on the average of crops for 1792–94.[78] In all, the planters probably lost around £4.5 million currency, or £2.5 million sterling, in damage to their estates. This loss comprised 7,000 enslaved labourers killed or deported and the destruction of sixty-five sugar and thirty-five coffee estates.[79] More significantly, for the small-scale planters who had invested considerable effort in building a life in the colonies, the chances of being able to start again were slim. Indeed, even those planters with access to large amounts of credit had to

> begin the world a second time, and at an advanced age return with their families, and settle again in a climate of late years so deadly noxious to European Constitutions, that life even in the young and vigorous is scarce worth one year's purchase, and, from the insubordination among slaves produced by the long continuance of the Insurrection, subject to continual repetition, which it cannot but cost years and many lives, to subdue.[80]

Despite these difficulties, which even the melodramatic pamphleteer failed to overstate, the owners of both Waltham and Westerhall did attempt to restore their estates. By July 1796, George Home had been informed that he would have to make an immediate investment of £3,000 sterling to rebuild the sugar works and to buy in sufficient labour and livestock. Even so, he was told not to expect any return from sales of produce until 1799.[81] Clearly, if the planters were unable to produce commodities for export, then the West India merchants who both shipped the goods, and often supplied the credit for planters, would find themselves in difficulties. As the London house of Simond & Hankey informed George Home, 'We have not the smallest hesitation in determining that so good a property should be carried on, the only difficulty is in procuring the means; As merchants we are willing to go as far as our means will bear, yet you must be aware how much we are curtailed by the same events as have reduced Waltham.' As they wrote this, Simond & Hankey were under the impression that only £3,000 would be required to re-establish the estate, at least part of which money they envisaged would be financed by 'a loan from Government' which they were then negotiating.[82] Unfortunately both for the merchants and for Home, the early estimate proved to be wholly inadequate. It increased incrementally over the next nine months, rising first to £5,000, then to £7,000 and finally to £11,000 sterling in March 1797.[83] While the estate continued to labour under the burden of debt, part of which was lessened by the granting of an Exchequer loan of £6,000 by the government in April 1797, it was rebuilt, and produced its first sugar crop in 1798 in time to capitalise on market prices that had been inflated by 50 per cent by the war with France.[84]

The trustees of Westerhall estate, including Sir William Pulteney, committed themselves to the re-establishment of the estate. By the spring of 1797, their manager on the plantation, John Ross, had spent £9,394 to this end.[85] This sum did not include the annual expenses involved in preparing the plantation for production. For the crop of 1797, the London-based firm of J. Petrie, Campbell & Co. dispatched supplies worth £2,567. Like Simond & Hankey, J. Petrie, Campbell & Co. were prepared to allow Westerhall to run a large debt which would be financed, eventually, by renewed sugar sales.[86] Westerhall resumed production rather more quickly than Waltham, perhaps because Sir William Pulteney was prepared to sacrifice the immediate needs of his own Grenadian estate, Port Royal, to those of Westerhall. In 1798, 144 enslaved workers, including fifteen invalids, were transferred from Port Royal to Westerhall, at an annual rent of £1,375. As a result, work could recommence at Westerhall with a full gang that would have cost £11,460 to purchase.[87] These labourers allowed Westerhall's production to increase from 284 hogsheads of sugar shipped in 1798 to 500 shipped in 1799, to be sold in London, Glasgow and Liverpool.[88] Ross oversaw a remarkable recovery in the fortunes of the estate, and even used the opportunity of reconstruction to experiment with different varieties of sugar cane.[89] Westerhall and Waltham were only two of dozens of estates which faced colossal problems in returning to profitability. Yet for some of these absentee landowners, the prospect of being without a valuable source of income was unthinkable. Sir George Cornewall, an English landowner who never visited his Grenadian plantation of La Taste, nevertheless invested £13,729 in re-establishing it, employing the Scottish-owned firm of Evan Baillie & Co. of Bristol to ship supplies to the island.[90]

Of course, where wealth was accrued from Caribbean plantations, it was dependent on the work of the enslaved. There was no single 'Scottish' response to enslavement. A strong sense of abolitionism belied a national ambivalence: although many Scots at home denounced enslavement, there were plenty more who happily profited from it in the colonies. There was no major difference between Scottish planters and those of other nationalities in their dealings with the enslaved. Records for the eighteenth century are patchy, but from them an image of Scottish planters and managers seeking to maximise the number of enslaved emerges. In 1748 Robert Stirling of Keir purchased the Frontier estate in Jamaica with the intention that 'in four or five years time will I hope inable me to come and pass the remainder of my days amongst you.' He based this estimate on an assumption of making an annual profit of about £2,200 currency. To purchase the estate, he drew on his family for financial support. For all his optimism, however, Frontier was not as profitable as planned, and a series of misjudgements were compounded by the acquisition, in 1753, of the Hampden estate in partnership with his brother James. By the 1760s Robert's estates were encumbered with debts amounting to about £60,000 currency. In 1770, the family bought out the estate to clear the debts, and to try to transform its fortunes. To do this, they planned

Table 3.1 The enslaved population on Hampden estate, Jamaica, 1771–80

Date	Men	Boys	Women	Girls	Total
31 July 1771	111	29	73	23	236
31 December 1772	108	29	90	23	250
1 January 1774	105	31	88	24	248
31 December 1774	104	36	85	24	249
1 January 1776	129	42	105	26	302
31 December 1776	124	45	102	34	305
31 December 1777	122	57	106	35	320
31 December 1778	127	65	106	48	342
31 December 1779	122	68	100	48	338
31 December 1780	119	72	99	54	344

Source: GCA, T-SK 22/5–6, Stirling of Keir papers.

to build new sugar works and to buy 100 more slaves.[91] As Table 3.1 indicates, they purchased women and children in preference to men. It seems clear that they hoped to develop a self-sustaining slave population.

This expansion of the labour force produced no consistent increase in the estate's output; with the exception of 1780, annual crops between 1772 and 1783 amounted to between 171 and 225 hogsheads. The prices gained at markets in Glasgow, Bristol and London displayed the effect of the American War, as annual revenues rose sharply before returning to a more typical £3,500. By the late 1780s, though, the estate was turning a healthy net profit, and it made over £6,000 in 1789 and nearly £3,500 in 1790.[92] Perhaps the Stirlings' patience paid off, and they certainly displayed optimism for the future of an estate they had once despaired of: 'if the Seasons continue good, I may safely say we will ship 100 hhds more than last year – It is certainly a most precarious property but with tolerable seasons & a little additional strength of hands, we will be able to reach 400 hhds in a few years.' Importantly, in 1790 John Stirling still believed that an investment in new Africans was worthwhile: 'if they were thoroughly taken care of, the difference of the returns would very soon pay for the Negroes'. Here, at least, there is no sign of abolitionist sentiment from either the planter or his Scottish gentry brother.[93]

Indeed, even after the abolition of the slave trade in 1807, Scots were no more enthusiastic about emancipating their enslaved than other planters. On the estates of key Scottish families there is no evidence either of sustained manumission or of a desperate desire to redirect their wealth into more morally acceptable investments, despite the costs of rebuilding discussed above. While Hermitage and Westerhall both saw declines, the former from 180 slaves to 150 and the latter from 304 to 256, Belmont and Waltham both had larger enslaved populations in 1834 than they had in 1817. They increased from 185 to 191 and from 186 to 244 respectively, with Waltham's increase occurring in the years immediately before abolition.[94] All four estates continued into the emancipation era, and the Baillies retained the Hermitage estate until 1875, following a public auction advertised in Bristol, Glasgow, Liverpool and London.[95]

Conclusion

Across the Caribbean basin, particularly after 1763, the number of plantations growing sugar cane, or producing coffee, indigo or cotton, increased. These plantations, many of which were owned by Scots, offered employment opportunities for other Scots from across the country. In utilising kinship and local connections, Scots on the plantations extended their links throughout the West Indies, purchasing land, engaging attorneys, managers, overseers and book-keepers, and welcoming new arrivals. Strikingly, many of the adventurers came from gentry families. The networks, almost uniformly, were based on pre-existing bonds. From this base, they were extended by individual contacts, both in the colonies and in Britain. In this way, the image of networks of Scots emerges. They were quite consciously transatlantic: investments by Scottish family members in Caribbean plantations were often rewarded by the appointment of a younger family member in the colonies. The patterns of support reflected those of Scottish society, almost as if there were no ocean between them. Some connections, as among the group in Tobago, were almost exclusively centred on a locality in Scotland. Others linked local, Scottish, British and transatlantic circles, facilitating their activities in several colonies and on both sides of the Atlantic. These networks, then, did not exist merely as a series of bilateral links for the transfer of goods, capital and people between Scotland and a colony; they established a lattice of connections that enmeshed Scotland, the Caribbean and Britain in a transatlantic complex.

Notes

1 NLS, Acc. 11910, Haldane papers, letter from Archibald Cameron to John Cameron of Fassfern, 1 April 1766 (formerly Aberdeen University History Department, H1766/1).

2 J. Roby, *Members of the assembly of Jamaica from the institution of that branch of the legislature to the present time* (Montego Bay: Alexander Holmes, 1831), p. 94; J. H. Lawrence-Archer, *Monumental inscriptions of the British West Indies* (London: Chatto & Windus, 1875), p. 340; W. A. Feurtado, *Official and other personages of Jamaica, from 1655 to 1790* (Kingston: W. A. Feurtado's Sons, 1896), p. 18; D. Dobson, *Scottish emigration to colonial America* (Athens, GA: University of Georgia Press, 1994), p. 133.
3 Feurtado, *Official and other personages*, p. 18.
4 E. Long, *The History of Jamaica, or general survey of the antient and modern state of that island* (1774; London: Frank Cass, 1970), vol. 2, p. 286.
5 A. I. Macinnes, 'Scottish Gaeldom: The first phase of clearance', in T. M. Devine and R. Mitchison (eds), *People and society in Scotland*, vol. 1: *1760–1830* (Edinburgh: John Donald, 1988), pp. 70–90.
6 NLS Map Library, EMAM.s. 5–7, J. Robertson, 'Map of the counties of Surrey, Middlesex and Cornwall in the island of Jamaica' 1804, map of Cornwall.
7 A. I. Macinnes, *Clanship, commerce and the House of Stuart, 1603–1788* (East Linton: Tuckwell Press, 1996), pp. 11–12.
8 UASCA, MS1160/5/2, Gordon of Cairness papers, James Barclay to David Gordon, 9 June 1729.
9 UASCA, MS1160/5/3, Gordon of Cairness papers, George Barclay to David Gordon, 30 June 1739; NAS, GD22/1/566, Cunninghame–Graham papers, almanack and register for Jamaica (1762), pp. f–g.
10 UASCA, MS1160/5/7, Gordon of Cairness papers, James Barclay to John Gordon, 3 August 1755; MS1160/5/8, John Gordon to James Barclay, 19 July 1756.
11 H. F. Barclay, *A history of the Barclay family with pedigrees from 1067 to 1933* (London: no imprint, 1933), vol. 2, p. 150; L. G. Pine (ed.), *Burke's landed gentry* (London: Burke's Peerage, 1952), pp. 1016–17; 317; A. L. Karras, *Sojourners in the sun: Scottish migrants in Jamaica and the Chesapeake, 1740–1800* (Ithaca: Cornell University Press, 1992), pp. 66–71.
12 NAS, GD345/1180, Grant of Monymusk muniments; NLS, MS1284, Delvine papers, Grant of Ballindalloch; D. Hancock, *Citizens of the world: London merchants and the integration of the British Atlantic community, 1735–1785* (Cambridge: Cambridge University Press, 1995), pp. 50–8.
13 NAS, GD248/51/2(9), Seafield muniments, Lewis Grant to Sir James Grant, 15 June 1774; GD248/61/2(67), J. Grant to Sir James Grant, 11 November 1774.
14 UASCA, MS1160/6/2/1, Gordon of Cairness papers, John Grant to Charles Gordon, 9 August 1778.
15 NLS, MS10925/5, Graham of Airth papers, Jamaica Papers, James Graham to William Graham, 19 June 1783; MS10925/7, James Graham to William Graham, 2 April 1785.
16 Long, *History of Jamaica*, vol. 2, pp. 287, 316–19; L. J. Ragatz, 'Absentee landlordism in the British Caribbean, 1750–1833', *Journal of Agricultural History*, 5, 1 (1931), 18.
17 NLJ, MS1655/2, Fyffe family letters, David Fyffe to Elizabeth Fyffe, Dundee, 31 May 1761.
18 NLJ, MS1655/3, Fyffe family letters, David Fyffe to 'Cousins', 23 June 1769; MS1655/4, David Fyffe to 'Dearest Cousin', November 1773; Feurtado, *Official and other personages*, p. 129.
19 NLJ, MS1655/4, Fyffe family letters, David Fyffe to 'Dearest Cousin', November 1773; MS1204, Fodringham indenture; MS1235, lease for Moor Park estate, 12 August 1788; NAS, GD121/3/80, Murthly Castle muniments, lease and release of Three Mile River plantation, 11 and 12 May 1781; George Cuthbert to Thomas Fotheringham, 10 February 1786.
20 HSP, 1582/29B, box 2 folder 2, Powell collection, Papers of Alexander Johnston, Hannicher to Alexander Johnston, 1 November 1777, Cosmo Gordon to Alexander Johnston, 10 November 1777; ACA, Baillie Court: propinquity books, 1637–1797, vol. 3, pp. 1465–6. I am grateful to Marjory Harper for this reference.

21 R. B. Sheridan, 'The rise of a colonial gentry: A case study of Antigua, 1730–1775', *Economic History Review*, 13, 3 (1961), 349.
22 R. B. Sheridan, *Sugar and slavery: An economic history of the British West Indies, 1623–1775* (Barbados: University of the West Indies Press, 1974), pp. 197–200; L. A. Timperley (ed.), *A directory of landownership in Scotland, c. 1770* (Edinburgh: Scottish Record Society, 1976), p. 24.
23 J. Schaw, *Journal of a lady of quality, being the narrative of a journey from Scotland to the West Indies, North Carolina and Portugal*, ed. E. W. Andrews and C. M. Andrews (New Haven: Yale University Press, 1923), pp. 81n., 100; V. L. Oliver, *Caribbeana, being miscellaneous papers relating to the history, genealogy, topography and antiquities of the British West Indies* (London: Mitchell, Hughes and Clarke, 1909–19), vol. 3, supplement, pp. 12, 15; Sheridan, 'Rise of a colonial gentry', 351; Sheridan, *Sugar and slavery*, p. 199; Timperley (ed.), *A directory of landownership in Scotland*, p. 21.
24 UASCA, MS1160/5/12, Gordon of Cairness papers, John Gordon to James Barclay, 23 November 1757.
25 NAS, GD248/51/2(4), Seafield muniments, Lewis Grant to Sir James Grant, 15 June 1774.
26 NAS, GD248/61/2(67), Seafield muniments, J. Grant to Sir James Grant, 11 November 1787.
27 D. H. Murdoch, 'Land policy in the eighteenth-century British Empire: The sale of Crown lands in the Ceded Islands, 1763–1783', *Historical Journal*, 27, 3 (1984), 553; L. J. Ragatz, *The fall of the planter class in the British Caribbean, 1763–1833* (1928; New York, Octagon Books, 1981), pp. 111–13; Oliver, *Caribbeana*, vol. 3, supplement, p. 275; D. Hamilton, 'Robert Melville and the frontiers of empire in the British West Indies, 1763–71', in A. Mackillop and S. Murdoch (eds) *Military governors and imperial frontiers c. 1600–1800: A study of Scotland and empires* (Leiden: Brill, 2003), pp. 181–204; R. H. Grove, *Green imperialism: Colonial expansion, tropical island edens and the origins of environmentalism, 1600–1800* (Cambridge: Cambridge University Press, 1995), p. 269.
28 PRO, CO106/9(30), Grenada, miscellanea, account of the first land sales in the island of Tobago, 20 May 1765; CO106/9(246–7), account of sales of plantation allotments in Tobago, 19 March 1767; CO101/14(127), Grenada, original correspondence: Secretary of State, Present state of the plantations now settling in Tobago, 1770.
29 PRO, CO106/9(31–4), account of the first land sale in St Vincent, 29 May 1765.
30 NAS, GD126/4, Balfour–Melville papers, docket register of plantations granted in Dominica.
31 PRO, CO106/9(36–7), Grenada, miscellanea, An account of the plantation lands at Prince Rupert's Bay in . . . Dominica, 25 June 1765.
32 PRO, CO106/9(35–6), account of the first sale of land in the island of Dominica, 35 June 1765; CO106/9(250–1), account sales of town lots in Roseau town, 14 May 1767, and account sales of town and garden lots in Portsmouth, 12 May 1767.
33 PRO, CO106/9(31), An account of the first land sale in the island of St Vincent, 29 May 1765.
34 W. Young, *Considerations which may tend to promote the settlement of our new West-India colonies, by encouraging individuals to embark on the undertaking* (London: James Robson, 1764), p. 19.
35 NAS, GD126/3/1, Balfour–Melville papers, An appraisement of Melvill-Hall estate in Dominica, 22 May 1769. On the rate of exchange see J. J. McCusker, *Money and exchange in Europe and America, 1660–1775* (Chapel Hill: University of North Carolina Press, 1978), pp. 272–3.
36 NAS, GD126/4, Balfour–Melville papers; GD126/3/1, appraisement of Melvill-Hall estate.
37 NAS, GD126/4, Balfour–Melville papers, docket register of plantations granted in Dominica.

38 NAS, GD44/34/46/1(1), Gordon Castle muniments, will of William Russel of Tobago, 28 August 1790; GD44/34/46/1(3), James Donaldson to William Logie, 1 October 1791; GD44/34/46/1(4), Alexander Tulloch to William Logie, 20 August 1792; GD44/34/46/1(10), Alexander Tulloch to Alexander Gordon, 24 July 1794.
39 NAS, GD44/34/46/1(9), Gordon Castle muniments, Mr Elder to Mr Logie, 5 April 1794.
40 NAS, GD44/34/46/1(15), memorandum to Charles Gordon Esq., 28 October 1795.
41 NLJ, MS375/4, letters to Sir William Young and Alexander Gordon of Tobago, Gordon to Young, 9 February 1796; Fergusson to Young, 13 June 1800.
42 NLJ, MS375/22, letters to Sir William Young and Alexander Gordon of Tobago, Elizabeth Stewart to Gordon, 19 November 1798; MS375/11, Neil Fergusson to Young, 15 September 1801.
43 NLJ, MS375/14, letters to Sir William Young and Alexander Gordon of Tobago, James Campbell to Young, 25 August 1801; NAS, GD44/34/46/2(3), Gordon Castle muniments, will of Alexander Gordon, 1801.
44 NLS, MS5513(188), Liston papers, James Baillie to Mrs Ramage, 10 May 1770.
45 HSP, 1582/29B box 2 folder 3, Powell collection, papers of Alexander Johnston, Alexander Johnston to James Johnston, 21 August 1784.
46 NAS, GD267/7/1/16, Home of Wedderburn manuscripts, Ninian Home to James Baillie, 6 June 1787.
47 *Ibid.*; NAS, GD267/5/32/10, Home of Wedderburn manuscripts, Evan Baillie to George Home, 26 Mach 1806.
48 *Ibid.*; PRO, CO101/34(12), Grenada, original correspondence: Secretary of State, state of His Majesty's council of the island of Grenada, 1 January 1795; Northern Infirmary, Inverness, subscription list 1799–1825; R. G. Thorne (ed.), *The History of Parliament: The House of Commons, 1790–1820* (London: History of Parliament Trust, 1986), vol. 3, p. 108.
49 PRO, CO104/1(48), Grenada, sessional papers, minutes of the council, 22 July 1767; BUL, DM1781/BRA2630, West Indies MSS, agreement for sale of Belmont estate, 10 October 1781.
50 NAS, GD267/1/18/22, Home of Wedderburn manuscripts, George Home to Patrick Home, 1 July 1795; GD267/5/39, catalogue of paintings at Paxton House, c. 1853. The paintings were transferred to Paxton House in 1813.
51 NAS, GD267/5/10/3, Home of Wedderburn manuscripts, Richard Landreth to George Home, 21 March 1799; GD267/5/32/10, Evan Baillie to George Home, 26 March 1806.
52 NAS, GD267/5/32/8, Home of Wedderburn manuscripts, Evan Baillie to George Home, 28 April 1806. Papers relating to the case may be found in GD267/5/9.
53 S. L. Hough and P. R. O. Hough (eds), *The Beinecke Lesser Antilles collection at Hamilton College, 1521–1860* (Gainesville: University of Florida Press, 1994), pp. 235–6.
54 Oliver, *Caribbeana*, vol. 3, supplement, p. 82; NAS, GD1/32/38(27), Miscellaneous accessions, An account of all the lands sold in the islands of St Vincent and Dominica.
55 *Scots Magazine*, 33 (June 1771), 317.
56 NAS, GD1/32/38(11), Miscellaneous accessions, Sir Alexander Grant to Sir Archibald Grant, 15 November 1769.
57 NLS, MS1284/203, Delvine papers, Grant of Ballindalloch, James Grant to ?, 1 February 1774; R. C. Simmons and P. D. G. Thomas (eds), *Proceedings and debates of the British parliaments respecting North America, 1754–1783* (Millwood, NY: Klaus International Publications, 1983), vol. 2, p. 36.
58 A. McFarlane, *The British in the Americas 1480–1815* (London: Longman, 1994), pp. 289–90.
59 NMM, DOU/6, Papers of Admiral Sir James Douglas, letterbook 1762–67, letter from William Brisbane, 14 April 1766.
60 *Ibid.*, James Douglas to 'Willy', 28 August 1766; letter from William Brisbane, 21 July 1767; letter from Robert Milne, 6 July 1767.

61 *Ibid.*, letters from Robert Milne, 1 July, 8 July, 25 July 1767.
62 NAS, GD23/364(10–11), Bught papers, letterbook of Thomas Cumming, 1799–1810.
63 InvM, Letterbook of George Inglis, George Inglis to Thomas Newburn, 10 April 1801; NAS, GD23/364(36), Bught papers, Thomas Cumming to George Inglis.
64 InvM, Letterbook of George Inglis, George Inglis to Evan Baillie, 6 April 1802; George Inglis to Hugh Inglis, Demerara, 22 October 1801; Thorne, *House of Commons, 1790–1820*, vol. 3, p. 110; Anon., *Monumental inscriptions, chapel burial ground Inverness* (Inverness: Highland Family History Society, 1996), pp. 73, 97.
65 PRO, CO101/34(12), Grenada, original correspondence: Secretary of State, list of the members of His Majesty's council in Grenada, 1 January 1795; Anon, *Brief enquiry*, p. 13.
66 'Letter from James Baillie, St. Eustatius, 20 July 1761', in C. Fraser-MacIntosh (ed.), *Letters of two centuries, chiefly connected with Inverness and the Highlands, from 1616 to 1815* (Inverness: A. & W. MacKenzie, 1890), pp. 254–5; PRO, CO 318/8(61–108), West Indies, original correspondence: secretary of State, list of burghers resident in St Eustatius, 20 February 1781.
67 NLS, MS8794(35–6), Alexander Houstoun & Co. papers, foreign letterbook F, letter to David McFarlane, 20 July 1778; Northern Infirmary, Inverness, subscription list 1799–1825; NAS, GD128/44/6b, Fraser–MacIntosh papers, Alexander Rose to John MacIntosh, 31 March 1782.
68 Ragatz, 'Absentee landlordism', 11.
69 Anon., *Considerations of the state of the sugar islands, and on the policy of enabling foreigners to lend money on real securities in those colonies* (London: no imprint, 1773), p. 27.
70 PRO, CO101/5(45), Grenada, original correspondence: Board of Trade, Governor Leybourne to Lord Hillsborough, 11 November 1771.
71 C. J. Cowton and A. J. O'Shaughnessy, 'Absentee control of sugar plantations in the British West Indies', *Accounting and Business Research*, 22, 85 (1991), 35–6; Ragatz, 'Absentee landlordism', 20.
72 UASCA, MS3175/Z61/1(5–6), Duff House papers, Peter Furnell to Gibson Dalzell, 12 October 1751 and 21 January 1753.
73 UASCA, MS1160/6/15(1), Gordon of Cairness papers, Francis Grant to Charles Gordon, 23 September 1781.
74 Ragatz, 'Absentee landlordism', 21.
75 InvM, Letterbook of George Inglis, George Inglis to Hugh Inglis, 29 April 1801 and 22 May 1801.
76 L. Namier and J. Brooke (eds), *The History of Parliament: The House of Commons, 1754–1790* (London: History of Parliament Trust, 1964), vol. 2, pp. 683–7; vol. 3, pp. 341–3.
77 BUL, DM41/63/1, West Indies MSS, Westerhall papers, schedule of the title deeds of Alexander Johnstone; DM41/32/1, inventory and valuation of . . . Baccaye, 1 December 1770; DM41/61/9, draft letter.
78 NAS, GD267/5/19/6, Home of Wedderburn manuscripts, Mather Byles to George Home, 9 October 1795; GD267/5/28/3, estimate of the losses sustained on Waltham estate, 28 October 1795.
79 Alexander Houstoun to the Duke of Portland, 30 July 1796, quoted in S. Seymour et al., 'Estate and empire: Sir George Cornewall's management of Moccas, Hertfordshire and La Taste, Grenada, 1771–1819', *Journal of Historical Geography*, 24, 3 (1998), 334.
80 Anon., *Brief enquiry*, 121, 123.
81 NAS, GD267/5/28/2, Home of Wedderburn manuscripts, Benjamin Webster to George Home, 31 July 1796.
82 *Ibid.*, Simond & Hankey to George Home, 28 September 1796.
83 *Ibid.*, Mather Byles to George Home, 23 November 1796, 21 January 1797 and 21 March 1797.

84 NAS, GD267/5/4/3, Home of Wedderburn manuscripts, Accounts of George Home with Simond & Hankey, 30 June 1799 and 30 June 1800; GD267/5/1/3, Richard Landreth to George Home, 21 March 1799; GD267/5/4/1, account of muscovado sugar sales in London, October 1790 to February 1791; GD267/5/4/13(1), account of sales at London of Waltham's muscovado sugar, 1807.
85 BUL, DM41/59/3, West Indies MSS, Westerhall papers, An account of the expenses incurred in reinstating the plantation, 9 April 1797.
86 BUL, DM41/61/16, West Indies MSS, Westerhall papers, Westerhall estate in account current with J. Petrie, Campbell & Co., 31 December 1797.
87 BUL, DM41/59/10, West Indies MSS, Westerhall papers, list of slaves belonging to Port Royal moved to Westerhall estate, 16 March 1798.
88 BUL, DM41/60/4, West Indies MSS, Westerhall papers, account of produce, 1798; DM41/59/15, John Ross to Messrs Forster, Cooke & Frere, 18 June 1799.
89 BUL, DM41/62/9, West Indies MSS, Westerhall papers, John Ross to William Otto, 6 May 1797; DM41/63/5, John Ross to Messrs Forster, Cooke & Frere, 4 November 1798.
90 Seymour *et al.*, 'Estate and empire', 330–1, 334, 336, 342.
91 GCA, T-SK11/2(38), Stirling of Keir papers, Robert Stirling to his brother, March 1748; T-SK22/2, James Stirling to Archibald Stirling of Keir, 4 June 1765, James Stirling to Robert Gordon, Bristol, 1 November 1771.
92 GCA, T-SK 22/11, Stirling of Keir papers, sales book, produce of Hampden estate for 1789 and 1790.
93 GCA, T-SK11/3, Stirling of Keir papers, John Stirling to William Stirling, 15 September 1790, same to same, 13 December 1790.
94 PRO, T71/266, 268, 273–6, 279–80, 284–5, 290–1, 299, 301, 305–6, 320–1, 323, slave registers, 1817–33.
95 PRO, CO441/10/9, papers, correspondence and plans: Baillie, Hermitage and Mount St Bernard. Advertisements were taken in papers in Bristol, Liverpool, London and Edinburgh.

CHAPTER FOUR

Mercantile connections

In many ways merchants embody the idea of an Atlantic world more clearly than any other group. Indeed, mercantile activity has been central to scholarly conceptions of the Atlantic as a transnational maritime world of exchanges.[1] This chapter's main characters (the firms of Alexander Houstoun & Co. and the Baillie family's houses in London and Bristol) demonstrate the transatlantic nature of Caribbean enterprise. As with plantation management, kinship networks underpinned the ways in which mercantile concerns organised themselves.

The partners in Houstoun & Co., the greatest of the Scottish West India houses, were among the most powerful members of Glasgow's 'sugar aristocracy', which, after 1783, usurped the pre-eminent position of the 'tobacco lords' in the city's merchant elite. Their location in Glasgow had particular importance for the manner in which they structured their affairs, and for the way they raised finance.[2]

The Baillies, on the other hand, were more geographically dispersed, and established centres of operation in two key English port cities. Although they were based in England, their local Scottish connections remained important for raising finance and recruiting personnel. Their significance as successful Anglo-Scots illustrates not only the flexibility of Scots and their networks, but also the increasingly integrated British society in which they flourished.

These companies were truly 'Atlantic': their operations crisscrossed the ocean as they plied trade between its eastern and western shores. The founders of Houstoun & Co. and the Baillies began their careers in the Leeward Islands of St Kitts and Nevis (although with four decades between them) and expanded their operations, most notably into the Windward Islands acquired in 1763, and developed networks that drew in different colonial centres. Houstoun & Co., in particular, employed mercantile strategies that were informed by intelligence imported from another part of the Atlantic world. This transfer of strategies was just one of a series of measures and innovations employed by merchants the better to exploit opportunities, and to address the challenges and crises confronting them in the transnational world of exchanges.

Transnational networks

While the principal function of the Scottish, and Scottish-owned, merchant houses was trade between Britain and the Caribbean, they did more than simply ply a route between the two. Instead, they were enmeshed in a lattice of personal financial and mercantile connections that stretched from Scandinavia to Africa and from the Caribbean to the Canadian Maritimes. Sinclair, Brebner & Co., for example, were based in Greenock on the Clyde. The partners in the firm were Robert and Alexander Sinclair, merchants at Greenock, and John Brebner and William Sibbald, both merchants in Leith. Around the world they had connections with Sibbald & Brown in London, with John Brebner and Sinclair & Fervie in New York and with Archibald Sinclair in Kingston. Each of the firms had a direct kinship link with the Greenock firm.[3] Houstoun & Co. maintained contacts in the Danish colony of St Croix and in the Dutch-owned entrepot of St Eustatius, as well in as the Dutch territories on the Guyanese coast and in the British islands.

Houstoun & Co.'s connections with the West Indies stretched back to the War of Spanish Succession, during which two British officers, Major James Milliken and Colonel William McDowall, acquired land in St Kitts and Nevis. After their return to Scotland as absentee planters, they founded James Milliken & Co. (the immediate forerunner of Houstoun & Co.) and brought sugar to Glasgow from the Caribbean. They also became involved with a number of the tobacco lords in other ventures in Glasgow. In 1750, McDowall's son became a partner in Dunlop, Houstoun & Co., better known as the Ship Bank.[4] These connections with other prominent merchants, financiers and industrialists in Glasgow were vitally important to Houstoun & Co., especially towards the end of the century.

Houstoun & Co.'s activities were intricately structured, in a way that ensured that Glasgow remained at the heart of its transnational empire. The company, originally under the guise of Milliken & Co., traded first with St Kitts and Nevis, but underwent a massive expansion from the middle of the century, especially after 1763, and carried commodities from Jamaica, Grenada, St Vincent and, later, Tobago, Demerara, the Danish island of St Croix and the Dutch colony of

St Eustatius. By the middle of the 1790s, it served over 220 clients in eighteen territories, an increase of over 36 per cent from the early 1770s. This expansion occurred mainly in Jamaica and the Windward Islands, while the previously central Leeward Islands of St Kitts and Nevis became of increasingly marginal importance.[5]

To look after these extensive concerns, Houstoun & Co. used a 'hub and spoke' structure in which Glasgow was in frequent contact with individuals or partnerships in each of the islands. Importantly, these agents had either a familial link to one or more of the directors, or had a strong association with Glasgow. As well as enforcing separation between the different island networks, the company maintained geographical cohesion within them to facilitate the transfer of produce from plantation to port, and of supplies from port to plantation. In the smaller islands of the Windward and Leeward archipelagos such cohesion was relatively easy to attain. Jamaica, a much larger island, was more problematic. Houstoun & Co.'s operations in Jamaica were therefore concentrated in a particular part of the island. The company's seventeen Jamaican clients between 1776 and 1780 all lived in the adjoining south-eastern parishes of St Thomas in the East and St David's. Both were coastal parishes and were well endowed with ports, especially at Port Morant and Morant Bay, where a number of the clients were located. These parishes also had relatively easy access to the main town, Kingston, under thirty miles along the coast.

The agent was at the centre of the island network. Houstoun & Co.'s main envoy in Jamaica was John Paterson, who acted as a link between Glasgow and the clients by passing on correspondence. He also acted as executor for deceased clients, and as the company's debt collector. He was responsible for keeping the company informed of developments in the island, and was consulted on how Houstoun & Co. could best proceed in their Jamaican enterprises. As well as helping the company, Paterson acted for the planters in the island. He communicated their thoughts to Glasgow, for example in the form of an appeal for lower freight or insurance charges, and suggested new clients to Houstoun & Co.[6]

Within the network itself, the company wrote to each client, while a number of the clients traded and corresponded with each other, or acted as each other's representatives. Dr Charles Irvine of the Friendship estate in St Thomas in the East communicated with the company in Glasgow, and he also acted with Paterson and another of the company's clients, David McFarlane, as executor of the will of John Lumsden, a Kingston merchant. Later he corresponded with James Renny and William Lambie, who were among the company's clients in the island by the 1780s.[7]

Different merchants reprised Paterson's role in Jamaica in other islands with links to Houstoun & Co. In St Kitts, Akers & Houstoun acted as the conduit between the parent house and the planters. In the Windwards, which became increasingly important for the company after 1763, similar arrangements were made. Until the dissolution of their partnership in 1779, Houstoun & Paterson were responsible for overseeing the interests of the company in Grenada. Alexander Houstoun Jun. (a principal shareholder in the parent firm and lieutenant-governor of Grenada between 1796 and 1802) and his business partner, Fergus Paterson, were charged with loading produce on to company ships and identifying new clients in the island. They also had a power of attorney to act on behalf of Houstoun & Co. Often, this led to Houstoun & Paterson being asked to ensure the payment of debts by planters – a notoriously difficult task. In St Vincent, Turner & Paul performed a similar role.

By the mid 1770s, the success of Houstoun & Co.'s exploits in the West Indies had encouraged expansion. In 1777, following an idea from Houstoun & Paterson, the company decided to open a store in Tobago, where there was a particularly high proportion of Scottish planters. The *Sally* was dispatched to Tobago in March 1777 with the intention that it return in the autumn with 400 hogsheads of sugar. Responsibility for the new store was entrusted to Turner & Paul of St Vincent rather than to Houstoun & Paterson, whose idea it had been: 'Our friend Coll Turner of St Vincent, who is now here, intends taking his passage in the *Sally*, to whom, on his arrival, we refer you for particulars as the ship will be under his direction.' The store was established despite the continuing conflict in North America, but the shipment of sugar in the autumn was considerably less than envisaged: the *Sally* returned to Glasgow that autumn carrying only thirty-five casks.[8]

The fact that Turner assumed responsibility for the new Tobago operation indicates the company's desire to maintain separation between its networks. Turner stayed on in Tobago, where he became a member of the assembly, while his partner Robert Paul handled affairs in St Vincent, where he became a member of the council. The company was quite specific that Houstoun & Paterson should not be given control in Tobago, largely because Grenada was so important that it would occupy their full attention. As the managers in Glasgow wrote, 'you should confine yourselves to Grenada and the Grenadilles, which we look upon as a sufficiently extensive field & will keep your business more compact & easy to be managed'.[9]

The decision to thwart Houstoun & Paterson's expansion into Tobago may have triggered a crisis in the partnership. In 1779, it broke up, as Fergus Paterson sought new opportunities in the Dutch island of St Eustatius. It is not entirely clear why the men went their separate ways. Houstoun & Co. seemed to be completely in the dark, and would have preferred that the partnership had remained intact. But they continued to support Paterson as he entered the provisioning trade. He supplied Houstoun & Co.'s estates in Grenada, using St Eustatius's status as a free port and calling on the financial help of Houstoun & Co.'s 'friends', Messrs Hope and Co. of Amsterdam. On the island, Paterson would have encountered a number of other Scots, including at least two with Glasgow mercantile pedigrees: John Leitch and Robert Dennistoun. For Houstoun & Co., their associates and others like them, the world did not stop at Britain's colonial shores: their world transcended international boundaries.[10]

Alexander Houstoun Jun. stayed on in Grenada and continued to run his firm, which retained the name Houstoun & Paterson. In early 1781, he was given greater responsibility, as the company in Glasgow transferred the ownership of estates in Grenada to Houstoun & Paterson. Passing control from absentee to resident ownership was a device to ensure that the occupying French forces did not confiscate the estates.[11] In 1777, Houstoun & Co. seized the Mount Alexander estate, after years of unsuccessful attempts to recover debts from Alexander Wilson. This diversification into Grenada planting was no whimsical advance. Although the level of debt attached to the estate continued to grow, Houstoun & Co. felt there was no alternative means of securing it. They installed a manager, William McFarlane, who was instructed to use 'the utmost care & frugality in the management of the Estate [so] that the great deal of debt now on it may be reduced as speedily as possible.' In fact, quite the opposite occurred; by 1798 the estate was indebted to the tune of £78,119.[12]

While the Houstouns, McDowalls and Millikens developed their Glasgow-based trading empire in the West Indies, members of the Baillie family became increasingly influential in West Indian mercantile circles. These men, like Houstoun & Co., forged a mercantile and plantation nexus that enabled them to prosper. Their operations indicate the cohesion that had emerged within the British Atlantic world. They also point to the ability of Scots to shift, apparently seamlessly, between the Highlands of Scotland, the islands of the Caribbean and major international port cities in England.

All four Baillies were born in the parish of Inverness: Alexander, James and Evan were the three eldest children of Hugh Baillie of Dochfour. George Baillie, their cousin, was the third son of Hugh's younger brother William. The Baillies belonged to one of the older families in the burgh and its hinterland, and the success of their ventures did much to further the family lands and political influence in the north of Scotland. All these men came of age at a time of great expansion of the empire in the Caribbean, and all were drawn to the region's new opportunities. As a result of their West Indian enterprises, James, Evan and George returned to Britain and established themselves as important actors on the mercantile stage. Unlike the founders of Houstoun & Co., the Baillies did not return to their home area. In part this was an issue of practicality: Inverness and the Highlands offered a much smaller market for West India goods, and could not muster sources of capital on anything like the scale of Glasgow.

Nonetheless, Alexander Baillie, the first of the brothers to go to the Caribbean in the employ of James Smith, did consider a direct trade between St Kitts and Inverness to undercut the 'extravagant prices at Glasgow': 'I am sure when rum is bought here at 2s ... and sold there for 6s or 7s sterling, and sugar bought here at 2d per lb, sold with you at 6d, there must be a good deal got by it; and on the other hand, the oats I fancy may be bought there at 40s per hhd at most, always sells here at £7.'[13] This notion also appealed to the political commentator John Campbell, who in 1774 recommended the construction of a canal from Inverness to the west coast to encourage the sale of Moray Firth herring (the 'fittest for the consumption of the People in the Sugar Islands') and to 'enable the active assiduous Merchant to transport the returns of his Trade with the West Indies the East side of the Island.'[14]

In 1755, Alexander's brother James, using his contacts to secure employment in St Kitts, joined him. He also spent time in Nevis and the Dutch island of St Eustatius, and built relationships and gained mercantile expertise to the extent that he felt able to display some self-satisfaction with his progress. He wrote, 'I have, since my settlement here, done very well, and better than I expected when I set out from Inverness.'[15]

By the early 1760s, the Baillie brothers no longer merely worked for James Smith, but had entered into a partnership with him in St Kitts. Messrs Smith & Baillies traded between Africa, the Caribbean and the American mainland; their most important connection on the mainland was with the merchant and politician Henry Laurens of Charleston, to whom Africans and West India produce were consigned and from whom plantation stores were purchased.[16] The partnership remained intact until 1770, by which time the range of the Baillies' interests had grown considerably.

Like many Scots, Alexander and James Baillie grasped the opportunities presented by the cession of the Windward Islands in 1763. In 1765, they purchased the Hermitage plantation in Grenada, while James bought the Mount St Bernard plantation.[17] These were the Baillies' first incursions into landownership outside Scotland, and represented a considerable investment. Their merchant operations, based in St Kitts, had been sufficiently profitable to allow them to begin producing merchandise as well as shipping and selling it. The great boom in landowning in St Kitts had passed, and much of the land was in the hands of absentee landowners like William McDowall. While this provided the Baillies, and others like them, with opportunities in trade and factoring, it severely limited their opportunities for landed investments. The expansion of the empire in the Windwards, however, opened up new swathes of plantation property. For both men to have remained in St Kitts and to have supervised their Grenada investments would have been impracticable. Therefore, following the expansion of their interests, the brothers divided responsibilities: Alexander remained in St Kitts, while James moved southwards to manage the new estates in Grenada.

At the Hermitage plantation in the parish of St Patrick, Baillie found a number of Scottish neighbours, among them Peter Gordon, Alexander Campbell and John Aitchison (who later sold his estate to Alexander Houstoun Jun.). These men formed the core of a mercantile and political network. Baillie had existing connections with Gordon, having acted for him in the sale of slaves in South Carolina, while the connection between Alexander Campbell and Baillie may have become a familial link by Baillie's marriage to Colina Campbell, daughter of Colin Campbell of Glenure.[18]

By 1770, Alexander and James had been joined in the West Indies by their younger brother Evan, and had co-founded the new firm of Alexander, James and Evan Baillie in St Kitts after the dissolution of Smith & Baillies in 1770. They were intent on continuing the business of the old company, and utilised its former contacts, while James Smith continued in his role of planter and merchant.[19] These long-standing acquaintances were certainly beneficial to the new firm as it consolidated its position. Henry Laurens was again important, directing their attention to a recently established firm in Charleston with which to deal, and he wished them 'all manner of success and happiness' in their new venture.[20] The new firm continued to prosper in St Kitts, but James, Evan and later George Baillie all increasingly focused their attention on the Windwards and extended the range of the family's network. James, for example, as well as having interests in the British islands, established a trade with St Eustatius, where James Fraser of Inverness was a resident.[21]

James Baillie lived in Grenada throughout the 1770s, and ran the Hermitage estate as well as building up his trading empire. His most important connection in the island was with Alexander Campbell, who was also a close friend of the speaker of the assembly, Ninian

Home. Baillie entered a partnership in Thornton, Baillie and Campbell that traded from a store in St George's in the 1780s and into the 1790s. Baillie and Campbell also collaborated in London, on both mercantile and political matters, up to Baillie's death in 1793, when he was MP for Horsham and agent for Grenada.[22]

His younger brother, Evan, stayed in St Kitts for about a year before he too sought out the opportunities of the Windwards. He went to St Vincent, where he acquired an estate through marriage to Mary Gurley, with whom he had several children. In St Vincent he quickly became a man of standing in the community, and was one of the relatively few Scots to sit in the island assembly between 1771 and 1774.[23] During the first half of the 1770s, Evan Baillie began to trade to Bristol, then Britain's second most important sugar market, a position it consolidated in the period between the end of the Seven Years War and the American War of Independence.[24]

The buoyancy in the Bristol market persuaded Evan Baillie of the efficacy of utilising his contacts in the city, in preference to other markets. His mercantile connection with the 'metropolis of the west' originated in a partnership formed in the early 1770s with Mr Garraway. The firm of Garraway & Baillie acted as merchants for planters in the island, including Baillie's new relative Peter Gurley (a member of the assembly) and Thomas Hackshaw (a member of the council). By 1774 Baillie and his young family had left St Vincent and settled in Bristol, where he managed the affairs of the merchant house. He became involved in another company, Bright, Baillie and Bright, which imported sugar into Bristol, before branching out on his own. By 1785, he was so well established in the city that he was a member of the common council, as well as one of the city's leading merchants.[25]

Jamaica was the principal supplier of sugar and its derivatives to the Bristol market, but Evan Baillie & Co. operated within a much broader context. Baillie's personal connections with both St Kitts and St Vincent ensured that both islands remained part of his company's network, to which were added Grenada, Nevis, Martinique and, to a lesser extent, Antigua and Barbados by the end of the century. The expansion into Martinique, in particular, demonstrated a real willingness on Baillie's part to seize new opportunities as they presented themselves. Martinique was a French colony occupied by British forces between 1794 and 1802, when it was returned after the Treaty of Amiens. Baillie's ships called there from the spring of 1795. In July 1795, the *Charming Eliza* arrived in Bristol from Martinique heavily laden with sugar, coffee, cocoa and cotton.[26]

By the 1780s, Baillie had established a connection that was to be of great importance to him and his family. The partners in the firm of

Pinney & Tobin had a West Indian pedigree stretching back to 1685, when Azariah Pinney first arrived in Nevis.[27] The alliance between the two firms allowed each company, on an informal basis, to use the connections and facilities of the other. Thus, in 1787, a prospective client in St Kitts was informed by Pinney & Tobin that 'Mr Baillie has assured us that the captains of his ship . . . shall take in any sugars consigned for us.' Although no formal mercantile arrangements between the Baillies and the Pinneys were entered into before 1813, they continued to operate under a series of these *ad hoc* 'understandings'. And by the end of the eighteenth century the two families forged a marital alliance by the marriage of John Pinney's daughter Elizabeth to Evan Baillie's eldest son, Peter, in 1797.[28] Peter had long been marked out as Evan's successor. In 1789 Evan wrote, 'If the mercantile line should be your object, I should hope that after three years close application you should be able to take much trouble and responsibility off my shoulders'.[29]

On his return from his grand tour, Peter entered the family business, and he was running parts of the company by the mid-1790s. Evan, meanwhile, became increasingly engaged with the wider mercantile community, as a director of the Bristol Fire Office insurance house.[30] After 1798, Peter assumed much greater responsibility for the West India house as Evan spent more time in Scotland, having inherited the family estate at Dochfour in 1796. Four years later, in 1802, Evan Baillie was elected a member of Parliament for Bristol with the backing of much of the city's merchant community, which necessarily led him to spend less time at the counting house. By this time Evan's third son, James Evan, had come of age; he began to involve himself in the running of the company, and took charge of the firm after Peter's untimely death in 1812. He also established himself in London. Early in the nineteenth century, he busied himself tidying up the affairs of the Paraclete estate, which had been owned by Alexander Campbell, his uncle James's partner and brother-in-law. Around this time he also entered a mercantile partnership in London, incorporating Messrs J. E. Baillie, Fraser & Co.[31] James Evan's later incarnation, as president of the British Guiana Association, stemmed from a further expansion of the Baillie's network into the Guyana colonies of Demerara and Berbice. The integration of this Scottish family into the Atlantic world, surviving as West India merchants for over a century from the 1750s until 1861, demonstrates the way in which old family ties were complemented by new alliances.[32] Whether fostered by marriage or by acquaintance between those planters and traders with shared interests, the new connections imbued the long-standing bonds with a fresh impetus that allowed them to operate over generations.

A world of exchanges

These and other complex transnational networks allowed the freer flow of trade goods around the Atlantic world. For Houstoun & Co. and the Baillies, the main commodities were Caribbean staples like sugar and cotton shipped to Britain, enslaved Africans and British goods, usually plantation stores, sent to the Caribbean.

The first Glasgow involvement in the sugar trade came almost half a century before the Act of Union, and in the later seventeenth century two or three ships from the Caribbean arrived annually in the River Clyde. After 1707, with an exponential growth in demand for Caribbean staples, commodities were landed at Scottish ports in greater and greater volumes. In 1743 and 1744 seventeen ships arrived in Glasgow from the Caribbean, while twenty-two cleared Glasgow for the West Indies. This was a small proportion of total shipping in the port, amounting to just over 6 per cent for arrivals and less than 8 per cent for departures. Eight ships imported about 16,000 hundredweight of sugar, while about 50,000 pounds of cotton were landed annually. At this stage, Caribbean trade was dwarfed by that of the tobacco colonies and Europe and Ireland but it expanded rapidly. Between September 1775 and August 1779, Houstoun & Co. alone imported around 45,000 hundredweight of sugar in twenty ships, with a total value of almost £110,000 sterling. This amounted to perhaps 15 per cent of annual Scottish imports of sugar in the 1770s. By 1790, $11\frac{1}{2}$ per cent of arrivals in Glasgow came from the West Indies, and almost 15 per cent of departures went there. In the number of ships, the Caribbean was more significant than the USA, and on a par with the whole of continental Europe. In terms of tonnage, the Caribbean was much more important. The larger transatlantic vessels meant that Caribbean ships accounted for over a fifth of tonnage entering the port, and over a quarter of that leaving it. Sugar imports had risen to 132,690 hundredweight by 1790, and more than doubled again to 311,342 by 1815. Total Scottish imports in this period increased from 135,369 to 334,093 hundredweight, indicating Glasgow's almost complete monopoly of sugar imports to Scotland.[33]

Some of this sugar was brought into Glasgow under the commission system prevalent in the West Indies and employed in all the major sugar markets in Britain. Under it, merchants imported the produce from the islands and sold it, often through brokers, on behalf of the planters, for which they were charged commission.[34] Houstoun & Co. initially employed this procedure for West India trade. For planters in the Leeward Islands and in Jamaica, they sold sugar in Glasgow and consigned supplies to them, as well as informing them individually of the sales of their sugars. In the Windward Islands acquired after 1763, they tried something different.

By the middle of the eighteenth century Glasgow was Britain's principal port for Chesapeake tobacco. In the Chesapeake, Glasgow merchant houses employed factors who bought tobacco from the growers, and then shipped it and sold it in Glasgow. While the burden of risk of the sale therefore fell on the merchant rather than the producer, the store system allowed tobacco to be shipped more quickly, and brought to market at an optimum time.[35] Houstoun & Co. applied this 'store system' to the West Indies. In managing their Grenadian concerns, Houstoun & Paterson entered into agreements that committed planters to send a certain amount of their crop of Houstoun & Co. every year. In March 1776, for example, the company reminded Robert Bogle Jun. of his commitment to ship fifty hogsheads of sugar every year.[36] Unlike their letters to planters in the Leewards, Houstoun & Co.'s correspondence with clients in the Windwards rarely mentioned the result of sugar sales, suggesting that by the time when the sugar entered the market, it was already the property of the merchants. In this way Houstoun & Co. functioned quite differently from other West India houses in London and the outports, and this was a factor in their great success and in their ultimate and ignominious collapse.

This was, for Houstoun & Co., a mixed-trade system, employed in geographically specific areas and involving the introduction of the store system alongside existing commission arrangements. The company's records do not make clear why they adopted this innovation in the 1760s, but it is, nevertheless, possible to speculate as to the reasons. One of the defining characteristics of the Chesapeake store system was that the stores serviced the produce and needs of small-scale backcountry farmers rather than the great tidewater planters. The initial land grants in the Windwards were limited in size, and although some planters were able over time to consolidate a number of grants into large estates, on the whole plantations were not above 300 acres. Many were considerably smaller, making the use of a store system particularly appropriate. This is not to imply that plantations in the Leeward Islands were too vast to be suited to the store system: many were not. But in Jamaica, on average estates were very much larger, at around 900 acres.[37]

In this context, the timing of Houstoun & Co.'s penetration of the Windward Islands was also important. When William McDowall I and James Milliken II began trading from St Kitts in the 1720s, sugar had been produced and exported under the commission system for three-quarters of a century. As relative newcomers to mercantile activity, not only were they bound by the conventions of the existing trade, but they were unaware of the use of the store system in the Chesapeake, which at that stage had yet to prove its value. By the time of the expansion into the Windwards in the 1760s, the partners in Houstoun & Co. were well known in Glasgow's merchant community. These connections were both professional, in ventures like banking, and social, through membership of one or more of Glasgow's gentlemen's clubs.[38] At close quarters they had witnessed the spectacular success of the Chesapeake trade, which was then approaching its apogee. The company, then, had a new system of trade that it was able to employ in newly acquired islands, in which the conventions of trade had yet to be established.

The introduction of a store system was a capital-intensive venture, in terms of physically establishing the store and in having funds available for credit advances. In Tobago, the store established by Turner in early 1777 represented an outlay of £4,500, a sum 50 per cent higher than a similar undertaking in the Chesapeake.[39] The experience of the tobacco merchants suggested that such investments would not quickly be recouped, which meant that Houstoun & Co. required access to considerable amounts of credit. In this respect, their location was critical. The credit surplus in Glasgow in the 1760s and 1770s, allied to 'a specific investment mentality [which] had been created in the West of Scotland by the later eighteenth century', was used to finance not only the tobacco trade, but also West Indian trade.[40] Moreover, Scots, many of them from the west of Scotland, quickly dominated the Windward Islands. Houstoun & Co. were thus able to deal predominantly, but not exclusively, with planters with whom they were familiar, and to whom they could comfortably extend lines of credit.

By the time of Turner's arrival in Tobago, a number of influential men in the Scots-dominated island had been informed of Houstoun & Co.'s imminent expansion into the colony. William Bruce, Thomas Wilson and Archibald Stewart were approached with a view to their making 'a tryal' of the Glasgow market. Houstoun & Co. also contacted the influential planters and merchants John and Alexander Campbell, explaining their expansion and seeking their assistance: 'we shall therefore be much obliged to you, for any Interest you can use in loading [the *Sally*] expeditiously, & that you would be so kind as to Inform any of the Planters you may meet with who have Glasgow connections or who may Incline to make trial of this Market.'[41]

Clearly Houstoun & Co. did not envisage entering into trade arrangements with just anybody: clients had to come recommended by people already known to them. In this respect, the satellite firms played a vital role in acting as referees for prospective clients. Without such a 'reference', Houstoun & Co. would not enter into a commitment with a planter: to be Scottish was not enough. They consistently refused to deal with Dr Robert Telfer of Jamaica, as they informed Duncan McFarlane of Morant Bay: 'With respect to the goods ordered for Dr. Robt. Telfer... we have declined shipping them, not being acquainted with the Dr nor have we ever had any Correspondence with him, and as you do not choose to become bound for him, we think it would be rather precipitate in us to engage an entire stranger.'[42] It was a particular advantage if the prospective clients had some kind of connection with Glasgow. For Houstoun & Co., the regional element was important in the network, and it reinforced familial and practical considerations: local connections made it easier for them to decide whether they were selecting suitable clients. Theoretically, it also allowed for the easier recovery of debts, although some proved to be extremely difficult to claw back from recalcitrant planters.

The Baillies were rather more conventional merchants. James returned to London and became a commodity merchant and financier. Credit was extended through the Caribbean through a series of agency houses operated by his cousin George. He was also a sugar merchant who, like virtually all London merchants, handled consignments on a commission basis. Even those London concerns with strong Glasgow connections, like J. Petrie, Campbell & Co., sold produce through brokers and then charged planters, like the owners of the Westerhall estate, the costs of duties, freight, pierage, wharfage, landing, weighing, housing, cooperage, sales charges and brokerage, as well as their own $2\frac{1}{2}$ per cent commission.[43]

In Bristol, Evan Baillie also operated the commission system. In partnership with the Brights, he imported sugar from St Kitts, Nevis, Grenada and St Vincent, landing 3,784 hogsheads of sugar (around 45,000 hundredweight) over five years in the 1770s. As Baillie's operations expanded during the last quarter of the century, he garnered an ever-increasing share of the Bristol sugar market. Across the years 1785, 1788 and 1791–99, Evan Baillie imported 20,271 hogsheads, and he imported a further 5,867 in 1799–1800 as Evan Baillie & Sons, becoming Bristol's sixth largest sugar importer between 1728 and 1800.[44] Within his mercantile network, Baillie used family and local connections from which to recruit. The captain of his ship, the *Maria*, which plied a trade between Bristol and St Kitts, was Hugh Inglis of Inverness, brother of the partner of Evan's cousin George.[45]

Once at the market, the process of selling sugar was no simple matter. Its price, for example, was affected by a number of variables. Most fundamentally, there were different kinds of sugar which commanded different prices. Under normal circumstances clayed sugar, which had already undergone a process of refinement in the Caribbean, fetched a higher price than muscovado sugars. At the London market, clayed sugar typically sold for 50 per cent more than muscovado, as the production costs were passed on to British buyers.[46] Furthermore, several different types of canes were grown, especially towards the end of the century, and this also affected the quality of the sugar produced and, as a consequence, its price.

Not only did the varieties of cane and their processing differ; the produce of each island also attracted varying prices, reflecting the reputation of each for the quality of its sugar. The fleet arriving in the Clyde in late September and early October 1777, for example, brought sugars that fluctuated wildly in price (see Table 4.1). The price variations suggest the difference in quality of the sugars produced, both in terms of the quality within each island and in comparison to each other. The sugar market was a very sophisticated organism that was even able to distinguish between the produce of different plantations on a given island. In October 1776, the current prices for the Grenadian estates of Mount Alexander and Mount Craven ranged from 30s to 32s and from 35s to 40s respectively. These sorts of fluctuations were not unique to the Glasgow market. Thirty-four hogsheads of sugar from the 1798 crop of Westerhall estate in Grenada arrived in London in the *Basseterre*, and were sold in three lots of 79s, 84s and 85s per hundredweight.[47]

There was also the additional complication of regional variations in the sugar markets. These took the form of differences in charges, prices and consumer preferences. Although sales prices tended to be highest in London, the cumulative charges were also generally higher there than in regional ports. In 1798 and 1799, for example, in London duties and freight were charged at 19s 4d and 17s 6d respectively, while at Glasgow the equivalent costs were 17s 6d and 7s.[48] To command the

Table 4.1 Sugar prices at Glasgow, autumn 1777

Date received	Island	Price range per cwt (sterling)	Value of cargo (sterling)
September 1777	Tobago	58s 6d–64s	£5073 7s 6d
4 October 1777	St Kitts	58s–70s	£5788 1s 1d
4 October 1777	Grenada	41s–67s	£4101 12s 1d
5 October 1777	St Vincent	55s 6d–69s	£9469 10s 3d
5 October 1777	Jamaica	54s 6d–63s	£6594 10s 1d

Source: NLS, MS8799(105, 118, 127, 138, 155), Alexander Houstoun & Co. papers, sale book C.

optimum revenue, planters often consigned parts of the same crop to different ports. In 1798, John Ross, manager of the Westerhall estate, consigned twenty-five hogsheads of sugar each to both Liverpool and Glasgow and a further thirty-four to London. Splitting the crop in this way represented not only an awareness that certain markets produced better prices at different times. It also showed an understanding that different markets expressed variations in demand for a different grade or quality of sugar. Grocers in Bristol preferred to judge sugar by its colour, and generally desired yellow or light brown sugar. Sugar refiners selected sugars by the strength of the grain. Barbados was regarded in Bristol as producing the best clayed sugar.[49] In Glasgow, clayed sugar was unpopular, and Houstoun & Co. informed its agents in Grenada that 'our Bakers and Grocers prefer Muscovadoes if of equal appearance'.[50]

Houstoun & Co. also imported cotton from the West Indies to the Clyde. From the 1770s, they carried cotton from St Croix, Carricaou and Grenada. This cotton connection, as we will see, was important for the company, not only because it had interests in cotton manufacturers in Scotland, but also because cotton industrialists were an important source of capital for the company. A number of other Glasgow merchants also brought cotton into Scotland, fulfilling the increasing demands of an industry that, by the end of the eighteenth century, was perhaps the country's most important.

The expansion of the British Empire into the formerly Dutch Guyanese colonies was a boon to cotton importers in the early 1800s. The Baillie family, as part of the Highland network operating there, made a number of incursions, in Demerara in particular. Evan Baillie acted as a merchant and adviser to a number of Demerara planters. His brother, James, had owned at least one estate there, the Northbrook plantation. And although Evan Baillie had a well-established trade connection with Bristol, he also asked other merchants to transport produce to markets in Liverpool or Glasgow. He wrote to his son to say, 'I forgot to ask you . . . whether Jno. Bolton or Dennistoun & Co. had made you any Remittance for our Cotton and Sugar sold by them, and perhaps it may be as well to draw now on Davidson & Graham, Bogle &c., &c. in the usual manner for the Shipments sent in the Fall on their Accounts.'[51] Baillie was not the only Inverness planter-merchant in Demerara to use John Bolton in Liverpool: George Inglis, his cousin's business partner, also dispatched cotton there. The Baillies' main connection with Liverpool was through George Baillie, who had been involved in the financing of slave voyages. In the early nineteenth century, having subsumed James Baillie & Co. into George Baillie & Co., he moved into cotton importing to London. He persuaded George Inglis to abandon his usual London importer, Messrs Lang, Irving & Co., and to consign cotton to Baillie's new merchant house. Inglis hoped this would 'prove the commencement of a Business, mutually advantageous to both of us'. Inglis had his own reasons for this: he was one of Baillie's creditors – it was in his interest that Baillie return profits, and he hoped not to drag Baillie into any further over-extension; 'As I have been able to pass my Bills at so long a date, I hope it will prevent you from being under any advance on this Occasion – which I shall always avoid as much as I possibly can.'[52]

The production of these commodities was dependent on enslaved labour. Because the enslaved were so central to the wealth of the West Indies, the Scottish role in their transatlantic transportation requires attention, despite a scholarly claim that Scots 'only indirectly profited' from the system of slavery.[53] While it is true that enslavement had been effectively banned in Scotland after the case of Knight versus Wedderburn in 1778 and that many Scots participated in the abolition campaign, virtually all Scots living in the Caribbean necessarily relied on the institution of enslavement, and on the trade that supplied it.

Scottish-owned firms, both in Scotland and more especially in England, did trade in Africans. David Hancock's study of Grant, Oswald & Co. has shown decisively a key Scottish interest in the trade through the slave fort at Bance Island in the mouth of the Sierra Leone River.[54] Nor was this involvement an isolated case. A number of Scots were active along the Guinea coast, some of them were in the service of the Royal African Company. Alexander Allerdyce of Dunnottar, MP for the Aberdeen Burghs between 1792 and 1801, was estimated during his time in Jamaica to have 'sold about as many blackmen as there are white in his native city [of Aberdeen]'. Elsewhere in Jamaica, the planter-medic Alexander Johnston, aware of the potential profits from enslavement, considered the possibility of buying a ship to bring Africans whom he would then sell in the parish of St Ann's and those adjoining it.[55]

Buchanan & Simpson of Glasgow carried Africans to the Caribbean and thence to Maryland and Virginia. They were partners in the voyages of the *Edgar*, captain John Baillie, which went from Liverpool to west Africa to Kingston in 1762 and 1763. They corresponded with a number of slave-trading concerns in Liverpool, and also tried to promote trade from Glasgow through a separate partnership that also involved the partners in the Ship Bank, Colin Dunlop and Alexander Houstoun.[56] In terms of the overall scale of the African trade, the number of voyages originating in Scotland was minute. Perhaps as few as ten slave ships left Scottish ports in the eighteenth century, all between 1717 and 1764, and half of those between 1760 and 1764.

The vast majority (eight) left from the River Clyde, from Glasgow and Greenock. Only two left from east coast ports: one from Montrose in 1735 and one from Leith in 1764. The ships touched the African coast in a number of places, from Bance Island in the north along the Gold Coast to Loango in the south. From there most sailed to the Caribbean, and only one to the upper James River in Virginia in 1760. One of the Greenock vessels was seized by the enslaved in 1730 and never reached the Caribbean, but the other nine between them carried perhaps 1,893 Africans to the Americas.[57]

Most Scots, whether captains of vessels like John Dunning of the *Mary* and the *Sally* or George Hamilton of the *Argyle*, or as ships' owners, like the Baillie family or Buchanan & Simpson, based their operations in England. The Baillies were involved in slave trading by the 1760s at least, as partners in the firm of Smith & Baillies of St Kitts. This company supplied Henry Laurens, among others, who was happy to recommend their services. Laurens believed that St Kitts was 'the best island in the West Indies to purchase Negroes', and he characterised Smith & Baillies as 'Men of honour & integrity ... also the principal African houses in those islands'.[58] The Baillies' interests in the trade in the Caribbean were considerable. In Grenada, James Baillie estimated that in the eighteen months preceding June 1772, 'our House (exclusive of the Business in the other islands, of which St. Kitts is the Capital place) sold Negroes here to the amount of £120,000 Sterling.'[59]

Such huge sums of money were clearly held a great attraction for James and Evan Baillie, and both maintained interests in the trade after their return to Britain. James was a partner in at least two voyages in the 1780s. One from London carried 445 Africans from Sierra Leone bound for Dominica. Forty-three did not survive the crossing. The other voyage, from Bristol, was undertaken in partnership with his brother. Evan retained a greater interest in the slave trade than James, and actively participated in it during the 1780s, before he turned attention more fully to sugar. Between February 1783 and March 1788, Evan, usually in partnership but once on his own, sent six voyages from Bristol to the Bight of Biafra. Despite mortality rates of almost 15 per cent, these crossings carried 2,073 Africans to Dominica, Grenada, Jamaica and the Virgin Islands. A single ship, the *Emilia*, made five of the crossings between 1783 and 1788. It made annual voyages in that time, remaining in Bristol for between two and four months in the year for cleaning and refitting. Each voyage collected Africans at Bonny and transported them to the Caribbean before returning to Bristol. The *Emilia* was away for between seven and eleven months at a time, but usually for only seven or eight. This suggests that a highly efficient organisation had secured Africans on the coast for collection – the ship rarely had to wait for long. The *Emilia*'s captain was James Fraser, who may have been related to Baillie. Baillie's mother was Emilia Fraser of Reelig, Inverness, sister of James Fraser, an Indian nabob. Baillie appears not have been ashamed by his means of making money, nor to have seen any reason to keep it secret.[60]

Crises

For all the success of these firms, and others like them, mercantile enterprise was not without its risks, and was beset by a series of crises throughout the final third of the eighteenth century. In early 1776, Houstoun & Co. displayed great optimism. They wrote to Houstoun & Paterson in Grenada that 'the prices of West India produce seem to advance wonderfully & we begin to entertain hopes that they will be maintained through the year.'[61] Even the impending crisis in the Thirteen Colonies did not concern them enormously as they contemplated plans to expand their operations in Nevis in the same month. As the year wore on, however, the company's normally circumspect managers became even more cautious. By April, they feared that the American War would cause uncertainty in the sugar markets, and warned their correspondents of their concern that 'the stagnation of the American Trade will have a bad effect.'[62]

This 'bad effect' began to manifest itself in delays to and cancellations of plans to expand operations in the region. The creation of a direct link between Glasgow and Nevis was deferred until the war was over, as were similar proposals for a connection with Dominica. Houstoun & Co. had been asked by John Cockburn of Roseau to ship goods to him, but they felt obliged to respond in the negative: 'When this American War is over, which we hope will be soon – we shall be glad to hear from you, as it may then be convenient for us to serve you, but at present we are averse to any new Connections. [I]n the present distracted condition of publick affairs, We are rather inclined to Wynd up than extend our business.'[63]

The caution of the parent firm notwithstanding, they were sufficiently impressed by Houstoun & Paterson's idea for a Tobago store to promote it. The expansion into Tobago, as well as Jamaica and the Windward Islands, brought new problems for Houstoun & Co. All three of their satellite firms in the Windwards in the 1770s (Houstoun & Paterson, Turner & Paul in both St Vincent and Tobago) had extended considerable credit to planters in their islands. By May 1777, Turner & Paul in Tobago owed Houstoun & Co. £10,469, part of which can be accounted for by the costs of establishing the new store. Despite

Glasgow's request, in the face of an imminent war with France in December 1777, 'to restrict our trade to the West Indies at least so as not to enter into any new engagements that may either require an advance of money, or the least risque of bad debts', by May 1778 they owed Houstoun & Co. £13,065. The two other companies owed similar amounts: Turner & Paul's operation in St Vincent owed £13,275, while Houstoun & Paterson were indebted to the tune of £13,910.[64] And while these debts were, strictly speaking, assets to the parent company, they remained so only if there was an expectation of their being repaid: an unlikely event in the case of a credit crisis, a loss of crop, an insurrection or a major war. It was Houstoun & Co.'s grave misfortune that all four struck simultaneously in the 1790s.

These credit extensions, despite the company's instructions to the contrary, indicate a shift in control in Houstoun & Co.'s operations. Signs of nascent tension between the aims of the company and the ambitions of its subsidiaries were already apparent by this time. But as the scale of the operations expanded under the store system, Houstoun & Co. became increasingly reliant on the local firms. With each of these firms expanding independently of the others, the cumulative effects were to enhance the power of the subsidiary and to lead Houstoun & Co. into ever more credit commitments. Within the company's empire, the metropole no longer dictated to the colonies.

The French treaty of alliance with the Americans in February 1778 struck fear into the hearts of the company's managers. Having already attempted to limit the actions of its subsidiaries, the company again expressed its anxiety to Turner & Paul and Houstoun & Paterson in March 1778.[65] The company was not alone in being concerned. British mercantile confidence was in tatters in spring 1778 because 'trade of every kind seems to be at a perfect stand owing to a most uncommonly great & general Scarcity of money over all three Kingdoms, where it will terminate God knows, but we have never known the like before'.[66]

Houstoun & Co.'s increasing pessimism led them to take measures to counteract the threat of privations by French and American ships. They employed more heavily armed ships. The *Sally* was provided with two extra guns and carried more crew, although the company was worried that this would limit the amount of freight and therefore reduce the profit. It also acquired a new, heavily armed vessel, the *Jupiter*, carrying eighteen guns and forty crewmen.[67] Ships' captains were provided with letters of marque, and sailed to the West Indies in convoys. This latter tactic not only had the advantage of greater security, but also brought a reduction in insurance premiums, which had rocketed since the start of the war.[68] Houstoun & Co.'s fleet was sufficiently large and well armed that it could continue to sail, even if it missed the official convoys. The captains of the *St Andrew* for St Kitts and Jamaica, the *Castlesemple* for Grenada, the *Sally* for Tobago and the *Britannia* for St Vincent were ordered to sail in convoy for as long as possible, until they had to go their separate ways in the Caribbean. They were told, 'Our only reason for this is that each of your Ships being well arm'd, Mann'd &c. you may be a mutual defence & protection to each other, in the event of your being attack'd by the Enemy. And we doubt not that in that case you will all make a proper resistance.'[69]

By the 1790s much had changed for Houstoun & Co., especially in Grenada. Houstoun & Paterson had been dissolved, and their business had become so extensive that it was no longer possible to entrust it to one company. Replacing Houstoun & Paterson in the island were six related firms, all of which had strong connections to Houstoun & Co. through family bonds and long-standing mercantile arrangements.[70] These companies became increasingly indebted to the parent firm as they drew on Houstoun & Co. to make advances to clients in the island. Houstoun & Co. had survived the financial crisis sparked in London in 1772 by the absconding of Alexander Fordyce with £243,000, which had caused mayhem across the Atlantic world.[71] But by the time of the collapse in West Indian credit, which began in London in 1793 and quickly spread to afflict companies across Britain and the empire, the satellite firms were running huge debts. The exponential increase in advances to planters led their debts to Houstoun & Co. to amount to £343,935 in 1796. Significantly, Houstoun & Co.'s ledgers show that the satellite firms, rather than the planters in the Windward Islands themselves, were indebted to the company.[72]

Three disastrous crops between 1789 and 1791 had dramatically increased the planters' debts to merchants, and credit was extended further as both merchants and planters sought to capitalise on the rebellion in the French colony of St Domingue in 1791. The slave rising essentially removed that island's previously enormous sugar production from the European markets, leaving the British islands as the most important suppliers of sugar. This generated a new chimerical confidence in the future of West Indian planting. The beginning of the French Revolutionary War in 1793 came hard on the heels of these credit advances. The British seizure of Martinique in 1794 led to a fall in the price of sugar in the British markets, and this, allied to losses from French privateering, insurrections in the islands and continuing uncertainty over the future of the slave trade, forced company after company into bankruptcy.[73] For these reasons the planters' sales of produce were insufficient to cover their debts, and the merchants in turn found themselves unable to pay their creditors.

As well as the mounting debts in Grenada, money was owed to Houstoun & Co. by firms in the Dutch colonies. Three firms in St Eustatius owed £38,764 between them, and Lambert Blair & Co. of Berbice owed £27,142.[74] What happened in St Vincent and Tobago is rather more difficult to discern. Turner & Paul do not appear in Houstoun & Co.'s ledgers after 1793, although a London firm, Turner & Co., owed Houstoun & Co. an increasing amount of money: the debt rose from £4,356 in 1793 to £25,649 in 1796. Robert Paul was certainly alive and resident in St Vincent in the mid-1790s, but seems to have ceased working with Houstoun & Co.[75] On the other hand, Coll Turner, who lived until September 1812, probably moved to London during the period of French occupation in Tobago between 1781 and 1793, and carried on the credit business of Houstoun & Co. from there.[76] In the islands themselves, Robert Glasgow, formerly speaker of the St Vincent assembly and a client of Houstoun & Co. at least since 1776, saw his debts almost treble from £5,104 in 1793 to £14,604 in 1796, which suggests that he took over from Robert Paul in the island. His debt was more than twice the size of the next biggest, in which he also had a share.[77]

The need for access to capital to finance West India trade (especially when undertaken through a store system) made Houstoun & Co.'s Glasgow location particularly significant. Tom Devine has shown that the surplus of capital in the west of Scotland could be invested in companies trading to the Chesapeake.[78] It was also, especially after 1783, directed towards the Caribbean. Before the 1790s, Houstoun & Co. did not look towards London for finance. If they ventured outside Scotland it was to the Netherlands, and usually to Dutch houses with a Scottish connection. By 1794 they owed Hope & Co. of Amsterdam and Crawfurd & Co. of Rotterdam over £61,000.[79]

The crisis of the 1790s was so acute, however, that for the first time Houstoun & Co. sought finance in London. Although not immediately successful, the company eventually became associated with Boyd, Benfield & Co. of London. Boyd was a Scottish banker who had fled the revolution in France, while Benfield was an extremely wealthy Indian nabob. From the outset of their relationship, Walter Boyd 'behaved with an unbounded confidence and liberality' towards Houstoun & Co., and advanced £255,000 in the first three months of their association in 1793. In return, McDowall worked to hard to solve his problems, as Paul Benfield told Walter Boyd in 1796: 'McDowall is moving Heaven and Earth to get his Business settled.'[80] Later in the 1790s, loans were raised on other prominent London houses, notably those of Salomans and J. J. Angerstein. Nonetheless, even in 1798, while ailing under the burden of debt, Houstoun & Co. raised finance in Scotland. In September 1798, the company secured loans of £5,000 from both the Thistle Bank and the Paisley Union Bank. As with the tobacco lords, however, the amount raised from banks was overshadowed by loans from individuals. Six days after the loans from the banks, Houstoun & Co. received a total of £30,500 from twenty-six of Glasgow's most senior merchants, along with £14,500 from Paisley merchants and manufacturers. All the loans were for six months, with interest at 5 per cent, and were financed by bills drawn on Boyd, Benfield & Co. A number of other loans amounting to £3,400 were raised in Glasgow, Greenock and Paisley.[81]

The timing of these loans is significant because while the pattern of raising local capital in this way was well established, the supply tended to dry up during war time as investors turned to the more secure and lucrative government stock, as the company well knew.[82] Nonetheless, despite the continuing war with France, and the company's well-documented financial troubles, the local merchant community was quite willing to back the company with hard currency, not just indicating faith in the company, but also suggesting an alliance of merchants, industrialists and gentry that rivaled the 'gentlemanly capitalists' of London described by Cain and Hopkins.[83]

The Baillies confronted many of the same crises. James Baillie was certainly under no illusions that his fortune was to be made overnight: 'I allow myself 15 Years from this date to the day I embark for Great Brittain . . . Provided my Health (which is at present very Good) permits me to continue here I shant see home before I can afford to live comfortably all my Remaining Days.'[84] And despite the political turmoil in his new home of Grenada, Baillie continued to flourish. The refusal of many of the British Protestant residents (including Baillie) to pay taxes to a government in which Catholics were represented was taken further by some planters and merchants, who used the crisis as a pretext for withholding the payment of business debts. Baillie managed to avoid being drawn into the quagmire of bad debts. He attributed his success in collecting most of the debts accruing from the sale of £120,000 worth of enslaved Africans to his careful selection of clients, bespeaking a caution and fear of debts similar to that of Houstoun & Co. in this period.

Even though these difficulties coincided with the 1772 credit crisis, Baillie survived unscathed, and continued to expand his interests (with the profits from his extensive slave trade enterprises) by acquiring 4,400 acres of land in St Vincent in 1773. The ever-increasing level of landownership, as well as trade in sugar and slaves from St George's and then London, formed the basis of James Baillie's wealth. In the 1780s, he also began to branch out into entrepreneurial credit arrangements with planters and other traders. He allowed planters to draw bills of exchange on his London house, which resulted in its supporting chains of credit, on large and small scales, throughout the islands.[85]

He took part in the great expansion of the West Indies in the early 1790s, which led him to have commitments of over £700,000, up to £500,000 of which was in West India bills at the time of his death in 1793. James Baillie's headlong rush to advance credit to planters was sustained after his death by his cousin George Baillie, who took over the firm of James Baillie & Co. Evan Baillie, for his part, seemed content with his sugar business in Bristol and some diversification into banking, land and industry, and did not enter the race to give credit. George Baillie, against Evan's advice, quickly changed the company name to George Baillie & Co. to prevent James's estate being declared bankrupt. By taking on his cousin's business, George was confronted by the crisis in credit that hit shortly after James's death, and it was he who faced the loss of crop in 1795, after the insurrections in Grenada and St Vincent.[86] George Baillie campaigned vigorously for government help, and wrote to William Pitt in September 1795 pointing out that he had to finance around £400,000 and had already sought the backing of his friends among the 'most respectable families', including Hope of Amsterdam, J. J. Angerstein and Francis Baring.[87] Despite the campaign, which, in alliance with the directors of Houstoun & Co. and with the backing of Henry Dundas, was successful, both Houstoun & Co. and George Baillie & Co. succumbed to the burden of their debts. George Baillie, as we have seen, tried again, as a cotton merchant in the early nineteenth century, but only Evan Baillie's firm survived. His more conservative approach allowed his company to ride out the storms of the 1790s, and to continue trading as sugar merchants until 1861.

Conclusion

The activities of these West India firms illustrate the complexity and the coherence of mercantile relationships in the Atlantic world. Houstoun & Co.'s arrangements in the Windward Islands were heavily influenced by intelligence about systems in the Chesapeake gleaned from Glasgow tobacco merchants. The four Baillies, born and raised in Inverness, all went to the West Indies in search of a fortune. That they were able to profit, not only in the islands, but in key English cities, demonstrates the opportunities available for those sufficiently mobile to capitalise on them, and the ability of (in this case) Scots to become thoroughly integrated in civic elites in England. The breadth of mercantile connections points to the existence of a transnational Atlantic world, where national boundaries, even between rival powers, did not prevent the transfer of goods or finance. Yet for all their internationalism, the Scots-owned firms remained bound to their kinship and local connections.

Evan Baillie's success translated itself into tangible investments in his native Scotland, and promoted his family's interests there. For Houstoun & Co., the enormous profits were also invested. Indeed, this was part of their problem: the assets of the directors were more than extensive enough to cover their debts, but they were tied up in assets, notably land, that could not be liquidated quickly enough. The extraordinary circumstances of the 1790s shattered the advances made by the innovations in their system of trading.

Notes

1 R. Pares, *A West-India fortune* (London: Longmans, Green & Co., 1950); J. M. Price, 'The rise of Glasgow in the Chesapeake tobacco trade, 1707–1775', *William and Mary Quarterly*, 11 (1954), 179–99; D. A. Farnie, 'The commercial empire of the Atlantic, 1607–1783', *Economic History Review*, 15, 2 (1962), 205–18; D. S. MacMillan, 'The "New Men" in action: Scottish mercantile and shipping operations in the North American colonies, 1760–1825', in D. S. MacMillan (ed.), *Canadian Business History: Selected studies* (Toronto: McClelland and Stewart, 1972), pp. 44–103; R. Davis, *The rise of the Atlantic economies* (Ithaca: Cornell University Press, 1973); T. M. Devine, *The tobacco lords: A study of the tobacco merchants of Glasgow and their trading activities, c. 1740–1790* (Edinburgh: John Donald, 1975); T. M. Devine, 'An eighteenth-century business elite: Glasgow–West India merchants, c. 1750–1815', *Scottish Historical Review*, 57 (1978), 40–67; K. Morgan, *Bristol and the Atlantic trade in the eighteenth century* (Cambridge: Cambridge University Press, 1993); D. Hancock, *Citizens of the world: London merchants and the integration of the British Atlantic community, 1735–1785* (Cambridge: Cambridge University Press, 1995); J. J. McCusker and K. Morgan (eds), *The early modern Atlantic economy* (Cambridge: Cambridge University Press, 2001).
2 D. Hamilton, 'Scottish trading in the Caribbean: The rise and fall of Houstoun and Co.', in N. C. Landsman (ed.), *Nation and province in the first British Empire: Scotland and the Americas, 1600–1800* (Lewisburg, PA, and London: Bucknell University Press, 2001), pp. 94–126.
3 NAS, CS96/1413(13, 35), Court of Session, unextracted processes, letterbook of Sinclair Brebner & Co., letters to William Sibbald and John Brebner, 7 December 1778 and 7 June 1789; CS96/1414(33, 65), journal of Sinclair, Brebner & Co., sundries account with Archibald Sinclair, and list of trading partners, 31 December 1781.
4 Hamilton, 'Scottish trading', pp. 98–100.
5 *ibid.*, p. 108.
6 NLS, MS8793(106), Alexander Houstoun & Co. papers, foreign letterbook E, letter to John Paterson, 2 December 1776; MS8794(34, 220–1), foreign letterbook F, letters to John Paterson, 20 July 1778, 1 June 1779.
7 ACA, Baillie Court: propinquity books, 1637–1797, vol. 3, pp. 1514–15; UASCA, MS2769/I/72/1, Davidson & Garden archive, papers of Dr Charles Irvine, inventory of accounts, title deeds and other papers in regard of Friendship estate, Jamaica, 25 September 1837; NLS, MS8797, Alexander Houstoun & Co. papers, ledger book L.
8 NLS, MS8793(97–8, 196), foreign letterbook E, letters to Alexander Houstoun Jun., 14 October 1776, and to John Hamilton, 17 March 1777; MS8799(238), sale book C.

9 NLS, MS8793(212–13), foreign letterbook E, letter to Houstoun & Paterson, 14 April 1777.
10 NLS, MS8794(232–3, 256), foreign letterbook F, letters to Houstoun & Paterson, 26 August 1779, and to Fergus Paterson, 3 January 1780; PRO, CO318/8(83–5), West Indies, original correspondence: secretary of State, An exact list of those that are received as burghers sints the 5th of August 1780 till the 29th of January 1781.
11 NLS, MS8794(443), foreign letterbook F, letter to Houstoun & Paterson, 15 January 1781.
12 NLS, MS8794(67), foreign letterbook F, letter to William McFarlane, 13 November 1778; MS8798(142), ledger book M.
13 Alexander Baillie, St Kitts, to Alexander Baillie, Dunzean, 26 May 1753, in C. Fraser-MacIntosh (ed.), *Letters of two centuries, chiefly connected with Inverness and the Highlands, from 1616 to 1815* (Inverness: A. and W. MacKenzie, 1890), pp. 239–40.
14 J. Campbell, *A political survey of Britain, being a series of reflections on the situation, lands, inhabitants, revenues, colonies, and commerce of this island* (London: no imprint, 1774), vol. 1, pp. 213, 215. Construction on the Caledonian Canal did not begin until 1804, and it was not opened until 1822.
15 Letter from James Baillie, 20 July 1761, in Fraser-MacIntosh (ed.), *Letters of two centuries*, p. 255.
16 Henry Laurens to Smith & Baillies, 8 February 1769, in G. C. Roger et al. (eds), *The papers of Henry Laurens* (Columbia, SC: University of South Carolina Press, 1968–92), vol. 4, pp. 29–31.
17 S. G. Checkland, 'Two Scottish West India liquidations after 1793', *Scottish Journal of Political Economy*, 4 (1957), 136; R. G. Thorne (ed.), *The History of Partiament: The House of Commons, 1790–1820* (London: History of Parliament Trust, 1986), vol. 3, p. 110.
18 Henry Laurens to Clay & Haversham, 26 October 1767, in Roger et al. (eds), *Papers of Henry Laurens*, vol. 4, p. 377; F. J. Grant (ed.), *Register of marriages in the city of Edinburgh* (Edinburgh: Scottish Record Society, 1922), p. 33.
19 NLS, MS8793(41–2, 55), foreign letterbook E, letters to James Smith, 19 June 1776, 1 October 1776.
20 Henry Laurens to James Baillie, 31 March 1770, and to Alexander, James and Evan Baillie, 3 August 1770, in Roger et al. (eds), *Papers of Henry Laurens*, vol. 7, pp. 263–4, 370.
21 'Obituary of James Baillie', *Gentleman's Magazine*, 63 (1793), 869; PRO, CO318/8(83), West Indies, original correspondence: secretary of State, An exact list of those that are received as burghers.
22 *St. George's Chronicle and New Grenada Gazette*, 15 October 1790; PRO, CO101/32 (no fol.), Grenada, original correspondence: Secretary of State, minutes of a meeting of the gentlemen connected with the island of Grenada, 5 September 1792.
23 PRO, CO263/2 (no fol.), St Vincent, sessional papers, journals of the house of assembly, 19 December 1771 and 11 May 1772.
24 Morgan, *Bristol and the Atlantic trade*, pp. 22, 289; W. E. Minchinton, *The port of Bristol in the eighteenth century* (Bristol: Historical Association Bristol Branch, 1962); Minchinton (ed.), *The trade of Bristol in the eighteenth century* (Bristol: Bristol Record Society, 1957), pp. ix–x.
25 BUL, DM1061, Papers of Captain David Duncomb, Messrs Garraway & Baillie to David Duncomb, 26 July 1775; Morgan, *Bristol and the Atlantic trade*, p. 194; Thorne (ed.), *House of Commons, 1790–1820*, vol. 3, p. 108.
26 BUL, Pinney papers, box 30 bundle 2, Peter Baillie in account current with Schimmelpinning & Co.; Minchinton, *Trade of Bristol*, p. 66.
27 For a history of the Pinney family, see Pares, *A West-India fortune*.
28 Pinney & Tobin to John Julius, 12 October 1787, in Minchinton, *Trade of Bristol*, p. 134; Pares, *A West-India fortune*, p. 213; BUL, Pinney papers, box U, marriage settlement, 8 May 1797; V. L. Oliver (ed.), *Caribbeana, being miscellaneous papers*

relating to the history, genealogy, topography and antiquities of the British West Indies (London: Mitchell Hughes & Clarke, 1909–19), vol. 3, supplement, p. 70.
29 BUL, Pinney papers, Evan Baillie to Peter Baillie, 24 May 1789; Pinney manuscripts, box 33, Alexander Baillie to Peter Baillie, 30 July 1796.
30 BUL, Pinney papers, insurance policy, 24 June 1797.
31 NLS, MS5599(146, 148–9), Liston papers, James Baillie to Robert Liston, 23 February 1803; NAS, GD267/5/9(4, 24, 34–6), Home of Wedderburn manuscripts; Pares, *A West-India fortune*, p. 213.
32 BUL, DM78/1, West Indies papers, memorandum and agreement to dissolve Evan Baillie, Sons & Co., 30 April 1861.
33 NLS, MS8799, Alexander Houstoun & Co. papers, sale book C; G. Jackson, 'Glasgow in transition, c.1660–c.1740', and 'New horizons in trade', in T. M. Devine and G. Jackson (eds), *Glasgow*, vol. 1: *Beginnings to 1830* (Manchester: Manchester University Press, 1995), pp. 75–6, 217, 219; Morgan, *Bristol and the Atlantic trade*, p. 184.
34 Pares, *A West-India fortune*, p. 32.
35 Devine, *The tobacco lords*, pp. 55–6; J. M. Price, 'Buchanan & Simson, 1759–63: A different kind of Glasgow firm trading to the Chesapeake', *William and Mary Quarterly*, 40, 1 (1983), 3–4.
36 NLS, MS8793(9–10), foreign letterbook E, letter to Robert Bogle Jun., 4 March 1776.
37 PRO, CO142/31, Jamaica, miscellanea, list of landholders in the island of Jamaica, 1754; L. J. Ragatz, 'Absentee landlordism in the British Caribbean, 1750–1833', *Journal of Agricultural History*, 5, 1 (1931), 8; M. Craton and J. Walvin, *A Jamaican plantation: The history of Worthy Park, 1670–1970* (London: W. H. Allen, 1970), p. 129.
38 J. Strang, *Glasgow and its clubs, or glimpses of the condition, manners, characters and oddities of the city, during the past and present century* (London and Glasgow: Richard Griffen & Co., 1856), pp. 52, 128–51, 263; D. J. Hamilton, 'Patronage and profit: Scottish networks in the British West Indies, c. 1763–1807', PhD thesis, University of Aberdeen, 1999, pp. 271–2.
39 NLS, MS8793(218–21), foreign letterbook E, n.d.; J. M. Price, *Capital and credit in British overseas trade: The view from the Chesapeake* (Cambridge, MA, Harvard University Press, 1980), p. 25.
40 T. M. Devine, 'Sources of capital for the Glasgow tobacco trade, c. 1740–1780', *Business History*, 16, 2 (1974), 126–7.
41 NLS, MS8793(202–3), foreign letterbook E, letters to Thomas Wilson, Archibald Stewart, William Bruce, and John and Alexander Campbell, 21 March 1777.
42 NLS, MS8793(106), foreign letterbook E, letter to Duncan McFarlane, 2 December 1776. A similar letter was sent a year later (MS8793(280)).
43 Checkland, 'Two Scottish West India liquidations', 137; BUL, DM41/59(6), West Indies MSS, Westerhall papers, account of sugar sales, 16 October 1794.
44 Morgan, *Bristol and the Atlantic trade*, pp. 194, 197.
45 Oliver, *Caribbeana*, vol. 2, p. 274; Minchinton, *Trade of Bristol*, p. 134.
46 R. Pares, 'The London sugar market, 1740–1769', *Economic History Review*, 9 (1956), 254–70.
47 NLS, MS8793(87), foreign letterbook E, letter to Houstoun & Paterson, 1 October 1776; BUL, DM41/59(12), account from J. Petrie, Campbell & Co., 24 April 1799.
48 ibid.; NAS, GD267/5/4(3), Home of Wedderburn manuscripts., account of George Home with Simond & Hankey, 10 September 1799.
49 Pares, *A West-India fortune*, pp. 189–90.
50 NLS, MS8793(306–12), foreign letterbook E, letter to Houstoun & Paterson, Grenada, 8 December 1777.
51 BUL, Pinney papers, Evan Baillie to Peter Baillie, 13 June 1804.
52 InvM, Letterbook of George Inglis, pp. 65–7, 89, 143, letters to Messrs Lang, Irving & Co. and to George Baillie, 22 April, 11 May, 29 August 1801.
53 A. L. Karras, *Sojourners in the sun: Scottish migrants in Jamaica and the Chesapeake, 1740–1800* (Ithaca: Cornell University Press, 1992), p. 7.

54 D. Hancock, 'Scots in the slave trade', in Landsman (ed.), *Nation and province*, pp. 60–93.
55 ACA, Baillie Court: propinquity books, 1637–1797, vol. 2, pp. 720, 862, 1047; Thorne (ed.), *House of Commons, 1790–1820*, vol. 3, p. 60; HSP, 1582/29B, box 2 folder 3, Powell collection, papers of Alexander Johnston, Alexander Johnston to James Johnston, 21 August 1784.
56 NAS, CS96/507(4a), Court of Session, unextracted processes, letterbook of Buchanan & Simpson, letter to Halliday & Dunbar, 19 October 1759; Price, 'Buchanan & Simson', 29–31; D. Eltis *et al.*, *The trans-Atlantic slave trade: A database on CD-ROM* (Cambridge: Cambridge University Press, 1999), entries 90969, 90970.
57 *Ibid.*, entries 20529, 21806, 24552, 24576, 25214, 25648, 77781, 90406, 91063, 94597.
58 Henry Laurens to James Penman and William Makdougall, 21 November 1767, in Roger *et al.* (eds), *Papers of Henry Laurens*, vol. 5, pp. 466–7.
59 NLS, MS5514(113), Liston papers, James Baillie to Mrs Ramage, 14 June 1772.
60 Eltis *et al.* (eds), *The trans-Atlantic slave trade*, entries 17920, 17933, 17952, 17967, 17988, 17990, 81807; C. Mosley (ed.), *Burke's peerage and baronetage* (Crans: Burke's Peerage [Genealogical Books], 1999), p. 436.
61 NLS, MS8793(18), Foreign letterbook E, letter to Houstoun & Paterson, 7 March 1776.
62 NLS, MS8793(31, 35–7), foreign letterbook E, letters to Duncan McFarlane, 19 April 1776, and Turner & Paul, 31 May 1776.
63 NLS, MS8793(62, 83), foreign letterbook E, letters to James Nesbit, and to John Cockburn, 1 October 1776.
64 NLS, MS8793(240, 325), foreign letterbook E, letters to Turner & Paul, Tobago, 2 May 1777; MS8794(10, 20, 22), foreign letterbook F, letters to Turner & Paul, Tobago; to Turner & Paul, St Vincent; and to Houstoun & Paterson, Grenada, 28 May 1778.
65 NLS, MS8793(323–5, 419–20, 422–4), foreign letterbook E, letters to Turner & Paul, 30 December 1777, 26 March 1778; and to Houstoun & Paterson, 26 March 1778.
66 NLS, MS8794(3), foreign letterbook F, letter to Turner & Paul, St Vincent, 27 May 1778.
67 NLS, MS8794(402–3), foreign letterbook F, letters to Turner & Paul, Tobago, 20, 26 February 1778.
68 NLS, MS8794(188), foreign letterbook F, letter to Turner & Paul, St Vincent, 22 March 1779; NAS, CS96/1414(5, 12), journal of Sinclair, Brebner & Co., 5 September 1778, 16 February 1779.
69 NLS, MS8794(175), foreign letterbook F, instructions to Captains Scott, McKinlay, McGregor and Buchanan, 13 March 1779.
70 NLS, MS8796–9, Alexander Houstoun & Co. papers foreign ledger books, K, L and M, 1793–98.
71 R. B. Sheridan, 'The credit crisis of 1772 and the American colonies', *Journal of Economic History*, 20, 2 (1960), 161–86; James Robinson to William Cunninghame, 23 June 1773, in T. M. Devine (ed.), *A Scottish firm in Virginia, 1767–1777* (Edinburgh: Scottish History Society, 1984), p. 74.
72 NLS, MS8796(135–8), ledger book K; MS8797(142–7), ledger book L.
73 Pares, *A West-India fortune*, pp. 175–6, 251, 263, 357; Checkland, 'Two Scottish West India liquidations'; Morgan, *Bristol and the Atlantic trade*, p. 29.
74 NLS, MS8796(133, 145–6, 223, 256), ledger book K.
75 NLS, MS8796(81–2), ledger book K; MS8797(77), ledger book L; PRO, CO260/13(9), St Vincent, original correspondence: secretary of State, minutes of a Council of War, 15 February 1795.
76 Oliver, *Caribbeana*, vol. 3, p. 295: will of Coll Turner of Tobago.
77 PRO, CO263/21 (no fol.), St Vincent, sessional papers, minutes of the assembly, 14 November 1789; NLS, MS8793(76), foreign letterbook E, letter to Turner & Paul, 1 October 1776; MS8796(123), ledger book K; MS8797(130–1, 259), ledger book L.

78 Devine, 'Sources of capital', 124–5.
79 NLS, MS8796(95), ledger book K.
80 S. R. Cope, *Walter Boyd: A merchant banker in the age of Napoleon* (London: Alan Sutton, 1983), pp. 41–2; Walter Boyd, *Letter to the creditors of the house of Boyd, Benfield & Co.* (London: Henry Reynall, 1800), appendix 5, Paul Benfield to Walter Boyd, 2 August 1796.
81 NAS, GD 237/12/26(1) MacDouall of Garthland papers, copy disposition in security, 3 November 1798 (registered 24 December 1798).
82 Devine, 'Sources of capital', 127–8.
83 P. J. Cain and A. G. Hopkins, *British imperialism*, vol. 1: *Innovation and expansion, 1688–1914* (London: Longman, 1993).
84 NLS, MS5513(187–8), Liston papers, James Baillie to Mrs Ramage, 10 May 1770.
85 NAS, CS96/1526(14, 21, 38), Court of session, unextracted processes, journal of a Glasgow merchant, bills drawn on James Baillie of London; GD126/9, bundle 2, Balfour–Melville papers, John and James Hamilton to Lt.-Gen. Robert Melville, 30 July 1790; S. G. Checkland, 'Finance for the West Indies, 1780–1815', *Economic History Review*, 10 (1957), 461–9.
86 Checkland, 'Two Scottish West India liquidations', 138–9.
87 *Ibid.*, 140; NAS, GD51/1/499(2), Melville Castle muniments, George Baillie to William Pitt, 17 September 1795.

CHAPTER FIVE

Scots doctors in the West Indies

One of the gravest risks for Europeans in the West Indies was that they would accumulate illnesses more quickly than wealth 'under the scorching sky of the tropics'.[1] Throughout the eighteenth century, new arrivals in the islands complained of the perils of tropical diseases. James Barclay reported from Jamaica in 1727 that the 'sickliness of the Climate ... is no better than it is said to be', while sixty years later, James Murray lamented, 'I am still alive & that is all – Sickness at home is very bad, but nothing to what a man must expect to suffer here.'[2]

A disease environment like the Caribbean's called for medical practitioners to attend to the white population. As life-threatening as a sojourn in the Caribbean was for whites, however, for the enslaved population it was worse. During the seventeenth century, slave-owners had given up 'trying to keep their Negroes alive ... and instead routinely bought replacement slaves'.[3] By the period under consideration, however, planters had been forced, by rising prices and the humanitarian impulse towards the amelioration of slave conditions, to provide better medical care for their enslaved labourers. These factors, allied to the expansion of the number of British-owned West Indian colonies and the number of people (both black and white) therein, increased the demand for doctors in the islands. Scotland, with established and reputable medical schools in its universities, was especially well placed to send doctors to the islands to provide medical care to the plantations, which were increasingly being owned or managed by Scotsmen.

The islands could be an attractive proposition for Scots doctors, providing, of course, that they lived long enough. Practice in the Caribbean often led to doctors acquiring considerable wealth, partly from their professional roles and partly from their diversification into other realms of West Indian profits: planting and trading. Beyond these mammonist motivations, a sojourn in this tropical environment granted Scottish doctors access to a laboratory for scientific and medical discovery and observation. The role of Scots in the collection and dissemination of medical and botanical intelligence extended the frontiers of European knowledge of the tropical environment. This production of knowledge contributed to the process of accommodation between the metropolitan state and the colonies.

Medical networks

> The government or treatment of the slaves is of so great importance, their health, and let me add, their happiness, so essentially connected with the interests of the proprietors, and of humanity, that the judgement and direction of the manager of a plantation, are best shewn by a proper attention to these objects.[4]

The need for white people to attend to the health of the enslaved and, indeed, to the care of the white elite was often met by networks. Dr Walter Tullideph had arrived in Antigua in 1726 at his cousin's invitation. By 1735, Tullideph believed that he needed more help in his practice and turned to his kinship network. He wrote to another cousin, William Dunbar, a sugar factor in London, asking him to find a 'Sober Young Surgeon who has been educated at Edinburgh (if possible) for three years'. As a result, Dr William Mercer was engaged at an initial salary of £30 *per annum*. A year later, Tullideph entered the planting business, acquiring, by marriage, a 127-acre estate, and turned his attention increasingly to his new venture.[5]

In 1736 he began to plan for the care of both his medical practice and his estate under future circumstances in which he might not be resident in the island. As was shown in Chapter Three, the value of engaging reliable representatives was apparent to absentee Scottish proprietors, and Tullideph sought to ensure that all his affairs would be properly superintended. Accordingly, he wrote to his brother Thomas in Scotland: 'If any of our nephews will study Physick and Settle as a Planter I can allow such a one £100 Sterlg. pr. Ann. to manadge my Estate and take care of my negroes when I resolve to come home...'[6] Unfortunately for Tullideph, none of his nephews evinced any desire to go to the Caribbean, which may explain why William Mercer became a partner in Tullideph's practice a year later. Yet the failure of the plan does not diminish its significance. Almost as soon as Tullideph became a planter, he entertained thoughts, rather than hopes, of returning home, and of leaving family members in charge of an emergent dynasty in Antigua. Moreover, his proposal to his nephews points to a logical conjunction of roles: the estate manager and doctor. William Turnbull also alluded to this dualism in the above quotation when he noted the need for the good governance of slaves by managers.

Although Tullideph's nephews declined his invitation, he was far from being the only Scottish doctor in Antigua. In 1731, Antigua had twenty-two doctors, around half of whom were Scots. The figures increased as the century progressed, so that by about 1750, there were thirty-two doctors, nineteen of whom either were Scottish or had been trained in Scotland. Of the nineteen medical practitioners with whom Tullideph corresponded, fourteen are likely to have been from Scotland.[7] Although these kinds of statistics are lacking for other islands, it is clear that this domination of the profession was not confined to Antigua.

A few years before Tullideph arrived in Antigua, Alexander Grant of Dalvey settled in Jamaica as a self-styled 'Practitioner in Physick & Chiurgery', having studied a little basic medicine in Aberdeen. He entered a practice in western Jamaica with two cousins before moving into planting and trading from the 1730s, and relocating to London in 1739.[8] This move was perhaps a blessing for the people of western Jamaica, because it removed an incompletely trained 'doctor' from their midst, and was certainly a boon for Grant, for he went on to acquire considerable wealth and status in London. This status was used to the benefit of several of his kinsmen, including Walter Grant of Jamaica.

Walter Grant travelled from Jamaica to study medicine at Marischal College in Aberdeen. His position in the college came as a result of being 'strongly recommended by Dr Alexander Grant of Dalvey, late of Jamaica'. A further member of the extended Grant clan, Sir Archibald Grant of Monymusk, stepped in and paid his kinsman's college dues, allowing him to graduate as a doctor of medicine in 1753. After graduation, Dr Grant returned to Jamaica, where he practised in Kingston 'as a surgeon in good repute in company with Andrew Rose'.[9] As well as practising medicine, Grant performed the kind of dual role that Tullideph had envisaged for his nephews, by monitoring and managing the plantation affairs of members of the Grant family around Kingston, along with yet another kinsman, Alex Grant.[10]

This kind of network was not used solely as a means of recruitment; it was also a vehicle by which young doctors could solicit employment, or have it solicited for them. Networking thus operated to the benefit of both recruiters and recruits. In 1763, Dr Alexander Johnston arrived in the Jamaican parish of St Ann's.[11] Dr Alexander Fullerton first employed him, and within two years they had become partners, albeit with Johnston as the junior. Indeed for the first two years of the partnership, he had to pay half the costs, but received only a third of the profits.[12] Despite these early tribulations, Johnston began to acquire land and wealth in St Ann's, news of which was communicated to Scotland by frequent correspondence with his brother James.

Johnston's successful presence in the island made him a natural contact for other members of the network in north-east Scotland. In early 1783, Dr Anderson of Strichen, 'a distant relative' of the Johnstons, arrived in Jamaica clutching a letter of introduction from James Johnston. In this letter, James wrote to Alexander, 'I sincerely wish you may have it in your powers to serve him which I flatter myself you will do if you have an opportunity.' Alexander, sensitive to the obligations bestowed by his familial and local connections, readily agreed, and promised to 'introduce [Dr Anderson] into good business, if he behaves well; – I like him very well.'[13] However favourable his early impressions of Anderson may have been, Johnston's opinion of his young charge deteriorated considerably over the course of a year. In August 1784, he told his brother that he was 'not pleased with Mr. Anderson' and feared that he had been 'too hasty with him... Besides I do not think he had any good Education – consequently not much ability.'[14]

Elsewhere in Jamaica, Scots were able to utilise valuable connections to procure positions for themselves in the island. Through the support of the noted improver Sir John Sinclair of Ulbster and of Mr Wemyss of Edinburgh, Dr John Williamson, formerly surgeon to the Caithness Highlanders, was introduced to Lewis Cuthbert, one of Lord Harewood's Jamaican representatives. Through Cuthbert and Harewood's other attorney, Alexander MacLeod, Williamson was introduced to Drs Clarke and Forbes. On 21 September 1798, Williamson concluded articles of co-partnership with these two gentlemen that bound him to the partnership for seven years and, on payment of a £700 sterling bond, entitled him to one-third of the profits.[15]

The Windward islands abounded with doctors. The Waltham estate in Grenada, formerly owned by Lieutenant-Governor Ninian Home, remained in his family's hands after his death in 1795. By the early part of the nineteenth century, the estate had almost recovered from its sacking during Fedon's Rebellion, and was operating as before. Dr William Stephenson was engaged by George Home to reside on the estate and to practise medicine there from December 1802. After nearly two years he left Waltham, perhaps as a result of a dispute with the manager, or because he was lured away by a more lucrative practice.

Thomas Duncan, another Scottish doctor in the island, who was acquainted with Stephenson, wrote to Home offering the services of his brother, who by then had been practising in Grenada for nine months. He stressed that the offer was his 'bourden duty out of gratitude to you'. Duncan's brother had seen in those nine months 'more practice & had more experience in the diseases of the Climate than any other person can possibly have in years upon one estate', and would, therefore, be a valuable addition to the staff at Waltham. There is no reason to doubt that Duncan was offering these services to Home out of friendship, and out of a concern for his affairs, yet the move would also benefit Duncan himself. He admitted to Home, 'I confess it would take some hard rides off my shoulder & so far be of service to me.'[16]

In the field of medicine, these kinship ties were augmented by professional connections. A variety of professional organisations through which medical men communicated and socialised grew in parallel with the expansion of the medical schools. Medical societies sprang up in the university cities. In Edinburgh, the first medical society was established in 1731, while the first student-based group, the Royal Medical Society of Edinburgh, was founded three years later. The earliest society in Aberdeen is generally believed to have been founded by James McGrigor and James Robertson in 1789, but there is firm evidence of a student medical society dating from at least 1761.[17] Furthermore, the institutions that legitimised the practice of trained doctors, rather than 'quacks', could also act as points of contact between medics. The Royal College of Physicians in London and that in Edinburgh licensed practitioners. Graduates of Scottish universities throughout the eighteenth century, in particular, swelled the ranks of the Royal College in London. The college roll shows an enormous increase in the Edinburgh graduates being admitted. Only two Edinburgh alumni entered in the first half of the century, but ninety-five did so in the second half. While the new upstart dwarfed the numbers from the other Scottish universities, they too increased substantially. The number of Aberdeen graduates grew from ten before 1750 to twenty-seven after it; St Andrews's increased from four to eighteen; Glasgow's from four to ten.[18] These institutions fostered the development of professional networks that could first be utilised to provide employment, and then function as vehicles for the dissemination of medical or scientific information.

Alexander Johnston's appearance in Jamaica is likely to have been facilitated by professional contacts focused through the lens of an Aberdonian connection. As the location of Johnston's home in Scotland is not known precisely, it is difficult to be exactly certain when he attended university. Enough is known, however, to suggest that he graduated AM (*artium magister*) from Marischal College, Aberdeen, in 1758. He was certainly in Aberdeen in 1761, as is indicated by his presence at, and participation in, the meetings of the Medical Society.[19] After he left Aberdeen, probably in 1762, Johnston went to London, where he continued his education under 'Hunter and Fordyce'. These two prominent and influential physicians, the former from Glasgow, the latter from Aberdeen, 'between them were the great private teachers in London in the latter part of the eighteenth century'.[20] After receiving Hunter's and Fordyce's contributions to his 'good education', Johnston appeared in Jamaica in 1763 as an employee of Fullarton, who was also from Aberdeen.

This pattern of professional connections applied elsewhere in the Caribbean. In May 1789, Jonathon Troup from Aberdeenshire arrived in Dominica. On his arrival he was met by Andrew Smith of Aberdeen, one of the 'Principal Gentlemen in the island', and in the evening he met Dr Andrew Fillan, his employer and one of sixteen doctors in the town and garrison of Roseau. Fillan was clearly pre-eminent among these medics, his business being responsible for two-thirds of the practice in the town. He had been in the island for fourteen years and over that time had become 'generally beloved by inhabitants' for being 'an excellent, attentive Practitioner'.[21] The provenance of Fillan's degree is unknown, but in 1791 a doctorate of medicine was conferred upon him by Marischal College around the same time as he received a fellowship from the Royal College of Physicians in Edinburgh.[22]

Fillan's partner, Dr James Clark, has also left a stamp on the historical record. Clark, an Aberdonian, received a doctorate of medicine from King's College, Aberdeen, in 1773, probably two years before he went to the West Indies. For much of 1789, Clark was absent from the island, to visit Aberdeen and to be received as a fellow of the Royal College of Physicians of Edinburgh, for which he had been nominated by the eminent Jamaican botanist William Wright.[23] Troup's arrival in Dominica was the result of his recruitment by Clark. Troup was later told that Clark had provided Fillan with an 'excellent' reference, and that he was aware that his presence in the island was a direct result of having been 'brought out' by Clark. It is unclear, however, what the precise connection was between Troup and Clark. One possibility is that Clark became aware of Troup's medical training as a result of a common local background. Alternatively, the connection may have been established through the medical community in the city. There is no evidence of a kinship link. At least one person in Dominica assumed there was, but was corrected by Troup himself.[24]

The regulation of medicine

> Planters should remember the sixth commandment. Those who presume to prescribe to the sick, and are not qualified by study and experience, must be murderers.[25]

James Grainger's dire warning was not without foundation in the Caribbean. Medical practice in the islands, while enormously important if conducted properly, was prone to rather too frequent bouts of malpractice by unqualified doctors whose antics undermined the reputation of the profession in the islands. The planter-historian Edward Long was especially critical of the group of men who styled themselves 'doctors', and he savaged those practitioners whose 'principal instruments of death were mercury and opium, ever mistakenly applied, and injudiciously combined.' Even worse, perhaps, he accused doctors of inventing medical-sounding terms to cover their own ignorance.[26] Jonathon Troup's later criticism of his employer, Dr Fillan, highlighted part of the problem: 'farewell to study & attention & recovery – making Money by flattery and attendance tho' you never cure one is the point here Hence a great error & incuriousity & slowness to the advancement of study.'[27] The medical profession itself served to confirm impressions of rather less than professional conduct.

At least one doctor in Dominica made speculative forays into veterinary medicine. Dr Spencer attempted to relieve the suffering of a hen by cutting it open and removing the excess food and stones it had eaten. He closed the two-inch incision with three stitches. The operation was spectacularly unsuccessful: the bird 'died of mortification' three days later. Troup was not in the least impressed, describing Spencer's actions as 'foolishness'.[28] But this spirit of experimentation was not confined to exploratory operations on poultry; it could also be applied to human patients. One doctor-planter argued at the turn of the century that estate managers should acquire some rudimentary medical knowledge which they ought to put to the test, commenting, 'you need not be deterred from the exercise of your talents, by the apprehension of committing mistakes: a little malpractice is common enough, even to those who are most familiar with the art, and yet death does not always ensue. Nature struggles hard for life, and, in her efforts to preserve it, rectifies many more of their errors than we are aware of, or they will acknowledge.'[29] Nature, of course, was not always capable of intervening in time. As Charles Gordon of Cairness lay gravely ill in Jamaica, he was given ten doses of bark. These 'satt very kindly upon his stomach'; the doctors thought they had cured him. He died two days later, probably as a result of an overdose.[30]

The over-prescription of expensive drugs was probably a result as much of ignorance on the part of the doctors as of a calculated attempt to lighten their patients' pockets. The use of opiates was designed to quell pain, while mercury was used to combat smallpox. What was not realised at the time was that some of the supposed symptoms of the disease were actually side effects of the ingestion of mercury. There were many critics of the use of mercury, but it was a matter of some debate among Caribbean doctors. The English doctor at Worthy Park in Jamaica, John Quier, made extensive use of mercury in this often-successful battle against smallpox, while Thomas Dancer believed the practice to be hazardous but sometimes necessary. John Williamson explicitly counselled against its use.[31] On the other hand, at least one Scottish doctor was a firm believer in the healing powers of mercury. Colin Chisholm of Grenada, in advocating the use of mercury in treating yellow fever, argued:

> it is to be presumed that those who maintain the opinion which militates against its utility and safety, are badly qualified to discuss the point. The principal arguments proposed against the practice, are drawn from either imperfect experience, or from those sources which false theory made an imaginary discovery of; or from indolent reliance on received opinions, promulgated by high medical authority, which time and imbecility have matured into ... 'supine scepticism'.[32]

Despite disputes over practice, and the evident incompetence of some doctors, the regulation of the medical profession in the West Indies was not a challenge that was immediately taken up. It was a matter of great concern to Edward Long that there was no means of ensuring that those men who practised medicine in Jamaica were actually trained for the task. 'It is the highest reproach, it is even an impiety,' he charged, that ill-trained doctors 'should be tamely permitted to over-run and depopulate [Jamaica], preying on the purses and lives of innocent men, with an impudence, ignorance, and rapacity, that is unparalleled.'[33] Long's solution was for legislative action to be taken to exclude from practice all those who were unable to produce certificated authentication of their credentials and qualifications. Yet four decades later, the issue of medical regulation had still to be resolved. In 1817, John Williamson wrote of the need for legislative sanction 'to prevent the admission of unqualified persons to the practice of medicine'. Still no action was taken. Indeed, it was not until 1826 that the Jamaica assembly and council responded, and even then the legislation did not receive gubernatorial approval and enter the statute book until 1833.[34]

Despite the well-founded grievances of many in the islands, it would be unfair to characterise all doctors as uneducated charlatans. The following examples demonstrate that many Scottish doctors were trained, diligent and innovative practitioners who made significant contributions to the health of the islands' inhabitants. Indeed, such contributions were acknowledged by the very critics of the state of medicine in the Caribbean. John Stewart of Jamaica conceded that there were many well-qualified doctors in the island even if 'Some of them who are set up as medical men in Jamaica are not the most competent that could be desired.' And even Long, so scathing in this assault on 'quacks', noted that Jamaica 'is happily supplied with several men of great ability.'[35] Among those men in Jamaica, a number are likely to have been Scots.

In Dominica, Scottish doctors were able to maintain a relatively good reputation. In another of Troup's attacks on his employer's good name, he accused Dr Fillan of tremendous incompetence, 'but *the name of a Scots Dr* & of the time he has been in the island . . . Protect his ignorance.'[36] It is unclear whether Troup's vitriol was inspired by a sense that his reputation might be tarnished by what he saw as Fillan's incompetence, or by a sense that the good name of the Scottish medical profession itself was being undermined by malpractice. But it does suggest that a Scottish doctor was assumed to be well qualified and professional. While Troup sought to act in a professional manner, the same could not be said of all those who practised medicine in his island. Troup, indeed, was scathing of 'empirics' among his colleagues who 'don't understand the reasonings' of their actions. To him they were little better than unqualified doctors. For all his bluster, however, Troup was not immune from error. By his own admission he 'inadvertently gave a vomit of T[artar] Emet[ic] to Boy for man [without] asking his complaint – he vomited blood from it.'[37]

Surgery practice

Having been recruited to the West Indies through familial, local or professional networks, doctors found themselves operating in one of two kinds of practice. Under the first system, the doctor, severally or in partnership, provided care to a number of plantations on a more or less *ad hoc* basis. The second involved the doctor being employed directly by the planter to attend the estate or estates in his possession.

In Jamaica in 1764, Alexander Johnston entered a practice that attended to a number of plantations in the parish of St Ann's. It was a busy and lucrative practice with 331 patients on its books between 1760 and 1772, around eighty-three of whom were probably Scottish or of Scots descent.[38] The practice attended to patients across the parish, and placed a discernible emphasis on the treatment of white people.

In treating Europeans, Johnston relied heavily on the customary medicines and techniques of the day. His accounts itemise frequent purgings and use of the bark (cinchona), along with the application of blisters and the prescriptions of vomits and mercurial solutions.[39] These medications were supplied by the pharmacy which was an integral part of firstly Fullerton's, and then the partnership's, practice in St Ann's. This conjunction of roles attracted some notable criticism, even among contemporaries. James Grainger alluded to the system's impropriety in 1764 when he argued that each estate should be supplied annually with medicines from England. Half a century later, John Williamson quite explicitly sought 'to change that system, which so exposes the sick to the designing and extravagant arts of the physician and apothecary, united in the same person.'[40] Williamson was well qualified to comment on the situation, having practised in St Thomas in the Vale in Jamaica between 1798 and 1812, in partnership with Clarke and Forbes.

In Dominica, Jonathon Troup's disillusionment with the conduct of his employer and colleagues did not begin immediately, and after his arrival in the island he applied himself to his task with enthusiasm. As a doctor based in surgery practice, he found himself visiting a number of plantations. During his time in the island, he attended to the white and black populations on twenty-four estates and to the inmates at the prison in Roseau. Although Troup complained that he was doing more than his share of the work, the practice in which he was employed seems to have been genuinely busy.

Troup attended to the enslaved as often as to white people, either collectively or on an individual basis. From time to time he inoculated slaves against smallpox. Against the practice of dirt-eating, Troup could not inoculate, and he was at something of a loss to comprehend one of the most perplexing killers of Africans in the Caribbean. Less baffling to Troup were the injuries to which he had to attend. A week after his arrival, he helped a man who had been attacked by his black mistress with a sharp saw. While he was seeing to the cut over the patient's left eye, he was called to Mr Laurie's estate. A recently arrived slave boy, knowing no better, had walked through an open window on an upper floor and had fallen twelve feet to the ground. In order to determine whether the boy's skull was fractured, Troup 'scalp[ed] the skull bone' and was pleased to find only a small scratch. Later in the year he treated a sailor whose finger had been shattered by an anchor, a knife wound, a dislocated collarbone, a gash caused by an axe and an African whose legs had been so horribly scalded by boiling rum that they were 'as white as any European'.[41]

Prescriptions for the myriad ailments encountered by Troup and his colleagues were usually, but not exclusively, furnished by the pharmacy. Like that of Alexander Johnston's practice in Jamaica, this pharmacy was an integral part of Fillan's practice where doctors could sometimes be found making up medicines, both for their own use and for sale to other doctors and customers. Owning the pharmacy was a lucrative part of Fillan's business, and one that Troup accused him of encouraging by 'pouring in Med[icine]s'. Troup believed that his employer's prescriptions were motivated more by the pursuit of profit than by a concern for the well being of his patients. This desire for wealth merely compounded Fillan's ineptitude, as Troup saw it, in prescribing medicines 'indiscriminately at random'.[42] Troup continued to use the conventional methods (blistering, purging, vomiting), including, on one occasion, the application of blisters to a patient's back as a cure for sore eyes. He generally used conventional medicines like bark, tartar emetics, jalap oil, James powder and opiates. But like several doctors, he sought to use discoveries to introduce innovations to his medical practice. While in cases like dirt-eating he was reduced to recording his observations rather than confronting them, at other times he utilised the medicines available naturally in the island. Thus he applied cassada, 'a poisonous herb of the island', to a child with a 'foul ulcer . . . deep & black'. He later used cow manure on an infected toe, and dressed a head wound with soot.[43]

Plantation practice

While Johnston and Troup were required to travel to visit patients on many estates, some other Scottish doctors in the West Indies remained on a single estate, caring for both the black and the white residents. Dr Colin Chisholm, for example, was employed on the Westerhall estate in Grenada at an annual salary of £330.[44] Employing a doctor to work alongside the manager was an obvious variation of Walter Tullideph's instinct to engage a man capable of being both. The importance of having someone with medical training to attend to an estate was highlighted by some contemporary writers, particularly around the turn of the century, when the need to maintain the enslaved population was becoming increasingly apparent.[45] For this reason, on Christmas Day 1802, 'after a good passage of five weeks and two days', Dr William Stephenson arrived at the Waltham estate in Grenada. His correspondence with his employer during the course of his residence claimed that the enslaved population at Waltham was relatively healthy. In his first letter to George Home, Stephenson noted, 'the people here, both <u>white</u> and <u>black</u> are all in very good health – There has not been a case of sickness of more than three or four days continuance, since I got here.'[46]

Apart from several cases of quinsy, which he attributed to the unsettled weather rather than to bacterial infection, Stephenson dealt primarily with the care of ulcers and small sores during the first three months. He noted that the stock of medicines on the estate would soon require replenishing, and expressed some alarm at the charges for medicines, which he felt were double or even treble the prices in Edinburgh. The real problem he seemed to be facing was that the cowpox matter, which was used to inoculate the enslaved against smallpox, had failed him, having been used two or three times before. Nevertheless, the fact that inoculation was supposed to be taking place indicates a desire on the part of the estate owner to maintain his workers in as healthy a condition as possible.

The practice of inoculation was long-standing in the Caribbean by the time when Stephenson arrived, having first been used in 1727.[47] In the aftermath of a smallpox epidemic in Antigua in the mid-1750s, Dr Thomas Fraser began a process of inoculation with great success. He treated around forty whites and between 270 and 300 enslaved. Treating the latter groups was problematic owing to the 'scanty allowance we have for the care' of the enslaved, which 'will not afford any great expense of medicines'.[48] Perhaps John Quier, an English doctor on Worthy Park plantation in Jamaica from 1767, made the greatest advances in smallpox inoculation in the islands. In the spring of 1768, Quier successfully inoculated 700 slaves, using matter freshly drawn from another patient rather than attempting, like Stephenson, to use old matter.[49]

Stephenson had clearly never read Quier's work, or had dismissed it, because he persisted with cowpox matter. In summer 1803, having considered the stock of medicines on the estate, Stephenson sent Home a list of those he required, rather than relying on local suppliers in pharmacies run by men like Fillan or Johnston.[50] By the time of the annual appraisement of the health of the enslaved population, Stephenson had received another supply of cowpox matter, which had proved as ineffective as the last. The situation had by then become more pressing, as he had six or seven slave children to inoculate.

At the time of the appraisement, fifty-one of the 205 slaves were sick, although only eight were 'incurable' and three 'doubtful'. The males appear to have been healthier than the females: only nineteen of the seventy-seven men were unwell, while thirty-two of the ninety-four women were sick. Nine of the women who were described as 'sick' either were pregnant or had recently miscarried, which suggests that the inability to work was the criterion for defining illness, and in particular that the twenty people described as 'invalids' were likely to have been elderly rather than genuinely unwell. Over the course of the previous year, there had been six deaths among the enslaved on the estate, including three 'very old people (invalids)', two infants and a woman who passed away as a result of her seventh or eighth abortion (no-one seemed sure how many she had endured). Despite all this, and almost a quarter of the enslaved population being sick, Stephenson was able to express himself satisfied with the health of the slaves.[51]

This satisfaction was a consistent feature of Stephenson's letters to Home. Indeed, by June 1804, he claimed that the slaves on Waltham were the healthiest in the whole island. He and his friend Mr Duncan had taken the opportunity of visiting slave hospitals on other estates, and he had seen how much busier they were than the hospital at Waltham. This he attributed to the healthy diet of the enslaved and to their being well clothed, 'not like the many that were starving for the want of common necessities of life' on other plantations. Moreover, the slave population at Waltham increased naturally over the year. Even though the hospital was fuller than normal, as a result of many of the slaves suffering from sores, induced, according to Stephenson, by very wet weather, Waltham was less badly affected than most other estates. 'Proof', Stephenson wrote, 'of the healthiness of the situation'.[52]

Although he had little to say about the well being of the white residents on the plantation, one remark implied that they too benefited from living in a healthy part of the island. He wrote, 'Notwithstanding the great mortality among the inhabitants of our colour, I inform you with heart-felt pleasure of the good health of all here.'[53]

The rewards

Like other Caribbean sojourners, Scots doctors tended to go to the West Indies with the intention of making money. For those practitioners who became established in a colony, there was money to be made from medicine alone. Andrew Fillan in Dominica, in garnering two-thirds of the market in Roseau (despite being one of sixteen practitioners) and in running a pharmacy, was well placed to make a comfortable living. His employees, on the other hand, were less likely to be able to finance a lavish lifestyle, as they were bound by indenture to the practice.

On the larger islands, a doctor might earn a substantial income from his practice. Alexander Johnston's partnership in Jamaica tended to regard treating the enslaved as generating a relatively meagre income: until 1784 the practice charged proprietors 5s per slave for an annual health check. In 1773, Dr George Gallimore was charged £24 15s for attention to ninety-nine slaves.[54] This rate remained unchanged for another decade, when it was increased to 7s 6d per person. The enslaved seen on an individual basis were charged more, but still considerably less than Europeans were charged for apparently similar treatments. In 1773, for example, Charles Arbuthnot of Aberdeenshire was charged 2s 6d for a purge to a slave, but 5s for a purge to a white.[55]

Not only were medicines for whites more expensive, but the call-out charge for a European was far from inconsiderable. A daytime visit by Johnston cost £1 3s 9d, while a nocturnal summons cost twice that. Visits by junior doctors were cheaper: in 1773 the charge for a night visit by the junior member of the practice, Dr Weir, was the same as Johnston's daytime charge. Clearly seniority had its advantages.[56] Dr Weir's arrival probably allowed Johnston to make fewer night visits and to cut back on his medical commitments. After 1771, Johnston attended far fewer patients than he had before, and it seems likely that he began to use his greater free time to extend his entrepreneurial activities in the island. Certainly by 1784, Johnston concentrated on the more lucrative treatment of Europeans and did very little 'negroe practice', leaving that function to the other fifteen or sixteen doctors in the parish.[57]

In addition to attending to a variety of plantations, between 1781 and 1783 Johnston provided medical care to the 99th Regiment garrisoned in the island. Garrison medicine, like that of the enslaved population, was far less lucrative than private practice for white planters, but it nevertheless provided a steady stream of income. Johnston was paid a *per diem* rate of 3s sterling. Thus his 169 days' duty in 1781 brought him £25 7s, 365 days in 1782 netted him £54 15s and the fifty-five days to 24 February 1783 generated £8 5s.[58]

For all that treating the enslaved seemed relatively unprofitable on an individual basis, in Jamaica it was far from unknown for doctors to have 4,000 or more slaves under their care. Using Johnston's charges as a guide, this would have generated an annual income of £1,000 currency before 1784 and £1,500 currency after that. In other islands, too, doctors found themselves with large slave practices in addition to their white and garrison practices.[59] Indeed, in spite of his reservations about the treatment of the enslaved, Johnston's practice in 1774 attended to 1,959 slaves on nineteen estates, bringing an annual income of almost £490, to which need to be added the costs of medicines and the treatment of whites.[60] In 1817, John Williamson recommended that the number of slaves under a doctor's care should be limited to 4,000 (implying that some were not), and that each doctor should earn 10s per person, making a potential annual income of £2,000 currency. Given the propensity of planters to run up considerable debts, however, this income might be more theoretical than actual. Williamson complained that the 'procrastinating system of payments' meant that doctors were not always paid promptly.[61]

Many doctors also sought alternative sources of income. For several, the route to riches often involved becoming a planter. We have already seen Walter Tullideph's rapid acquisition of wealth through planting in Antigua. Others, like Colin Chisholm of Inverness, did similarly. An alumnus of King's College, Aberdeen, he was awarded the degree of MD by that institution in 1793, having been recommended by John Rollo, himself the author of a study of West Indian medicine. By this time, Chisholm practised in Grenada, where he witnessed the outbreak of the yellow fever epidemic that swept along the Atlantic coast of the Americas between 1793 and 1796. He was also a landowner and a key figure in an important trans-colonial network. He acquired sufficient wealth to relocate in the early nineteenth century to a fashionable new area of Bristol, where he sponsored the medical studies of young Bristolians in Aberdeen.[62]

In 1771, Alexander Johnston began to acquire land in St Ann's parish. By 1784, he owned two pens totalling 3,000 acres and worth £19,300, including the enslaved and stock thereon. This sum, Johnston believed, was a low valuation of the worth of his estates, but nevertheless represented considerably more than the assets with which he had arrived in the island.[63] Despite his complaints about the valuation of property, it was profitable, even after his death in 1787. At the time of this death, the value of his property, not including the land itself, was £10,263. Included in this was the value of his library in Jamaica, which neatly represented the interests of a Scottish doctor, educated in Enlightenment Scotland, who became a landowner. In addition to works by Cullen and Boerhaave on chemistry, six volumes of Linnaeus's works and Priestly's *Opticks*, he had books on farming and gardening, books on law and works by Hume, Locke and Pope.[64] After his death, his estates were retained by his heirs, and made annual profits of over £1,000 in 1789, 1790 and 1791.[65] Similarly, in the parish of St Thomas in the East, the Friendship estate, which had been owned by Dr Charles Irvine until his death in 1794, remained in the hands of his family. In 1806, while under the care of Thomas Urquhart, the estate was appraised by Thomas MacKenzie and James Johnston. They found that it amounted to 1,112 acres of land, 191 slaves and a quantity of stock. In all they estimated it to be worth £45,590 currency.[66] But if the pursuit of wealth was a considerable motivation for doctors, many were also concerned to garner some professional reward for their work.

The advancement of knowledge

In yet another of Edward Long's tirades against doctors and their medicine in Jamaica, he lamented the failure of those practitioners, to whom he attributed some ability, 'to publish the fruits of [their] knowledge and practice.' Too often, he believed, when a good doctor died 'his treasure of experimental knowledge has been buried with him.'[67] When Long's work was published in 1774, there were indeed few books based on empirical experience available, among the most notable being those by Thomas Trapham, Sir Hans Sloane, William Hillary and James Grainger. The final quarter of the century saw a ballooning of the literature relating to disease in the islands. Thus the colonies began to play a far more important role in the production of knowledge. Given the extent of Scottish involvement in medical practice in the Caribbean, it is unsurprising that Scots wrote many of these volumes.

The purpose of these books was the dissemination of knowledge which was acquired in the colonies and which could not be learned from the study of medicine in European universities. In each of the volumes, the writers described their experiences in treating diseases, and published them as contributions to knowledge. Thomas Dancer's discussion of the waters at the Bath in St Thomas in the East was intended not for the medical community as such but for the literate members of white society, and was heftily subscribed to by the Jamaican elite.[68] John Rollo's *Observations on the means of preserving and restoring health in the West-Indies* was directed primarily to 'the Officers of the Army' in the islands. Written in Barbados in 1782, his chapters formed a series of recommendations to the officers on the best means to limit the appalling loss of life from disease among soldiers garrisoned in the Caribbean. He outlined the measures necessary to ensure proper dress, diet, lodging and employment in the Caribbean, along with comments on the climate. In these, he noted that the circumstances would be not be the same in all the islands, meaning that certain variations would be required.[69]

Scots doctors who practised in the Caribbean in the later eighteenth century made significant contributions to the growing corpus of literature on West Indian medicine. In addition to the works of Chisholm, Clark, Collins, Dancer, Grainger, Rollo and Williamson, volumes by other Scots added to the advancement of medical knowledge. Some wrote in general terms on medicine and disease in the islands. James Lind's *Essay on diseases incidental to Europeans in hot climates*

(1768) was in its fifth edition by 1794.⁷⁰ John Hunter MD, of Perthshire, wrote his *Observations on the diseases of the army in Jamaica* in 1788, while Thomas Dancer's *The medical assistant, or the Jamaica practise of physic* was published in 1801. Other publications dealt primarily with specific diseases. Included in this group was James Hendy, whose *Treatise on the glandular fever of Barbadoes* was published in 1784. Of particular importance to sailors trying to get to the West Indies was Sir Gilbert Blane's *Observations on the diseases incident to seamen* (1785). Blane was instrumental in the introduction of lemons into seamen's diets as an anti-scorbutic measure, more than three decades after James Lind had advised such a course of action.⁷¹ Later, in 1801, Robert Robertson published a book on the same subject, having already written his *Physical journal kept ... during three voyages to the coast of Africa and the West Indies* in 1779.

Publications also engaged with botanical debates over the medical properties of certain plants. In December 1777, the Royal Society of London published two communications from Dr William Wright in Jamaica, later president of the Royal College of Physicians of Edinburgh. The first concerned the uses of the Caribbean Jesuit's bark tree (a source of quinine), and compared its properties to those of the Peruvian variety. In the second, he discussed the medical uses of the Jamaican cabbage-bark tree, describing its powerful narcotic effect and its uses as a purgative. This latter piece joined the discussion begun by Peter Duguid, formerly of Jamaica, in a collection of *Edinburgh Essays*. Wright challenged the writers of the *Edinburgh Medical Commentaries*, who had asserted that 'the decoction of cabbage-bark always excited vomiting'. Wright had found 'no such effect from it here', and ascribed the Edinburgh findings to their use of mouldy bark. Clearly, the colonies were not to be regarded simply as repositories of scientific material for study in Europe, but were increasingly at the forefront of providing the analysis too.⁷²

John Williamson's *Medical and miscellaneous observations* excited controversy when it was first published in Edinburgh in 1817. It was reviewed at length in the *Edinburgh Review* in a piece which discussed not only the medical aspects of Williamson's book. The reviewer launched an assault on Williamson for his ambivalent attitude towards slavery, and for his close association with West Indian planters. The *Review*'s rival, *Blackwood's Edinburgh Magazine*, responded with a stinging attack, defending Williamson and lambasting the *Review* for advocating 'whatever appears hostile to the views of those, who from their local knowledge, are most conversant with colonial affairs, and attempts to stigmatize them with every odious epithet that can be conceived.'⁷³

Other Scottish doctors sought simply to advance knowledge of the Caribbean plants themselves. Dr John Lindsay in Jamaica made a considerable contribution to the understanding of the process by which ferns and other cryptogamous plants reproduce. He did this by observing eighteen species of tropical fern in their natural habitat and publishing his findings in the *Transactions of the Linnean Society* in 1794. It was surely this kind of discovery, made in 'foreign climes' as the result of 'indefatigable industry', that Edward Forbes, in his inaugural lecture as professor of botany at King's College, London, in 1843, lauded as having been so important in advancing the study of botany.[74]

One of the more common diseases discussed by doctors in the 1790s was yellow fever. The high incidence of the disease in the West Indies was a function both of an environment that allowed diseases and their vectors to flourish and of demographic movements associated with the plantation system.[75] But opinions were divided in the 1790s over the origin of the disease. James Clark believed that the outbreak which swept through Dominica between 1793 and 1796 arose naturally in the island from marsh effluvia, and was not infectious. On the other hand, Colin Chisholm, writing of his experience in Grenada, argued that a ship introduced the disease from Boullam on the African coast in February 1793.[76]

In some senses, both Chisholm and Clark correctly identified some of the causes of the disease, while in others they were utterly wrong. Chisholm asserted that the Boullam outbreak arose among people 'confined in a sultry, most atmosphere' on board the *Hankey* and was spread to those who visited the ship at St George's and to those ships anchored near it. Clark, on the other hand, was correct in believing that yellow fever was not contagious. In attributing it to 'foul air', he suggested that the lack of storms through the hurricane season had adversely affected the air. The unusually hot conditions in Dominica were replicated in Jamaica and in Philadelphia shortly before the disease struck there. The temperature may have allowed mosquitoes to flourish, and because they bred in clean water collections in man-made containers and niches, like those found around sugar estates and depots, the absence of rain was not a particular disadvantage.[77] But Clark erred in insisting that the 'foul air' was the problem. Equally wrong-headed was his suggestion that purifying the air with fire and smoke would eradicate the problem. This view echoed that of Edward Long, who, like many of his more medically learned contemporaries, noted that the enslaved were less afflicted by the 'malignant effluvia' than Europeans. Their habit of lighting fires to drive away mosquitoes had the happy effect of 'correcting the night air' and so, the argument ran, reducing the likelihood of yellow fever.[78] In short, Clark and Long identified a means to curtail the spread of the disease, but without ever realising that their rationale was wholly wrong.

What is not clear is whether the enslaved knew any better. Their attempts to banish mosquitoes from their sleeping quarters were entirely understandable from the point of view of comfort. But if they knew, from information brought from Africa, that the mosquitoes were also carriers of disease, they kept it to themselves. It was not until the 1890s that European medicine fully understood this question. For Europeans in the tropics in the eighteenth century, the mosquito was little more than an irritant: 'the musquestoe is a most annoying insect, and possesses a watchful, yet enterprising character ... Moisture, and the foul air of marshes, seem to be particularly their element.'[79] This lack of understanding of the disease, its causes and its means of transmission resulted in the deaths of thousands of people from the Caribbean to the cities of Philadelphia and New York in the 1790s. Jonathon Troup was much closer to the truth than he realised when he remarked on mosquitoes, 'You don't feel the insect bite you but the effects come after.'[80]

Many of the medical volumes ran to more than one edition, and there was clearly a demand for them and for their information. Their comments on health and the management of the enslaved became especially important as the price of Africans increased, and as the clamour for the amelioration of their conditions grew ever louder. The books were of interest not only to planters and managers in the Caribbean. In the American South, volumes written by Scots doctors in the islands were used as guides. Indeed, it has been asserted that the only books available in English in Virginia were the compendious work by Dr Collins's *Practical rules* and James Thomson's *Treatise on the diseases of negroes, as they occur in the island of Jamaica, with observations on the country remedies* (1820).[81]

Print was not, of course, the only means of promoting the advancement and exchange of medical and scientific intelligence. Knowledge was produced and exchanged through a variety of media, ranging from private correspondence to plant transfers and the institution of botanical gardens and museum collections.

Many Scottish doctors in the Caribbean believed that they were in a strong position to contribute to the general advance of science. As a result, one of the major forms of this contribution came in the form of correspondence with influential figures in Britain. Walter Tullideph in Antigua sent plants to Sir Hans Sloane in London. Later Jonathon Troup wrote to the then president of the Royal Society in London, Sir Joseph Banks. The principal part of his letter to 'the Protector of

Science' dealt with the case of a slave woman who gave birth to quadruplets. Not content with that, Troup rambled on about a tour through Scotland and a storm in the Bay of Biscay and commented on the 'negligence of Physicians here'.[82] In Jamaica, William Wright and James Thomson were both active in collecting botanical and medical information. Wright's practice, it has been argued, was established with the express intention of advancing medical science. One of the earliest members of the American Philosophical Society in Philadelphia, and proposed for a fellowship of the Royal Society by Joseph Banks, Wright assembled a significant natural history collection, much of which he donated to Kew Gardens.[83]

On a rather less extensive scale, Troup in Dominica sought also to collect the local flora and fauna. A few days after his arrival in the island, he captured a small serpent, which he kept. By the end of September he had added ants, land crabs and the head and jaw of a shark to his collection. These 'curiosities' attracted a number of visitors to what he rather grandiosely described as his 'museum'. Troup's interest in the local environment did not pass uncriticised, however. His employer was noticeably unimpressed by Troup's exploits, charging him with having come to 'make a tool of us to collect curiosity for the Royal Society'.[84] Later, in the 1820s, the newly established Northern Institution for the Promotion of Science and Literature in Inverness received a number of items from the Caribbean for display in its museum, and used Dr John MacIntosh in Berbice as a local agent, to whom Caribbean artefacts were sent for onward shipment to Inverness.[85]

One of the most significant manifestations of the spirit of scientific discovery was the foundation of botanical gardens. The first West Indian garden was established in St Vincent in 1765 by Governor Robert Melville under the guidance of Dr George Young, who was also principal surgeon to the island hospital.[86] Melville's interest in botany and science, which led him to join the Society of Arts in London, was carried over into the management of his Caribbean estates. In 1769, Mount Melvill estate in Grenada experimented with the cultivation of European crops. In particular, vegetables to feed the expanding enslaved population were introduced on the estate. This innovation was not confined to Grenada. In Jamaica, Thomas Thistlewood began a similar process at around the same time and using largely the same kinds of plants, at Breadnut Island Pen in Westmoreland parish.[87] The most notable of the new plants brought to the garden at St Vincent in 1765 was breadfruit imported from Tahiti. This was the first appearance of the breadfruit in the western hemisphere, and it was introduced as a food staple for the enslaved population. A nutritious diet was noted by many doctors as being crucial to the maintenance of a healthy enslaved population. Plant transfers of the kind, carried out institutionally by the botanical gardens and privately by men like Melville, were designed to increase the longevity of the enslaved. On St Vincent, however, widespread use of the breadfruit failed to materialise. By 1801, Alexander Anderson, the curator of the garden, was 'the only person who ... obliges his Negroes to eat it'.[88]

Contemporary observers frequently commented on the value of the St Vincent garden. John Campbell, in his *Political survey of Britain* in 1774, remarked not only on the 'many good Consequences' arising from acquiring a greater knowledge of plants and trees, but also on the 'innumerable good effects' of promoting a spirit of scientific discovery. Sir William Young, MP and son of the former governor, during a tour of his Caribbean estates in 1791 and 1792, said of the garden at St Vincent, 'The variety, beauty, growth and health of the plants, from all parts of the globe, is most striking.'[89]

The gardens, furthermore, were repositories of plants which could be used in medicine. In particular, they were the breeding grounds for plants which, like the breadfruit, were not native to the West Indies. In 1774, in advocating the establishment of a botanical garden in Jamaica, Edward Long catalogued a list of 'foreign plants, as might properly be introduced, and cultivated, in Jamaica, with great propriety'. Notable on the list were medical and nutritional plants like Turkish opium seed, camphor trees from Sumatra, Jesuit's bark from Peru, 'true' jalap from Mexico, East Indian cardamoms, turmeric and breadfruit, and gum ammoniac from Africa. Many of these plants were already growing in St Vincent, a point not lost on Long: 'I cannot but consider it a reproach to the gentlemen of Jamaica, that they should have suffered the little colony of St Vincent to get a start of them, in the execution of so truly laudable and useful a plan.'[90] Long also proposed establishing a separate garden near the school he wanted to be built. The garden, he hoped, would be stocked with local plants and those from the 'southern continent' most noted for their medicinal and commercial uses.[91]

Edward Long was not the only Jamaican proponent of botanical gardens, and at least two had been opened in the island by 1774. Hinton East had built a private garden near Kingston, while another citizen, Matthew Wallen, began his garden in the early 1770s. In 1775, the assembly acquired land to establish a public botanical garden situated near the mineral waters at the Bath, in St Thomas in the EaSt Dr Thomas Clarke was appointed botanist to the island in 1777, and by the 1780s his compatriot Thomas Dancer was physician to the Bath. The Scottish influence ran deeper still. The island's then governor,

Sir Basil Keith, had been encouraged to promote the establishment of the garden by John Hope, professor of botany and *materia medica* at Edinburgh University. And it was on Hope's recommendation that his former student Thomas Clarke was appointed.[92]

The inauguration of these gardens represented, too, the regard for aesthetics and a desire to beautify the islands as significant offshoots of medicine in the eighteenth-century British Caribbean. Indeed, in many ways, this urge to create gardens also reflected an important aspect of the culture of improvement so prevalent in Scottish society. Thomas Dancer, in cataloguing the plants for the garden at the Bath, listed only those that he considered 'the most remarkable for use of beauty'.[93] Senior policy makers had been concerned about the dangers of excessive deforestation at least since the 1760s. As William Young wrote, 'certain portions of land in wood, will be preserved on the tops of hills on other convenient places, for the publick benefit, and to prevent that drought, which, in these climates, is usual consequence of a total removal of the woods'. By the late 1790s, Alexander Anderson, curator of the St Vincent garden, went further than highlighting the environmental and medical ramifications of the process. He was also at pains to point out the aesthetic implications. He was astonished that 'the idea of ornament alone' did not lead to the preservation of natural flora.[94]

Indeed the attractiveness of aspect played a role in the designs that doctors proposed for the construction of hospitals and sick-houses. James Grainger, writing in the 1760s, described his ideal self-contained plantation hospital, complete with herb garden and lemon bushes. As well as providing a source of medical supplies, it was to provide a pleasing scene for the convalescents enjoying a 'walk round the square'. Another Scottish doctor, John Williamson, echoed such sentiments half a century later. He desired that the hospital be separated from other buildings by fruit and other trees. These, he argued, would provide fruit beneficial to recovering patients, as well as looking attractive.[95]

The scale of, and attention given to, this upsurge in the dissemination of scientific discovery also represented the emergence of a new dynamic in the relationship between colony and metropole. Until the later part of the century, responsibility for medical advances lay in the compass of European theory. The work of these doctors and botanists undertaken in the practices and gardens of the West Indies challenged the dominance of Eurocentric approaches. Empirical experience gleaned in the colonies came not only to affect imperial decision making regarding the environment, but to acquire influence in the metropolitan academy.[96] Over the final third of the century, an increasing number of doctors with Caribbean connections were elected fellows of the Royal College of Physicians of Edinburgh. As late as 1773 there were no West Indians in the college, but in 1786 two of the fifty-four fellows (James Walker and William Wright) were based in Jamaica. In 1790, five of the sixty-six fellows practised in the Caribbean, and by 1795, there were seven Caribbean residents and one returnee among the sixty-nine fellows.[97]

British academics, moreover, wanted to import as many plants as possible. John Hope at Edinburgh University was instrumental in founding the Society for the Importation of Foreign Seeds and Plants, which existed between 1763 and 1773. After its demise, he continued to trade plants and correspondence. His network included Linnaeus and Joseph Banks; Benjamin Franklin, Benjamin Rush and John Bartram in Philadelphia; Alexander Garden in Charleston; and Gavin Hamilton in India. As well as these luminaries, he communicated with acquaintances in the Caribbean, including William Wright in Jamaica, George Young in St Vincent and Dr Munro in Grenada.[98] Robert Hamilton and William Cullen, respectively professors of botany and anatomy and of medicine at the University of Glasgow, wrote in a memorial of 1754 that 'it would be highly ornamental to the Garden & very usefull towards promoting botanical knowledge in this University to plant the quarters of the Garden with such curious exotic Trees and Shrubs as our soil and climate will bear.'[99] As the botanical gardens at Glasgow and Edinburgh were employed as teaching tools in medicine, and lectures in botany discussed the use of non-British plants, it is likely that West Indian knowledge filtered into the teaching of scientific subjects in Scotland by the latter part of the century.[100] At the University of Glasgow, the medical department in particular was considered to be less bound to 'old institutions and prejudices' than others in the university. As a result, the department was

> enabled to accommodate their lectures to the progress of knowledge and discovery, and to those improvements which have, of late years, been introduced into all the sciences connected with the art of medicine. The progress of botany and natural history, and the wonderful discoveries in chemistry, have now extended the sphere of these useful branches beyond the mere purpose of the physician, and have rendered a competent knowledge of them highly interesting to every man of liberal education.[101]

Conclusion

It is clear that the recruitment of doctors for the Caribbean plantations relied on Scottish networks. The webs of connections emanating from family or local units that drew Scottish managers and overseers to the islands were also able to meet some of the demand for physicians. In this professional field, however, the bonds were complemented by links forged in the medical institutions in Britain, and in Scotland particularly. The great expansion of medical learning in the Scottish universities in the eighteenth century, especially in Edinburgh, was allied to an increase in the influence of associated institutions like the royal colleges and medical societies. The identification of Scotland with medical learning was a function of this expansion, and one that allowed many Scots to meet the Caribbean demand for trained doctors.

Once in the islands, the doctors found themselves dealing with challenges very different from those at home, and challenges for which their European education may have ill prepared them. For many, a sojourn in the islands represented an opportunity not only to make money, but also to make a significant contribution to the understanding of tropical medicine. The exchange of information flowing through these Scottish conduits facilitated a transatlantic dialogue, and had the profound effect of challenging the metropolitan state's prerogative as the source of knowledge about colonies. This new dynamic in metropolitan–colonial relations, as the next chapter will discuss, was replicated in the realm of island politics.

Notes

1 Alexander von Humboldt, *Personal narrative of travels to the equinoctial regions of America, during the years 1799–1804*, trans. T. Ross (London: Henry G. Bohn, 1852), vol. 1, pp. 141–42.
2 UASCA, MS1160/5/1, Gordon of Cairness papers, James Barclay to Charles Gordon, 5 December 1727; MS3575/15, papers of Murray families, James Murray to John Murray, 16 May 1787.
3 R. S. Dunn, *Sugar and slaves: The rise of the planter class in the English West Indies, 1624–1713* (Chapel Hill: University of North Carolina Press, 1972), p. 301.
4 G. Turnbull, *Letters to a young planter, or observations on the management of a sugar plantation* (London: J. Strachan, 1785), p. 36.
5 R. B. Sheridan, 'Mortality and the medical treatment of slaves in the British West Indies', in H. Beckles and V. Shepherd (eds), *Caribbean slave society and economy* (New York: The New Press, 1991), pp. 205–6; R. B. Sheridan, 'The rise of a colonial gentry: A case study of Antigua, 1730–1775', Economic History Review, 13, 3 (1961), 350.
6 Walter Tullideph to Thomas Tullideph, 28 April 1736, quoted in Sheridan, 'Mortality and the medical treatment of slaves', p. 206.
7 *Ibid.* p. 204–6.
8 D. Hancock, *Citizens of the world: London merchants and the integration of the British Atlantic community, 1735–1785* (Cambridge: Cambridge University Press, 1995), pp. 50–1.
9 P. J. Anderson (ed.), *Fasti Academiae Marischallanae Aberdonensis: Selections from the records of the Marischal College and University, 1593–1860* (Aberdeen: New Spalding Club, 1898), vol. 2: *Officers, graduates and alumni*, p. 117.
10 NAS, GD345/1180, bundle 1761(110), Grant of Monymusk muniments, Dr Walter Grant to Capt. Archibald Grant, 14 April 1761. See also bundles 1762 and 1763.

11 Aspects of Johnston's career have been reviewed in A. L. Karras, 'The world of Alexander Johnston: The creolization of ambition, 1762–1787', *Historical Journal*, 30, 1 (1987), 53–76.
12 HSP, 1582/29B, box 2 folder 1, Powell collection, papers of Alexander Johnston, memorandum, September 1766. The partnership was based on an oral understanding: no articles of co-partnery were written.
13 HSP, 1582/29B, box 2 folder 3, James Johnston to Alexander Johnston, 23 December 1782; Alexander Johnston to James Johnston, 24 June 1783.
14 *Ibid.*, Alexander Johnston to James Johnston, 21 August 1784.
15 J. Williamson, *Medical and miscellaneous observations, relative to the West India islands* (Edinburgh: Alexander Smellie, 1817), vol. 1, pp. 40, 47, 49.
16 NAS, GD267/5/12/1, Home of Wedderburn manuscripts, Thomas Duncan to George Home, 13 December 1804.
17 J. Jenkinson, *Scottish medical societies, 1731–1939: Their history and records* (Edinburgh: Edinburgh University Press, 1993), pp. 10–11; J. D. Comrie, *History of Scottish medicine* (London: Baillière, Tindall and Cox, 1927), p. 158. Both give 1789 as the date for the first Aberdeen group, but see HSP, 1582/29B, box 1, book of discourses read to the Medical Society at Aberdeen, 1761.
18 W. Munck (ed.), *The roll of the Royal College of Physicians of London* (London: Royal College of Physicians, 1878). The figures for Aberdeen are an aggregate of those for King's College and Marischal College.
19 Anderson (ed.), *Fasti Academiae Marischallanae*, vol. 2, pp. 325, 329. Two Alexander Johnstons from the north-east graduated AM in this period, one in 1758, the other in 1762. The latter became a minister. Johnston's papers contain lecture notes on Mathematics from John Stuart's lectures in 1756. From 1753, the Marischal curriculum stipulated the study of mathematics in the second year. For a graduate in 1758, second year would have been 1756. His papers also contain notes of William Cullen's chemistry lectures, suggesting that he spent some time at Edinburgh, where Cullen was Professor of Chemistry and Medicine from 1755 to 1766.
20 HSP, 1582/29B, box 2 folder 3, Alexander Johnston to James Johnston, 20 January 1784; Z. Cope, 'The private medical schools of London, 1746–1914', in F. N. L. Poynter (ed.), *The evolution of medical education in Britain* (Baltimore: Williams and Wilkins, 1966), p. 94.
21 UASCA, MS2070, Journal of Jonathon Troup, fol. 11, 11 May 1789. Troup graduated AM from Marischal College, Aberdeen, in 1786: Anderson (ed.), *Fasti Academiae Marischallanae*, vol. 2, p. 359.
22 *Ibid.*, vol. 2, p. 134.
23 UASCA, MS2070, Journal of Jonathon Troup, fol. 20, 19 June 1789; D. F. Clyde, *Two centuries of health care in Dominica* (New Dehli: Gopal, 1980), pp. 2, 5–6; P. J. Anderson (ed.), *Officers and graduates of University and King's College, Aberdeen, 1495–1860* (Aberdeen: New Spalding Club, 1893), p. 134. Clark was the author of an account of the yellow fever epidemic in Dominica: J. Clark, *A treatise on the yellow fever, as it appeared in the island of Dominica in the years 1793–96* (London: Murray and Highly, 1797).
24 UASCA, MS2070, Journal of Jonathon Troup, fols 67, 71v, 130v, 30 August, 4 September, 21 November 1789.
25 J. Grainger, *An essay on the more common West-India diseases; and remedies which that country itself produces* (London: Becket and de Hondt, 1764). James Grainger (1721–1766) graduated in medicine from the University of Edinburgh in 1753. Best known for his poem *The sugar cane* (1759), he lived in St Kitts from 1759 until his death.
26 E. Long, *The history of Jamaica, or general survey of the ancient and modern state of that island* (1774; London: Frank Cass, 1970), vol. 2, pp. 584, 587.
27 UASCA, MS2070, journal of Jonathon Troup, fol. 59v, 25 August 1789.
28 *Ibid.*, fol. 29v, 19 July 1789.

29 Dr Collins, *Practical rules for the management and treatment of negro slaves in the sugar colonies* (1803; Freeport: Books for Libraries Press, 1971), p. 207.
30 UASCA, MS1160/5/7, Gordon of Cairness papers, James Barclay to John Gordon, 3 August 1755.
31 J. Quier et al., *Letters and essays on the smallpox and inoculation* (London and Edinburgh: J. Murray and C. Elliot, 1778), pp. 22–3; T. Dancer, *A short dissertation on the Jamaica Bath waters* (Kingston: D. Douglas and Alex. Aikman, 1784), p. 80; Williamson, *Medical and miscellaneous observations*, vol. 2, p. 152.
32 C. Chisholm, *An essay on the malignant pestilential fever introduced into the West Indian islands from Boullam* (London: J. Mawlam, 1801), vol. 1, pp. 419–20.
33 Long, *History of Jamaica*, vol. 2, p. 591.
34 Sheridan, *Doctors and slaves: A medical and demographic history of slavery in the British West Indies, 1680–1834* (Cambridge: Cambridge University Press, 1985), pp. 36, 49–51.
35 J. Stewart, *A view of the past and present state of the island of Jamaica* (1823; New York: Negro Universities Press, 1969); Long, *History of Jamaica*, vol. 2, p. 583.
36 UASCA, MS2070, Journal of Jonathon Troup, fol. 79, 12 September 1789 (My italics).
37 Ibid., fol. 75v, 8 September 1789.
38 HSP, 1582/29B, box 1, ledger book, 1760–72.
39 Ibid., journal, 1773.
40 Grainger, *essay on the more common West-India diseases*, p. 74; Williamson, *Medical and miscellaneous observations*, vol. 2, p. 181.
41 UASCA, MS2070, Journal of Jonathon Troup, fols 13v–14, 17v, 22v, 77v.
42 Ibid., fols 67, 68, 71, 77v.
43 Ibid., fols 12v, 14, 81v.
44 BUL, DM41/21/2, West Indies MSS, Westerhall papers, Westerhall estate accounts, 1 January 1796.
45 Collins, *Practical rules*, pp. 205–06; Stewart, *A view of Jamaica*, p. 195.
46 NAS, GD267/5/11/1, Home of Wedderburn manuscripts, William Stephenson to George Home, 26 March 1803.
47 Sheridan, *Doctors and slaves*, p. 252.
48 'An account of Inoculation for the small-pox in the island of Antigua, in the years 1755 and 1756, by the late Sr. Thomas Fraser, physician in that island', in Quier et al., *Letters and essays*, pp. 105–7.
49 Ibid., pp. 4–29; M. Craton and J. Walvin, *A Jamaican plantation: The history of Worthy Park, 1670–1970* (London: W. H. Allen, 1970), pp. 132–3.
50 NAS, GD267/5/11/2, Home of Wedderburn manuscripts, Stephenson to Home, 20 July 1803.
51 NAS, GD267/5/11/3(1–2), Home of Wedderburn manuscripts, Stephenson to Home, 2 February 1804.
52 NAS, GD267/5/11/4, Home of Wedderburn manuscripts, Stephenson to Home, 6 June 1804; GD267/5/11/5(1), Stephenson to Home, 2 October 1804.
53 Ibid.
54 HSP, 1582/29B, box 1, journal, 1773, account with Dr George Gallimore.
55 Ibid., account with Charles Arbuthnot Jun., 1773.
56 Ibid., and account with James and Henry Tucker, 1773.
57 HSP, 1582/29B, box 2 folder 3, Alexander Johnston to James Johnston, 20 January 1784; Karras, 'The world of Alexander Johnston', 62. Karras noticed a 46 per cent decline in visits in January and a reduction of 33 per cent in July.
58 HSP, 1582/29B, box 1, ledger, 1782–86, fol. 253.
59 Sheridan, *Doctors and slaves*, pp. 300–1, 306.
60 HSP, 1582/29B, box 1, journal, 1773.
61 Williamson, *Medical and miscellaneous observations*, vol. 2, pp. 178, 180.
62 Anderson (ed.), *Officers and graduates of University and King's College*, p. 139.

63　HSP, 1582/29B, box 2 folder 1, An estimated value of... all the property of Dr Alexander Johnston, 7 July 1784; box 2 folder 3, Alexander Johnston to James Johnston, 21 August 1784; Karras, 'The world of Alexander Johnston', 66–7.
64　JMA, IB/11/3/7/1(170), Jamaica inventories, inventory and appraisement of the goods and chattels of Dr Alexander Johnston, 11 June 1787.
65　HSP, 1582/29B, box 2 folder 1, account of the profits and proceeds of Murphy's Penn.
66　UASCA, MS2769/I/72/1, Davidson & Garden Archive, papers of Dr Charles Irvine, account book, abstract of the valuation of Friendship estate, Jamaica, 7 July 1806.
67　Long, *History of Jamaica*, vol. 2, p. 582.
68　Dancer, *Short dissertation*, p. 19.
69　J. Rollo, *Observations on the means of preserving and restoring health in the West-Indies* (London: C. Dilly, 1783); D. Geggus, 'Yellow fever in the 1790s: The British army in occupied St Domingue', *Medical History*, 23, 1 (1979), 38–58.
70　Sheridan, *Doctors and slaves*, p. 23.
71　D. A. Baugh, *British naval administration in the age of Walpole* (Princeton: Princeton University Press, 1965), pp. 379, 384.
72　W. Wright, 'Description of the Jesuits bark tree' and 'Description and use of the cabbage-bark tree of Jamaica', *Philosophical Transactions of the Royal Society*, 67 (December 1777), 504–6, 507–11.
73　'Present state of West India affairs', *Edinburgh Review*, 28 (1817), 340–71; 'Strictures on an article in no. LVI of the Edinburgh Review, entitled "Present State of West India affairs"', *Blackwood's Edinburgh Magazine*, 7, 2 (1817), 41–6, quotation from p. 41.
74　A. G. Morton, *History of botanical science* (London: Academic Press, 1981), pp. 324, 357n.; E. Forbes, *An inaugural lecture on botany, considered as a science and as a branch of medical education* (London: Jan van Voorst, 1843), pp. 16–17, 19.
75　S. Watts, *Epidemics and history: Disease, power and imperialism* (New Haven: Yale University Press, 1997), pp. 88–92; Sheridan, *Doctors and slaves*, p. 4.
76　Clark, *Treatise on the yellow fever*, pp. 23, 78; Chisholm, *Essay on the malignant pestilential fever*, vol. 1, pp. 107–11; J. D. Goodyear, 'The sugar connection: A new perspective on the history of yellow fever', *Bulletin of the History of Medicine*, 52, 1 (1978), 5, 10–11; Geggus, 'yellow fever in the 1790s', 38.
77　Chisholm, *Essay on the malignant pestilential fever*, vol. 1, pp. 107, 121–3; Goodyear, 'The sugar connection', 12, 18–19; Geggus, 'Yellow fever in the 1790s', 44.
78　Clark, *Treatise on the yellow fever*, pp. 49, 67–8; Long, *History of Jamaica*, vol. 2, p. 510.
79　Williamson, *Medical and miscellaneous observations*, vol. 1, p. 43.
80　UASCA, MS2070, Journal of Jonathon Troup, fol. 16, 31 May 1789.
81　Sheridan, *Doctors and slaves*, p. 69.
82　Sheridan, 'Mortality and the medical treatment of slaves', p. 205; UASCA, MS2070, Journal of Jonathon Troup, fols 34v–35, 1 August 1789.
83　Sheridan, 'Mortality and the medical treatment of slaves', pp. 201–2; R. P. Stearns, 'Colonial fellows of the Royal Society of London, 1661–1778', *William and Mary Quarterly*, 3, 1 (1946), 261–3.
84　UASCA, MS2070, Journal of Jonathon Troup, fols 14v, 91, 94v–95, 99v, 130v.
85　J. Anderson, *Prize essay on the state of society and knowledge in the Highlands of Scotland* (Edinburgh: William Tait, 1827), appendices 1–5. In 1836 Anderson went to St Vincent as a special magistrate: R. A. McDonald (ed.), *Between slavery and freedom: Special Magistrate John Anderson's journal of St Vincent during the apprenticeship* (Kingston: University of the West Indies Press; Philadelphia: University of Pennsylvania Press, 2001).
86　Long, *History of Jamaica*, vol. 2, pp. 912–13; R. H. Grove, *Green imperialism: Colonial expansion, tropical island edens and the origins of environmentalism, 1600–1800* (Cambridge: Cambridge University Press, 1995), pp. 267–8.

87 NAS, GD126/3, bundle 1, Balfour–Melville papers, account of Robert Melville Esq. for his estate Mount Melvill with John Knight; D. Hall, 'Botanical and horticultural enterprise in eighteenth-century Jamaica', in R. A. McDonald (ed.), *West Indies accounts: Essays on the history of the British Caribbean and Atlantic economy in honour of Richard B. Sheridan* (Barbados, University of the West Indies Press, 1996), pp. 101–25.
88 IHR, 'Lady Liston's journal, December 1800 to April 1801', in C. Taylor (ed.), 'Journeys through the Caribbean' (unpublished transcript, IHR), p. 36.
89 J. Campbell, *A political survey of Britain, being a series of reflections on the situation, lands, inhabitants, revenues, colonies, and commerce of this island* (London: no imprint, 1774), vol. 2, p. 263; 'A tour through the several islands of Barbados, St Vincent, Antigua, Tobago and Grenada in the years 1791 and 1792: by Sir William Young Bart.', in B. Edwards, *The history, civil and commercial, of the British colonies in the West Indies* (London: John Stockdale, 1801, 3rd edition), vol. 3, p. 262.
90 Long, *History of Jamaica*, vol. 3, pp. 903, 913.
91 *Ibid.*, vol. 2, p. 259.
92 Dancer, *Short dissertation*, p. 95 and list of subscribers; Hall, 'Botanical and horticultural enterprise', p. 101; 'Letter from John Hope to Linnaeus, 18 April 1776', in A. G. Morton, *John Hope, 1725–1786: Scottish sotanist* (Edinburgh: Scottish botanical Garden Trust, 1986), pp. 34–5.
93 Dancer, *Short dissertation*, p. 95.
94 W. Young, *Considerations which may tend to promote the settlement of our new West-India Colonies, by encouraging individuals to embark on the undertaking* (London: James Robson, 1764); A. Anderson, 'The history and geography of St Vincent', quoted in Grove, *Green imperialism*, pp. 302, 306.
95 Grainger, *Essay on the more common West-India diseases*, p. 72; Williamson, *Medical and miscellaneous observations*, vol. 2, p. 148.
96 Grove, *Green imperialism*, pp. 292–7.
97 *Edinburgh Almanack and Scots Register* (1773), p. 152; (1786), p. 70; (1790), p. 110; (1795), p. 58.
98 Morton, *John Hope*, pp. 13–15.
99 'To the Honourable the Rector & other members of the University of Glasgow', in A. D. Boney, *The lost gardens of Glasgow University* (London: Christopher Helm, 1988), p. 88.
100 *Ibid.*, pp. 193–6; J. Geyer-Kordesch, 'Comparative difficulties: Scottish medical education in the European context, c. 1690–1830', in V. Nutton and R. Porter (eds), *The history of medical education in Britain* (Amsterdam: Rodopi, 1995), pp. 94–115.
101 'The statistical account of the University of Glasgow', *OSA*, vol. 1, p. 237.

CHAPTER SIX

Scots in West Indian politics

As Chapters Three, Four and Five demonstrated, the operation of networks provided a general underpinning for Scottish activity in the West Indian empire in the later eighteenth century. The next two chapters consider more closely the functioning of this process in the political sphere. The island legislatures were responsible for introducing and discussing innovations designed to order society better in each of the colonies. In passing legislation governing the islands, these institutions concentrated on matters of local but often contentious concern. The demands of the white islanders, as expressed through their elite, could bring the elected assemblies into conflict with the requirements of the government in London, as represented by the governor. Conflict was very evident in the island legislatures, and it took two main forms. The first consisted of internal conflicts between branches of the government. These disputes often took place between the elected and the appointed politicians in the islands, and could, on occasion, be complicated by antagonism between English and Scottish settlers. The second set of conflicts saw British settlers pulling together in the face of external foes. From time to time, the enemy could be the government in London seeking to extend rights to Catholics, or rebellious colonies, or a foreign power. As in some of the mainland colonies, differing perceptions of the rights of the imperial government and the colonial legislatures led to disagreements between them. These disagreements, though occasionally heated, never deteriorated into the level of confrontation witnessed on the American mainland.

West Indians consistently displayed a desire to uphold what they saw as British ideals informed by the revolutionary rhetoric of 1688 rather than of 1776. Their conflicts with London, with the governors or among themselves revolved around the extension of arbitrary government and its limitations on liberty, or what they saw as the seeping of Catholicism into the British colonies. The strategies employed during these crises and those surrounding assembly privileges, revenues and the American and French revolutions all summoned the language of 1688. In doing so, they employed tropes prevalent in Britain among staunch supporters of both the government and its radical opposition.[1]

The extent of the Caribbean colonists' attachment to Britain, despite the periodic disputes, remained consistently strong throughout the final third of the century. Although the colonies in the West Indies were vulnerable to attack, from both within and without, and were reliant on British trade and defence to a greater extent than the mainland colonies, their fidelity was not motivated by security considerations alone. Three major crises (over the easing of restrictions on Catholics in Grenada, the American Revolution and the insurrections of the 1790s) prompted reactions which demonstrated their very 'Britishness'. These sections argue that the transient nature of the white population in the islands ensured that the 'home' country remained central to their consciousness. Moreover, the influence of substantial numbers of Scots in the islands' polities had profound implications for the legislatures' responses, and for fostering both integration and continuity in the Atlantic empire throughout an exceptionally turbulent period.

The role of the legislatures

The constitutional structure of the islands comprised a governor appointed in London, a council nominated by the governor and an assembly elected by the white propertied inhabitants. This attempt to translate the roles of the king and Houses of Parliament to the colonies was not untroubled or uncriticised. The planter-historians Edward Long and Bryan Edwards both believed that neither the governor nor the council could emulate the king or the House of Lords. Long was a particular critic of the holders of gubernatorial office. His attitude was shared by many members of assemblies throughout the British Caribbean, who found themselves at loggerheads with a governor and, by implication, with the imperial government in London. On the other hand, they both believed the that assembly (of which they had both been members) closely resembled the House of Commons, with Edwards even asserting that the members of the assemblies were 'more fairly and equally chosen by their constituents, than those of the British House of Commons'.[2]

The sizes of the governments varied across the islands. In Jamaica, the legislature comprised forty-two representatives in the assembly and twelve council members appointed by the governor. In the Windwards, the assemblies were smaller: Grenada's had twenty-four members, Dominica's nineteen and St Vincent's thirteen.[3]

The colonial governors, appointed in London, held extremely powerful positions. Indeed, their powers over the colony exceeded those 'which the laws of England allow to the sovereign himself', and on occasion this great influence proved too tempting for some governors, who blurred the line between public service and private ambition.[4] The duties of the governor included command of the land forces in the island. He also appointed the judges, justices of the peace and councillors. He had the power to call and dissolve the assembly, and could veto any legislation passed by the assembly or council. He presided over the Court of Chancery and Court of Error, as well as having the disposal of civil posts not controlled by London. The monetary rewards came from a variety of sources, including court fees, a share of customs house seizures and the sale of commissions, in addition to a salary voted on by the assembly. At £10,000 per annum (of which only £3,000 was salary) the Jamaican post was the third most lucrative in the British Empire, behind the lord-lieutenancy of Ireland and the governor-generalship of India.[5]

The council formed the upper house of the legislature, and had responsibility for considering legislation sent up from the assembly. Without the council's consent, no legislation could be passed on to the governor for his assent. Its members had a number of other responsibilities. As a group they advised the governor, in a manner analogous to the Privy Council in Britain, and formed a court of appeal. Individually, the councillors were also justices of the peace. The assembly, elected by freeholders in parochial constituencies, framed and voted on laws for the colony, and, apart from introducing trade laws contrary to those of Britain, 'there [were] no concerns of a local and provincial nature, to which the authority of colonial laws [did] not extend.' Although the assembly was subordinate to the council, and could be dissolved by the governor at his pleasure, it had one power that was hugely significant. It had the right to control and examine the island treasury, and voted on the levying of taxes and supply.[6] Any attempts by the council or governor to interfere with these rights were swiftly and vigorously resisted.

For the most part, the legislature dealt with practical matters of local concern, upon which decisions were made without regard to a particularly national perspective. Legislation discussed in either of the chambers typically included measures to raise public funds to pay salaries or finance the construction of defences, harbours or roads; to ensure proper weights and measures; to prevent excessive drinking by visiting sailors; and to suppress any internal dangers, particularly from runaway slaves.[7]

The legislation introduced to Grenada in 1767 to ease these problems was insufficient for many in the island's elite. In 1769, the Grand Jury petitioned the assembly for further action to secure boats on which the enslaved could escape. Moreover, it sought reassurances that ships' captains would be prevented from landing 'sick & Disabled Seamen' on the island to put a stop to their 'daily dying in the Streets in the Town of St. George'. This, the memorialists argued, was 'a great Grievance & Nuisance'. They also demanded further controls on the sale of bread, the price of meat and the vending of 'diseased unwholesome Cattle'.[8]

Measures to restrict and, if necessary, to recover runaway slaves were high on the list of priorities for the Grenada legislature. In April 1767 a bill requiring that masters of ships do their utmost to prevent stowaways was passed in the island. A joint committee of the council and the assembly was formed to prepare a bill to allow the captain-general of the island (i.e., the governor) to send a detachment of the enslaved and free people of colour and, if necessary, white inhabitants, in pursuit of runaways. The composition of the joint committee gives a clear indication of the level of involvement by Scots in the island's political process. On the five-man committee, one of the two councillors was Scottish, as were all three of the assembly's representatives.[9]

Scots in the island legislatures

In Jamaica, members of the Campbell family became increasingly important political actors as the century progressed. James Campbell was the first of the family to serve in the island assembly, and did so for Westmoreland parish between 1706 and 1708. Yet despite his and John Campbell's efforts, the family did not become a real force in the area until the second half of the century. In 1755, another John Campbell was elected for the Hanover parish, which had been formed following a parochial restructuring in 1723. Between 1755 and 1781, there were only eight years in which neither of the parish's representatives was a Campbell, and in three of those years another Argyll man, Dugald Malcolm, was returned. This political constituency was at the centre of the Argyll community. The picture of the Campbells emerging as a political force in Jamaica from mid-century mirrors the experiences of other Scots in the island. The vast majority of Scots who sat in the assembly did so in the period after 1750. Indeed, there were twice as many Scottish representatives in the assembly in the half-century after 1763 as in the fifty years before. In the parish of St George, there were only nine years between 1758 and 1820 when none of the representatives was a Scot. Similarly, in Portland, there was a Scottish member of the assembly in all but four of the fifty-four years between 1772 and 1826. In the last quarter of the century, Scots served consecutively for Vere and Port Royal for thirty and thirty-eight years respectively.[10] It is clear that Scots made great strides in entering the island's political elite. What is particularly significant, and is suggested by the case of the Campbells, is that Scottish involvement in Caribbean politics was driven by the need to represent their networks as much as their constituencies. In Jamaica the networks were sufficiently well grounded in the constituencies to be able to dominate them.

Other Scottish groups in the island were similarly represented. Two key associations, the 'realms' of Alexander Johnston and Francis Grant, both featured in the assembly.[11] In the case of Johnston's network, Dr Alexander Fullerton may be singled out as the group's most influential politician. As well as being Johnston's partner, he was a member of the assembly for St Ann's parish from 1768 to 1770, and then again from 1774 to 1801. He was also a member of the council between 1790 and 1796.[12] Francis Grant enjoyed an even closer tie to the island's political elite. His brother John was chief justice of the island, and represented the parish of St Dorothy between 1777 and 1790. The Dundee grouping in St Elizabeth was also represented. Its contacts included Dr William Elphinstone (1775–87) and James Wedderburn (1795–97).[13] Also in this group was Dr Duncan McGlashan, who was Elphinstone's partner in a Kingston medical practice.[14]

By the early nineteenth century Scots had entrenched their position in Jamaica. Around 1806, their representation mirrored Edward Long's oft-quoted observation that a third of whites in Jamaica were Scots. The then governor of Jamaica, George Nugent, included at least fourteen Scots in his list of the forty-three 'principal people' in the island.[15] This kind of Scottish political involvement was not unique to Jamaica. The remarkable Caledonian influx to the Windward Islands after 1763 was matched, and occasionally surpassed, by the elevation of Scots into the political elites these islands. As the statistics in Table 6.1 suggest, Scots were an extremely significant minority in three of the island legislatures, and an overwhelming majority in the fourth. Such representation not only points to their political significance, but implies the size and status of the Scottish populations in the islands.

Table 6.1 Scots in the Windward Island legislatures, c. 1766–96

Island	Council (%)	Assembly (%)
Dominica	40.3	26.9
Grenada	38.9	44.7
St Vincent	23.3	31.6
Tobago	61.9	75 (to 1780 only)

Sources: PRO, CO71/1, 71/26, CO74/1, 74/3, 74/6A, 74/6B; CO101/7, 101/25, 101/30, 101/32–4; CO102/15; CO104/1–3; CO260/13; CO263/1–2, 263/21; CO285/3; CO288/1–3.

Some trends emerge from these figures. In the years of British rule, Scots dominated the political structures of the islands. Grenada, the most important island in the archipelago, saw its assembly headed by Scots as the largest single national group. In 1770, of the twenty-four assemblymen, nine were Scots and five were Irish, and there were four Frenchmen, three Englishmen, two 'creoles' and an American.[16] The extent of Scottish participation in elective politics came to have a significant effect on the island. St Vincent had the smallest number of Scots, while Dominica was the only island where the appointed council was more densely packed with Scots than the elected assembly. This tended to exacerbate tensions between the legislative branches during the 1760s. Perhaps the most startling figures are those indicating the sheer scale of Scottish representation in Tobago until the period of French occupation. The statistics suggest that Scots dominated Tobago more than any other island, and perhaps more than any other colony. These are, nevertheless, fairly general statistics which, while useful for suggesting important trends, disguise considerable fluctuations in representation.

It is important to be clear that these were not stable electoral blocs. Disputes could often arise in the legislatures between Scots. Votes in the councils and assemblies usually saw divisions among Scots. As in Jamaica, members of the assemblies were often as attached to their networks as to their constituencies more broadly, although it was frequently the case that a network was based in a particular parish. In Tobago, for example, the Moray network was represented on the council in 1794 by two members, Alexander Gordon and John Robertson.[17] Two decades earlier, both men had sat in the assembly, where two others, James Elder and Walter Robertson, both held seats.[18] This profusion of Scots in island politics was not entirely unproblematic, however.

Internal conflicts

Both branches of the legislature were resolute in defence of their privileges. This led, on occasion, to conflict between them. The Dominica assembly, like those elsewhere, was intent on pushing its position in the legislature as far as it could. An early dispute between the council and the assembly arose when the assembly demanded the attendance of two councillors, John Weir and Robert Seaman, to answer accusations of partiality in their roles as returning officers. The council responded that to summon councillors in this way breached the privileges of their offices. The assembly argued that because the two men were called in their capacity as returning officers, not as councillors, it was within its rights. To push its point the assembly declared the disputed election void, and replaced Thomas Clarkson and Duncan McIntosh with two new members, Edward Bryce Smith and John Boone.[19] The council refused to swear in the new members, the assembly refused to admit the old ones, and the whole legislative process ground to a halt. Both sides of the dispute became increasingly entrenched. The assembly began to cite legal precedents for its actions that quickly elicited alternative precedents from the council, which also tried to seize the moral high ground. The council asked that although it was in the right, and could prove it, 'Will Quotations from Tedious Law Books; Will Message upon Message upon trivial points, pass laws to save a sinking Country?'[20] This had absolutely no effect on the assembly. The president of the council, Walter Pringle, a confidant of Governor Melville, acquired from his friend the power to prorogue the assembly on 19 February 1768. The assembly eventually acquiesced, but remained determined nonetheless to retain, and obtain, as much power for itself as possible.

The antagonism between the council and assembly had a particular piquancy in Dominica. As Table 6.1 shows, of the Windward Islands only Dominica had proportionately more Scots in the council than in the assembly. The role of the governor in appointing the council had led to the appointment of a disproportionately high number of Scots, and friends of Melville, in the council. There was English resentment at the prevalence of Scots in the senior chamber, a factor which appears to have been unique in the Windwards: nowhere else was there a conflict between an elected, predominantly English, assembly and an appointed, largely Scottish, council.

This animosity was not confined to the legislature. The works of the satirist Charles Churchill, a noted supporter of John Wilkes, were the subject of a subscription in Dominica in 1767. Among the varied topics available was *A prophecy of famine: A Scots pastoral*, which was described as

> A most acrimonious Satire on the Kingdom of Scotland, widening national Breaches, and fermenting divisions; (which it is every one's Duty to stifle and compose) and yet the Author discovers in this Performance, such Strength of Sentiment, nervous Expression, and elegant Numbers, & there is so much Humour throughout the Whole, that even a NORTH-BRITON might forgive all he meets within reading it.[21]

The final point is probably debatable, but the presence of this kind of satire is indicative of the success that Scots were having in seizing the opportunities of the empire, just as it was of their incursion into the British state. As a result, it is unlikely to have been coincidental that the two members of the assembly whose elections were fixed by Melville's associate John Weir were Scottish, and those who replaced them were English.

In seeking to resolve the problem, the Scottish president of the Scottish-led council turned to the Scottish governor to protect the rights of other Scottish councillors and assemblymen. But it is far from clear that the English-run assembly was in the wrong. The unique national aspect of this dispute points to the anomalous position of Scots in Dominica. Their unusually and disproportionately high representation in the council was almost certainly the result of Robert Melville's attempts to run the island as his personal fiefdom.

Under the federal structure operating in the Windward Islands, the governor in Grenada had responsibility for all four main islands, as well as smaller ones like the Grenadines and Bequia. Melville also owned 1,000 acres of land in Dominica, which he had acquired through means that approached illegality. By 1767, discussions over the expediency of separating the government of Dominica from the government of Grenada were under way. Governor Melville expressed his guarded opinion on the matter to Lord Shelburne in January that year: 'I long ago & repeatedly signalled my readiness to constitute a separate Council and Assembly there as soon as it should be practicable by a sufficiency of Freeholders which hitherto has not been the case and it appears that till there are more residing Purchasers of lands (there now not being above 17 or 18) it will be difficult'.[22]

A petition signed by 159 people from Dominica and merchants from London and Liverpool was sent to George III in July 1767 seeking the establishment of a government in Dominica independent from

Grenada. Of those 159, only thirteen were Scots. This is a surprisingly small number, given the level of Scottish involvement in the Dominica elite. Striking, too, is the absence of men connected with Melville. John Weir, deputy provost marshal and seller of land to Melville, did not sign. Nor did either of the Pringle brothers, who were closely tied to Melville.

To an extent Melville's apparent acceptance of a separate legislature at some future date may have been genuine. But in the short term, he was far more concerned that this would also mean a separate governor being appointed. By 1768 he had indicated his dissatisfaction with the plan, and his concern about absenteeism was a cover for his wholesale opposition to any diminution of his little empire in the Windwards. Having made his views known to Lord Hillsborough at the Board of Trade, Hillsborough responded rather indignantly: 'Does Governor Melville really think that if it should happen upon this subject, His Majesty's Board of Trade and his Privy Council should differ from him in regard to this Establishment that it would be an affront to him or of Consequence an Injury to the Colony, and that such a difference of opinion would evince His Majesty's Administration is neither just nor enlightened?'[23]

The Dominica council voted unanimously in favour of separation, concurring with the assembly and the majority of opinion in the island. Even Weir voted in favour, perhaps not coincidentally during Melville's furlough in London. Melville thus saw a part of his government placed in the hands of Lieutenant-Governor William Young, who in 1770 became governor of the island, entirely independent of Grenada.[24] Young's star continued to rise. He was later responsible for the suppression of the Black Caribs in St Vincent. His power base was derived from his former position as chairman of the Land Commission, to which he had been appointed by the then prime minister, George Grenville. As a result of this post, his network of contacts stretched widely throughout the islands: he, like Melville, had acquaintances in each of the four island councils.

Melville was never explicit about his loss of influence, at least never on paper. But he was not prepared to sit back and watch that influence be undermined, despite the opinion of the imperial government that the separation of the government of Dominica was 'in the Interest of the Proprietors of Land there'.[25] The particular bone of contention he chose to fight over arose from the failure of the Land Commission to report the sales of land in Dominica to him in February 1771. Previously, these reports, along with those for Tobago and St Vincent, had been sent to Robert Melville as governor-general of the Grenada and Neutral Islands. Melville was noticeably displeased when the

Dominica reports were sent to the governor of that island, who happened to be the former head of the Land Commission. His displeasure was deepened by the news that the sales were being granted under the Great Seal of Dominica rather than of Grenada. As the commissioners had received no formal instructions from London to act in this fashion, Melville was, strictly speaking, quite justified in raising the issue, even though he was demanding powers for his government over the affairs of another.[26]

All this created the (probably accurate) impression of Scots benefiting to an unfair extent. Yet this was not just a national contest between Scots and the English for control of the island. It was more a battle over the power of Melville and his cohort to generate an unwarranted influence over Dominican affairs. The perceived 'Scottishness' of the council and the 'Englishness' of the assembly thus exacerbated, rather than caused, animosity between the branches.

Neither the decline of Melville's authority nor the decline in Scottish representation in the council ended the war of attrition inside the legislature. The assembly caused considerable problems for the governor and council of Dominica in 1771 when they tried, eventually successfully, to pass a bill for the governor's salary of £2,000. The new governor, William Young, commented, 'I perceive...a strong jealously in the Assembly of the Power of the Crown; and in every Business respecting the raising and disposing of Monies, they are strugling to keep the control more in their own hands, than is consistent with the Honor and Independency of His Majesty's Govt., and of the several offices appointed by the King's authority. This occasions public Business to pass slowly.'[27] The assembly remained determined to limit expenditure by the executive, as a statement of its own power as much as a desire to curtail fiscal imprudence. In 1786 it decided that to continue to pay for a large force to search for runaway slaves was unnecessary during the rainy season. The council viewed this as the assembly once again exceeding its authority and commented that it had acted in a 'very improper' and 'very unparliamentary' manner. It recommended that the force be twice the size proposed by the assembly.[28]

The most striking aspect of the functioning of the system in Dominica was the frequency with which its constituent organs were in conflict. This 'essentially confrontational' approach applied across the British West Indies and meant that assemblies fought with governors, councils squabbled with assemblies, and both resisted the encroachment of control from London.[29]

In the 1760s Jamaica was also convulsed by a confrontation between the assembly and Governor Lyttleton over privileges of assembly members. The dispute, inflated from a minor squabble to a major constitutional crisis, demonstrates the importance to the Jamaica elite of being seen as Britons, with the same rights and privileges as those 'at home'. Moreover, as has been argued persuasively, this conflict was part of a 'more or less continuous process of negotiation' between London and the colonies.[30] Even more important was the realisation that the colonies could gain substantial victories over the representatives of the Crown. To be sure, the imperial government's position was undermined by another major imperial crisis, but the assembly was able, despite the colony's dependence on Britain, to extract a major concession without recourse to outright revolution.

External disputes

While the Jamaicans were engrossed in their own internecine strife, much of the rest of the Atlantic empire was responding to the introduction of the Stamp Act in 1765. This dissent has more commonly been associated with the mainland colonies, but the Act also met with vociferous opposition in the some of the Caribbean islands.[31] The response was most violent in St Kitts, where organised riots took to the streets on 31 October and 5 November 1765, destroying stamps and burning effigies. The first of these riots occurred the day before the introduction of the Act, while the second coincided with a critical date in the British Protestant calendar. It marked the anniversary of both the Gunpowder Plot and the landing of William of Orange at Torbay in 1688. It was surely no accident that those who opposed the Act as the undermining of British liberty invoked the triumph of the Glorious Revolution in their campaign. While the legacy of the revolution was interwoven with a variety of ideologies in the eighteenth-century Britain, it was widely employed, as in the Caribbean, both as an example of direct popular political action and as a justification for it.[32]

Throughout the Leeward Islands, the payment of duties was prevented. The duties were paid in Jamaica without any great opposition, as was the case in newly acquired Grenada, then the seat of government for the Windwards. This difference in response has been explained in terms of the Leewards' greater reliance on American trade for provisions. This reliance forced them, under pressure from the Americans, to 'either rise in opposition or face the spectre of famine'.[33] Undoubtedly this was a factor, but the scale of rioting, especially in St Kitts, where the stamp distributor was forced by a mob of 500 whites to resign or face the gallows, suggests more than simple acquiescence to an American agenda. The fact that the Leewards did not feel bound to follow the Americans into revolution a decade later further implies that the Caribbean islands were capable of independent action. The organised nature and timing of the riots points to a widespread response to a perceived extension of arbitrary government to an island which had, since 1726, had the right to vote the revenue for imperial administration and defence through the assembly.

Jamaica did not witness large-scale opposition, though the Act did not pass unnoticed. There was some dissent among the elite. A Scot, Robert Graham, collector of customs for the island, saw the imposition of the Act as an infringement of Jamaicans' 'rights as Brittains', but believed that opposition was out of the question. '[W]e must submit', he wrote.[34] Jamaican acquiescence was, in part, a result of its greater independence from the American colonies. It was also a function of its assembly being in dispute with the governor, and, indeed, being prorogued for much of the period of anti-Stamp Act agitation. While both disputes recalled fears of the encroachment of tyranny, the Jamaica assembly saw the threat coming from the governor, not the imperial government.[35] Indeed, to defeat Lyttleton, the Jamaica assembly relied on the British ministry. Why the Windwards did not oppose the Act is more difficult to discern. Their recent establishment as British colonies and their 'settling' nature, with a small white population, probably militated against any large-scale opposition. But whatever passiveness they may have shown in the face of the Stamp Act, the Windward Islands soon showed themselves to be anything but politically inert.

Controlling the revenues

The St Vincent assembly, like its counterparts elsewhere, sought to ensure that actions taken by either the governor or the council did not undermine its constitutional position. As in Dominica, the assembly's competence in financial affairs made the passing of revenue bills occasions of political controversy. As Governor Leybourne wrote of the St Vincent legislature,

> I have little expectation of their passing a Revenue Law without making the Consent of the Assembly necessary to the Issuing of Money, these ideas are so strongly implanted in the minds of the People in this Country that every Person I have conversed with on the subject, entertain the same sentiments, and as they have the example of the Old Islands they seem so unanimous in their opinion upon this point.[36]

The control of the money required by the governor to run the colony was the assemblies' most potent and jealously guarded privilege.

Imposing a 4½ per cent duty on all exports from the islands was the standard means of raising revenue in the Windward Islands. It was exacted originally by royal proclamation from London. The assemblies of Grenada and Dominica, like that of St Vincent, opposed the imposition of what they saw as arbitrary government. The Grenada assembly, aware of the need to generate revenue, proposed in 1769 that a law be enacted enabling it to order the application of the duty, which it would then vote to the Crown. This law, it argued, would mirror that of St Kitts of 1726, which was in turn based on an act passed in Barbados in 1663.[37] Two years later, in the midst of Governor Young's struggle with the Dominica assembly, it became apparent to him that the assembly was firmly resistant to the raising of duty by proclamation. Its opposition to it, he believed, was based on 'a presumption that the Mode by which the Duty is now exacted it illegal'. Significantly, it was widely held among the whites that 'whenever this matter is brought to a tryal in England the decision will be in their favour.'[38] Three years later this belief proved to be well founded.

In 1774, the Scottish planter Alexander Campbell began litigation against the collector of the duty in Grenada, to recover duties paid on his exports of sugar. Campbell argued that the Crown, having established a local legislature, had abrogated its right to set taxes in the colony. Drawing on a case in Jamaica in 1722, he argued that the establishment of Grenada as a colony, rather than a conquered territory, meant that 'no tax could be imposed upon the inhabitants, but by an assembly of the island or by an act of Parliament.' Judgement was passed on the case of *Campbell* v. *Hall* on 28 November 1774. Lord Mansfield found for the plaintiff, and effectively ended the right of the imperial government arbitrarily to raise taxes in the Windwards without the consent of the local population.[39]

It is clear from Campbell's case, which invoked the articles of capitulation that enshrined the Grenadians' 'rights, liberties and properties' as 'subjects of Great Britain', that the inhabitants of the 'new' islands sought not only the same constitutional rights as settlers in the 'old' islands, but those due to any 'true-born Briton'. The same motivations fired, most forcibly, revolutionaries in the continental American colonies. The constitutional implications of acknowledging the right of the Windward Islands to set taxes bolstered the authority of the assemblies. And, like the success of the Jamaica assembly in 1766, Campbell's ability to force a concession from London probably confirmed the impression among the white West Indian residents that the colonial system worked. This, as will be shown, strengthened their commitment to the metropole two years later.

Although the islands never countenanced outright revolution, the conflicts outlined above highlight tensions in the political structure of the empire. In the Caribbean context, these tensions served as a check on the rule of policy makers in London and their representatives in the islands, the governors. The implications of this tension were not lost on ministers. In 1792, in his instructions to Ninian Home, Henry Dundas counselled that 'an uniform and assiduous endeavour to cultivate a mutual good understanding between the assembly and the executive Government, an open and manifest attention to the Interest of the Island, to the expenditure of all Monies granted by it, whether appropriated or not, and a readiness to lay all accounts before the assembly, form the best and most prevailing claim to their confidence and liberality...'[40]

Significantly, though, the disputes arose at times of relative calm in the islands. Through the wartime storms of the late 1770s and 1790s, constitutional squalls were overshadowed. The islanders sought an accommodation with the British authorities, demanding the rights of Britons but never, as in the mainland colonies, rejecting rule by Britons. There are strong echoes of the West Indian demands in the campaigns of Scottish radicals in this period. In their agitation for the reform of the burgh franchises in 1775 and again in 1782, Scottish radicals claimed 'we are Britons, without possessing the rights of Britons'.[41] In Grenada, while there were relatively mundane issues on which Scots disagreed with each other, on the most contentious problem in the first decade of British rule they tended towards agreement, in opposition to a perceived threat to the rights of Britons.

The crisis in Grenada

In Grenada, like the other Windward islands, Scots emerged quickly as a large group in the white population. By 1766, Scotsmen filled thirteen of the twenty-one occupied seats in the Grenada assembly. Fewer than three years later, however, this number had plummeted to six out of twenty-two. The decline coincided with a period of considerable 'Heat and Animosity' in the Grenada legislature and across the island. When the Treaty of Paris transferred Grenada formally to British rule in 1763, it came with a large French Catholic population, many of whom remained in the island as His Majesty's 'New Subjects'. As in the rest of the British Empire, the franchise was based on property, and, as the French had retained the rights to their property, they formed the largest part of the electorate.

The presence of this large body of French Catholics was highly problematic for the imperial government. It was bound by the terms of the Treaty of Paris to safeguard the rights of the French *colons*. Consequently, it had to balance the need to establish the legitimacy of its rule, in the eyes of this large and potentially hostile population, with the prevailing attitudes of the British Protestant settlers. The legal requirements of the Grenada constitution also militated against any large-scale French involvement. This, of course, occurred in a period soon after a long-drawn-out war against France, in which memories of the Jacobite rebellions were still fresh in the minds of Protestant Britons. Moreover, divisions in Protestantism itself appear to have been glossed over on the western shores of the Atlantic, perhaps in response to perceived threats from Catholicism. This was certainly true for the Caribbean, and also appears to have been the case in the more religiously diverse North American colonies.[42]

There are certain parallels between Grenada and Quebec, which was acquired at the same time and which had an even more overwhelmingly large French Catholic population. In Quebec, the small British Protestant population was vocal in expressing opposition to any extension of rights to *Canadiens*. Problems were heightened in Quebec because the Protestant community was too small to administer the colony effectively, and this led to a level of accommodation with established French practices. In the mid-1760s, it was not at all apparent that such an accommodation was envisioned. On the contrary, both Quebec and Grenada were to be subjected to a policy of anglicisation. The Stamp Act, had it not been repealed in 1766, would have charged additional levies on all publications in French in both colonies.[43] In Grenada, where the Protestant population was proportionately larger than in Quebec and maintained a far more cordial relationship with the Presbyterian governor, Melville, than the Canadians did with the Episcopalian James Murray, moves towards assimilating Catholics were more effectively opposed.[44]

The dispute arose in late 1767 when the returning officer for St George Town, Walter Roberston, refused to accept the candidacy of a French resident in an election to the assembly. This provoked a round of petitioning and led the council to elect a committee to consider 'the present unhappy state of the island'.[45] The committee reported to the council that blame for the conflict lay entirely with the French settlers and their 'late attempt . . . to intrude themselves into the Legislature is a Manifest Violation of the Laws of Great Britain, & of the Constitution & Laws of this Country.'[46]

The councillors were further outraged later in the year. In Grenada, everybody who held public office was required to take certain oaths of

'Allegiance, Supremacy and Abjuration' as well as making and subscribing a declaration against transubstantiation. For Catholics, this posed fundamental difficulties. Following a report by the Committee of the Council for Plantation Affairs on 13 August 1768, Lord Hillsborough sent instructions to Ulysses Fitzmaurice, acting lieutenant-governor in Melville's absence. These informed him that two Catholics could sit in the council, three could hold seats in the assembly, one might be an assistant judge, and there might be one Catholic appointed as commissioner of the peace for each town, parish or district. Moreover, they were 'required to make no other oaths than those of Allegiance and Supremacy'. As a result, some 1,200 French people applied their signature to the oaths by 1771.[47] The council and the governor were thus set on a collision course in which councillors opposed concessions to Catholics as unconstitutional, while Fitzmaurice attempted to carry out his instructions.

In February 1769, French justices of the peace were appointed in each parish but, at this stage, there were still no Frenchmen on the council. Lord Hillsborough in London sent word that this was an important objective: 'As the Appointment of two of His Majesty's New Subjects to be Members of the Council ... shall be the completion of His Majesty's gracious Plan for the satisfaction of His Majesty's New Subjects in Grenada, I shall take the King's pleasure thereupon the moment I receive intelligence from you of those measures having been carried into execution...'[48] Accordingly, Fitzmaurice nominated Messrs Devocuna and Chanteloup, and a number of the existing councillors threatened to resign. They argued that the constitution of Grenada allowed for there to be only twelve members sworn at one time, and, as there were already that number, no more could be nominated. Fitzmaurice pressed the issue, whereupon Messrs Graham, Lindow, Corsar, Melvill, Townsend and Williams left the chamber and were subsequently suspended by the governor.[49] Unsurprisingly, this enraged the councillors. They petitioned George III, arguing that Fitzmaurice had suspended them for opposing a measure which was 'in express Contradiction to your Majesty's Instructions hitherto communicated to your Council'. By charging Fitzmaurice with preparing to make 'a most dangerous innovation', the councillors raised the spectre of arbitrary gubernatorial rule.[50]

The issue aroused enormous controversy in Grenada, and also in Britain, where those opposing the admission of Catholics waged a high profile propaganda war. Seventeen members of the Grand Jury of Grenada (including seven Scots) petitioned the king to revoke the instruction, which 'hath drawn after it a train of evils'. They pointed out that the new subjects, so recently their sworn enemies, were passing laws in a language they did not understand, and passing judgement on Britons on the basis of statutes they could not read. Furthermore, they expressed concern that the concessions applied only to French Catholics. This, they declared, was a 'partial and unnatural preference, over Your Majesty's natural born Roman Catholic Subjects, many of whom are residing in this island, and who dutifully submit to the Laws, which have precluded them from the like benefits'.[51] In 1770, Governor Robert Melville returned to Grenada, allowing Fitzmaurice to return to St Vincent. Melville, during his furlough in London, had tried to persuade Hillsborough to take a tougher line on the Catholics, and once back in the island was far more sympathetic to the grievances of the Protestant settlers. One of his first actions, after being petitioned by British nationals, was to prorogue the assembly, whose legislation was in any case being widely ignored by the Protestant community. They believed that as the legislature was unconstitutional, they were under no obligation to obey its strictures. Indeed, they averred that it was quite wrong to pay taxes levied by it, or adhere to laws passed by it. Prominent among this group were Scots, many of whom, like Melville himself, displayed a profoundly anti-Catholic bias.

In 1767 legislation had been passed before the council proposing the levying of additional taxes on a number of estate proprietors in the parish of St Patrick to establish and regulate Grenville Harbour. By November 1770 many of these proprietors were refusing to 'pay their Shares of the Tax imposed on them for the support of it; which Tax they alledge to be illegal, as having been imposed on them since the admission of Roman Catholics in the Assembly.'[52] Most of the proprietors named in the original legislation (Roger Smith, Peter Gordon, John Aitchison, Alexander Campbell and James and Alexander Baillie) were Scots. Campbell later found fame as the plaintiff in *Campbell* v. *Hall*, while James Baillie's disgust with the whole affair led him to remark in 1772, 'Politics I have given up, and may they go to the D__l their own way, which they are fast doing.'[53]

As well as flouting the laws of Grenada, the protestors demonstrated against the institutions in which Catholics were represented, and against those who were seen to be co-operating with them. Those who failed to comply with the law were brought before the Grenada courts, but even there a spirit of opposition could be discerned. Judge Israel Wilkes, brother of John, instructed the jury to acquit the defendant who had refused to pay a tax. Another judge tried to intercede to prevent Wilkes acting in this way, leading to demonstrations in the streets of St George's: 'We had at night illuminations and bonfires. The Senior Judge was burnt in effigy, and several barrels of porter drank to the health of Judge Wilkes, or Grenada Wilkes, the British Constitution, and No Dispensing Power.'[54]

The riots took a similar form to those in St Kitts over the Stamp Act in November 1765. And as in St Kitts, and the dispute over the Jamaica privilege controversy, the response to the crisis was couched in terms that tied it to the defence of other British rights. In St Kitts, the anti-Stamp Act riot took place on the anniversary of the beginning of the 1688 revolution. Nicholas Bourke's *A letter concerning the privileges of the island of Jamaica vindicated* (1767) drew expressly on the precedent of the seventeenth-century struggle between Parliament and the Stuart Crown.[55] In Grenada, the toast to 'No Dispensing Power' was a specific reference to the prerogative powers of the Stuarts which had led to the revolution against James II and reinforced the attack on the admission of Catholics.

The furore drifted across the Atlantic and was replicated in the press in Britain. Articles and letters were published in support of the rebellious Protestants, who continued to claim that they acted in accord with the values of any true patriot. The crisis hit a particularly tender nerve among contributors to the *Scots Magazine*. Articles warned of the 'danger of anarchy and confusion' if the authorities persisted with their policy of admitting Catholics to the island's institutions.[56] Others condemned Hillsborough and Fitzmaurice for their connivance with the Catholics, and compared the laudable intentions of the Grenada Protestants with the more self-serving aspirations of 'patriots' in Britain, who were lambasted as 'unprincipled imposters'. A 'London merchant trading to the Grenades' commented:

> I have been led to a detection of the false patriotism of Messrs. Sawbridge, Oliver, Townsend, Crosby, Wilkes, Bull, and a thousand more of the same stamp, without going out of my way to seek for *damning proofs* of their political hypocrisy and deceit. I found them in the field of fair comparison, and collated them from the similarity of the circumstances of the aggrieved subjects of the island of Grenada, and of the freeholders in Middlesex.

The author highlighted particularly the respective actions of the brothers Wilkes and, by comparing John Wilkes's position with that of the Grenadians, reaffirmed the role of Scots in the moral guardianship of Britishness. Among officialdom, only Governor Melville's 'truly laudable concern for the liberties of the people' escaped the author's wrath.[57] It is likely that this kind of propaganda was inspired by a group of Grenadians in London, who were kept informed of developments by friends or family in the island. Within this group, Scots were influential. William Mackintosh, a Grenada planter, was 'consider'd as the

Chief Instrument of the factious Grenadians residing in England'. Mackintosh, indeed, tried to use the dispute to settle his own score with the Walter Robertson, and to remove him from the office of assistant judge. Yet Robertson's anti-Catholic credentials were impeccable: it was his refusal to allow the candidacy of a Frenchman in the 1767 election that had sparked off the controversy in the first place. His position was hardly threatened, however. He had been appointed by Melville, who remained steadfast in his support.[58]

Melville himself was involved in campaigning against the admission of Catholics during his time in the capital between 1768 and 1770. Melville was profoundly anti-Catholic. In 1751, he had joined the Old Revolution Club in Edinburgh, which explicitly celebrated the overthrow of 'popery' in 1688. His views were widely shared among contemporary Scots, and the presence of a large Scottish community in Grenada was an important factor in the fierce resistance to the admission of Catholics.[59]

The *Scots Magazine* was certainly enthusiastic about informing its readers of attacks on Britishness in Grenada. Doubtless this both responded to, and continued to fuel, a particularly anti-Catholic constituency in Scotland. The level of animosity towards Catholicism was inversely proportional to the size of the Catholic population in Scotland. In 1755, there were about 33,000 Catholics in Scotland, or about 2.6 per cent of the population. By 1800, before the start of large-scale Irish immigration, the proportion had declined to 1.8 per cent, or about 30,000 souls. In Glasgow, like Edinburgh, there were clubs that celebrated the triumph of Protestantism, and where there was a reported 'long-established affection for the severest Presbyterianism and... a deep-rooted hatred of Popery.'[60] But it was not only in the two major Lowland cities that anti-Catholicism was rife. Many other towns in Scotland, in addition to Glasgow and Edinburgh, were represented among the 356 petitions sent to Parliament in 1778 in protest at the Scottish Catholic Relief Bill. The depth of the hostility to the bill sparked rioting in Edinburgh and Glasgow in January and February 1779, and led to its collapse.[61] These riots prefigured the Gordon Riots: a week of burning, looting and destruction in London in June 1780 that followed Lord George Gordon's presentation of the Protestant Association's petition for the repeal of the Catholic Relief Act in England. There was a considerable delegation from Scotland among the rioters. The fact that a Scottish mob travelled to London to oppose Catholic relief in England, having already banished it from the Scottish political agenda, indicates a profound and wide-ranging anti-Catholicism north of the border.[62] After all, the protests in England sought to *repeal* legislation that had been allowed to pass, rather than, as in Scotland, to oppose its introduction.

Scots in Grenada, although seeing a slump in political representation during the late 1760s, recovered their position in 1770, a development perhaps coinciding with the return of Governor Melville to the island. Of the sixty signatories of a petition to Melville, twenty-six were Scots around the same time that seven of the seventeen councillors were Scottish, and nine of the twenty-four assemblymen.[63] Although the crisis came to an end in 1774, there was continued mistrust between the communities. In the 1790s the issue of Catholic participation was still a matter of pressing concern. Henry Dundas, in his first instructions to the new lieutenant-governor, Ninian Home, noted the 'necessary qualification to sit in the Assembly, vizt., the making and subscribing the Declaration against Transubstantiation &c.'[64] Such an instruction was perhaps painful for Dundas as the promoter of the ill-fated Scottish Catholic Relief Bill, but was hardly likely to have upset Home, who had campaigned in the 1760s against the extension of privileges to French Catholics.

Elsewhere in the Windwards, the presence of French inhabitants did not cause major constitutional difficulties to the same extent. While the Protestant inhabitants of Dominica, St Vincent and (perhaps especially) Tobago were unlikely to be more disposed towards Catholicism, the situation never developed as in Grenada. In part this was a result of the much larger French population in Grenada, and in part a function of their retention of property rights. The Treaty of Paris safeguarded only Grenadian land rights; in the other islands the treaty led to many French settlers leaving, and to the disenfranchisement of those who remained.

The 'war of Britishness'[65]

One of the most striking aspects of the British settlers' response to government plans to extend rights to Catholics was the level of loyalty to the British 'constitution' claimed by them. When the possibility of revolution, rather than resistance, emerged in the 1770s, the island legislatures, still with a strong Scottish presence, were swift to declare their loyalty to the Crown, their disapprobation of the events being perpetrated by what the Grenada assembly described as the 'deluded people of several Provinces of North America'. The council of St Vincent wrote, 'It is with the deepest concern we reflect on the unnatural Revolt of Several of the American Colonies... We flatter ourselves that your Majesty's Efforts supported by the Wisdom of

Parliament cannot fail speedily to restore Union and tranquillity to the Nation.'[66]

These responses were unequivocal, but equally significant is the colonists' sense that a British 'nation', of which they were part, was being split by the American actions. Such an attitude was mirrored in the reaction of the St Vincent assembly. It informed the governor that there were no people 'more loyal or more firmly Attached' to the king than those in the island. They would, moreover, 'at all times be willing to show their submission to the Constitutional Claims of his Parliament'. Their claim was not unchallenged. The Grenada assembly believed that *its* members were the most loyal of the king's subjects. It noted, 'It is with the gravest concern we have beheld the Spirit of rebellion which has for some time prevailed amongst so many of the Inhabitants of North America.'[67] While this seems an ironical sentiment in an island which had spawned anti-Catholic riots and the *Campbell* v. *Hall* case in opposition to government policy, it serves to illustrate the distinction made between resistance, which was acceptable, and outright revolution, which was not.

The loyalty of the Windward Islands was reinforced by the presence of so many Scots, especially in the legislatures. Although Scots were more than willing to disagree with each other on matters relating to the internal affairs of the islands, and to disagree with London when they felt their rights were being infringed, they nevertheless demonstrated remarkable solidarity with Britain in the face of an external threat. As we have seen, some of the key tenets of Britishness were of fundamental importance to Scots. Protestantism and liberty were as much watchwords for Scots as for other Britons, and, as Chapter Four noted, commerce was also a central aspect of Scottish life. Overarching these factors was the empire (or Greater Britain), from which Scots had derived great material advantages but also a sense of participation in a shared British enterprise. This overseas success had done much to rehabilitate Scots in the later eighteenth century after the Jacobite Rebellion had so tarnished their reputations. The American Revolution gave Scots in the Caribbean a chance to demonstrate their British credentials.

Throughout the Thirteen Colonies, from Georgia to Massachusetts, Scots were regarded, and regarded themselves, as being particularly loyal to the Crown. Among the multi-ethnic composition of the Atlantic colonies, it is not always possible to discern the actions of one group as being separate from another, but as far as many Americans were concerned there was no doubt about the Scots. As Washington's aide-de-camp reported, 'the Scotchmen are worse than I thought'.[68] It is true that not all Scots in the colonies were averse to the actions of the Americans, but even John Witherspoon, sixth president of the College of New Jersey, was forced to concede in his 'Address to the natives of Scotland residing in America' in May 1776 that most Scots were loyal. The 'Address' had been intended to limit the denigration of Scots. This animosity towards Scots manifested itself in popular toasts calling for 'a free exportation of Scotchmen and Tories', and in numerous satirical plays and poems.[69] All this took place in the context of an interruption of the normal channels of communication between Scotland and America through which many Scots had influenced the development of education and medicine in North America. But such a hiatus suggests that the bonds between the two were rather weaker than the image of a shared cultural identity which some historians have proposed. It suggests instead that the majority of Scots, whether in Scotland or in the colonies, saw themselves as partners in the empire as part of the metropole, rather than as subordinate provincial associates like North Americans or the Irish.[70]

While Scots on the mainland were seen as especially loyal, in the Caribbean such a distinction on ethnic grounds is more difficult to identify. This is not to suggest that Scots in the Caribbean were less loyal than those in the Thirteen Colonies. Rather it is because virtually everybody was loyal. Most whites of British descent never seriously contemplated severing their links with the metropole. This loyalty is ascribed to a variety of reasons. For some the islands' particular social, strategic and economic circumstances forced a reliance on Britain. As Andrew O'Shaughnessy has argued, enslavement 'reinforced metropolitan ties and made whites a besieged minority dependent on Britain for their ascendancy.' For others, the absence of a white artisan class meant that there was no-one to push the elite into revolution.[71]

In the Caribbean, absenteeism had profound implications. Firstly, it generated an unusual degree of social mobility, and allowed those who were not substantial landowners to enter the political elite. In this way members of the lower (white) orders, such as they were, had no real need to use revolution as a means of acquiring power. Secondly, absenteeism, and the more general transience of the population, meant that white Caribbean society was far less settled than groups on the American mainland. The islands were, for many, and particularly for Scots, a site for the acquisition or renewal of a fortune, rather than a place for permanent residence. As a result of a short-term commitment to the islands, Scots maintained very strong ties with home. Even for those who spent years in the West Indies, the extent of their letter writing is testimony to the continued presence of 'home' in their thinking. The reliance on Britain for education, at both school and university levels, reinforced the centrality of the metropole in West Indian minds. Furthermore, the rhetoric of the islanders repeatedly summoned the spectres of arbitrary government, tyranny and Catholicism, all of which were at variance with their image of British Protestant liberty. At the heart of the West Indians' response to the American Revolution was a profound sentimental attachment to Britain. This attachment was seen by them, through the political struggles of the 1760s and 1770s, to have been rewarded. For despite their devotion to Britishness, they were not blinded to the failings of London or its edicts. On the contrary, there were moments in Jamaica in 1764, in St Kitts in 1766 and in Grenada between 1768 and 1772 when members of the white communities were in open rebellion against the imperial government. But never, it seems, did they contemplate secession. And it is highly significant that in each of these cases, as in the *Campbell v. Hall* case, their campaigns were successful. For them the empire worked. And, as a result, there was great reluctance to countenance supporting their colonial brethren in 1776.

Facing insurrections

The Caribbean did not survive the American War unscathed. The islands' trade was badly hit, and several were occupied by French forces; Tobago was retained by them until the 1790s, when yet another challenge was laid down. From the 1760s, local politicians in St Vincent viewed the Carib question as the island's most pressing problem. The president of the council reported in May 1769 that the 'Black Charibbs' had prevented the surveying of part of the island. A fortnight later, the council sent an address to the king complaining of the risks of a Carib rising. In particular it warned of the strategic implications of an enemy within.[72] The Caribs rebelled occasionally against the British colonists with the clandestine encouragement of the French authorities in St Lucia. Evidence of this collusion led Governor Leybourne in Grenada to conclude that 'it will be impossible to bring these Savages to a proper sense of duty to His Majesty'.[73] William Young, lieutenant-governor of Dominica, was dispatched to St Vincent to suppress them in 1772. In 'reducing them to His Majesty's Sovereignty', Young sought the word of the French governor of St Domingue that he would not provide aid to the Caribs. In practice, however, it proved virtually impossible to prevent private French traders from supplying the rebels.[74] In January 1773, a treaty was signed between George III and the Caribs in which some of their lands were reserved, and under the terms of which they swore allegiance to the British king. It proved not to be a long-term solution, as the conduct of the Caribs in the American War showed. Governor Edward Lincoln noted that 'this is the only island that has any internal enemy, who by their treacherous manner of fighting & insincerity are now more formidable than their numbers import, & who from their behaviour during the war discovered their inveteracy to us.'[75] During the spring of 1784, Lincoln pleaded with the administration in London to sanction the removal of the Caribs to the Bahamas. He warned that French guns and ammunition from Martinique were reaching the Caribs. From the safety of London, Lord Sydney responded that it was too difficult to remove the Caribs to another island.[76]

The general level of mistrust of the French authorities in the Caribbean reached new heights in the 1790s. In some respects the French Revolution of 1789 had little immediate impact on people in the British Caribbean. Jonathon Troup in Dominica, usually a man with more than enough to say for himself, reported on 2 October 1789 only that twenty rebellious slaves had been executed in Martinique, and that 20,000 people had been killed in Paris. Thereafter, he restricted himself to thoughts on Dominica.[77] But this general ambivalence was to change. In December 1791, Governor Mathews of Grenada informed London of the scale of the insurrection in St Domingue. He reported that 68,640 enslaved had rebelled, and had destroyed 1,126 estates on the island.[78] This clearly unsettled the British residents in the Caribbean, and heightened their fears of rebellion in their islands. The non-white population was considered particularly suspect: they were seen as potential agents of the French Revolution, the ideals of which were so inimical to Britons in the Caribbean. Such an environment led the free people of colour in Grenada to issue an explicit statement of their loyalty: 'At this period when much anarchy has arisen and mistaken notions of freedom have infected the inhabitants of foreign colonies, we are happy to express our steadfast resolution . . . to enjoy the blessings which we partake of under your Mild, Virtuous and Benevolent Government.'[79]

Ninian Home, as the newly appointed lieutenant-governor of Grenada, was warned by his benefactor, Henry Dundas, to be especially wary of 'movements in the neighbouring Foreign Islands'. Home reluctantly granted asylum to fleeing French Royalists, but was steadfast in refusing to admit any of their slaves. He was informed by Dundas that he 'should take immediate and effectual measures for sending away all those who may have reason to believe are likely, by principles or conduct . . . [to] in any ways affect His Majesty's interests in . . . Grenada.'[80] It is clear that Dundas was determined to restrict the spread of revolutionary ideas among the enslaved in the British islands. And Home used the opportunity to attack the long-standing French population as well as to restrict newcomers. He had been a staunch opponent of the extension of rights to Catholics in the 1760s, and his attitude had, if anything, hardened over the years. 'White people are much wanted in this Island,' he wrote, 'for many of the French... are gone and many more must go soon, and it would be happy for the Island if we were rid of them all.'[81]

The islanders' fears, and those of the London government, were not misplaced. Inspired and encouraged by Victor Hugues in Guadeloupe, insurrections ignited in Grenada and St Vincent in the early spring of 1795. The Scottish presence in Grenada continued in the emergency council established following the capture of Ninian Home and others, including his friend Alexander Campbell. Four of the seven members of the council were Scots, with Kenneth Francis MacKenzie as president. The council remained steadfast in its opposition to the rebellion, believing that its way of life was being threatened by an alliance of the French and the enslaved. MacKenzie, along with Mather Byles (a key figure in a number of Scottish networks in the island), issued proclamations condemning the 'most horrid acts of barbarity' that threatened to usurp their 'mild Government and Laws, affording equal protection to every individual'. This was palpable nonsense, but it underpinned the Grenadians' beliefs and provided justification for the rewards payable for insurgents who were brought to justice, dead or alive. This language enraged Victor Hugues, the leader of the French Revolution in the Caribbean. He denounced MacKenzie as 'despicable' and enjoined the insurgents to press on. He declared that 'where any deliberate act a Republican dies by the hands of our enemies', his men should 'put to the sword all such, until their name and memory are blotted out.'[82]

In confronting the trauma of rebellion by the enslaved, Caribs and the French, the Caribbean islands relied heavily on the Scottish contingent in the island elites. The scale of the combined threats made this sometimes desperate battle for survival more important than disputes between branches of the legislatures. And this battle for survival was underpinned by their belief in certain 'British' principles. The kind of liberty envisioned by Victor Hugues, still less that of the enslaved, was clearly not that which the British held so dear.

Conclusion

From the earliest British settlement of the Windward Islands, Scots were influential in island politics, and were well represented in all the legislative bodies. Their representation was proportionately higher than elsewhere in the Caribbean, including Jamaica. But there, too, there was a considerable expansion in Scottish influence in the second half of the eighteenth century. Scots in the Windwards tended to be slightly better represented in the elected assemblies than in the appointed councils. The important exception to this was Dominica, where the machinations of Robert Melville contrived to maintain a network responsive to his interests.

Elsewhere, while Scots were not especially prominent in the agitations in Jamaica and St Kitts in the mid-1760s, they did appropriate the same language of dissent in their disputes with the imperial government. During the crisis in Grenada from the late 1760s, a virulent strain of anti-Catholicism emerged which was similarly and contemporaneously apparent in Scotland. In summoning the rhetoric of the Glorious Revolution, as those in Jamaica and St Kitts had done, they defined themselves as dissenters determined to be British.

Indeed, for all their willingness to argue among themselves, and with London, the legislatures of the Caribbean remained committed to Britain during the American Revolution. In the Windward Islands, the presence of many Scots cemented their loyalty. The commitment to British views of the Crown, liberty and Protestantism demonstrates the perception among West India Scots of their part in a Greater Britain in which they would play a political role. As the next chapter will show, this role was not entirely predicated on direct representation in Parliament, but on networks of important connections. The bonds drew together in an imperial embrace the interests of the islands and the demands of Scottish politics.

Notes

1 D. W. Livingstone, 'Hume, English barbarism and American independence', in R. B. Sher and J. R. Smitten (eds), *Scotland and America in the age of the Enlightenment* (Edinburgh: Edinburgh University Press, 1990), pp. 136–42; K. Wilson, 'Inventing revolution: 1688 and eighteenth-century popular politics', *Journal of British Studies*, 28 (1989), 349–86; C. Kidd, 'The ideological significance of Robertson's History of Scotland', in S. J. Brown (ed.), *William Robertson and the expansion of empire* (Cambridge: Cambridge University Press, 1997), pp. 122–44.
2 E. Long, *The history of Jamaica, or general survey of the antient and modern state of that island* (1774; London: Frank Cass, 1970), vol. 1, p. 11; B. Edwards, *The history, civil and commercial, of the British colonies in the West Indies* (London: Whittaker, 1819), vol. 2, p. 386.
3 PRO, CO101/3(1), Grenada, original correspondence: Board of Trade, minutes, 7 September 1768; CO102/15 (no fol.), Grenada, entry books, additional instructions to Robert Melville, 12 October 1768; CO288/1(8–9), Tobago, sessional papers, journal of the assembly, 12 July 1768.
4 Edwards, *History of the West Indies*, vol. 2, p. 391; D. Hamilton, 'Robert Melville and the frontiers of empire in the British West Indies, 1763–1771', in A. Mackillop and S. Murdoch (eds), *Military governors and imperial frontiers c. 1600–1800: A study of Scotland and empires* (Leiden: Brill, 2003), pp. 181–204.

5   Edwards, *History of the West Indies*, vol. 2, pp. 386-90, 428; J. Stewart, *A view of the past and present state of the island of Jamaica* (1823; New York: Negro Universities Press, 1969), pp. 131–2.
6   Edwards, *History of the West Indies*, vol. 2, pp. 398–420.
7   PRO, CO101/2(28), Grenada, original correspondence: Secretary of State, letter from Robert Melville to Lord Shelburne, 15 January 1767.
8   PRO, CO104/3(73), Grenada, sessional papers, minutes of the assembly of Grenada and the Grenadines, 18 July 1769.
9   PRO, CO104/1(38), Grenada, sessional papers, minutes of the separate-council for Grenada, 17 and 29 April 1767; CO104/1(43), minutes, 29 April 1767.
10 J. Roby, *Members of the assembly of Jamaica, from the institution of that branch of the legislature to the present time* (Montego Bay: Alexander Homes, 1831), pp. 5–102, especially pp. 32–3, 62–3, 75, 80–2, 91–3, 94.
11 A. L. Karras, *Sojourners in the sun: Scottish migrants in Jamaica and the Chesapeake, 1740-1800* (Ithaca: Cornell University Press, 1992), pp. 137–54.
12 Roby, *Members of the assembly of Jamaica*, p. 39.
13 *Ibid.*, pp. 23, 81, 96–7.
14 NLJ, MS1655, Fyffe family letters, David Fyffe, Black River, to cousins, Dundee, 23 June 1769; W. A. Feurtado, *Official and other personages of Jamaica, from 1655 to 1790* (Kingston: W. A. Feurtado's Sons, 1896), p. 63.
15 F. Cundall (ed.), *Lady Nugent's journal* (London: West India Committee, 1939), pp. lxviii–lxxv.
16 A. J. O'Shaughnessy, *An empire divided: The American Revolution and the British Caribbean* (Philadelphia: University of Pennsylvania Press, 2000), p. 256n19.
17 PRO, CO285/3(74), Tobago, original correspondence: Secretary of State, minutes of the council, 6 January 1794.
18 PRO, CO288/3(3), Tobago, sessional papers, minutes of the council, 7 January 1777.
19 PRO, CO74/1 (no fol.), Dominica, sessional papers, minutes of the council, 9 January – 19 February 1768.
20 *Ibid.*, minutes of the council, 18 January 1768.
21 *The Freeport Gazette, or the Dominica Advertiser*, 2, 83 (10 January 1767), in PRO, CO101/2(34–5), Grenada, original correspondence: Board of Trade.
22 PRO, CO101/2(27), Governor Melville to Lord Shelburne, 15 January 1767.
23 PRO, CO102/15(14), Grenada, entry books: letters from the Secretary of State, letter from Lord Hillsborough, 12 February 1768.
24 PRO, CO74/1 (no fol.), Dominica, sessional papers, minutes of the council, 30 June 1768; CO71/1 (no fol.), Dominica, original correspondence: Board of Trade, order of the king-in-council, 6 June 1770.
25 *Ibid.*
26 PRO, CO 106/9(11–18) Grenada, miscellanea, papers relating to the sale of lands in the Ceded Islands, 18 May – 10 July 1771.
27 PRO, CO72/3 (no fol.), Dominica, entry books: letters to the Secretary of State, Sir William Young to Lord Dartmouth, 31 October 1771.
28 PRO, CO74/6A (no fol.), Dominica, sessional papers, minutes of the council, 4 July 1786.
29 M. Watson, 'The British West Indian legislatures in the seventeenth and eighteenth centuries: An historiographical introduction', in P. Lawson (ed.), *Parliament and the Atlantic empire* (Edinburgh: Edinburgh University Press, 1995), p. 91.
30 J. P. Greene, 'The Jamaica privilege controversy, 1764–66: An episode in the process of constitutional definition in the early modern British Empire', *Journal of Imperial and Commonwealth History*, 22, 1 (1994), 16–53; T. R. Clayton, 'Sophistry, security and socio-political structures in the American Revolution; or, why Jamaica did not rebel', *Historical Journal*, 29, 2 (1986), 325–6.
31 A. J. O'Shaughnessy, 'The Stamp Act crisis in the British Caribbean', *William and Mary Quarterly*, 51, 2 (1994), 203–26; *Scots Magazine*, 28 (January 1766), p. 50.
32 Wilson, 'Inventing revolution', 349, 352–3, 362; O'Shaughnessy, 'The Stamp Act crisis', 208.

33 O'Shaughnessy, 'The Stamp Act crisis', 216.
34 Clayton, 'Sophistry, security and socio-political structures', 324.
35 *Ibid.*, 325.
36 PRO, CO101/5(39), Grenada, original correspondence, William Leybourne Leybourne to Lord Hillsborough, 20 November 1771.
37 PRO, CO104/3(59), Grenada, sessional papers, minutes of the assembly, 2 March 1769.
38 PRO, CO72/3 (no fol.), Sir William Young to Lord Dartmouth, 31 October 1771.
39 'The genuine speech of Lord Mansfield... in the case of Campbell versus Hall', *Scots Magazine*, 36 (December 1774), 641–3; L. J. Ragatz, *The fall of the planter class in the British Caribbean, 1763–1833* (1928; New York: Octagon Books, 1981), p. 128.
40 PRO, CO101/32 (no fol.), Grenada, original correspondence, Henry Dundas to Ninian Home, 5 October 1792.
41 Thomas McGrugar, quoted in J. Vance, 'Constitutional radicalism in Scotland and Ireland in the era of the American Revolution, c. 1760–1789', PhD thesis, University of Aberdeen, 1998, p. 328; C. Kidd, 'North Britishness and the nature of eighteenth-century patriotism', *Historical Journal*, 39, 2 (1996), 361–82.
42 L. Colley, *Britons: Forging the nation, 1707–1837* (London: Pimlico, 1994), pp. 11–54; P. J. Marshall, 'Who cared about the Thirteen Colonies? Some evidence from philanthropy', *Journal of Imperial and Commonwealth History*, 27, 2 (1999), 57–64.
43 P. Lawson, *The imperial challenge: Quebec and Britain in the age of the American Revolution* (Montreal: McGill-Queen's University Press, 1989), p. 91.
44 'Introduction', in Mackillop and Murdoch (eds), *Military governors*, p. xliii.
45 PRO, CO104/1(61–2), Grenada, sessional papers, minutes of the council, 17 December 1767, 4 January 1768.
46 PRO, CO104/1(64–5), report of a committee of the council, 15 January 1768.
47 PRO, CO101/3(3), minutes, 7 September 1768; S. L. Hough and P. R. O. Hough (eds), *The Beinecke Lesser Antilles collection at Hamilton College, 1521-1860* (Gainesville: University of Florida Press, 1994), pp. 231–2.
48 PRO, CO101/3(112), Lord Hillsborough to Lieutenant-Governor Fitzmaurice, 13 May 1769.
49 PRO, CO101/3(81), Fitzmaurice to John Forbes, deputy clerk of the council, 29 September 1769; CO101/3(114–15), Fitzmaurice to Hillsborough, 26 August 1769.
50 PRO, CO101/3(89), petition to the King's Most Excellent Majesty, 5 October 1769.
51 PRO, CO101/4(56–7), petition of the grand jury, 10 September 1770.
52 PRO, CO104/1(48), minutes of the council, 22 July 1767; CO101/4(80), Melville to Hillsborough, 25 November 1770.
53 NLS, MS5514(113), Liston papers, James Baillie to Mrs. Ramage, 14 June 1772.
54 *Scots Magazine*, 33 (July 1771), 383.
55 Greene, 'The Jamaica privilege controversy', 20, 31–7.
56 'Letter to the Earl of H__b__h, His M__'s s__y of S__te for the c__l__s, on the present situation of affairs in the island of Gr__n__da', *Scots Magazine*, 31 (December 1769), 648–50.
57 'Grenada and London patriotism compared', *Scots Magazine*, 33 (December 1771), 641–2.
58 PRO, CO101/3(134), Melville to Hillsborough, 6 April 1770; CO101/4(66), Melville to Hillsborough, 31 October 1770.
59 NAS, GD126/9/1, Balfour–Melville papers; O'Shaughnessy, *An empire divided*, p. 285.
60 J. Darragh, 'The Catholic population of Scotland since the year 1860', *Innes Review*, 4 (1953), 58; R. K. Donovan, 'The popular party of the Church of Scotland and the American Revolution', in Sher and Smitten (eds), *Scotland and America in the age of the Enlightenment*, p. 89; J. Strang, *Glasgow and its clubs, or glimpses of the condition, manners, characters and addities of the city, during the past and present century* (London & Glasgow: Richard Griffen & Co., 1856), pp. 116–18, 240–4.

61 M. Fry, *The Dundas despotism* (Edinburgh: Edinburgh University Press, 1992), pp. 70–6; Vance, 'Constitutional radicalism', p. 218.
62 G. Rudé, 'The Gordon Riots: A study of the rioters and their victims', in G. Rudé, *Paris and London in the eighteenth century* (New York, Viking Press, 1971); Fry, *The Dundas despotism*, p. 77; R. K. Donovan, 'Voices of distrust: The expression of anti-Catholic feeling in Scotland, 1778–81', *Innes Review*, 30 (1979), 62–76.
63 PRO, CO101/4(61), petition from the inhabitants of Grenada, 22 October 1770; CO101/4(56–7), petition from the grand jury to George III, 10 September 1770.
64 PRO, CO101/32 (no fol.), Dundas to Home, 5 October 1792.
65 P. J. Marshall, 'A nation defined by empire, 1755–1776', in A. Grant and K. J. Stringer (eds), *Uniting the kingdom? The making of British history* (London: Routledge, 1995), p. 222.
66 PRO, CO101/19(146), Grenada, original correspondence: Secretary of State, address to the king . . . from the council of St Vincent, 17 April 1776; CO101/19(148), petition to Lt. Governor William Young by the assembly of Grenada, 19 April 1776.
67 PRO, CO101/19(154), petition to William Young by the assembly of St Vincent, 2 March 1776; CO101/19(150), petition to William Young by the assembly of Grenada, 25 March 1776.
68 A. Hook, *Scotland and America: A study of cultural relations, 1750–1835* (Glasgow and London: Blackie, 1975), p. 50; M. Fry, 'A commercial empire: Scotland and British expansion in the eighteenth century', in T. M. Devine and J. R. Young (eds), *Eighteenth-century Scotland: New perspectives* (East Linton: Tuckwell Press, 1999), p. 64.
69 Hook, *Scotland and America*, pp. 51–64; N. C. Landsman, 'Scotland, the American colonies and the development of British political identity', in L. Stone (ed.), *An imperial state at war* (London & New York: Routledge, 1994), pp. 275–6.
70 J. Clive and B. Bailyn, 'England's cultural provinces: Scotland and America', *William and Mary Quarterly*, 11 (1954), 200–13; Landsman, 'Scotland, the American colonies and the development of British political identity', pp. 258–87; N. C. Landsman, *From colonials to provincials: American thought and culture, 1680–1760* (New York: Twayne Publishers, 1998).
71 O'Shaughnessy, *An empire divided*, p. 57; O' Shaughnessy, 'The Stamp Act crisis', 204; Clayton, 'Sophistry, security and socio-political structures', 329–44.
72 PRO, CO263/1 (no fol.), St Vincent, sessional papers, speech by the president of the council, 10 May 1769; address to the king, 24 May 1769.
73 PRO, CO101/5(41), Governor Leybourne to Lord Hillsborough, 30 December 1772.
74 PRO, CO72/3 (no fol.), Sir William Young to Lord Dartmouth, 28 July 1772.
75 PRO, CO260/7 (no fol.), St Vincent, original correspondence: Secretary of State, Governor Lincoln to Lord Sydney, 8 March 1784.
76 *Ibid.*, correspondence between Lincoln and Sydney, 2 May, June and 6 August 1784.
77 UASCA, MS2070, Journal of Jonathon Troup, fol. 95, 2 October 1789.
78 PRO, CO101/32 (no fol.), Governor Mathews to Henry Dundas, 8 December 1791.
79 PRO, CO101/32 (no fol.), loyal address by the free coloureds of Grenada, 10 January 1792.
80 PRO, CO101/33 (no fol.), Grenada, original correspondence: Secretary of State, Henry Dundas to Ninian Home, 21 February 1793. For Home's efforts to prevent non-whites entering Grenada, see his proclamation of January 1793.
81 NAS, GD267/7/3(4), Home of Wedderburn manuscripts, Ninian Home to George Logan, 17 June 1794.
82 PRO, CO101/34(28), Grenada, original correspondence: Secretary of State, proclamation, 4 March 1795; 'A declaration of the commissioners delegated by the National Convention to the Windward Islands', in Anon., *A brief enquiry into the causes of, and conduct pursued by the colonial government, for quelling the insurrection in Grenada* (London: R. Faulder, 1796), p. 13.

CHAPTER SEVEN

Scots, the Caribbean and British imperial politics

The expansion of Scottish involvement in politics in the Caribbean mirrored the Scots' increasingly prominent position in the imperial polity in London. Significantly, as the number of Scots acquiring political influence with the national government increased, so too did the opportunities for political advancement in the islands. Moreover, as well as providing access to opportunities, well-placed Scots in London acted as vehicles for the articulation, in government circles, of the concerns of West India Scots.

The process of acquiring official positions in the West Indies by and for Scots was both a concomitant of, and a further contribution to, the integration of Britain. This, of course, did not pass unnoticed, nor was it uncriticised. Nonetheless, a remarkable number of Scots were able to enter high office in the colonies. The presence of these people in official positions, in the Caribbean and in Britain, provided the networks with access to the highest echelons of government, and thus made them effective lobby groups. The influence of the lobby groups was predicated, to a large extent, on the number of parliamentary votes they could muster. This relationship between the interests of the islands and political authority in Britain can be emphasised still further. Political decisions in Britain influenced affairs in the islands, just as wealth and prestige acquired by Caribbean involvement affected Scotland's political landscape. The nature of the political relationship between metropolitan authority and colonial sphere was not simply a question of the London government imposing its will on the colonies. The layers of individual and network connections, and their patronage links, added to the shared beliefs in 'British' ideals like liberty, Protestantism and loyalty to the Crown that have been outlined in the previous chapter.[1] As a result, political events in one part of the British Atlantic world could affect those in another, which, in turn, had implications for the government of the whole. These bonds between Scotland, Britain and the Caribbean survived the rupture in the British Atlantic world in 1776, and provided an element of continuity in imperial relations in the area.

The network associations provided for both the generation and the freer flow of patronage, which was an integral part of eighteenth-century British society. While there were profoundly corrupt elements at work within the British polity, there was no automatic correlation between patronage and underhand activity. As one noted historian has pointed out: 'Every eighteenth-century political actor was fully aware of the distinction between the justifiable and illegitimate uses of "influence", just as they were familiar with the distinction between venality and patronage. Private connection and public duty were not necessarily incompatible.'[2] While Scots' access to patronage was occasionally derided at the time, it was, in an imperial context, of enormous benefit to policy makers. In a world where transatlantic communication involved a delay of at least three months between the sending of a dispatch and the receipt of the reply, even assuming fine weather and an absence of hostile ships, the ability to appoint someone to one's bidding, without frequent consultation, was imperative. In short, patronage was essential to the operation of an extended imperial polity in which the modes of communication were at best extremely slow.[3]

Procuring political office

As Chapter One noted, Lord Bute was the target of a great deal anti-Scottish abuse, but as vitriolic as it may have been, the commentary on Bute's disbursement of patronage was not without foundation. During his period in office, the islands of Dominica, Grenada, St Vincent and Tobago were ceded to Britain, along with East and West Florida and Quebec. In 1763, General Robert Melville was appointed governor of the Ceded Islands. His compatriot General James Grant of Ballindalloch, using his friendship with Sir Harry Erskine as a means of influencing Bute, became governor of East Florida, while West Florida went to George Johnstone on Bute's recommendation. As George III wrote, 'I wish to hear what my D. Friend has thought of decisively for Capt. Johnston. Florida was thought on.'[4] In short, the three new governorships in the Caribbean region were all filled by Scots, at the same time as General James Murray, also a Scot with access to Lord Bute, was confirmed as Quebec's first British civilian governor. In West Florida, Johnstone found among his staff James MacPherson, the author of *Ossian*, who acquired his post as a direct consequence of Bute's intervention.[5]

Bute's brief tenure of office ended in 1763, although his manager in Scotland, his brother James Stuart MacKenzie, survived until 1765. Thereafter, the management of Scotland was entrusted to the lord advocate in Edinburgh. Although direct access to the leading figure in high office had been cut off, Scots still maintained avenues through which patronage could be directed. Bute himself still had parliamentary influence. During the debates over the repeal of the Stamp Act in February 1766, Bute's parliamentary 'interest' included twenty-four of the thirty-nine Scottish MPs who voted, as well as another nineteen English MPs.[6] Other connections, which could be used to gain (or seek to gain) offices in the Caribbean empire, were maintained with the ever-increasing number of Scots MPs.

People seeking assistance, either for themselves or for relatives, frequently approached James Duff, Second Earl of Fife. Lord Fife was MP for Banffshire from 1754 to 1784, and thereafter for Elginshire until 1790. He was something of a political maverick, but by the time of his successful re-election in 1774 he was, in general, a supporter of the government, particularly with regard to Lord North's handling of the crisis in the American colonies.[7] Around this time, his kinsman Patrick Duff of Banff became aware of a number of government vacancies in the West Indies and wrote to Fife asking him to use his influence to procure an office in one of the islands for his son. Fife replied that although competition was fierce, because Duff's son had impressed him on the occasion when they had met, he would ask Lord Dartmouth 'to appoint your son to some proper Office in the Customs when there is any vacancy in any of the West Indian islands.'[8] Fife was also the recipient of requests for patronage from the West Indies themselves. Charles Baird was one the Scottish community in Antigua visited by Janet Schaw in December 1774. He was comptroller of customs at St John's, and a particularly persistent seeker of Fife's support. At least four times between December 1774 and March 1775, Baird wrote to Fife pointing out the current vacancies for collectors of customs in Caribbean islands. Unfortunately for Baird, Fife showed far less inclination to help him as he did his kinsman Duff.[9]

If Bute had been vilified as a focus for favours in the 1760s, and men like Lord Fife had often been recipients of requests for patronage, the key figure from the 1780s until the turn of the century was Henry Dundas. Dundas came from a well-established legal family in Scotland, and he qualified as an advocate in 1763. He entered Parliament in 1774, and a year later was appointed lord advocate. His influence over patronage in Scotland was cemented when, in 1779, he became sole keeper of the Signet in Scotland. His pragmatism enabled him to serve in Lord North's government, and then to continue as lord advocate under Rockingham and then Lord Shelburne in 1782. Spurned during the Fox–North coalition in 1783, he was restored with the accession of William Pitt the Younger later that year. Dundas provided Pitt with unstinting support during the first few troubled months of his administration, and became one of the prime minister's most trusted colleagues. From the middle of the 1780s, Dundas's hold over Scottish patronage, as well as his extraordinary influence in the running of the empire, allowed him to exert an ever-increasing degree of control over politics in Scotland. By 1790, he had the firm backing of thirty-two of the forty-five MPs in Scotland, and the general support of another seven.[10]

Dundas's position in Scotland provided an important basis for his continuing imperial influence. It was remarked at the time, 'Scotland and India Dundas ruled and fed the one with the other'.[11] Historical emphasis on Dundas's involvement with India, dating from his appointment to the Board of Control in 1784, has tended to overshadow his influence in the rest of the empire. By the time of his apogee in the early 1790s, his domination of Scottish politics, as overseen by his nephew Robert Dundas, was tied into his imperial influence at the Board of Control and, between 1791 and 1794, his tenure as Home Secretary. This latter post gave him control over the colonies, and gave him great leverage in the West Indies. Yet even before this time, so pervasive was his role in government, and so important was he to Pitt, that he influenced the direction of patronage.[12] More than any other political figure of the century, Dundas represented the connections between Scotland, Britain and the empire. Although the older managers of Scotland had access to Indian patronage, their sphere of influence was never so extensive as that of Dundas. And Bute, although enormously powerful, lacked Dundas's longevity.

Dundas's power and 'interest' were perceived to be such that he attracted requests for patronage for offices at all levels of colonial government. In 1790, he received a letter from William Armstrong of Basseterre in St Kitts informing him that the collector of customs at Basseterre was seriously ill. Armstrong wrote, 'would I be so fortunate as to interest you in my behalf for his Succession it would make me extremely happy and truely grateful.' As predicted, the poor man passed away, but was replaced by a Mr Barkley, much to Armstrong's disgust. He railed against the iniquities of gubernatorial patronage and against Barkley, 'who from his understanding the Governor perfectly, generally succeeds to every vacancy when the temporary gift is in his power – this surprises many, as Mr. Barkley whose consequence and Abilitys are by no means above mediocrity should constantly be the first in every promotion.'[13]

That a man of apparently inferior ability was engaged ahead of Armstrong does not mean that Dundas's influence was less than that of the governor, although colonial governors did control the distribution of some patronage in the islands. The explanation lies in the problem of communication. A mere seventeen days had passed between Armstrong's letter requesting assistance and the second one damning Barkley's appointment. In these circumstances, it is unlikely that Dundas would even have known the job was likely to be vacant, before it had been filled again. This particular episode demonstrates clearly how widely patronage was sought and employed in the colonies. Armstrong was certainly undaunted by the experience and continued to seek patronage. By 1800 he planned to return home. Accordingly, he wrote to Thomas Coutts, an influential Scottish banker in the Strand, London, and a friend of the Erskine family into which Armstrong had married. Coutts, considering that he was not best placed to help, directed his request to Dundas in November 1800. Here the ways in which kinship connections provided access to high-level patronage can be seen in operation. Nor was this an isolated case. Earlier, in 1794, William Gloag of Edinburgh had asked Dundas to use what influence he had to provide his brother-in-law, Philip Wilson, with the secretaryship of Grenada or, failing that, a customs post in either Grenada or St Vincent.[14]

Dundas's most significant interventions were in the appointment of governors in the islands, and here too the use of kinship connections is evident. What is also significant is the fact that some of the requests for assistance came before Dundas had responsibility for the colonies. In 1788, Governor James Seton of St Vincent wrote to Dundas asking him to bring about an increase in his pension, so as not to leave his family 'without one farthing'. The two men had discussed this very matter the last time they had seen each other.[15] Seton remained in St Vincent until after the insurrection in 1795, at which time he applied to the Duke of Portland for permission to return home. Portland had replaced Dundas as Home Secretary, but as Seton was unacquainted with him, he asked Dundas to intervene as the 'letter will be more likely to have the desired effect when seconded by a friend with whom I have long had the pleasure of being acquainted.'[16]

Dundas's influence also played a key part in furthering the careers of Scots resident in the West Indies, in addition to those appointed to go there. In October 1766, one of the thirteen Scots elected to the new assembly in Grenada was Ninian Home. He was also nominated the first speaker. Thereafter, Home's political career in the island developed quickly. He became a member of the council before being appointed an assistant judge in 1784. This position was described by the Home's brother, George, as 'rather honourable than profitable', and he went on to say that '[t]here are always three or four of the Principal People in the Island named Assistant Judges who occasionally lend their aid to the Chief Judge.'[17]

Not content with being merely one of the 'Principal People', Ninian Home called on Henry Dundas for help to obtain an official position in government. He particularly had his eye on the governorship of Dominica, to succeed Governor Orde.[18] That honour evaded him, which did not particularly surprise his brother. Indeed, George Home found this desire for office rather frivolous, especially as Ninian was £5,000 in debt to Joseph Smith, who was in turn bound to Sir James Cockburn, a West India merchant and former MP for the Linlithgow Burghs.

Although in 1786 George Home was not optimistic about Ninian's chances of acquiring a more prestigious office, he sought nonetheless to encourage Dundas to bear his brother in mind. Dundas had already secured the Berwickshire constituency for Patrick Home, who held the seat between 1784 and 1796. As an ally of Dundas, Patrick Home was invited to partake of 'burgundy and blasphemy' at parties at Dundas's house near Wimbledon Common. On one such occasion, in March 1787, Patrick Home hoped to speak with Dundas on the subject of Ninian's promotion, but as it was to be a large party, he was uncertain whether an opportunity would present itself.[19] The particular link between Dundas and the Homes is even more evident in letter in March 1792 in which George Home remarked to Dundas, 'I had the pleasure of seeing you at Denira and renewed the application for my brother in case of a vacancy in the Government of Grenada.' Indeed, George Home and Henry Dundas had been acquainted since at the least the middle of the 1770s. Both were lawyers by profession, and both became members of Edinburgh's Poker Club, founded originally in 1762 by leading literati to stoke the flames of agitation for a Scottish militia, and later a meeting place for the Edinburgh elite.[20]

Ninian Home was appointed lieutenant-governor of Grenada to replace Edward Mathews in October 1792. Dundas had been impressed not just by him, however. George Home, a clerk of session, was approached by the lord advocate, Robert Dundas, in December 1792 with the offer of undertaking the internal management of Scottish politics. In this role, Home would have been required 'to correspond with the friends of the Government in different quarters of the Country and with Mr. Dundas in London'. Home declined the offer to be *sous ministre*, citing age, ill health, other engagements and, most tellingly, a determination not to 'risk the disgrace of undertaking what I cannot be sure of executing well'.[21] Whether Dundas expected George Home to accept as an exchange for the promotion of Ninian Home is a matter for speculation. Nevertheless, Ninian's elevation to the lieutenant-governorship clearly took place within the context of a long-standing and intimately connected legal and political network centred in Enlightenment Edinburgh.

Appeals to Dundas's better nature continued to come from individuals who had already reached the upper echelons of colonial government, even after Dundas became secretary of state for war and responsibility for the colonies had passed to the Duke of Portland in July 1794. Indeed, Dundas was still widely perceived as being able to influence decisions relating to the Caribbean: in the five months after this change, he received seven requests for appointments in the West Indies. Even some time later, the representations from well-connected individuals continued to flood in, despite Dundas telling some petitioners to direct their requests to Portland.[22]

In 1795, William Lindsay, lieutenant-governor of Tobago, appealed to Dundas for assistance. At the time of the correspondence between the two, the Revolutionary War with France was raging with a particular and subversive intensity in the West Indies. The great uncertainty engendered by France's promotion of the revolution in the French islands, and the sponsorship of the insurrection then current in Grenada, had clearly affected Governor Lindsay. He believed that if his time were up in Tobago, even he, as a former colonial governor, would need some assistance in furthering his career. He wrote,

> If . . . Tobago be restored to the French, I should be very much obliged to you if you would have the goodness to use your influence in preventing my being left unprovided for . . . I wish most ardently to continue exerting myself for the Public Service in however distant a region, & as you have been so kind as to protect me once in a manner I shall never forget, I cannot help but hoping & requesting that you will not allow me to be put by.[23]

By May 1795, Lindsay's panic appeared to have abated slightly, and, having returned to Tobago from Barbados, he sought to promote the rights of British inhabitants, many of whom were Scots, to over-run the estates owned by French planters. He also made a point of noting that he had found employment for a clergyman, with a four-fold increase in his salary, when it became clear that the clergyman had a connection with Dundas. It seems likely that Lindsay was trying to return the favour with Dundas, as well as ensuring that Dundas would be supportive of any future requests for patronage.[24]

Nor was Lindsay the only man to seek Dundas's help after 1794. As late as 1799, Dundas acted as a conduit between his Scottish correspondents and William Pitt. In 1798, Dundas informed Pitt that 'Mr. Geo. Home is anxious that Mr. Byles be confirmed in the Office of Resident Commissary of Grenada'.[25] Home was a friend of Dundas, while Mather Byles was Home's attorney in Grenada. A few days after this, Dundas sent Pitt another memorandum, this time enclosing a letter from Mr Hepburn in St Vincent (via Mr Elder, lord provost of Edinburgh) 'soliciting either the office of Comptroller or Searcher in that Island'. Clearly, Hepburn had been a persistent agitator for the position, as Dundas noted, 'this application has been renewed, at different times, for these five years.'[26]

Requests also came from one of the most powerful governors in the empire. Alexander Lindsay, Sixth Earl of Balcarres, governor of Jamaica, wrote to Dundas in January 1798 asking that his tenure be extended. He remained in Jamaica until 1801. He wrote again in April 1799, this time 'very warmly soliciting you for the Situation of a writer to Bengal for my second son Charles Lindsay.' Three members of the Lindsay family were employed in the service of the East India Company in the late eighteenth century.[27] Considerable as their presence was in India, the Lindsays were especially well represented in the Caribbean in the 1790s. As well as Alexander in Jamaica and William in Tobago, Balcarres's brother, Colin Lindsay, suppressed the Grenada insurrection in 1795 before committing suicide.[28]

The promotion of Home to lieutenant-governor and the approaches by William Lindsay, Lord Balcarres and others are important indications of the role played by patronage in the governance of the empire, and of Dundas's pivotal place within it. It is certainly the case that the patronage system favoured the well placed and well connected. Yet it does not necessarily follow that those who were promoted were unworthy. A number of those Scots who attempted to use connections with Dundas or Lord Fife found their efforts thwarted, sometimes by competition, sometimes by timing and sometimes by lack of ability. While George Home's discussions over with Dundas at Dunira gave his brother an edge over other candidates for preferment in Grenada, Ninian Home's years of experience in the island and his sound reputation there probably weighed heavily with Dundas. He was ultimately responsible for the colonies; it seems improbable that he would appoint someone to such a senior position in so important an island simply because a candidate's brother had asked. The patronage connection was important for Dundas because it enabled him to appoint someone well known to him, and someone on whom he could rely, in order to circumvent the problems of transatlantic communication.

The need of legislators to employ patronage was mirrored by the desire of others to receive it. This was particularly the case for Scots, whose long-established patronage networks made available to the empire a store of young, able individuals who were willing to take a chance on life in the tropics in return for the prospect of advancement.

The metropolitan–colonial nexus

Despite the rupture in Greater Britain caused by American independence, the strength of the connections between Britain and its colonies in the Caribbean remained. As the preceding sections have shown, this nexus was maintained through individual connections and by common beliefs. Just as individuals acting through networks were the distributors and recipients of patronage, so too did they bind the empire. By holding land, wealth or status in both the metropole and the colonies, these people ensured that what took place in Scotland could influence events in the Caribbean. More significantly, perhaps, the fact that their West Indian enterprises could also influence the domestic political map in Scotland demonstrates a true symbiosis in the relationship.

One of the most blatant attempts to link a vote in Scotland with a Caribbean boon was made in 1795. Patrick Cruickshank of Stracathro, a landowner in St Vincent, had failed to secure the purchase of a tract of land in St George's parish in the island, despite having offered to pay £2,000 directly to the Treasury in 1793. Cruickshank was plainly aggrieved by this. He believed that his voting in accordance with Dundas's wishes at the previous three elections in the county of Forfarshire entitled him to succeed in his application. Consequently, he promised his vote to Sir David Carnegie rather than to Dundas's candidate, the sitting MP, David Scott, who was an influential figure in the East India Company. Cruickshank commented that it was with the 'greatest reluctance' that he 'went against [his] former friends', and he offered a solution to the impasse. If he was sent to St Vincent as lieutenant-governor, or as commissioner of the sale of undisposed lands, he would 'set out as soon as Necessary and will send home my Brother James Cruickshank of Langley Park to vote for Mr. Scott he is now in St. Vincent.' If not, he warned, he would continue to vote for Carnegie. Moreover, he pointed out that, as he had just purchased Alexander Turnbull's land, it was 'in [his] power to strike him off the Roll or continue him as I please next Michaelmas head count', meaning that he effectively controlled two votes. In the context of the pre-1832 Scottish electoral system, a four-vote swing could determine the outcome of a county election.[29]

Although his remarkable piece of electoral blackmail failed ultimately to encourage Dundas to intervene on Cruickshank's behalf, it demonstrates the perception that what did, or did not, happen in the Caribbean (in this instance a land deal and a piece of self-promotion) had ramifications for events in Scotland. The fact that Carnegie won the election in 1796 suggests that Cruickshank was true to his threat and voted against Dundas's wishes.

One of the most striking examples of one family's emergence in British politics, as a result of its interconnected Scottish and Caribbean interests, was that of the Baillie family of Dochfour, just south-west of Inverness. James Baillie was the first of the family to enter Parliament, as MP for Horsham in Surrey in 1792. At the time he was also a prominent West India merchant in London, and agent for the island of Grenada.[30] His brother Evan also entered Westminster politics, as did two of Evan's sons, Peter and James Evan. The engineered election of Peter for the Inverness Burghs in 1807 offers a glimpse of the intertwining of Scottish and Caribbean political interests.

Evan, like James, was born in Inverness, and ventured to the West Indies before settling in Bristol. From the 1780s, he became increasingly involved in the city's mercantile and political elite, serving in turn as councilman in 1785, as sheriff in 1786 and 1787 and ultimately as the one of the city's two MPs between 1802 and 1812. As he developed his standing in south-western England, using his wealth and status as a prominent West India merchant, he also consolidated his interests in the north of Scotland. In 1798, his eldest brother, Alexander, passed away, and with James Baillie having died in 1793, Evan inherited the family estate at Dochfour. During the first decade of the nineteenth century, Evan Baillie paid ever more attention to the affairs of the Scottish estate, and invested both in its expansion and in other ventures. A concomitant of this was the interest which Evan's eldest son, Peter, took in the estate. While Evan had been born and raised in Inverness, Peter had been born in St Vincent and brought up in Bristol. Following his return from his grand tour, he became a partner in his father's merchant house and moved easily among the elite in Bristol. In 1806 he was sent north, to oversee the Dochfour estate, and to prepare the ground for the forthcoming election. In 1807, he became the MP for the Inverness Burghs, while his father remained MP for Bristol.

His acquisition of the seat owed much to his family's centuries-old residence in the burgh, and probably to its increased standing and wealth. But the actual process of election was carried through a local network. In securing the election in 1807, Baillie had to win over the freeholders of the towns of Inverness, Fortrose, Forres and Nairn, which comprised the Inverness Burghs constituency. To do so, he used key figures in the four towns. Evan Baillie's cousin, James Grant of Bught, was provost of Inverness, and had been a partner of both Peter and Evan Baillie in the Inverness Thread Factory since 1805. As a result of Grant's influence, Inverness Council was brought into line. In Fortrose, the Baillies relied on Sir Alexander Munro, brother of the former MP. Like the Baillies, he had used imperial wealth (his was derived from India) to purchase land in England, where he lived at Novar House near Cheltenham. And like the Baillies, Munro had retained interests in the north of Scotland; he continued to be an influential member of the Fortrose Council until after the 1807 election. Henry Dundas, by this time Lord Melville, was not enthusiastic about Baillie's candidature, and decreed that it was not to be encouraged. In the event, though, Melville's opposition proved to be insufficient, as did the opposition of George Cumming, backed by the Nairn and Forres burghs, and Baillie was duly elected, on Fortrose's casting vote, on 30 May 1807.[31]

The network had not yet completed its work, however, for the next councils had to be voted by the existing members. In the summer of 1807, shortly after Baillie's successful election, the key figures who had assisted in the campaign made arrangements to consolidate his still slightly precarious position. Sir Alexander Munro assured Baillie that following his departure 'for the North' from London in June 1807, 'I will use all my endeavours to strengthen and promote your Interest in the Boroughs of Inverness and Fortrose'. More particularly, he counselled that if in Fortrose 'there are any inimical to your interest you must turn them out of the Council . . . and subscribe such of your own friends as you can depend on.' Munro's concern was fuelled by his impending departure from the council and by the need to ensure Baillie's election to it as his replacement. In order to do this he advised Baillie (who had returned to Bristol) to contact his factor, George Munro, who would be better placed to offer advice.[32]

On his arrival in Fortrose, Munro went about winning over the doubters by entertaining all the magistrates and council of the town: 'I made them happy and merry as far as the help of Sherry Wine, Madeira, Port, Claret, Hock, Burgandy Champagne, Constancia, and other sweet wines could make me: to wash down Turtle & Venison &c. &c. in short they confirmed their attachment to me, and I believe they will do everything in the Compass of their power, that I can wish or desire.' Just as he recounted this tale of electoral hospitality to Peter Baillie's cousin James in London, he implied that the situation had been prepared in Fortrose; all that remained was the arrival of the candidate. At Michaelmas 1807 Baillie was duly appointed to the Fortrose Council, the control of which was delivered to him by Munro.[33]

On the same day as Munro corresponded with James Baillie, James Grant wrote to Peter Baillie in Bristol, confirming that the situation in Inverness was also being secured. He wrote, 'I think I have arranged our Town Politicks for the coming year. Mr. Gilzean has agreed to second me and there will be other changes which will strengthen our Interest.' It is also apparent from Grant's letter that there was collusion not only between Baillie and his friends in the north, but also among his friends, as Grant made reference to the plan being fixed by Munro and the Fortrose Council.[34]

The efforts of these men were not in vain. While such shameless vote-rigging was not at all uncommon in their political world, it has a particular resonance here. For these events, in one of the constituencies furthest from Westminster, secured, using local and kinship ties, the election of a Bristol merchant, with strong West Indian mercantile and proprietorial connections, to a House of Commons that had just overseen the abolition of the slave trade. Battle was still to be joined over the abolition of enslavement itself, however, and these votes secured the election of another member of the West India interest, from a family which clearly supported its retention.

Influencing the imperial polity

The West India lobby in London became increasingly well organised during the later eighteenth century, largely as a response to the challenges facing the West Indies in the era of the American Revolution.[35] Within this group were those influential planters and merchants resident in Britain who comprised the West India Committee. Many of these individuals were MPs and some were the agents for colonial territories. The colonial agents were representatives of the islands and acted as conduits for the flow of information between metropole and colony, and furthered the ambitions of the islands at Westminster, either jointly or severally. For example, in 1792 James Baillie, as agent for Grenada, along with Alexander Campbell (himself a former agent and Baillie's neighbour in Grenada), visited Henry Dundas and was informed that the government planned to withdraw one of the regiments from the garrison. As a result, a meeting of sixteen prominent Grenadians chaired by Campbell was convened at the London Tavern. The minutes recorded that 'Mr Baillie ... be requested to draw up a

Memorial to be presented to the Rt. Honble. Henry Dundas'.[36] Dundas thus acted not only as a kind of imperial employment agency. He was also an access point to the highest levels of government for people with specific concerns.

A few months before the Grenadians discovered the proposed troop cuts, Dundas found himself at the centre of a battle over the Caribbean islands' monopoly on sugar production. On one side were those seeking a reduction in sugar prices and the right to produce sugar outside the West Indies. On the other side were the West Indians, who lobbied hard for the maintenance of the 'implied compact' between the islands and the British government for 'a natural monopoly'. The committee formed to press for an end to the monopoly railed against the 'present extravagant and oppressively high price of sugar'; it was, they believed, 'very injurious, and a very extensive public grievance'.[37] The planters and merchants responded vigorously. They not only cited the 'compact' between Britain and the colonies, but also conflated this dispute with that against the abolition of enslavement, and argued that those campaigning against them sought to dictate to the colonists and 'to excite a spirit of insurrection among their labourers'. This, they asserted, would 'produce an injury to the Colonies, which must necessarily react upon the Mother Country.'[38]

The dispute drew in the directors of the East India Company, who wanted to export sugar from India, and sugar brokers. It was the colonial agents, however, who launched the most powerful salvo of the dispute. Their memorial outlined the long relationship between the islands and Britain, as the planters and merchants had done, but they went further. They implied that to breach the compact in this way would undermine the whole fabric of the imperial relationship: 'this measure, if carried into effect, cannot fail to excite the greatest alarms in the minds of His Majesty's Subjects resident in the West India Colonies, as it directly militates against a long succession of Acts of Parliament for near a century and a half past; and must entirely destroy the Confidence which the West India Colonies have hitherto reposed on the Faith and Protection of Great Britain.'[39]

That the sugar monopoly remained intact does not necessarily mean that the agents were able to scare the government into compliance with their wishes, but their implied threat of independence must have caused some concern in London. Once more James Baillie was involved, along with the agents Stephen Fuller (Jamaica), John Brathwaite (Barbados), Charles Thomson (St Kitts), William Hutchinson (Antigua) and Mr Knox. The influence of the agents was allied to that of the MPs and those attached to them in two other key areas of campaigning.

The Exchequer loans

By the 1790s, merchants had granted enormous levels of credit to the planters and traders in the Caribbean islands. There was a bubble of confidence surrounding these large-scale investments that was burst spectacularly by the convulsions occasioned by the outbreak of war with revolutionary France. The insurrections in the Windward Islands, as petitioners to the House of Commons were swift to point out, were inspired by their French enemies, and had caused devastation to parts of the islands. This had profound implications for the export of crops and the remittance of debts. The razing of estates not only destroyed the planters' assets, but also adversely affected mercantile companies, which lost their trade goods and found their debtors destitute.[40]

Scottish-owned firms like Alexander Houstoun & Co. of Glasgow and George Baillie & Co. of London had invested heavily in the Windward Islands. Houstoun & Co., for example, were owed £324,118 from Grenada alone.[41] George Baillie & Co. (formerly James Baillie & Co.) carried similarly huge debts. The crisis in West Indian credit left these and other firms in such dire straits after 1795 that the acquisition of public money appeared to be the only solution. Through Henry Dundas, George Baillie was introduced to William Pitt, who was initially unprepared to grant Exchequer bills. Baillie, however, was able to generate considerable support for his application on behalf of the West India merchants from Liverpool and Bristol, where his cousin Evan was a prominent merchant and politician. He was also able to draw on the considerable legacy of his deceased cousin, James Baillie, whose company he had taken over.

On 11 June 1795, a petition from the merchants trading to St Vincent and Grenada was presented to Parliament and was referred to a House of Commons committee and to Henry Dundas. The committee found that the problems caused by the loss of crop in 1795 and the investment required to rebuild the plantations necessitated financial assistance from the government. On 16 June, the Chancellor of the Exchequer and Dundas were instructed to prepare a bill to allow the disposal of not more the £1.5 million to the Grenada and St Vincent merchants. The bill received its royal assent on 27 June 1795. Of the £1.5 million, George Baillie & Co. received £250,000 and Alexander Houstoun & Co. collected £170,000 as a result of this first Act, and a further £70,000 in 1797.[42] Allocations on this scale indicate the importance of these firms, and also the influence their principal shareholders could wield. Dundas certainly played a role in introducing the merchants to Pitt, as Baillie acknowledged: 'I take the liberty of inclosing for your perusal copy of a letter I had this day the Honor of adressing to Mr. Pitt on the subject of the Exchequer Loan, and altho' the business lay principally in the department of the Chancellor of the Exchequer, we consider ourselves indebted to you as being the promoter and supporter of it, and to your friendly interference we all attribute, entirely, our success.'[43]

There case was strengthened by the presence of William Johnstone Pulteney as a commissioner in the Exchequer Loan Office. Through a judicious marriage into the Pulteney family in 1760, William Johnstone had become one of the richest commoners in Britain. By the time of the loans he was MP for Shrewsbury, having been MP for Cromartyshire in northern Scotland between 1768 and 1774.[44] Pulteney's family, the Johnstones, originated in south-west Scotland, and had a number of West Indian interests: Pulteney owned the Port Royal estate in Grenada and, after 1799, the Bon Accord estate in Tobago.[45] His elder brother, Alexander, had purchased the Baccaye estate in Grenada in 1766, which he renamed Westerhall. By 1794, Pulteney was a trustee of the estate, which was also indebted to him. In August 1795, in the wake of the insurrection which had caused considerable damage to Westerhall, Pulteney was of the opinion that Lady Johnstone would be able to raise 'the sum she wants', because the commissioners were 'authorised by the Act of Parliament to Lend on Landed property'. Pulteney's faith in his fellow commissioners was not misplaced: £10,000 was laid out in government loans for the reestablishment of Westerhall.[46]

Nor was this the only occasion that Scots MPs with West Indian interests found themselves on important British committees considering Caribbean business, and in particular the concerns of the planters of Grenada and St Vincent. In 1803, the chairman of the parliamentary committee investigating the claims of those planters for financial relief was Evan Baillie, himself a St Vincent planter, trustee of a Grenadian estate and cousin of one of the principal lobbyists for the 1795 Exchequer loans.

Houstoun & Co., which also benefited enormously from the loans, were equally well represented in Parliament. William McDowall, one of the principal shareholders in Houstoun & Co., was MP for the Glasgow Burghs at the time of the credit crisis. Furthermore, McDowall's brother, his brother-in-law and a number of influential friends were also MPs at the time. As a result, not only was McDowall extremely wealthy; he was also one of the most important figures in Scottish politics, perhaps second only to Dundas himself and, significantly, a loyal supporter of Pitt.[47] Almost inevitably, he had maintained links with Dundas over a number of years. In the run-up to the 1790 election, so closely aligned were they that Dundas consulted

McDowall over the suitability of candidates. On one occasion, Dundas was prepared to allow McDowall to select the candidate, noting only that his choice, Mr Blair, would be 'a proper person' because he was 'entirely attached to our Political Principles'.[48] At the time of the loan there were thirteen or fourteen other Scots MPs, in addition to Henry Dundas, William McDowall and William Pulteney, not all of whom represented Scottish constituencies, with West Indian connections of one kind or another.

The successful lobbying of Parliament for the original Exchequer loans proved to be insufficient to solve the long-term problems of the islands. It soon became apparent that the crisis was considerably deeper than was first thought. Mather Byles wrote to George Home in November 1796 to inform him that it would take £5,000 sterling to re-establish Waltham, £2,000 more than originally planned. Around the same time, on 16 December, the planters and merchants of both St Vincent and Grenada petitioned the Commons for more time to repay the loans. A committee of the whole House recommended that an additional £600,000 be made available to the petitioners. Of this sum, the stricken estate of Waltham received £6,000, which was used to repay its debt to the merchants Simond & Hankey.[49] Nevertheless, in December 1798 and 1799, the petitioners again made it clear that they would be unable to fulfil their obligations to pay on 5 January the following year. Again and again payments were deferred. The loan to George Home for Waltham estate was finally repaid in 1804.[50] By the end of 1799, Houstoun & Co. had managed to repay less than half of the interest on their loans and only a fraction of the capital sum. Having been granted an initial loan of £170,000, the firm now owed the government £265,008. In February 1800, William McDowall sought recourse in yet another petition, in which he outlined the calamitous situation in the islands that had led to the present crisis, which had been deepened by the slump in the market for West Indian produce, and he asked for more time to repay the loan.[51] In making his case, McDowall produced letters from the treasurer of the Bank of Scotland (the governor of which was Henry Dundas), the cashier of the Royal Bank of Scotland, and the chairman and secretary of the Glasgow Chamber of Commerce, all of whom attested to the respectability of Houstoun & Co. and pointed out the deleterious consequences of the failure of the House: 'the Directors are humbly of the Opinion, that any Embarrassment in the Affairs of a Company of such respectability would be attended with Consequences prejudicial to the Commercial Credit of the Country; and that, therefore, the Intervention of the Government for its Support... appears to them to be a Measure of Public Utility.'[52]

The support from the Edinburgh banks represented not only recognition of the importance of the firm. Key partners in Houstoun & Co. also maintained personal connections with the banks: Alexander Houstoun was a director of the Bank of Scotland, while William McDowall was deputy-governor of the British Linen Bank in Edinburgh.[53] The select committee which reviewed the request also dealt with the joint pleas of the executors of Charles Ashwell and William Johnston, who owed respectively £16,000 and £10,000. All three petitions were considered minutely by the committee, then twice by a committee of the whole House, before a bill was moved and finally enacted on 28 July 1800.[54]

The anti-abolition campaign

If the acquisition of Exchequer loans and the continual deferment of repayments were cases of prominent lobbying of Parliament by West India Scots, during the controversy surrounding the abolition of the slave trade Scots acted rather less publicly in support of their West India colleagues. The great wealth of the West Indies had been generated by the export of agricultural commodities whose production was particularly labour-intensive. Towards the end of the eighteenth century this seemingly inexhaustible labour supply was threatened, as the planters saw it, by misguided and malevolent interests in Britain bent on the destruction of the West Indies, and ultimately on the undermining of the basis of British wealth. As the campaign for the abolition of the trade gathered pace in Britain, Parliament was inundated with petitions advocating abolition. Within this campaign, a number of Scots were prominent figures. Across Scotland, petitions calling for abolition were drawn up, indicating widespread popular opposition to the institution of enslavement, even in areas where West Indian opportunities had provided employment and wealth.[55] But those Scots who benefited from enslavement were swift to respond in kind. Whether these petitions came from the mayor, burgess and commonality of Bristol, the Birmingham manufacturers or one of the island agents like Stephen Fuller of Jamaica, they conformed to a standard template. They all outlined the devastating effects of abolition for their way of life (whatever form it took), as well as stating that the trade was vital for the very survival of the islands and, indeed, for British trade and manufacturing. The petitions frequently remarked on the consequences for domestic British employment if the trade were abolished. They argued that abolition 'would not only be ruinous ... to the Petitioners ... but the mischief would extend most widely, throwing many Hundreds of Common Labouring People ... wholly out of Employment, and of course reducing them to the Necessity of emigrating to Foreign Countries.'[56]

The anti-abolition campaign forged an unholy alliance between the sugar producers of the West Indies and the sugar refiners in Britain. Previously those groups had been diametrically opposed to each other, as the one tried to maintain the monopoly and price of the sugar supply, while the other sought to open the trade and lower costs. Yet when faced with the prospect of a serious decline in sugar supplies, if not their complete cessation, the two groups were able to put aside their differences and co-operate against what they perceived to be a common enemy.[57]

Liverpool, as Britain's principal slave trade port, presented numerous petitions to Parliament, and again the petitioners represented a number of trades. In May 1789, for example, petitions were received from merchants trading to Africa, from manufacturers of iron, copper, brass and lead, from the sailmakers, joiners, shipwrights, ropemakers, coopers, gunmakers, blockmakers and bakers of Liverpool.[58] Bristol, too, showered the Palace of Westminster with petitions, demonstrating the importance of the slave trade as the general underpinning of the entire Atlantic mercantile community. What is slightly surprising, then, is the relative infrequency of petitions from Scotland. Scots in the islands, and those with strong links there, were quite open about opposing abolition, and did not attempt to hide their practices from those at home. Indeed, Alexander Rose of Jamaica wrote to John MacIntosh in Inverness in 1792 saying, 'we hope this Bill will be lost in the middle passage & never come safe into port'. Despite concerns about abolition, though, Rose continued in his unpleasantly sarcastic style, 'we are as yet in a state of tranquility respecting our Black Planters – the word slave being abolished, as obnoxious to the nice feelings of the modern votaries of transatlantic humanity'.[59]

The Glasgow merchants and planters petitioned Parliament in 1789, but otherwise appear to have left that job to their counterparts in Liverpool or Bristol in the 1790s.[60] There were a number of reasons for this. Firstly, and perhaps most obviously, the slave trade was never as essential a feature of the economy in Glasgow as it was in Bristol and, particularly, in Liverpool. So while there were Caribbean planters and merchants in Glasgow who feared the consequences of abolition, there was not a widespread fear of ruin for a series of ship manufacturers and suppliers, or for manufacturers of goods for Africa in the city. The second explanation is organisational. West India merchants and planters in Glasgow had no formal organisation until 1807, when the West India Association was founded in the city.[61] That is not to say that they had no communication with each other, but their meetings were on a more *ad hoc* basis through a series of fora. One of the meetings resulted in the petition to Parliament, while James McDowall chaired at least one other meeting in February 1795.[62] Most of the merchants were acquainted with each other through membership of either the Glasgow Chamber of Commerce, which was founded in 1783, or one of the many clubs in the city.[63]

In the later part of the eighteenth century there was a proliferation of gentlemen's clubs in Glasgow that, as well as providing a social distraction, fostered contacts between merchants, politicians and city notables. Most of the leading West India merchants in Glasgow were members of the Gaelic Society of Glasgow, which was less concerned with the promotion of Gaelic than in securing the interests of its influential members.[64] Some of the clubs had been founded in the heyday of the tobacco ascendency, but after the collapse of the Chesapeake trade after American independence, and as merchants diversified their operations into the Caribbean, the clubs increasingly became bastions of the sugar aristocracy. Among the members of the Hodge Podge Club were the merchants William Mure, William McDowall, Robert Houstoun Rae, Henry Glassford, Andrew Buchanan, the Grenadian planter John Graham of Dougalston and the Jamaica merchant and planter Charles Stirling. Stirling and his business partner, John Gordon, were central figures in the Tory party. Leading Tories would gather to meet in their offices, where they would decide upon the suitability of parliamentary candidates. As a result of their patronage of Alexander Campbell of Blythswood, the merchants 'derived through the great Parliamentary influence of that gentleman, a reciprocal power in matters connected with the Government and its patronage.'[65] Thus, men in Glasgow with mercantile and planting concerns in the Caribbean established social and political networks in Glasgow in ways that allowed them to advance their specific interests in London.

Although these clubs, and contacts created in them, were not ostensibly political, nor were they wholly concerned with the West Indies, they promoted patronage connections between individuals. And these patronage connections, tied into broader networks in Britain and the West Indies, created more conduits through which Scots with Caribbean links could articulate their concerns, and largely obviated the need for a specific Glaswegian, or Scottish, group.

Most Scots seem to have raised their concerns through the media of island agents or lobby groups in the key English cities. They were certainly present in the commercial and political elites of slaving ports like Liverpool and Bristol, and were involved in lobbying there. In Liverpool, Scots agitated against the abolition of the slave trade: in June 1788 Archibald Dalzel (whose brother Andrew was professor of classics at the University of Edinburgh and a prominent abolitionist) was one of five men deputed to petition Parliament by the Committee of the Liverpool African Merchants. He went on to become governor of Cape Coast Castle and author of the avowedly pro-slavery *The history of Dahomey* (1793).[66] In Bristol, a group of merchants including the prominent Anglo-Scots Evan Baillie and John Gordon met in April 1789 and voted to defend the trade 'on which the welfare of the West India islands and the commerce and revenue of the kingdom so essentially depend', and, consequently, sent petitions to Parliament.[67] A few weeks later, the merchants met again and determined to establish a fund 'for the expences which will attend the opposition to the Abolition of the Slave Trade.' The levy was set at 6*d* per hogshead and puncheon on 'our imports with this port from the Sugar Islands from the 24 April 1789 to the 24 April 1790.' In this year, probably somewhere over 20,000 hogsheads of sugar were imported to Bristol by seventy-six merchants.[68]

Some years later, while the battle over abolition still raged, Evan Baillie expressed surprise at the 'phrenzy that has seized all parties on the subject', and then proceeded to add to it by commenting 'how feeble our attempts have been to oppose the abolition of the Slave Trade' and articulating his fear for 'a most fatal stab to the West India credit as it renders all security on Estates highly precarious, having no promise of engagement to prevent any fanatical Minister from Sanctioning even a measure of emancipation.'[69]

Similarly, a number of Scottish-based West India concerns maintained tied to figures in London. Donald Malcolm of Poltalloch, whose family had amassed a considerable fortune from its plantations in Jamaica, paid subscriptions to the 'Merchants of London' for the specific purpose of opposing the Slave Bill in 1790. Although the money came through Malcolm's Glasgow agent, the actual lobbying was done through a London organisation.[70]

Sir Alexander Grant of Dalvey, an important London merchant, acted as an agent for the various branches of the extended Grant family, including Grant of Monymusk and Grant of Grant. These families continued to exploit enslaved labour, and, although Grant of Dalvey had been dead for many years, his former company's campaigning against abolition redounded to their benefit. The new proprietors of the Bance Island factory, John and Alexander Anderson, were the nephews of Grant's partner, Richard Oswald. In May 1798, they petitioned Parliament against the bills before the House of Commons for the abolition of the African trade. Their particular concern was with Bance Island, a slave fort in the mouth of the Sierra Leone River. It had been purchased by Grant, Oswald & Co. in 1748, and, according to the petitions, had required not only a substantial initial investment but also another £20,000 injected in 1794 to repair the damage caused by a Franco-American attack. They argued, furthermore, that the right of the company to trade in slaves as recompense for its initial expense was enshrined in an Act of Parliament that allowed the original owners and their heirs to 'be at Liberty to continue in the quiet possession of the said Island, Fort and Buildings thereon.'[71]

Even a decade after full emancipation, the merchants of Glasgow were sufficiently interested in the West Indies to petition Parliament for a preferential duty in favour of British West Indian sugar. The terms in which they did so paid little attention to a moral imperative but made much of the 'sacrifices' they had made for abolition. These sacrifices, they argued, were 'useless so long as the Planters of sugar by means of free labour are not enabled successfully to compete with Planters in States where slavery continues.'[72] So while there was active Scottish participation in the anti-abolition campaign, the majority view in Scotland tended to support the end of the trade, despite Scottish involvement in it, and despite the profits and opportunities accruing to Scots from the institution of enslavement. There were very few anti-abolition petitions from Scotland, compared with a flurry from Scottish churches and burghs advocating it. Slavery had been regarded as illegal in Scotland since 1778, after the Court of Session in Edinburgh had found in favour of the black servant Joseph Knight in the *Knight* v. *Wedderburn* case. This ruling went further in declaring slavery illegal than the ruling on the Somerset case in England in 1772. Popular abolitionism curtailed an especially vocal anti-abolition campaign north of the border.

In Parliament itself, a similar picture of relatively low-profile but keenly felt anti-abolitionism was evident among some Scots MPs. Only six Scottish MPs participated in the debates on the various slave trade bills after 1789, and three of them represented English constituencies. Sir William Young, MP for St Mawes in Cornwall and agent for St Vincent between 1795 and 1802, was one of Wilberforce's most frequent and measured critics as well as being one of the few, if not the only one, to mention the effect of abolition on Glasgow as well as the English ports.[73] Rather less restrained was James Baillie, then MP for Horsham and agent for Grenada. Shortly before his death, he accused the abolitionists on being bent on the destruction of the British West Indies, and dismissed some of the witnesses they produced as 'ill-informed, ignorant and low men'. Perhaps one of the seemingly least rational statements in the debates came from another Scotsman, John Petrie, who had extensive connections with Tobago, where his brother, Gilbert, was Speaker of the assembly. In 1799 he informed the Honourable Members that 'The abolition of the slave trade would be the scourge of Africa; as a planter he wished it to take place; but as a cosmopolite, he desired its continuance out of humanity to the inhabitants of the coast of Africa.'[74] This kind of contradiction was evident in much of the anti-abolitionist rhetoric. It was present in the Anderson brothers' concern with their *liberty* to run the Bance Island slave fort, and in the words in General James Grant of Ballindalloch, former governor-general of East Florida, who opined to Lord Cornwallis in 1792 that abolition would be 'contrary to the rights of men'.[75]

Conclusion

The changing face of politics in Scotland from the 1760s, as the result of the emergence of a younger generation of Scots with an eye for London's political opportunities, and an empathy towards its values, coupled to the culmination of a successful 'British' war, impelled more and more Scots to look southwards in search of advancement. Many of these opportunities appeared overseas in the West Indies, where the aftermath of the Seven Years War had resulted in the expansion of British territory. The frequency of these openings grew, not only as the empire expanded, but also with the consolidation and greater integration of the home country. This allowed Scots greater access to power in London, increasingly through English constituencies, and provided conduits for the disbursement of political patronage to other Scots. These were the circumstances which ensured that between 1763 and 1784 there was always at least one Scottish governor in the West Indies. In 1795, each of the Ceded Islands, as well as Jamaica and St Lucia, had a Scottish governor.[76] Additionally, the influence of governors and of powerful figures in London provided employment for Scots in other offices. At this level, kinship and local networks operated: the first avenue of approach for assistance or preferment in London might be the local MP, who, as in the case of the Duffs, might also be a relative.

Nobody, however, was more powerful in this political world than Henry Dundas, whose influence over the Caribbean has tended to be obfuscated by his role in Indian affairs. Dundas, of course, distributed patronage to people all over the empire, and was often approached by long-standing political allies. In the Scottish context, the bartering nature of patronage allowed a pay-off between electoral stability in Scotland and parliamentary votes for Dundas, and imperial advantage for the recipient of his patronage. This political dynamic between events in the West Indies and those in Scotland is amply demonstrated by the attempts by Patrick Cruickshank to force Dundas into providing employment in the Caribbean in exchange for a vote in Scotland. Anglo-Scots were also in a position to intervene in Scottish affairs, wedding their colonial power-base to local, pre-existing kinship connections. The layers of interconnection between those Scots who were clearly a part of the West India lobby and those who were not also softens the distinction between the two.

The final sphere, founded on the same kind of influence that drove the second, saw the articulation of West Indian interests and grievances in the most powerful circles in London. As a result, the needs of the largest networks were attended to by the careful cultivation of key groups and individuals to produce legislation favourable to the network. On other occasions the networks were used to act in opposition to a broader theme affecting the islands more generally.

All this indicates that the bonds holding the Caribbean colonies and Britain held fast into the final quarter of the eighteenth century. Despite the threats of the West Indian colonial agents, and the riots outlined in Chapter Six, it is clear that rumours of the death of the 'first empire' in 1783 have been exaggerated. To this enduring imperial unity Scots made a fundamental contribution. As the involvement of Scots in the politics of both the West Indies and Britain extended concurrently, a cyclical pattern of influence and power emerged. As the political role of Scots in the empire increased, and as the importance of the empire to Britain grew, so the importance of Scots for Britain increased. At the same time, as Scots gained prominence in Britain, they were in a position to dispense patronage through the networks, and to raise still further the status of Scots in the West Indies. The symbiotic nature of this transatlantic political dynamic meant that Scottish politics could be altered by Caribbean influence. As the next chapter argues, so too was much of Scottish society.

Notes

1 See also L. Colley, *Britons: Forging the nation, 1707–1837* (London: Pimlico, 1994); S. J. Connolly, 'Varieties of Britishness: Ireland, Scotland and Wales in the Hanoverian State', and P. J. Marshall, 'A nation defined by empire', in A. Grant and K. J. Stringer (eds), *Uniting the kingdom? The making of British history* (London: Routledge, 1995), pp. 193–207, 208–22.
2 J. Brewer, *The sinews of power: War, money and the English state, 1688–1783* (London: Unwin Hyman, 1989), p. 74.
3 On the problem of communication see I. K. Steele, *The English Atlantic 1675–1740: An exploration of communication and community* (New York and Oxford: Oxford University Press, 1986); D. Sobel, *Longitude* (London: Fourth Estate, 1996).
4 R. Sedgwick (ed.), *Letters of George III to Lord Bute, 1756–1766* (London: Macmillan, 1939), p. 203.

5. L. Namier and J. Brooke (eds), *The History of Parliament: The House of Commons, 1754–1790* (London: History of Parliament Trust, 1964), vol. 2, pp. 95–6.
6. R. C. Simmons and P. D. G. Thomas (eds), *Proceedings and debates of the British parliaments respecting North America, 1754–1783* (Millwood, NY: Kraus International Publications, 1983), vol. 2, pp. 289–92.
7. Namier and Brooke (eds), *House of Commons, 1754–1790*, vol. 2, pp. 346–54; L. Namier, 'Lord Fife and his factor', in L. Namier, *Crossroads of power: Essays on eighteenth-century England* (London: Hamish Hamilton, 1962), pp. 23–6. Fife held an Irish peerage and was entitled to sit in the Commons.
8. UASCA, MS3175, bundle 56/2, Duff House papers, Patrick Duff to the Earl of Fife, 24 February 1775; Fife to Duff, 14 March 1775.
9. UASCA, MS3175, bundles 56/1 and 56/2, Duff House papers, Charles Baird to the Earl of Fife; J. Schaw, *Journal of a lady of quality, being the narrative of a journey from Scotland to the West Indies, North Carolina and Portugal in the years 1774 to 1776*, ed. E. W. Andrews and C. M. Andrews (New Haven: Yale University Press, 1923), p. 81.
10. M. Fry, *The Dundas despotism* (Edinburgh: Edinburgh University Press, 1992), p. 150.
11. Quoted in R. G. Thorne (ed.), *The History of Parliament: The House of Commons, 1790–1820* (London: History of Parliament Trust, 1986), vol. 3, p. 636.
12. Fry, *The Dundas despotism*; J. Dwyer and A. Murdoch, 'Paradigms and politics: Manners, morals and the rise of Henry Dundas, 1770–1784', in J. Dwyer *et al.* (eds), *New perspectives on the politics and culture of early modern Scotland* (Edinburgh: John Donald, 1982), pp. 210–48.
13. NLS, MS6524(166), Melville papers, William Armstrong to Henry Dundas, 13 January 1790; MS6524(170), Armstrong to Dundas, 30 January 1790.
14. NLS, MS17(25), Melville papers, Thomas Coutts to Henry Dundas, 27 November 1800; MS6524(162), William Gloag to Henry Dundas, 12 July 1794.
15. NLS, MS 6524(164), Governor Seton to Henry Dundas, 26 May 1788.
16. PRO, CO260/13(100), St Vincent, original correspondence: Secretary of State, Governor Seton to Henry Dundas, 25 September 1795.
17. NAS, GD267/3/11(19), Home of Wedderburn manuscripts, George Home to Patrick Home, 3 August 1784.
18. NAS, GD267/1/6(5), Home of Wedderburn Manuscripts, Ninian Home to George Home, n.d.
19. NAS, GD267/1/12(7), Home of Wedderburn Manuscripts, Patrick Home to George Home, 24 March 1787. See also Fry, *The Dundas despotism*, p. 107.
20. PRO, CO101/32 (no fol.), Grenada, original correspondence: Secretary of State, George Home to Henry Dundas, March 1792; J. Robertson, *The Scottish Enlightenment and the militia issue* (Edinburgh: John Donald, 1985), pp. 118, 189–91. Dunira was the Dundas family residence in Midlothian.
21. NAS, MS267/1/5(12), Home of Wedderburn Manuscripts, George Home to Patrick Home, 15 December 1792.
22. NLS, MS21(19, 25, 53, 62, 64, 66, 71), Melville papers, secretary's minute book, August 1794 – January 1795; MS1075(9), Melville papers, John Brathwaite to Henry Dundas, 13 March 1795. Brathwaite was agent for Barbados between 1792 and 1805, and a member of the West India Committee.
23. NLS, MS3844(1), Melville papers, William Lindsay, Barbados, to Henry Dundas, 31 March 1795.
24. NLS, MS3844(3–4), William Lindsay, Tobago, to Henry Dundas, 6 May 1795.
25. NLS, MS9370(69), Melville papers, Mr Secretary Dundas to Mr Pitt, 30 December 1798.
26. NLS, MS9370(28), Mr Dundas to Mr Pitt, 4 January 1799.
27. NLS, MS3844(5, 7), Lord Balcarres to Henry Dundas, 2 January 1798, 12 April 1799; G. J. Bryant, 'Scots in India in the eighteenth century', *Scottish Historical Review*, 64, 1 (1985), 22–41.

28 W. I. Addison (ed.), *The matriculation albums of the University of Glasgow, from 1728 to 1858* (Glasgow: James Maclehose & Sons, 1913).
29 NAS, GD51/5/16, Melville Castle muniments, Patrick Cruickshank to Henry Dundas, 30 August 1795.
30 Thorne (ed.), *House of Commons, 1790–1820*, vol. 3, p. 110.
31 *Ibid.*, vol. 2, p. 607; vol. 3, pp. 111–12; BUL, Pinney papers, box 30 bundle 2, letter and agreement from James Grant to Peter Baillie, 10 June 1805.
32 BUL, Pinney papers, box 30 bundle 1, Alexander Munro to Peter Baillie, 6 June 1807.
33 BUL, Pinney papers, box 30, papers of Peter Baillie, Alexander Munro to James Baillie, 25 August 1807; Thorne (ed.), *House of Commons, 1790–1820*, vol. 2, p. 608.
34 BUL, Pinney papers, box 30, James Grant to Peter Baillie, 25 August 1807.
35 A. J. O'Shaughnessy, 'The formation of a commercial lobby: The West India interest, British colonial policy and the American Revolution', *Historical Journal*, 40, 1 (1997), 71–95.
36 PRO, CO101/32 (no fol.), Minutes of a meeting of the gentlemen connected with the island of Grenada, 7 September 1792.
37 NAS, GD51/1/361(2), Melville Castle muniments, memorial from the Committee ... for Lower Sugar Prices, 12 January 1792.
38 NAS, GD51/1/361(8), memorial from the West India planters and merchants, 28 February 1792.
39 NAS, GD51/1/361(13), memorial of the agents of the West India sugar colonies, 20 March 1792.
40 *Journals of the House of Commons*, 50 (1794–95), 591, 'Petition of the merchants trading to Grenada and St Vincent', 11 June 1795.
41 S. G. Checkland, 'Two Scottish West India liquidations after 1793', *Scottish Journal of Political Economy*, 4 (1957), 132; *Journals of the House of Commons*, 55 (1799–1800), p. 426, 'List of Annual Balance due to Alexander Houstoun & Co.'
42 *Journals of the House of Commons*, 55 (1799–1800), 424, 'Report on Mr McDowall's petition, 28 April 1800'; Checkland, 'Two Scottish West India liquidations', 133.
43 NAS, GD51/1/499(1), Melville Castle muniments, George Baillie to Henry Dundas, 17 September 1795.
44 Thorne (ed.), *House of Commons, 1790–1820*, vol. 4, pp. 902–4.
45 BUL, DM41/59/10, West Indies Mss, Westerhall papers, list of negroes belonging to Port Royal estate, 16 March 1798; V. L. Oliver (ed.), *Caribbeana, being miscellaneous papers relating to the history, genealogy, topography and antiquities of the British West Indies* (London: Mitchell Hughes and Clarke, 1909–19), vol. 3, pp. 294–5.
46 BUL, DM41/32/1, West Indies MSS, Westerhall papers, 'Inventory and valuation of the plantation commonly called Baccaye', 1 December 1770; DM41/53/2, case history, 12 March 1790–8 April 1799; DM41/62/1, letter from Sir William Pulteney, 26 August 1795; DM41/62/2, Petrie, Campbell & Co. to Robert Keith Esq., 25 September 1795.
47 Thorne (ed.), *House of Commons, 1790–1820*, vol. 3, pp. 108–9.
48 NAS, GD237/12/46(7), Macdouall of Garthland papers, Henry Dundas to William McDowall, 22 June 1790.
49 *Journals of the House of Commons*, 52 (1796–97), 210–11, 228, 235; NAS, GD267/5/4(2), Home of Wedderburn Manuscripts, George Home's current account with Simond & Hankey, 14 November 1795 to 30 June 1798.
50 NAS, GD267/5/4(10), account, March 1804.
51 *Journals of the House of Commons*, 55 (1799–1800), 424–5, 'Report on Mr McDowall's petition'; pp. 170–1, 'petition of Mr William McDowall Esq.'
52 *Journals of the House of Commons*, 55 (1799–1800), 437, 'Report on Mr McDowall's petition', appendix B, resolution of the directors of the Glasgow Chamber of Commerce and Manufactures; Fry, *The Dundas despotism*, p. 134.
53 *Edinburgh Almanack and Scots Register* (1773), 130; (1786), 65–6; (1790), 53.

54 *Journals of the House of Commons*, 55 (1799–1800), 206, 543–4, 616, 668, 744, 759, 784.
55 For this, and other, imperial ambiguities, see P. J. Marshall, 'Britain and the world in the eighteenth century, iv: The turning outwards of Britain', *Transactions of the Royal Historical Society*, 6th series, 11 (2001), 2–3.
56 *Journals of the House of Commons*, 44 (1788–89), 353, 'Petition of the West India planters, West India merchants and others residing in the city of Bristol', 20 May 1789. See also 'The manufacturers of African goods of Birmingham', 20 May 1789, *Ibid.*, p. 380.
57 *Ibid.*, p. 353.
58 *Ibid.*, pp. 381–3.
59 NAS, GD128/44/6b, Fraser–MacIntosh papers, Alexander Rose to John MacIntosh, 1 July 1792.
60 *Ibid.*, p. 294, 'Petition of the proprietors of estates in the West India islands, and merchants trading to the West Indies, residing in the city of Glasgow and its neighbourhood', 25 April 1789.
61 T. M. Devine, 'An eighteenth-century business elite: Glasgow–West India merchants, c. 1750–1815', *Scottish Historical Review*, 57 (1978), 41.
62 *Edinburgh Evening Courant*, 7 March 1795, 1.
63 H. Hamilton, 'The founding of the Glasgow Chamber of Commerce, 1783', *Scottish Journal of Political Economy*, 1 (1954), 33–48.
64 J. Strang, *Glasgow and its clubs, or glimpses of the condition, manners, characters and oddities of the city, during the past and present century* (London & Glasgow: R. Griffen & Co., 1856), pp. 128–51.
65 *Ibid.*, pp. 52, 264.
66 Liverpool Public Libraries Record Office, minutes of the common council, 4 May 1788. I am grateful to Roy C. Bridges for drawing this reference to my attention. See also A. Dalzel, *The history of Dahomey: An inland kingdom of Africa* (1793; London: Frank Cass, 1967), introduction by J. D. Fage, pp. 5–22.
67 J. Latimer, *The history of the Society of Merchant Venturers of the city of Bristol* (1903; New York: Burt Franklin, 1970), pp. 185–6; *Journals of the House of Commons*, 44 (1788–89), 352–3, 'Petitions from the Corporation of Bristol, the Merchant Venturers of Bristol, the African Merchants of Bristol, and the West India Planters and Merchants of Bristol against the abolition of the slave trade', 12 May 1789.
68 L. M. Penson, *The colonial agents of the British West Indies: A study in colonial administration, mainly in the eighteenth century* (1924; London: Frank Cass, 1971), p. 289; K. Morgan, *Bristol and the Atlantic trade in the eighteenth century* (Cambridge: Cambridge University Press, 1993), pp. 191–2.
69 BUL, Pinney papers, Evan Baillie to Peter Baillie, 13 June 1804.
70. A. I. Macinnes, 'A strategy for history: Inaugural lecture', *Aberdeen University Review*, 192 (1994), 356.
71 D. Hancock, *Citizens of the world: London merchants and the integration of the British Atlantic community, 1735–1785* (Cambridge: Cambridge University Press, 1995), pp. 52, 64; *Journals of the House of Commons*, 53 (1797–98), 624, 'Petition from the proprietors of Bance Island', 25 May 1798.
72 Anon., *A view of the Merchants House of Glasgow* (Glasgow: Bell and Bain, 1866), pp. 460–2.
73 Hansard, vol. 32, 3 March 1796, col. 868.
74 Hansard, vol. 29, 2 April 1792, col. 1,078; vol. 34, 1 March 1799, cols. 528–9.
75 Marshall, 'Britain and the world, iv', 2.
76 D. P. Henige (ed.), *Colonial governors from the fifteenth century to the present* (Madison: University of Wisconsin Press, 1970), pp. 112, 114, 128, 168–9, 180.

CHAPTER EIGHT

Repatriation from the West Indies

One of the defining characteristics of Scottish residency in the Caribbean was its transience. It is clear that many Scots went to the West Indies with the intention of making money and then leaving as soon as possible. Alexander Baillie of Dochfour noted shortly after his arrival in Nevis in 1752 that 'great Numbers . . . from all nations resort hither, from a very mistaken Notion indeed that Gold may be got for the gathering of it; There is no People more deceived in this respect than the Scots, who flock to the foreign Settlements in Numbers every year, And I'm very sorry to say that I have hitherto seen few of them in a Capacity to return.'[1]

Pessimism about his own situation was short-lived. Indeed his family profited hugely from their Caribbean enterprises and returned to Britain to enjoy and consolidate their wealth. Scots often went back to the places from which they had originated, investing in various enterprises. The first part of this chapter deals with the impacts felt across Scotland of the return of Caribbean revenue, a feature of Scottish society that was evident to contemporaries. The authors of the 1791 account of Inverness in the *Statistical account of Scotland* remarked upon 'the great influx of money from the East and West Indies' as a contributing factor in 'the increasing prosperity of this burgh.'[2]

A return to Britain did not always involve a home-coming to Scotland, however. For many Scots, settlement in England was as attractive as a return to their home locality. London was an especially popular destination, as were areas with strong West Indian connections like the south-west of England. The lure of the capital as the centre of financial, mercantile, political and social life had obvious attractions for wealthy Scots. The south-west benefited from proximity to the major Atlantic port at Bristol and the fashionable spas at Bath and Bristol Hot Wells. This region, in particular, was notable not only for the amenities and attractions of its cities, but also for the manner in which Scottish networks relocated there. In analysing one such network, it is clear to see how the group originated in Scotland, was developed in the West Indies, and finally settled in and around Bristol and became an integral part of the civic community there, as it continued to be in Inverness. This chapter also reviews the ways in which the returnees spent their Caribbean fortunes. While Eric Williams's argument that wealth from the West Indies and from enslavement helped finance the industrial revolution has received much criticism, it is clear that returnees from the Caribbean and their wealth had a profound influence on late eighteenth-century Scottish society.[3]

Not everyone who went to Scotland from the West Indies was a returnee in the strictest sense. In some cases, young West Indians were sent to Scotland to be educated. Often, these students were the children of Scottish migrants to the Caribbean, who were sent back to their parents' *alma mater* or to the bosom of their Scottish family. For others, the lure of an education at a Scottish university, especially in medicine, was sufficient to attract those with no existing Scottish connections. As a result, the pervasive and enduring influence of the Caribbean on Scotland, and of Caribbean Scots on Britain, becomes apparent.

Investment in Scotland

As the opening chapter noted, Scots adventurers to the Caribbean were often scions of noble or gentry families, or drawn from the aspiring 'middling sort'. On their return it was natural that they would seek to invest their imperial revenue in land. As well as being a means of conferring status, land purchases represented safe investments, unlike the far riskier enterprises of Caribbean planting, trading and finance. Moreover, the ownership of land provided security upon which to raise further loans to finance continuing West Indian ventures. The acquisition and improvement of land were thus desirable goals for Scots from a variety of backgrounds and from various parts of the country.

Some Scots began to plan for their return years before they were in a position to travel. From his base in Antigua, Dr Walter Tullideph purchased the Baldovan estate in Angus. In 1739, the Kingston merchant George Barclay planned to return home after a period in the Caribbean. Despite his misgivings about returning to a climate as cold as Aberdeen's, he went home to his Cairness estate, near Peterhead, where he died in 1756.[4] Building from this estate, the Gordons of Buthlaw, to whom the Cairness family was related by marriage, emerged as one of the largest landowning families in Aberdeenshire by the beginning of the nineteenth century, its wealth based on purchases financed by Jamaican capital.[5] John Grant, chief justice of Jamaica, began in 1787 to make preparations for his return to Scotland after many years in the Caribbean. During his frequent correspondence with Sir James Grant of Grant, he asked his kinsman to reserve a plot of land at Glenbrown for him to settle on when he returned. Although John Grant regarded Glenbrown as 'one of the ugliest and most barren' places on Sir James's estate, he believed it would 'satisfy the hankerings of imagination towards the natal spot'. Significantly, it was his intention to 'improve' on the 'nakedness of the Country', by planting as many trees as possible.[6] This concern with 'improvement' recurred among West Indian returnees, and locates their activity within an important stream of Scottish Enlightenment thinking.

John Grant was not the only Scot with Caribbean interests to ally imperial wealth with Scottish estate improvement. This was the classic age of improvement in Scotland, and West Indian wealth contributed to it. One of the most noted improvers of the eighteenth century, Sir Archibald Grant of Monymusk, had begun the process of estate change in the 1720s, around the same time as he invested in mining and in the London financial markets. This did not go entirely according to plan, and after his expulsion from the House of Commons following his implication in a financial scandal, he retired to concentrate on the improvement of his Aberdeenshire estate. Although he was something of a pariah in financial circles, he continued undaunted to seek external revenue, largely because his improvements could not be funded by domestic wealth. By the 1760s, he and his son owned estates at Liguanea in Jamaica and in the newly acquired British colony of East Florida. In part, his kinsman Sir Alexander Grant of Dalvey, whose fortune had been made and sustained by planting and trading in the Caribbean, guided the process of Grant's acquisition of colonial land. He also benefited from the fact that another Grant, Sir James of Ballindalloch, was the colonial governor of East Florida during the 1760s.[7]

Allan Macinnes's work on Argyll in western Scotland has demonstrated that during the 1780s, the Malcolms of Poltalloch, headed by Neil Malcolm, made extensive use of profits from their Jamaican enterprises when improving their Argyll estate. The Malcolms enjoyed a long association with western Jamaica, distributing the produce of their plantations in Westmoreland and Hanover through the port of Lucea. The wealth generated there far out-stripped the revenue raised from the land they had held in Scotland for two centuries. From the 1780s into the nineteenth century, Jamaica was the principal source of the Malcolms' income. As well as providing capital for investment on their lands, this money was used to variously construct and refurbish four mansions on the expanding Poltalloch estates between 1793 and 1848. The last, constructed between 1848 and 1852, cost £100,000. And not only did their estates 'improve', but their social standing was heightened. In 1856, Jessie Elizabeth Malcolm, third daughter of Neil Malcolm, married into the English aristocracy by becoming the wife of Egremont William Lascelles, second son of the Third Earl of Harewood. The Lascelles had risen from minor Yorkshire gentry to the aristocracy by similar means, and at about the same time, as the Malcolms.[8]

This means of capitalising estate improvement was not wholly a Scottish phenomenon, of course. Sir George Cornewall's La Taste plantation in Grenada generated an income four times greater than that of his Moccas estate in Hertfordshire, while in Yorkshire, the Lascelles family acquired huge tracts of land which they then 'improved'.[9] Yet this does not diminish the importance of the Caribbean for Scotland. Importantly, the use of imperial wealth to acquire and improve land in Aberdeenshire and Argyll indicates the role of Caribbean money as a means for upward social mobility across eighteenth-century Scotland. Consideration of the application of merchants' capital to land around Glasgow and Inverness reinforces this point.

As Tom Devine has remarked, the 'ownership of land was an essential feature of the career of a *successful* colonial merchant' in Glasgow.[10] With so many successful merchants in the city, Caribbean-generated wealth had a profound impact on the market for land in the area. Indeed almost half of the seventy-six merchants identified by Devine as partners in the various Glasgow West India houses owned land close to the city.[11] Matching the demand among Glasgow merchants for land in the eighteenth century was opportunity. The collapse of Douglas, Heron & Co. (the Ayr Bank), with its imposition of insolvency on many large landowners, and the collapse of the defunct York Buildings Company made considerable tracts of land available for purchase in the 1770s. Moreover, the risks attending the great profits of Atlantic trade meant that even wealthy landowning merchants could face bankruptcy. Insolvencies among the tobacco lords after 1776, or periodic catastrophes like the collapse of Alexander Houstoun & Co., provided a stock of land.[12] For some Caribbean merchants, these investments represented their families' first incursions into landownership. For others, West Indian wealth made possible the consolidation and expansion of existing holdings.

In south-western Scotland, one of the most successful merchant families, the McDowalls, expanded their landholding. Colonel

William McDowall, a younger son of Garthland in Wigtonshire, used wealth acquired in St Kitts to purchase the Castlesemple estate in 1727. Later, as the family wealth increased, the colonel's son, William, bought the Garthland estate from his then impoverished cousin. In short he was able to buy the land denied to his father by birthright. William McDowall II also strengthened further the bonds between land, commerce and the Caribbean. He married Elizabeth Graham of Airth in Stirlingshire, whose family developed Jamaican interests by intermarriage with the Stirling family.[13] William McDowall III, grandson of Colonel McDowall, after inheriting from his father, continued to expand his family's land holding by purchasing tracts in Ayrshire and Lanarkshire. In 1800, the imminent collapse of Houstoun & Co. had been delayed by both government and private loans secured on McDowall's land in Scotland, valued at over £286,000.[14] The Milliken family, partners with the McDowalls in their Caribbean ventures, owned large estates in Renfrewshire, close to Castlesemple.[15] The Millikens, moreover, were soon to be bound even more closely by marriage to the other major players in the Caribbean firm: the Houstoun family. The Houstouns, too, invested heavily in land before being forced to sell the Jordanhill estate when Houstoun & Co. went bust in 1801.

The Baillies in Inverness, like the McDowalls, were not merely wealthy interlopers into landed society. Both came from old, established landed families, and used the vast revenues accrued from involvement in Caribbean trade to further their holdings. In 1796, Evan Baillie inherited the family estate at Dochfour, just south-west of Inverness, after the death of his eldest brother. From this time onwards, he increasingly entrusted his son with responsibility for his Bristol merchant house, to allow him to spend more time in Scotland. As early as 1777, the estate had been valued at £13,340, and Baillie was clearly determined to increase its value as well as its extent.[16] As far as the Dochfour estate was concerned, he wanted to press forward with improvements because, as he informed his son Peter, 'it is highly disreputable to us all, if that favorite object of our little Family was suffered to go to decay.' He instructed his son, then at Dochfour, to press on with the planting of young hardwood trees at Kinmylies, and also to improve 'all practicable and flat lands planted with Firs' for 'corn land'. Furthermore, he advised cutting the old ash trees, and in consultation with James Grant to 'secure a purchaser for them at a good price'.[17]

Not content with developing the land he already owned, Baillie expressed a clear wish to acquire more. In the summer of 1806 he intimated his interest in acquiring neighbouring land at Dochgarroch and Kinmylies. In part, this desire for new land was a means of compensating for Dochfour and Kinmylies land that had been lost to the planned Caledonian Canal. Baillie was paid nearly £2,000 for land appropriated by the commissioners for the canal. Additionally he hoped to gain compensation for timber on the land, and advised his son Peter to take up the matter with Thomas Telford himself.[18] Even before the new canal took away part of his estate, however, Baillie set about acquiring additional land in the north. In 1804, he purchased a tract of land on the island of Skye for £1,700 from George Inglis, who had moved from Inverness to Bristol and seemed intent on limiting his connections with Scotland.[19]

Evan Baillie's most concerted attempts to acquire more land came in autumn 1806. His pursuit of the Dochgarroch estate proved fruitless, but in October he was still negotiating over the sale of additional land at Kinmylies. He expected his acquisition of the Balruddery estate for £20,000 to be completed by November. Around the same time, he paid £4,500 for an instalment on an estate in Ross-shire on behalf of Alexander Fraser, who was then managing the Baillies' Hermitage plantation in Grenada.[20] Here, the network worked both ways.

There are a number of reasons to explain Baillie's apparently sudden interest in acquiring new land in Scotland. The expansion of his landed interests took place within the context of renewed hostilities between Britain and France. The war curtailed British trade and increased investment in government stock as the costs of the war mounted. The country, and perhaps Scotland especially, had been rocked by financial crises in 1797, when convertibility had been suspended across Britain, and again in 1803, when the renewal of hostilities shattered the credit confidence of the previous year. In Argyll, these liquidity crises had taken a heavy toll on smaller landowners, who lacked the financial resources to insulate themselves from losses. The vulnerability of all but the largest and wealthiest landowners was exposed.[21] Elsewhere in the Highlands, Baillie, with his Caribbean wealth, was able not only to ride out these storms, but also to extend his more secure landed investments. The desire for land fitted with a general diversification of his interests. The Baillie family increased their holding in the Inverness Thread Factory in 1805, when Peter Baillie replaced George Inglis as a partner and joined his father, James Grant, John Mackintosh and Charles Jameson. Grant later played a pivotal role in Peter Baillie's election to the Inverness Burghs constituency.[22]

The Baillies also branched out from the mercantile to the financial domain in Bristol. Despite being 'as much averse to speculative or hazardous business as any Man can possibly be', Evan Baillie encouraged his son to accept an invitation in August 1806 to become a quarter shareholder in Messrs Elton, Edwards and Skinner, otherwise known as the Bristol Old Bank.[23] This diversification away from a hugely profitable West India merchant house was (at least in part) representative of the uncertainty surrounding the future of planting in the Caribbean. Baillie's concerns about the effect of the continuing war with France compounded his fears about the effect of the abolition of enslavement, and led him 'to think of abridging [his] West India business within very limitted bounds'.[24]

The Baillie family's appetite for Highland land did not diminish with Evan's death in 1835. His third son, James Evan, continued to purchase land in the north. Building on the opportunities provided by his father, James Evan became MP for Tralee, and later for Bristol. He was the principal of Evan Baillie, Sons & Co. in Bristol after his father's retirement in 1812, and a partner in J. E. Baillie, Fraser & Co. of London. As chairman of the British Guiana Association, president of the Whig Anchor Club of Bristol and a member of Brook's Club in London, he moved easily in powerful circles in England. He was, moreover, a prominent opponent of the abolition campaign.[25] Almost immediately after his father's death, he began to purchase large acreages of land. In 1835 he bought Glentrome in Badenoch for £7,350. Thereafter he made much more considerable purchases. He acquired the Glenelg estate in the western Highlands for £77,000 in 1837, and a year later he picked up the Glenshiel estate for £24,500. He spent a further £20,000 in 1851 buying the Letterfinlay estate. As a result, James Evan Baillie became one of the largest landowners in the western Highlands.[26] In these purchases, Caribbean revenue was important, especially in the form of slave compensation money. In 1835–36, James Evan Baillie received £53,964 in compensation for emancipated slaves, as well as owning shares in two partnerships, one with his brother Hugh Duncan and another with his brother and Henry Ames, which were awarded a further £57,042. Yet another £25,990 worth of awards were subjects of cases in Chancery.[27]

Baillie was one of a large number of substantial investors in the western Highlands in this period, many of whom were outsiders, a fact that has led them to be described collectively as a 'new elite'.[28] There are two points worth emphasising in particular. The first is that James Evan Baillie's purchases fitted into a longer pattern of land acquisition and improvement. And while his acquisitions were on a larger scale than those of his father, reflecting the new interest in the Highlands among the elite, and were begun immediately after Evan's death, they were a continuation of a process begun by him. Secondly, unlike many of the 'new elite', James Evan Baillie, although identified as a Bristol merchant, came from a family with a long-standing Highland social, political and landed pedigree. In this sense, he was part of an older, indigenous group that was revitalised by empire. As Allan Macinnes has pointed out for Argyll, 'not all landowners with a hereditary connection to the Highlands were on the defensive from the 1820s'. The land market was increasingly crowded and expensive, even from the 1790s, and the Highland landowners' resilience in the face of this new competition is testimony to the influence of Caribbean revenue.[29]

While Baillie and McDowall embodied the interconnections between planter, merchant and Scottish landowner, there were also institutions that fostered relations between landed and commercial interests. The previous chapter noted the importance of clubs in Glasgow as a means of facilitating communication between merchants in the city. They also served to connect landowners with Caribbean merchants. In 1780, the Gaelic Club was founded in Glasgow.[30] Initially a Highland connection was a prerequisite for membership, but the club soon became a place where members of the landed, professional and mercantile classes mingled. By 1798, when the club was subsumed by the Highland Society of Glasgow (established in 1727), it was less a Gaelic institution and more a meeting place for a unified elite. From its inception, the club had a strong Caribbean representation in its membership, and frequently consumed Caribbean goods. The opening dinner of the new club was marked by the offering of 'a splendid turtle' presented by Alexander Campbell of Hallyards, one of the leading sugar merchants in the city. In the nineteenth century, the club came to be presided over by Kirkman Finlay, sometime lord provost and one of the leading cotton merchants in Glasgow.[31]

It is clear that there was considerable acceptance of overseas merchants among the landed class. Atlantic merchants involved in the trades to the Chesapeake and the Caribbean, including McDowall and the Houstouns, were members and officers of institutions like the Caledonian Hunt and the Grand Lodge of Scotland, alongside their aristocratic brethren.[32] Imperial revenue acted as a means of social elevation for these merchants, and imperial interests formed common bonds among the landed and mercantile elites. In short, these connections point towards the emergence of a homogenous elite that shared both mercantile and agrarian concerns.

Just as the Baillies diversified into the alternative ventures of industry and banking in Scotland and England, so too did other families connected with the West Indies. Glasgow merchants had displayed a propensity towards the diversification of their interests long before the crisis resulting in American independence in 1776.[33] Some merchants invested in banking, and, by the final third of the eighteenth century, West India merchants invested in a great variety of industries, including iron production, coal extraction, ropemaking, leather tanning, brewing and glasswork. The Houstouns, firstly Alexander and then his son, Andrew, were heavily involved in coal mining, and purchased land with the intention of promoting extractive industry on it. In 1800, the lease of coal mines on the estates of Andrew Houstoun and his brother, Robert Houstoun Rae, were valued at £30,000.[34] Occasionally, planters had an eye to certain industries when ordering their supplies. James Stirling in Jamaica quite explicitly linked his Caribbean interests with his industrial ventures: 'if the tartan comes out Cheap I will have all my Negroes decked with it as it will help to encourage our Woollen manufactory.'[35]

What is especially striking about the industrial investments by West India merchants is that the two enterprises most commonly chosen related to cotton manufacturing and sugar production. Of the seventy-six Caribbean merchants identified by Tom Devine as having made industrial investments, twenty-one were partners in firms in the cotton industry, and fourteen in sugar production in Glasgow. While this has been noted before, no real explanation has been offered as to why these, rather than others, were chosen.[36]

It is no coincidence that the raw materials for both these industries came from the Caribbean, carried by the same merchants who invested in their manufacture, and who, in come cases, owned the plantations on which the staples were produced. Sugar was clearly the main Caribbean commodity shipped to Scotland, and among those who owned interests in sugar houses in Greenock, Port Glasgow and Glasgow were Alexander Campbell, John Campbell Sen., James Campbell, Arthur Connell, William Cunninghame, Richard Dennistoun, Robert Dennistoun, Robert Dunmore, James Garden, Andrew Houstoun, John Leitch, James McDowall, William McDowall III and Robert Houstoun Rae.[37] Of this group, at least three were plantation owners as well as merchants. For these men at least, the apparently separate roles and competing interests of planter, merchant and refiner became conflated.

Caribbean merchants investing in cotton manufacturing were also engaged in the shipping and sale of the raw material. Cotton was imported to Glasgow from Scottish-owned plantations in the islands of Grenada, Tobago and St Croix, from the more marginal islands of Carriacou and Mustique and from the South American colony of Demerara. Among those prominent investors in cotton manufacturing in western Scotland were John Campbell Sen., who handled cotton shipments and sales for Robert Melville's Carnbee estate in Tobago, for Ninian Home in Grenada and for George Inglis's plantation in Demerara.[38] Similarly the Dennistouns of Glasgow handled some of the cotton consignments for Evan Baillie of Bristol, who, like George Inglis, also sold cotton through Liverpool, using the offices of John Bolton & Co. Three of the partners in the West India firm of Dennistoun, Buchanan & Co. (James Sen., and Richard and Robert Dennistoun) all held shares in cotton spinning companies. The biggest cotton producer in Scotland, James Finlay & Co., was also heavily supported by West India capital, including considerable investment by Stirling, Gordon & Co., one of Glasgow's largest West India houses.[39]

Alexander Houstoun & Co., renowned as sugar merchants, were also involved in the shipment and manufacture of cotton. William McDowall III and his younger brother, James, were partners in cotton manufacturing firms in the later part of the century. At least from the mid-1770s, their West Indian firm imported cotton from the Caribbean directly from St Croix, Carriacou and Grenada. By April 1800, McDowall owned interests in cotton mills to the value of £20,000.[40] The extent of McDowall's importance in manufacturing in the Glasgow hinterland is suggested by the level of investment in Houstoun & Co. by manufacturing concerns in the 1790s, as noted in the previous chapter. In this way, the partners in Houstoun & Co., as well as those other merchants who invested their wealth in industries dependent on Caribbean commodities, at the same time integrated their affairs and limited the risk on their investments. If, for example, cotton or sugar sold quickly or expensively at Glasgow, the planting and mercantile branches of their investment benefited most. Conservely, their manufacturing concerns stood to gain if the prices of raw materials fell.

Investment in Scotland was not, however, driven only by the pursuit of profit. While the Williams thesis lays emphasis on the impact of money on industry and land, little attention has hitherto been paid to the social consequences of the repatriation of wealth and capital from the Caribbean. But it is clear that continuing attachment of Scots to their home areas, and to their families still resident there, encouraged some Scots to invest in local social infrastructures. At the end of the eighteenth century, the establishment of a new infirmary in Inverness attracted subscriptions worth more than £2,000 from the Caribbean.[41] The most considerable inward social investments, in terms of people as well as capital, came in the field of education.

Education

In January 1787, a group of gentlemen gathered to devise a plan to establish an academy in Inverness. They were concerned that existing provision in the burgh did not adequately educate their children. Instead, they believed 'that their young people should be more completely instructed in the most useful and necessary parts of learning.'[42] Such an institution, they argued, would be of the utmost benefit not only to the children of Inverness, but to those of all the counties of northern Scotland. These proposals were one of a series that were made in Scottish towns in the second half of the eighteenth century. From the foundation of the academy in Perth in 1760, these institutions promoted practical as well as classical instruction, and were designed primarily to provide a better source of wide-ranging education than the grammar schools. As such they were the educational embodiment of the culture of 'improvement' in Georgian Scotland. They were designed to attend to the needs of children from certain social backgrounds. In Inverness, there was no lack of schools: there were four run by the Scottish Society for Propagating Christian Knowledge with 230 pupils, and a further six schools with 200 pupils. The academy, founded by important members of the town, charged fees for each class, and so established itself as an institution for the mercantile and professional classes. Academies were also founded with financial and moral imperatives in mind, and offered a challenge to the universities. The breadth of their curricula was designed to attract students who would otherwise have attended university for a year or two, but avoided its expense, and the danger of an unsupervised slide into depravity.[43]

Establishing a new academy was, however, a costly business: the committee in Inverness reckoned that £4,000 would be required to create the school. In order to raise this considerable sum, the committee, headed by the provost, turned to wealthy individuals for donations. Significantly, they sought contributions not only from residents of Inverness, but also from those 'sons of clachnacuddin' living in different parts of Britain and overseas. These people, it was thought, would 'cheerfully contribute to so laudable an undertaking as the establishment of a good seminary of learning in this place so happily situated for it.'[44]

The prediction proved to be well founded. The committee was able to raise substantially more than the £4,000 it had hoped for. In addition to the annual provision of £70 from the town magistrates, some £6,277 was raised by subscriptions by July 1792. Of this, £1,301 came directly from residents of the West Indies, all but £30 being identified as coming from Jamaica.[45] This, though possible, appears an unlikely proportion of Caribbean contributions, given the strong Inverness connections with other West Indian islands. One explanation is that

'Jamaica' was used as a generic term for the West Indies as a whole. What is clear, though, is the manner in which the committee used networks to facilitate the gathering of this revenue.

The committee sent letters directly to correspondents in India and the Caribbean. A subscriber in Jamaica, John MacGillvray, was thanked for his donation of £200, and was asked to 'exert your Influence among your Acquaintances to procure us aid for accomplishing as noble an Object.'[46] The subscription papers were also distributed through a series of networks. James Baillie in London, as well as being encouraged to promote the scheme in the capital, was asked to send a batch of subscription papers to his contacts throughout the Caribbean. Similarly, Lewis Cuthbert in Edinburgh was approached to send papers to Jamaica, where he was justifiably believed to wield considerable influence.[47] Cuthbert, one the Lascelles family's attorneys in Jamaica, was only temporarily resident in Edinburgh, and returned to Jamaica shortly after receiving the letter. Once back in Spanish Town, he set about the task of raising money from Jamaica residents with Inverness connections. In this task he was assisted by Hugh Fraser of Westmoreland parish, who took responsibility for raising and remitting money from the western part of the island. Even Cuthbert's method of passing on money to the academy relied on a network of local association. Rather than wait for the pledged money to arrive, and then send it back to Scotland, Cuthbert paid the sum himself, and kept the pledges as they came in. Cuthbert instructed his 'commissioners', John Baillie of Dunain (a cousin of the Baillies of Dochfour) and William Inglis (brother of George, and later town provost), to pay the sum from money raised by the sale of some of his land in Scotland.[48]

The academy that these West Indians funded reflected the desire for 'useful learning' in its curriculum. In 1792, the academy advertised its existence by listing the classes that would be taught. The first three classes were fairly traditional: the first consisted of English (to be taught by an Englishman); the second, Latin and Greek; the third, writing, arithmetic and book-keeping. The fourth class, to be taught by Mr Douglass, formerly of the Marine Academy at Edinburgh, was far more innovative. In it, students were to study the branches of mathematics, 'geography with use of the globe', 'navigation with lunar observations', fortification and 'practical gunnery'. Under the guidance of the rector, the fifth class would consider natural and civil history, natural philosophy, chemistry and astronomy. A further class, 'in compliance with the desire of the Highland Society of London', would be devoted to Gaelic.[49]

This curriculum had obvious attractions for Scots in the Caribbean seeking a suitable educational establishment for their children. It also promised much for those Scots planning to set out on a career in the Caribbean, or another part of the empire. The denomination of the subjects, especially those in the fourth class, as 'useful' indicates the founders' awareness of the world beyond the Highland line, and of Scots within it. Subjects like 'geography with use of the globe' or 'navigation with lunar observations' could have had only a limited utility for those planning to remain in the Highlands. In many ways this was an imperial curriculum for the aspiring 'middling sort'.

Also striking about the curriculum are the perceptions regarding the value of teaching English and Gaelic. These perceptions also speak to a desire among Scots, and particularly Highlanders, to position themselves in the British world. The directors of the academy in Inverness were explicit in promoting their English class as being based on a method devised by an Englishman. They also actively sought an Englishman to teach it.[50] Conversely, they showed little interest in the Gaelic class, which was promoted by expatriate Scots who were members of the Highland Society of London. Indeed, the society withdrew its annual subscription of £35 in 1802 because 'the professor has received no additional aid from the funds of the Academy and consequently has not been able to bestow the necessary attention to the preservation of the Gaelic language in its ancient purity which alone can be effected by public countenance and instruction.'[51]

In the early years of its existence, the academy attracted a number of students from the Caribbean. Class registers for the period 1804–10 not only indicate the numbers arriving from the West Indies, but also hint at their reasons for coming. In the spring and autumn sessions of 1804, there were respectively seventeen and eighteen students from the Caribbean. With a total roll of around 200, it is apparent that this was a small minority of the student body. The English class, which in spring 1804 had the largest number of Caribbean students, saw them outnumbered by eight to one. After 1804, the number of students identified as hailing from the West Indies fell considerably. In the autumn session of 1805, there were only nine explicitly listed as being from the Caribbean, and by spring 1807 there were eleven. Although they were a minority in the school, they considerably outnumbered students from other parts of the empire. Between 1804 and 1807 there were twenty-three pupils from the Caribbean in Inverness, against one from East India and three from North America. In this context, and considering the distances involved, the presence of so many West Indies pupils is remarkable.[52]

Many of the students arriving at the academy from the Caribbean had kinship connections with Inverness. Indeed, of the twenty-three students, only four had names that seem to have dissociated them from the town. It is likely that the four students by the name of Inglis from Demerara were related to the Inglis family that owned the Bellefield plantation in the colony, and were merchants in Inverness. Dr Colin Chisholm, connected with the Inglis family in Demerara and, by this period, in Bristol as well as Inverness, may also have been related to the pupils William and Hugh Chisholm, who both attended the academy. In addition, William Cuthbert of Jamaica, a classmate of Hugh Inglis and Hugh Chisholm, may have been related to the Cuthbert brothers, Lewis and George, who played key roles in raising subscriptions in Jamaica. Both invested heavily enough to qualify as directors.[53]

The desire to send offspring back to Scotland was not confined to those from Inverness. In Fortrose, on the north shore of the Moray Firth, an academy was founded in 1791. In 1811, it received £210 from Grenada, along with £725 from India. A few miles to the north, in Tain, an academy was founded under the influence of Hugh Rose of Glastullich, whose own fortune, much of which he had used to improve his Easter Ross estate, derived from an earlier career in the Caribbean. Just like the academy in Inverness, it received subscriptions from donors across the Atlantic, including thirteen landowners from the West Indies and the United States. In particular, a number of planters from the Guyana colonies of Berbice and Demerara sent money amounting to £1,000 in 1814, the year after it opened.[54]

Outside the Highlands, Scots like the sons of Dr Alexander Johnston of Jamaica were sent home to study. As the American War of Independence approached its end in 1783, Johnston considered sending two of his Jamaican-born sons, aged nine and five, to Scotland to be educated. He intended to send them to his mother and his brother James in Aberdeenshire.[55] Throughout the summer of 1783, he mulled over his plan. His greatest concern was how he would cope with being parted from his two eldest sons. As an alternative, he considered travelling with them, seeing them settled in a good school, and then returning to the Caribbean without them after a year. By 1784, he had decided that this was impractical, and had resolved to send his sons to London, where they would be met by his brother and escorted back to Aberdeenshire.[56] Also in north-east Scotland, education benefited to a considerable extent from West Indian profits into the nineteenth century. James Dick of Forres went to Jamaica in the later part of the eighteenth century, and there amassed a considerable fortune. Following his death in 1828, he bequeathed £113,000 sterling to contribute to the salaries of parish teachers in the counties of Aberdeen, Banff and Moray. Dick's determination to support teachers was fired by a desire to see the children of his home area prepared for entrance to King's and Marischal colleges in Aberdeen.[57]

For parents like Alexander Johnston, the decision to send children home was a difficult one. Contemporary observers commented on the ill effects of the parting. Janet Schaw and Edward Long both regretted it, particularly as they believed that students frequently preferred to lavish money on themselves in Britain, rather than returning to the West Indies to share the benefit of their educations. Nonetheless, Caribbean education was widely seen as second-rate, and the general migration of students to Britain quickened. It has been shown that 148 pupils from the West Indies were enrolled at Eton College between 1753 and 1776, compared with only twenty-two from the Thirteen Colonies.[58] Among the Caribbean students at Eton there were certainly some Scots, and this process continued throughout the century. Education at Eton, which by this period had become England's principal private school, was a means of entrance into the British elite. West Indian parents evidently saw the benefits of education outweighing the perils and traumas of a lack of parental guidance. Yet for those students returning to Scotland in particular, the headlong rush into moral turpitude could be slowed. While they went without parental supervision, they remained within their network and often, as in the case of the Johnston boys, within their close family. These students were not cast adrift with money as their sole companion.

The process of educating children in Scotland implies also the importance of 'home'. Parents preferred to pay to send children home, rather than use their money to develop an educational infrastructure in the Caribbean. It was not that they were unwilling to invest in a school for their children: the financing of the academies in Inverness, Fortrose and Tain indicates quite the opposite. Rather, their decision came from a positive desire to see their children educated in Scotland, particularly in the area from which they came, and attests to the utility, as well as the classical grounding, of Scottish education. The practice of sending children home in this way also demonstrates the continuing importance of kinship and local connections. And this process, as much as planter absenteeism, denoted the islands as places of short-term residence.

Most of the students were white males. In Inverness the exceptions to the rule were Helen Inglis of Demerara and the McRae brothers, Alexander, Colin and John, from Jamaica. The three boys were all listed as 'coloured' in the register for spring 1806.[59] The presence of non-white children in what was otherwise a racially homogenous town is a clear indicator of Scottish involvement in miscegenation, a point that must have been recognised at the time. It also implies a willingness of the part of at least some parents of illegitimate children to take responsibility for them. Not only did educating coloured children in the father's home town represent a financial cost; it made it very plain to the family at home exactly the sorts of thing that went on in the West Indies. More importantly, perhaps, this was return migration that literally changed the way society looked. Free people of colour may have been common enough in the Caribbean, but in Inverness they were something of a rarity. Nor was this the only instance of coloured children being sent to Scotland. In the late 1780s and 1790s, for example, John Robertson of Tobago paid, on a regular basis, for the board and lodgings in Scotland for Charles and Daniel Robertson, 'two Molato boys', while there was at least one 'mulatto' at Dollar Academy.[60]

Assessing how the local population reacted to the arrival of black children is difficult because just as there was no single response to the institution of enslavement, attitudes towards non-whites varied in Scotland. Black people had been known in Scotland at least since the beginning of the sixteenth century, when a number were attached to the Stuart court.[61] By the eighteenth century, the national ambivalence was fully evident. As well as the willingness to enslave Africans overseas, there was a perception that black people ought not to be free in Scotland: June Evans noted the eighteen Africans who were subjects of adverts for runaways in Scottish newspapers, one of which read: 'Taken up a strolling Negro, whoever owns him, and gives sufficient Marks of his being theirs... may have him again upon Payment of Expenses laid out in him, otherwise the present possessor will dispose of him at his Pleasure.' Indeed, slave sales were known in Scotland in the 1760s, while David Hume's assertion of the inferiority of blacks had recently been made.[62] Against this background were heard ever louder calls for the abolition as the awfulness of enslavement and the unprecedented verdict in favour of Joseph Knight in 1778 entered the public consciousness.

If the provision of school-level education in the West Indies was patchy, then at university level it was non-existent. As a result, in addition to sending educated Scots out to the Caribbean, Scottish universities attracted students from the West Indies. Some fifty-one students from the Caribbean matriculated in arts at Marischal College, Aberdeen, between 1769 and 1807. Twenty-nine of them came from Jamaica to study. What is especially notable is the presence of thirteen doctors' sons among those from Jamaica. Among this group were three of Alexander Johnston's sons: John, James and Robert. The latter two also became doctors: James entered the service of the East India

Company, and Robert became a surgeon in London. But these two were among only fifteen of the fifty-one matriculants to graduate. To these graduates may be added the two doctorates of divinity and fourteen of medicine conferred on West Indians between 1743 and 1813.[63] Marischal out-stripped its city rival, King's College, in drawing students from the islands, reflecting the general trend in fortunes of the two colleges. After the period of renewal that saw curriculum changes at both in the 1750s, internal division, and the loss of key faculty members like Thomas Reid, resulted in King's relapsing 'into a torpid collegiate existence'. On the other hand, Marischal, while not without its problems, was able, under capable management and the patronage of Lord Bute, to attract greater investment and gifted staff, to build on the changes of 1753 and to expand through the later eighteenth century.[64] Between 1754 and 1815, thirteen West Indians entered the doors of King's to study arts, only three of whom graduated. Unlike Marischal, King's awarded many more medical degrees (twenty-two) than arts degrees to Caribbean students. In turn, Marischal's Caribbean intake was vastly outnumbered by the influx to the universities in Glasgow and Edinburgh. Between 1731 and 1810, 119 students from the Caribbean matriculated at Glasgow. At Edinburgh, 114 West Indians *graduated* in medicine alone between 1744 and 1810; many others took classes there and continued to do so well into the nineteenth century.[65]

Not only did the reputation of Edinburgh's medical school allow it to attract many more students than other Scottish universities, but it also drew many more non-Scots than the others. Of the 114 medical graduates, probably slightly fewer than half were of children of Scottish descent. This was in marked contrast to Glasgow, where around three-quarters of the Caribbean students were Scottish, and to the Aberdeen colleges, where over 80 per cent were of Scots descent.[66] In part this represented the wider international reputation of Edinburgh as a centre of medical excellence. It also suggests that the importance of local connections, perhaps as a result of a less exalted reputation, remained stronger for longer in Glasgow and Aberdeen. Most of their students came from families (like the Johnstons) with existing connections to the university or the city, which appears not to have been the case for Edinburgh.

Investment in England

While a great many Scots returning to Britain went to Scotland, just as some non-Scots arrived in Scotland from the Caribbean, a significant group of Scots established themselves in England. They tended to be drawn to centres of major economic and political activity. London was thus significant: many Scots with Caribbean interests developed and maintained a connection with the imperial capital. Others also pursued connections elsewhere in England. George Baillie had considerable interests in Liverpool, as did several other Scots, while scholarly research has suggested the need to consider Caribbean Scots' penetration of provincial England, notably Lincolnshire and Yorkshire.[67] The most significant area was the south-west of England, which had much to attract West India Scots. Its climate was rather more temperate than that of the northern lands, a concern articulated by some Scots returnees. More significantly, the region was centred on Britain's third most important Atlantic port at Bristol, and amply supplied with parliamentary constituencies. Although the growth of Bristol in the later eighteenth century was slower than that of the more northerly ports of Liverpool and Glasgow, Bristol remained Britain's second most important sugar market into the 1790s. The perception in the north of Scotland of the city's enduring prosperity is apparent from Simon Fraser of Moniack's request to Peter Baillie for help in 1807: 'It has since occurred to me that in your opulent City, & Country, or among your correspondents & friends in London other parts of England, you may have occasion to learn, that Sums of Money may wish to be invested on Landed Securities in a country like ours, where debts are registered.'[68]

The south-west also provided Scots with a source of parliamentary constituencies. Although Scotland had only forty-five seats at Westminster in the unreformed Parliament, Cornwall had forty-four, Devon twenty-six and Dorset twenty, while Gloucestershire and Somerset between them shared a further twenty-six. From the 1760s, Scots had found seats in this region, including three of Lord Bute's sons and Alexander Wedderburn. The tradition of Scottish aristocratic representation from the south-west continued into the 1790s: James Archibald Stuart, second son of Lord Bute, was MP for Bossiney, while George Campbell, Marquis of Lorne, represented St Germans. In Parliament, wealthy Scots with Caribbean interests joined them. For example, James Gordon, a West India planter, formerly chief justice of the Ceded Islands, sat for Truro; Sir James Johnstone, owner of the Westerhall estate in Grenada, was MP for Weymouth and Melcome Regis; his brother Sir William Pulteney sat for Shrewsbury; and Sir William Young represented St Mawes. Walter Boyd, the Scots banker who had such an interest in the fortunes of Alexander Houstoun & Co., was MP for Shaftsbury in Dorset between 1796 and 1802.[69]

During the later eighteenth century, this region was also an extremely fashionable place to be. The spas at Bristol Hot Wells and especially at nearby Bath drew wealthy metropolitans from London to the provinces on a regular basis. It was in many ways an area ideally suited to Scots with an eye to the Caribbean and with money to spend.

Connections linking Scotland, the Caribbean and the English regions illustrate the tendency of Scots to engage in multi-layered networks. Perhaps the clearest manifestation of these links can be seen in Bristol. As noted in Chapter Four, when Evan Baillie of Dochfour returned to Britain after a period in the West Indies, he went to Bristol to establish his merchant house. In running his firm, Baillie had employed his connections with Inverness alongside those more recently acquired in the Caribbean and in his new home. Around the turn of the century, his presence in Bristol drew other Invernessians with Caribbean interests more closely into his multi-layered network. Dr Colin Chisholm of Inverness, medical practitioner in Grenada, landowner in Demerara and author of *An essay on the malignant pestilential fever*, relocated to Bristol at the beginning of the nineteenth century. As well as bolstering the link between Inverness, Bristol and the Caribbean, Chisholm sponsored students from Bristol who attended his *alma mater* in Aberdeen.[70]

Shortly after Chisholm's decision to move to Bristol, George Inglis of Inverness decided to relocate himself and his family. The connections between the Inglis, Baillie and Chisholm families were strong. All were from Inverness, all had interests in the Caribbean, and George Inglis and Colin Chisholm were also cousins. Their fortunes were intertwined as one acted on behalf of another: from Demerara, Chisholm informed Inglis in Inverness that his cotton would be shipped to Bristol on Baillie's ship the *Emilia*. Inglis had mercantile links with both Evan Baillie and his cousin George. Additionally, Hugh Inglis, brother of George, had been employed by Evan Baillie, and was buried at St Michael's Church in Bristol.[71] In 1802, George Inglis wrote to Evan Baillie, 'I must take the liberty of troubling you to assist me in procuring a Comfortable Temporary residence for my family either in Clifton or Bristol for a few months until I can fix on something more permanent.'[72]

The decisions to move to Bristol were taken by Chisholm and Inglis shortly after the Treaty of Amiens returned the colony of Demerara to Dutch rule after 1802. This caused considerable uncertainty among those Britons with interests there. The fact that 'it [was] difficult to form a conjecture with any accuracy respecting the effects which the Restoration of the Dutch Colonies may have on our properties in Demerara' probably played a large part in Chisholm's decision. It also affected Inglis's thinking, even though he lived in Inverness. He wrote, 'If my affairs abroad Succeed but tolerably – I shall be enabled to live as comfortably as I could desire, Should the reverse be the case, we can with more care and comfort reduce our expenditure to our then limited means in a place where we are strangers than we could here.'[73] This should not imply that Bristol was a cheaper place to live than Inverness. Any loss of wealth would have been immediately apparent in Inverness, where the Inglises had been one of the town's most influential mercantile families. In Bristol, where they were largely unknown, their sense of shame occasioned by their straitened circumstances would have been much diminished.

The Baillies' connections with people from the north of Scotland, allied to the mercantile, political and marital bonds they forged with important Bristol families, indicates the extent of their role as exemplars of the kind of connections that integrated Britain at a practical level. Their place as an elite Caribbean, Bristol and Inverness family formed the kind of nexus that helped unite the kingdom. Nor were they the only West India Scots in south-western England. As well as Hugh Inglis, a number of other Scots who returned from the Caribbean were buried at churches in Bristol and Bath in the late eighteenth and early nineteenth centuries. Duncan Campbell of St Vincent died in the fashionable area of Clifton in Bristol in 1797 and was buried in the city's cathedral. Twenty years later John Campbell of Trewlany, Jamaica, joined him. A few miles away, the graveyards of Bath were littered with dead West India Scots. Gilbert Ramsey of Barbados and James Bruce of St Vincent were buried at Bath Abbey Church. At Bath Abbey, three generations of the MacKinnons of Antigua were interred along with another of their kinsmen, William McKinnon, grandson of the clan chief. They were joined by William Kennedy Lawrie of St Thomas in the East in Jamaica, Dr John Gordon of St Croix and Matthew Munro of Grenada. Munro had been employed by Houstoun & Co. in that island but died before witnessing the final demise of the company.[74]

The interplay between the different loyalties evident among West India Scots who settled in the south-west is equally apparent among those who headed for London. Evan Baillie's brother James, on his return from the Caribbean, settled in the south-east of England, establishing his company in London. It is quite clear that James Baillie had little or no intention of returning to Inverness having made his fortune; instead he had long coveted residence in London.

There are two major reasons why James Baillie based himself in London during the 1780s. He had first visited the city in 1767, and appears to have been awe-struck by it, to an extent that fuelled a desire to live there. He described it as a place 'where I had Company & plenty of Deversion of every kind – It certainly is a wonderful place for altho'

I walked about for three weeks, till I was hardly able to crawl, I don't believe I saw the half of it.'[75] More important, however, was London's place as the principal British mercantile and political centre. As such it attracted Scots with different but often complementary interests. Some, like Baillie, or Alexander Grant of Dalvey, resided more or less permanently in or near London. Others, like the major Scottish-based West India houses, maintained subsidiaries in London to handle their affairs in that market. Sinclair, Brebner & Co. of Greenock, for example, were linked to Sibbald and Brown, while Houstoun & Co. were connected with Houstoun, Clerk, Crichton & Co. There were also Scottish politicians and financiers in the city, into whose networks the returnees were able to fit. A further groups of repatriated Scots, like Charles Gordon of Cairness, preferred to spend part of their time on their Scottish estates, and part in London.[76]

James Baillie owned a large town house in Bedford Square in London, where he was a near neighbour of another prominent West India merchant, Thomas Hankey. His wealth also enabled him to purchase a property with which to bolster his status as a member of the city's mercantile and political elite. He bought a country mansion called Ealing Grove in Middlesex from the Duke of Argyll, who in turn had bought it from the Duke of Marlborough.[77] His distaste for residence in Scotland nevertheless belied a lingering concern for the north. When the harvest of 1782 failed, Baillie acted swiftly to contribute towards measures to alleviate the crisis. The contributors to the *Statistical account of Scotland* in 1791 remarked, 'Mr. Baillie's munificence at this season of sore calamity, does him the highest honour.'[78] He also, as noted above, made a personal contribution to the establishment of the Inverness academy, and became a director as well as helping to promote the school's subscription in the Caribbean.

London was home to a number of other West Indian planters and merchants of Scottish extraction. As well as Baillie, and his sidekick in the Grenadian group, Alexander Campbell, Sir Alexander Grant of Dalvey moved easily among a coterie of elite Scots in the capital, including the Duke of Argyll and Lords Erskine, Findlater and Hopetoun. Yet his social connections were not confined to Scots: he was also accepted in the royal circle, and was a regular visitor to the spas in Bath and Bristol.[79] He and his business partner Richard Oswald were also connected to important Scottish financiers in the city, among them the Herries family, who could also, through Charles Herries, boast personal experience of life in the Caribbean and who provided credit for those resident there.[80] The Coutts brothers oversaw the financial affairs of the Homes of Wedderburn, as well as those of Henry Dundas and the royal family.

Conclusion

It is clear that the process of imperial engagement with the Caribbean impacted significantly on Scotland in a variety of ways. The influx of capital from Caribbean activities had profound effects on agriculture and industry in Scotland, ensuring that people in all walks of life, and in all parts of Scotland, were in some way affected by Caribbean involvement. And while it is clear that the flood of commercial wealth into land was a 'contribution of the first order to the complex of factors which made up the Scottish "agricultural revolution"', it is also apparent that the income from Caribbean estate ownership also affected patterns of landowning in Scotland.[81] Caribbean wealth allowed some old-established families to consolidate, expand and improve their lands, while allowing others to enter the land market for the first time. By promoting this activity in the land market, West Indian-generated income (along with that from other imperial ventures) contributed to the increase in land prices.

Those with Caribbean interests were not concerned solely with land. Investments in industry promised healthy returns, with less risk than was entailed by Caribbean trade. Moreover, for companies like Houstoun & Co., an expansion of cotton manufacturing in the west of Scotland enabled them to find a ready market for the raw material grown on estates in the Caribbean, including their own plantations, which they carried to Scotland in their own ships. In short, they developed an integrated manufacturing process from planting to fabrication. More striking still was the reliance on Scotland for education. That the University of Edinburgh should attract many students to its medical school is unsurprising. But the fact that groups of Caribbean residents should prefer to send children thousands of miles to attend school, or to invest in the establishment of academies in Scotland, is of profound importance. It quite explicitly demonstrates perceptions about both the Caribbean as a place of temporary residence, and the place of Scotland as 'home'. For some, though, 'home' could mean Britain.

It is not just the fact that some Scots settled in England that is important, but the manner in which they did so. Their emergence in the political and mercantile elites in London and Bristol denotes the extent to which Britain was becoming integrated in the final third of the eighteenth century. For all the scottophobic bluster of the 1760s, it is clear that Scots were able to get ahead in England, and to take their place in an Anglo-Scottish landowning, political and commercial elite. By succeeding in the south, Scots with Caribbean connections demonstrated the flexibility of their networks.

Notes

1. HCA, D456, Baillie of Dunain papers, Alexander Baillie to Alexander Baillie, 18 March 1752.
2. OSA, vol. 17, p. 96.
3. E. Williams, *Capitalism and slavery* (Chapel Hill: University of North Carolina Press, 1945).
4. UACSA, MS1160/5(3), Gordon of Cairness papers, George Barclay to David Gordon, 30 June 1739; MS1160/5(8), John Gordon to James Barclay, 19 July 1756.
5. R. F. Callander, *A pattern of landownership in Scotland* (Finzean: Haughend Publications, 1987), p. 8.
6. NAS, GD 248/61/2(67), Seafield muniments, Grant correspondence, John Grant to Sir James Grant, 11 November 1787.
7. A. J. G. Cummings, 'The business affairs of an eighteenth-century lowland laird: Sir Archibald Grant of Monymusk, 1696–1778', in T. M. Devine (ed.), *Scottish elites* (Edinburgh: John Donald, 1994), pp. 43–61; NAS, GD345, bundle 1762, Grant of Monymusk muniments, Alexander Grant to Capt. Alexander Grant, May 1762; GD1/32/38(11), Miscellaneous accessions, Grant of Monymusk, Alexander Grant to Sir Archibald Grant, 15 November 1769.
8. A. I. Macinnes, 'Scottish Gaeldom from clanship to commercial landlordism, c. 1600–c. 1850', in S. Foster *et al.* (eds), *Scottish power centres* (Glasgow: Cruithne Press, 1999), pp. 174–5, 179; J. Foster, *Pedigree of the county families of Yorkshire* (London: W. Wilfred Head, 1874), vol. 2, n.p. On the Lascelles see R. Pares, 'A London West India merchant house, 1740–69', in R. Pares and A. J. P. Taylor (eds), *Essays presented to Sir Lewis Namier* (London: Macmillan, 1956), 75–107; S. D. Smith, 'Merchants and planters revisited', *Economic History Review*, 55, 3 (2002), 434–65; D. Hamilton, 'Private enterprise and public service: Naval contracting in the Caribbean, 1720–50', *Journal for Maritime Research* (April 2004), www.jmr.nmm.ac.uk.
9. S. Seymour *et al.*, 'Estate and empire: Sir George Cornewall's management of Moccas, Hertfordshire and La Taste, Grenada, 1771–1819', *Journal of Historical Geography*, 24, 3 (1998), 342.
10. T. M. Devine, 'Glasgow colonial merchants and land, 1770–1815', in J. T. Ward and R. G. Wilson (eds), *Land and industry: The landed estate and the industrial revolution* (Newton Abbot: David and Charles, 1971), p. 207.
11. T. M. Devine, 'An eighteenth-century business elite: Glasgow–West India merchants, c. 1750–1815', *Scottish Historical Review*, 57 (1978), 43.
12. Devine, 'Glasgow colonial merchants and land', pp. 214–15, 219.
13. NAS, GD237/12/29, Macdouall of Garthland papers, nomination of tutors by William McDowell of Castlesemple, 26 October 1768.
14. Devine, 'Glasgow colonial merchants and land', pp. 210, 256; *Journals of the House of Commons*, 55 (1799–1800), 428, 'Report on Mr. McDowall's petition', 28 April 1800.
15. L. A. Timperley (ed.), *A directory of landownership in Scotland, c. 1770* (Edinburgh: Scottish Records Society, 1976), pp. 291–5.
16. BUL, Pinney papers, box 31, notebook entry, 1777.
17. BUL, Pinney papers, box 30 bundle 1, Evan Baillie to Peter Baillie, 27 July 1806; Pinney papers (domestic), Evan Baillie to Peter Baillie, 21 September 1806.
18. BUL, Pinney papers, box 30 bundle 1, Evan Baillie to Peter Baillie, 10 August 1806; box 33, Conveyances . . . Evan Baillie Esq. to the commissioners appointed for the carrying on of the Caledonian Canal, 16 May 1806.
19. BUL, Pinney papers (domestic), Evan Baillie to Peter Baillie, 9 June 1804; Pinney papers, box 33, Evan Baillie to Peter Baillie, 12 June 1804.
20. BUL, Pinney papers (domestic), Evan Baillie to Peter Baillie, 28 September 1806.
21. S. G. Checkland, *Scottish banking: A history, 1695–1973* (Glasgow and London: Collins, 1975), pp. 220–5; A. I. Macinnes, 'Landownership, land use and elite enter-

prise in Scottish Gaeldom: From clanship to clearance in Argyllshire, 1688–1858', in Devine (ed.), *Scottish elites*, p. 27.
22 BUL, Pinney papers, box 30 bundle 2, letter and agreement from James Grant to Peter Baillie, 10 June 1805.
23 BUL, Pinney papers, box 30 bundle 1, Evan Baillie to Peter Baillie, 10 August 1806; Evan Baillie to Peter Baillie, 28 August 1806.
24 BUL, Pinney papers (domestic), Evan Baillie to Peter Baillie, 13 June 1804.
25 R. G. Thorne (ed.), *The History of Parliament: The House of Commons, 1790–1820* (London: History of Parliament Trust, 1986), vol. 3, pp. 110–11; P. Marshall, *Bristol and the abolition of slavery* (Bristol: Historical Association, Bristol Branch, 1975); R. Pares, *A West-India fortune* (London: Longmans, Green & Co., 1950), p. 213.
26 T. M. Devine, 'The emergence of a new elite in the Western Highlands and Islands, 1800–80', in T. M. Devine (ed.), *Improvement and Enlightenment* (Edinburgh: John Donald, 1989), pp. 111, 137.
27 *British parliamentary papers: Slave trade 87: Papers relating to negro apprenticeship slavery and the abolition of the slave trade* (Shannon: Irish Universities Press, 1969), pp. 166, 173, 191, 206, 229, 384–6, 392, 396.
28 Devine, 'The emergence of a new elite', pp. 108–42.
29 Macinnes, 'Landownership, land use and elite enterprise', pp. 26–7; Macinnes, 'Scottish Gaeldom from clanship to commercial landlordism', p. 179; *OSA*, vol. 17, pp. 93–4, 96;
30 J. Strang, *Glasgow and its clubs, or glimpses of the condition, manners, characters and oddities of the city during the past and present century* (London and Glasgow: Richard Griffen & Co., 1856), p. 129.
31 *Ibid.*, pp. 128–51; Macinnes, 'Landownership, land use and elite enterprise', p. 22; H. C. G. Matthew and B. Harrison (eds), *Oxford dictionary of national biography* (Oxford: Oxford University Press, 2004), vol. 19, pp. 607–8.
32 Lists of the members of the Caledonian Hunt and officers of the Grand Lodge of Scotland, can be found in the *Edinburgh Almanack and Scots Register*. The 1795 edition, for example, records William McDowall as treasurer of the Caledonian Hunt, along with members Andrew and Alexander Houstoun. Andrew Houstoun was grand warden of the Grand Lodge.
33 T. M. Devine, 'The colonial trades and industrial investment in Scotland, c. 1700–1815', *Economic History Review*, 29, 1 (1976), 11.
34 *Ibid.*, 7–8; Devine, 'An eighteenth-century business elite', 55–65; *Journals of the House of Commons*, 55 (1799–1800), 428, 'General abstract of the affairs of the house of Messrs. Alexander Houstoun & Co. . . . ', 28 April 1800.
35 GCA, T-SK22/2, Stirling of Keir papers, James Stirling to William Stirling, 5 September 1766.
36 Devine, 'The colonial trades and industrial investment', 4–5, 11.
37 Devine, 'An eighteenth-century business elite', 55–65.
38 NAS, GD126/9, bundle 1, Balfour–Melville papers, Messrs John & James Hamilton to Lieutenant-General Robert Melville, 30 July 1790; GD267/7/1(7), Home of Wedderburn manuscripts, Ninian Home to John Campbell Sen., 29 May 1787; InvM, Letterbook of George Inglis, letter to Messrs John Campbell & Co., 18 March 1801.
39 BUL, Pinney papers (domestic), Evan Baillie to Peter Baillie, 13 June 1804; Devine, 'An eighteenth-century business elite', 58.
40 NLS, MS8793(4), Alexander Houstoun & Co. papers, foreign letterbook E, letter to Frederick Corsar, 4 March 1776; MS 8793(31), letter to David McFarlane, 19 April 1776; MS8793(54–5), letter to Walter McFarlane; NAS, GD267/7/1(24), Ninian Home to Alexander Stevenson, 26 June 1787; *Journals of the House of Commons*, vol. 55 (1799–1800), 428, 'General abstract of the affairs of the house of Messrs. Alexander Houstoun & Co.'
41 A full list of subscribers 1799–1825 can be found on a plaque in the lobby of the Northern Infirmary, Inverness.
42 IRA, A1(4–6), Directors' minute book, 1787–98, minutes of a committee meeting, 29 January 1787.

43 D. Withrington, 'Education and society in the eighteenth century', in N. T. Phillipson and R. Mitchison (eds), *Scotland in the age of improvement* (Edinburgh: Edinburgh University Press, 1970), pp. 177–9; *OSA*, vol. 17, p. 99.
44 IRA, A1(1–2), (4–6), Directors' minute book 1787–98, minutes of a committee meeting, 29 January 1787. The *clachnacuddin* is a symbol particularly associated with Inverness. Literally a 'washing stone', it was the communal washing place in the River Ness.
45 *OSA*, vol. 17, p. 98; IRA, A1, Directors' minute book, 1787–98.
46 IRA, A1(19), William Mackintosh to John MacGillvray, 4 March 1787.
47 IRA, A1(16–17), William Mackintosh to James Baillie and Lewis Cuthbert, 16 February 1787.
48 IRA, A1(130–1), Lewis Cuthbert to William Mackintosh, 17 July 1791.
49 IRA, A1(197), advertisement, 29 June 1792.
50 *Ibid.*; IRA, A1(163), William Mackintosh to M. John Hoyes, 2 February 1792.
51 IRA, A2(143), Directors' minutes, 1787–1847, Highland Society of London to the directors of the academy, 9 January 1802.
52 IRA, B1, Class registers, 1804–10; *OSA*, vol. 17, p. 99.
53 IRA, A1(49, 86), lists of subscribers, 1789; B1, Class registers, spring 1804, autumn 1804, autumn 1805.
54 R. W. Munro and J. Munro, *Tain through the centuries* (Tain: Tain Town Council, 1966); I. R. W. Mowat, *Easter Ross 1750–1850: The double frontier* (Edinburgh: John Donald, 1981), pp. 42, 123.
55 HSP, 1582/29B, box 2 folder 3, Powell collection, papers of Alexander Johnston, Alexander Johnston to James Johnston, 24 June 1783.
56 HSP, 1582/29B, box 2 folder 3, Alexander Johnston to James Johnston, 14 September 1783, 16 February 1784.
57 A. Morgan, *The rise and progress of Scottish education* (Edinburgh and London: Oliver & Boyd, 1927), pp. 115–16.
58 A. J. O'Shaughnessy, *An empire divided: The American Revolution and the British Caribbean* (Philadelphia: University of Pennsylvania Press, 2000), pp. 20–1. J. M. Flavell, ' "The school for modesty and humility": Colonial American youth in London and their parents, 1755–1775', *Historical Journal*, 42, 2 (1999), 377–403.
59 IRA, B1, Class registers, 1804–10.
60 NAS, CS96/1526, Court of Session, unextracted processes, journal of a Glasgow merchant, fols 91, 96, 104, 113, 115, 120, 123, 133, 144, 153, 163, 165; J. Evans, 'African/Caribbeans in Scotland: A socio-geographical study', PhD thesis, University of Edinburgh, 1996, p. 77.
61 Evans, 'African/Caribbeans in Scotland', pp. 43, 52–82; P. Fryer, *Staying power: The history of black people in Britain* (London: Pluto Press, 1987), pp. 2–3. See also William Dunbar's poem 'On ane black-moir ladye' of 1507.
62 Evans, 'African/Caribbeans in Scotland', pp. 52–63.
63 P. J. Anderson (ed.), *Fasti Academiae Marischallanae Aberdonensis: Selections from the records of the Marischal College and University, 1593–1860* (Aberdeen: New Spalding Club, 1898), vol. 2, pp. 85–6, 114–16, 340–402.
64 P. B. Wood, *The Aberdeen Enlightenment: The arts curriculum in the eighteenth century* (Aberdeen: Aberdeen University Press, 1993), pp. 61–80.
65 P. J. Anderson (ed.), *Officers and graduates of University and King's College, Aberdeen, 1495–1860* (Aberdeen: New Spalding Club, 1893), pp. 128–44, 244–74; W. I. Addison (ed.), *The matriculation albums of the University of Glasgow, from 1728 to 1858* (Glasgow: J. Maclehose and Sons, 1913); Anon., *List of graduates in medicine in the University of Edinburgh, from 1705–1866* (Edinburgh: Neill and Co., 1867); R. B. Sheridan, *Doctors and slaves: A medical and demographic history of slavery in the British West Indies, 1680–1834* (Cambridge: Cambridge University Press, 1985), pp. 58–61.
66 Anon., *Graduates in medicine in the University of Edinburgh*; Addison, *Matriculation albums of the University of Glasgow*; P. J. Anderson (ed.), *Roll of alumni in arts of the University and King's College of Aberdeen, 1496–1860* (Aberdeen: New

Spalding Club, 1900); Anderson (ed.), *Officers and Graduates of University and King's College*; Anderson (ed.), *Fasti Academiae Marischallanae*.

67 For Liverpool see *Gore's Liverpool Directory* for 1766, 1767, 1773 and 1777. For provincial England see Macinnes, 'Scottish Gaeldom from clanship to commercial landlordism', p. 176; R. Rocher and M. E. Scorgie, 'A family empire: The Alexander Hamilton cousins, 1750–1830', *Journal of Imperial and Commonwealth History*, 23, 2 (1995), 202–5.
68 BUL, Pinney papers, Simon Fraser to Peter Baillie, 4 November 1807.
69 L. Namier and J. Brooke (eds), *The History of Parliament: The House of Commons, 1754–1790* (London: History of Parliament Trust, 1964), vols 1–3; Thorne (ed.), *House of Commons, 1790–1820*, vols 1, 3–5.
70 Anderson (ed.), *Officers and graduates of University and King's College*, p. 139.
71 V. L. Oliver, *Caribbeana, being miscellaneous papers relating to the history, genealogy, topography and antiquities of the British West Indies* (London: Mitchell, Hughes and Clarke, 1909–19), vol. 2, p. 274.
72 InvM, Letterbook of George Inglis, letter to Evan Baillie, 6 April 1802.
73 *Ibid.*
74 Oliver, *Caribbeana*, vol. 1, pp. 22, 26–7, 29, 76–7; vol. 2, pp. 186, 188, 232.
75 NLS, MS5513(67), Liston papers, James Baillie to Robert Liston, 12 November 1767.
76 UASCA, MS1160/6/16, Gordon of Cairness papers, Alexander Forbes to Charles Gordon, 28 September 1781.
77 'Obituary of James Baillie', *Gentleman's Magazine*, 63 (September 1793), 869.
78 OSA, vol. 17, p. 106.
79 D. Hancock, *Citizens of the world: London merchants and the integration of the British Atlantic community, 1735–85* (Cambridge: Cambridge University Press, 1995), p. 56.
80 Henry Laurens to Michael Herries, 27 June 1771, in G. C. Roger *et al.* (eds), *The papers of Henry Laurens* (Columbia, SC: University of South Carolina Press, 1968–92), vol. 7, p. 542; PRO, CO104/3(52), Grenada, sessional papers, minutes of the general assembly of Grenada, 17 February 1769; NAS, CS96/1526(38, 97), Court of Session, unextracted processes, journal of a Glasgow merchant.
81 Devine, 'Glasgow colonial merchants and land', p. 206.

CONCLUSION

To make the transition from a Scotland in a state of flux to a Caribbean beset by enormous challenges, Scots drew on the support and patronage of their networks. These groupings were, at their most fundamental level, based on precisely the kind of social relations within kinships that had characterised Scottish society for generations. More significantly, these apparently archaic forms of social relations, under attack at home, were adapted to provide the springboard for Scottish influence in what was regarded as a truly modern imperial enterprise. In the Caribbean, the networks operated in a context where Scots were, at least by the period in question, considered to be integral parts of the white minority communities. Indeed, they could scarcely be considered anything but central to the white population of the Windward Islands.

Networks based on ties of kinship (broadly defined) and local association underpinned virtually all Scottish activity in the West Indies in the later eighteenth century. Although based on long-standing connections, they were sufficiently flexible to accommodate different layers of involvement. The eighteenth-century Scots in the Caribbean needed to be able to shift between a number of contexts. They were not just an 'ethnic' group. Networks of Scots were highly complex and adaptable phenomena which were at once familial, Scottish, British and Atlantic. As a result of the activity of the networks, the Scottish–Caribbean interaction emerges as a dynamic and symbiotic relationship, as an underpinning of the Atlantic world as a transnational world of exchanges.

As influential members of the colonial elite, especially in the Windward Islands, Scots made important contributions to the political stance adopted by the islands in response to perceived injustices perpetrated by the imperial government and its governors, as well as to the threats from the American and French revolutions. The response to governmental plans to introduce Catholics to the Grenada legislature, for example, wore a particularly Scottish aspect. The widespread anti-Catholicism prevalent in Protestant, and especially Presbyterian, Scotland during this period was evident on the other side of the Atlantic.

Away from the political sphere, Scots, as an important group in the white elite, significantly affected the eighteenth-century Caribbean. Throughout much of the later part of the century, the medical profession in the British West Indies was dominated by Scottish and Scottish-trained doctors. Although not all medics were highly qualified, or necessarily motivated by a desire to improve the lot of the enslaved, Scots played an important role in furthering medical advances in the islands, and in communicating them to Britain.

Scots and their firms contributed to the extension of credit and mercantile facilities which fostered an increase in the production of Caribbean staples. Significantly for the Caribbean, Scots who made money in the islands almost overwhelmingly sought to remove it, and to make their long-term investments in Britain. As production was increased, so too was demand for enslaved Africans. Not only were Scots active users of enslaved labour, and occasionally willing suppliers of it, but they also conducted a series of affairs with enslaved women. While some Scots took responsibility for the children of these relationships by providing manumission and bequeathing legacies, it is also the case that many did not. But the return to Scotland of those who did literally changed the face of Scottish society.

This impact on Scotland, as well as the impacts of the application of colonial profits, was felt across the country. Investments in land and industry in Scotland fostered upward social mobility for merchants and gentry, while the attraction of large profits drew in powerful aristocratic families, and in turn fostered the coalescence of the mercantile, landed and industrial elites. Investments were also made in education. These brought money into schools and helped finance the establishments of new institutions, which in turn were able to supply the empire with a stock of 'usefully educated' young people.

The relationship affected both parties, and it casts new light on the functioning of the empire. In a British context, the increasing coalescence of the elite provided opportunities for Scots to advance in British and imperial politics. Key Scottish politicians, from the Argethalian managers to Henry Dundas, formed focal points for the distribution of patronage. Yet this integration was more widespread than simply acceptance by a few politically astute individuals in London. The Baillie family's dispersal around Britain is indicative of the ability of Scots to settle and prosper south of the border. And just as Scottish penetration of the highest echelons of the imperial government was predicated on the influence of Scots in London, so the increasing importance of their role in the empire heightened their prestige on the metropolitan stage.

In a wider sense, the Scottish–Caribbean interaction throws into sharp relief the idea of the imperial relationship as a process of accommodation. The colonial elite of the Caribbean, of which Scots were an integral part, was determined to remain British and part of the empire,

CONCLUSION

but it was not prepared to accept unquestioningly the decisions and opinions emanating from London. In political terms, this much is apparent from the conflicts between the island legislatures and the governors, and between the colonists and London, over issues like the voting of supply and the levying of taxes. Notions of colonial agency, or at least of the white elite, and of a process of accommodation went beyond the political sphere to suffuse the entire relationship between colony and metropole.

The management of long-distance transatlantic trade necessitated a considerable devolution of responsibility on to the satellite firms. As a result, parent companies were not always in control of their mercantile strategies, a situation which sometimes had disastrous results. The role of doctors in transmitting medical and scientific information between the Caribbean and Scotland offers another example of the interaction at work. White Caribbean doctors, predominantly Scottish-trained, travelled to the islands to attend to needs of the population there. But the spirit of enquiry fired by their attendance at enlightened centres in Scotland led them to pursue medical and botanical discovery in the Caribbean. They used networks formed in the universities and associated organisations to send back colonial intelligence that advanced knowledge in the metropole.

These kinds of connections were the essential bonds that held together the Atlantic world. This was a world in which events on one shore of the ocean impacted on events on the other. For Scots this was not so much a nexus between provinces marginal to England as a transnational world that allowed its citizens and their goods, finances, and ideas to be transferred around and between the colonial empires of different European powers.

BIBLIOGRAPHY

Manuscripts

Aberdeen City Archives
Baillie Court: propinquity books, 1637–1797

American Philosophical Society, Philadelphia
APS, 361 5a2, records of the St Andrew's Society of Philadelphia

Bristol University Library
Pinney papers
DM41, West Indies MSS, Westerhall papers
DM78-7, West Indies papers
DM470, Society of Merchant Venturers of Bristol: books of proceedings, 1605–1900
DM1061, Papers of Captain David Duncomb
DM1781/BRA2630, West Indies MSS, sale of Belmont estate, Grenada

Glasgow City Archives
T-SK, Stirling of Keir papers

Highland Council Archives, Inverness
D456, Baillie of Dunain papers
Inverness Royal Academy minute book, 1798–1823

Historical Society of Pennsylvania, Philadelphia
462/Am.111, Orr, Dunlope & Glenhome letterbook, 1767–69
1582/29B, Powell collection, papers of Alexander Johnston
1688/149.L.S, MacPherson family papers: correspondence

Inverness Museum
Letterbook of George Inglis, 1801–03

Inverness Royal Academy
A1, Directors' minute book, 1787–98
A2, Directors' minutes, 1787–1847
B1–2, Class registers

Jamaica Archives, Spanish Town
IB/II, Jamaica inventories

BIBLIOGRAPHY

The National Archives, Public Record Office, Kew

CO71/1, Dominica, original correspondence: Board of Trade, 1770–76
CO71/2, Dominica, original correspondence: secretary of State, 1730–1801
CO71/26, Dominica, original correspondence
CO72/3, Dominica, entry books: letters to the secretary of State, 1770–79
CO72/6, Dominica, entry books: précis of correspondence, 1794–97
CO74/1, Dominica, sessional papers, minutes of the council, 1767–70
CO74/3, Dominica, sessional papers, minutes of the assembly, 1769–76
CO74/6A, Dominica, sessional papers: minutes of the council and assembly, 1786–90
CO74/6B, Dominica, sessional papers: extracts of minutes of the council, 1771–91
CO101/1–7, Grenada, original correspondence: Board of Trade
CO101/14, Grenada, original correspondence: Secretary of State, 1769–70
CO101/19, Grenada, original correspondence: Secretary of State, 1775–76
CO101/25, Grenada, original correspondence: Secretary of State, 1784
CO101/30-4, Grenada, original correspondence: Secretary of State
CO102/15–16, Grenada, entry books: letters from the Secretary of State
CO104/1–3, Grenada, sessional papers
CO106/1, Grenada, miscellanea: shipping returns 1764–67
CO106/9–12, Grenada, miscellanea: papers relating to the sale of lands in the Ceded Islands
CO142/31, Jamaica, miscellanea: list of landholders in the island of Jamaica, 1754
CO152/68, Leeward Islands, original correspondence
CO260/1, St Vincent, original correspondence: Board of Trade, 1773–78
CO260/7, St Vincent, original correspondence: Secretary of State, 1783–86
CO260/13, St Vincent, original correspondence: Secretary of State, 1794–96
CO261/6, St Vincent, entry books, précis of correspondence, 1794–97
CO263/1–3, St Vincent, sessional papers
CO263/21, St Vincent, sessional papers: minutes of the assembly, 1786–93
CO285/1, Tobago, original correspondence: Board of Trade, 1778–81
CO285/3–4, Tobago, original correspondence: Secretary of State
CO288/1–3, Tobago, sessional papers
CO318/8, West Indies, original correspondence: Secretary of State
CO441/10/9, Papers, correspondence and plans: Baillie

T71/266, 268, 273-6, 279-80, 284-5, 290-1, 299, 301, 305-6, 320-1, 323, slave registers, 1817–33

National Archives of Scotland, Edinburgh

CS96, Court of Session, unextracted processes
GD1, Miscellaneous accessions
GD21, Cuninghame of Thornton muniments
GD22, Cunninghame–Graham papers
GD23, Bught papers
GD34, Abercairney papers

GD44, Gordon Castle muniments
GD51, Melville Castle muniments
GD121, Murthly Castle muniments
GD126, Balfour–Melville papers
GD128, Fraser–MacIntosh papers
GD160, Drummond Castle papers
GD205, Ogilvy of Inverquharity papers
GD224, Buccleuch papers
GD225, Leith Hall muniments
GD237/12, Macdouall of Garthland papers
GD248, Seafield muniments
GD267, Home of Wedderburn manuscripts
GD345, Grant of Monymusk muniments

National Library of Jamaica, Kingston
MS179, Letterbook of George Ferguson
MS287, Acts of the assembly of the island of Jamaica 1681–1791
MS375, Letters to Sir William Young and Alexander Gordon of Tobago
MS577, Letters of Charles Hamilton of Montego Bay
MS1066, Fotheringham indentures, 1788
MS1204, Fodringham indenture
MS1235, Lease for Moor Park plantation, St James's
MS1236, Conveyance of release of Tivoli estate
MS1655, Fyffe family letters, 1750–1821

National Library of Scotland, Edinburgh
MS17, 21, 22, 60, 1075, 3835, 3844, 6524, 9370, 14828, Melville papers
MS1284, Delvine papers, Grant of Ballindalloch
MS5513–15, 5538, 5555, 5704–5, 5599, Liston papers
MS8793–800, 8895–6, Alexander Houstoun & Co. papers
MS10924–5, Graham of Airth papers, Jamaican papers
Map Library, EMAM.s. 5–7, J. Robertson, 'Map of the counties of Surrey, Middlesex and Cornwall in the island of Jamaica', 1804
Acc. 11910, Haldane papers

National Maritime Museum, Greenwich
DOU/6, Papers of Admiral Sir James Douglas

University of Aberdeen, Special Collections and Archives
MS661, Letter collection: miscellaneous accessions
MS966/1–10, Letters of Lord Adam Gordon, 1783–95
MS1160, Gordon of Cairness papers
MS2070, Journal of Jonathan Troup, 1789–90
MS2226/1/-351, Taylor manuscripts
MS2769, Davidson & Garden archive
MS3027, Journal of Jonathan Troup

MS3175, Duff House papers
MS3575, Papers of Murray families, 1753–1859
MS3652, Shand papers

Printed primary sources

Aberdeen Journal
Blackwood's Edinburgh Magazine
Calendar of state papers, colonial series, America and the West Indies
Edinburgh Almanack and Scots Register
Edinburgh Evening Courant
Edinburgh Review
Gentleman's Magazine
Gore's Liverpool Directory
Hansard's parliamentary history of England
House of Lords sessional papers (reprinted, New York: Oceana Publications, 1974)
Inverness Journal and Northern Advertiser
Journals of the House of Commons
Philosophical Transactions of the Royal Society
Scots Magazine
St. George's Chronicle and New Grenada Gazette

Books and articles

Addison, W. Innes, *The matriculation albums of the University of Glasgow, from 1728 to 1858*, Glasgow, 1913
Agnew, L. R. C., 'Scottish medical education', in C. D. O'Malley (ed.), *The history of medical education*, Los Angeles, 1970
Akenson, Donald H., *If the Irish ran the world: Montserrat, 1630–1730*, Liverpool, 1997
Anderson, Benedict, *Imagined communities: Reflections on the origins and spread of nationalism*, London and New York, 1991
Anderson, J., *Prize essay on the state of society and knowledge in the Highlands of Scotland*, Edinburgh, 1827
Anderson, P. J. (ed.), *Officers and graduates of University and King's College, Aberdeen, 1495–1860*, Aberdeen, 1893
Anderson, P. J. (ed.), *Fasti Academiae Marischallanae Aberdonensis: Selections from the records of the Marischal College and University, 1593–1860*, Aberdeen, 1898
Anderson, P. J. (ed.), *Roll of alumni in arts of the University and King's College, Aberdeen, 1496–1860*, Aberdeen, 1900
Anon., *Considerations on the state of the sugar islands, and on the policy of enabling foreigners to lend money on real securities in those colonies*, London, 1773

BIBLIOGRAPHY

Anon., *A plain state of the argument between Great Britain and her colonies*, London, 1775

Anon., *An account of the island of Jamaica, with reflections on the treatment, occupation and provisions of the slaves*, Newcastle, 1788

Anon., *A brief enquiry into the causes of, and conduct pursued by the colonial government, for quelling the insurrection in Grenada*, London, 1796

Anon., 'Present state of West India affairs', *Edinburgh Review*, 28 (1817), 340–71

Anon., 'Strictures on an article in no. LVI of the Edinburgh Review, entitled "Present state of West India affairs"', *Blackwood's Edinburgh Magazine*, 7, 2(1817), 41–6

Anon., *The British poets*, vol. 59: *The poems of Grainger and Boyse*, Chiswick, 1822

Anon., *A catalogue of the graduates in the faculties of Arts, Divinity and Law in the University of Edinburgh since its foundation*, Edinburgh, 1858

Anon., *A view of the Merchants' House of Glasgow*, Glasgow, 1866

Anon., *List of graduates in medicine in the University of Edinburgh, from 1705–1866*, Edinburgh, 1867

Anon., 'The rise of Glasgow's West Indian trade, 1793–1818', *Three Banks Review*, 51 (1961), 34–44

Anon., 'An early Glasgow-West Indian miscellany', *Three Banks Review*, 54 (1962), 29–38

Anon., *Monumental inscriptions, chapel burial ground Inverness*, Inverness, 1996

Armitage, David, 'The Scottish vision of empire: Intellectual origins of the Darien venture', in J. Robertson (ed.), *A union for empire: Political thought and the Union of 1707*, Cambridge, 1995

Armitage, David, 'Making the empire British: Scotland in the Atlantic world, 1542–1707', *Past and Present*, 155 (1997), 34–63

Armitage, David, 'Greater Britain: A useful category of historical analysis?', *American Historical Review*, 104, 2 (1999), 427–46

Armitage D., and Braddick, M. (eds), *The British Atlantic world, 1500–1800*, Basingstoke, 2002

Armytage, Frances, *The freeport system in the British West Indies: A study in commercial policy, 1766–1822*, London, 1953

Arnold, David (ed.), *Imperial medicine and indigenous societies*, Manchester, 1988

Atwood, Thomas, *The history of the island of Dominica*, London, 1791

Bailyn, Bernard, *Voyagers to the west: A passage in the peopling of America on the eve of the revolution*, London, 1987

Bailyn, Bernard, 'The idea of Atlantic history', *Itinerario*, 20 (1996), 19–44

Bailyn, B., and Morgan, P. D. (eds), *Strangers within the realm: Cultural margins of the first British Empire*, Chapel Hill, 1991

Barclay, H. F., *A history of the Barclay family with pedigrees from 1067 to 1933*, 3 vols, London, 1933

BIBLIOGRAPHY

Baugh, Daniel A., *British naval administration in the age of Walpole*, Princeton, 1965
Bayly, C. A., *Imperial meridian: The British Empire and the world, 1780–1830*, London, 1989
Beckles, Hilary M., '"Black men in white skins": The formation of a white proletariat in West Indian society', *Journal of Imperial and Commonwealth History*, 15, 1 (1986), 5–21
Beckles, H., and Shepherd, V. (eds), *Caribbean slave society and economy*, New York, 1991
Blackburn, Robin, *The making of New World slavery: From the Baroque to the modern 1492–1800*, London, 1997
Boney, A. D., *The lost gardens of Glasgow University*, London, 1988
Bowen, H. V., *Elites, enterprise and the making of overseas empire, 1688–1775*, Basingstoke, 1996
Bowen, H. V., 'British conceptions of global empire, 1756–83', *Journal of Imperial and Commonwealth History*, 26, 3 (1998), 1–27
Boyd, Walter, *Letter to the creditors of the house of Boyd, Benfield & Co.*, London, 1800
Brathwaite, E., *The development of Creole society in Jamaica, 1770–1820*, Oxford, 1971
Brewer, J., *The sinews of power: Money, war and the English state, 1688–1783*, London, 1989
Brewer, J., and Porter R. (eds), *Consumption and the world of goods*, London, 1993
British parliamentary papers: Slave trade 87: Papers relating to negro apprenticeship slavery and the abolition of the slave trade, Shannon, 1969
Broadie, Alexander (ed.), *The Scottish Enlightenment: An anthology*, Edinburgh, 1997
Bryant, G. J., 'Scots in India in the eighteenth century', *Scottish Historical Review*, 64, 1 (1985), 22–41
Buettner, Elizabeth, 'Haggis in the Raj: Private and public celebrations of Scottishness in late imperial India', *Scottish Historical Review*, 81, 2 (2002), 212–39
Bull, Ida, 'Merchant households and their networks in eighteenth-century Trondheim', *Continuity and Change*, 17, 2 (2002), 213–31
Bumsted, J. M., *The people's clearance: Highland emigration to British North America, 1770–1815*, Edinburgh and Winnipeg, 1982
Burnard, Trevor, 'European migration to Jamaica, 1655–1780', *William and Mary Quarterly*, 53, 4 (1996), 769–96
Bush, Barbara, 'White "ladies", coloured "favourites" and black "wenches": Some considerations on sex, race and class factors in social relations in white Creole society in the British Caribbean', *Slavery and Abolition*, 2 (1981), 245–62
Cage, R. A., *The Scots abroad*, London, 1985
Cain, P. J., and Hopkins, A. G., *British imperialism*, vol. 1: *Innovation and expansion, 1688–1914*, London, 1993

BIBLIOGRAPHY

Calder, Angus, *Revolutionary empire*, New York, 1981
Callander, R. F., *A pattern of landownership in Scotland*, Finzean, 1987
Cameron, V. R. (ed.), *Emigrants from Scotland to America, 1774–1775*, Baltimore, 1965
Campbell, John, *A political survey of Britain, being a series of reflections on the situation, lands, inhabitants, revenues, colonies, and commerce of this island*, 2 vols, London, 1774
Campbell, R. H., 'An economic history of Scotland in the eighteenth century', *Scottish Journal of Political Economy*, 11 (1964), 17–24
Campbell, R. H., *Scotland since 1707: The rise of an industrial society*, Edinburgh, 1985
Canny, Nicholas (ed.), *The Oxford history of the British Empire*, vol. 1: *The origins of empire*, Oxford, 1998
Carmichael, A. C., *Domestic manners and social conditions of the white, coloured and negro populations of the West Indies*, London, 1833
Carrington, S. H. H., 'The American Revolution and the British West Indies' economy', *Journal of Interdisciplinary History*, 17, 4 (1987), 823–50
Cathcart, Alison, 'Patterns of kinship and clanship: The MacIntoshes of clan Chattan, 1291–1609', PhD thesis, University of Aberdeen, 2001
Checkland, S. G., 'Two Scottish West India liquidations after 1793', *Scottish Journal of Political Economy*, 4 (1957), 127–43
Checkland, S. G., 'Finance for the West Indies, 1780–1815', *Economic History Review*, 10 (1957), 461–9
Checkland, S. G., *Scottish banking: A history, 1695–1973*, Glasgow and London, 1975
Clayton, T. R., 'Sophistry, security and socio-political structures in the American Revolution; or, why Jamaica did not rebel', *Historical Journal*, 29, 2 (1986), 319–44
Chisholm, C., *An essay on the malignant pestilential fever introduced into the West Indian islands from Boullam*, London, 1801
Christie, O. F. (ed.), *The diary of William Jones, 1777–1821*, London, 1929
Clark, James, *A treatise on the yellow fever, as it appeared in the island of Dominica in the years 1793–96*, London, 1797
Clive, J. and Bailyn, B., 'England's cultural provinces: Scotland and America', *William and Mary Quarterly*, 11 (1954), 200–13
Clyde, D. F., *Two centuries of health care in Dominica*, New Delhi, 1980
Cochran, L. E., *Scottish trade with Ireland in the eighteenth century*, Edinburgh 1985
Colley, Linda, *Britons: Forging the nation, 1707–1837*, London, 1994
Collins, Dr, *Practical rules for the management and treatment of negro slaves in the sugar colonies*, 1803; Freeport, 1971
Comrie, J. D., *History of Scottish medicine*, London, 1927
Cooper, J. C., *A Cooper family from north east Angus*, Elmvale, 1992
Cope, S. R., *Walter Boyd: A merchant banker in the age of Napoleon*, London, 1983
Cope, Z., 'The private medical schools of London, 1746–1914', in F. N. L. Poynter (ed.), *The evolution of medical education in Britain*, Baltimore, 1966

BIBLIOGRAPHY

Cowton, C. J., and O'Shaughnessy, A. J., 'Absentee control of sugar plantations in the British West Indies', *Accounting and Business Research*, 22, 85 (1991), 33–45

Cox, Edward L., 'Fedon's Rebellion 1795–96: Causes and consequences', *Journal of Negro History*, 67, 1 (1982), 7–19

Craig, W. S., *History of the Royal College of Physicians of Edinburgh*, Oxford, 1976

Craton, Michael, *Testing the chains: Resistance to slavery in the British West Indies*, Ithaca, 1982

Craton, M., and Walvin, J., *A Jamaican plantation: The history of Worthy Park, 1670–1970*, London, 1970

Crosby, Alfred W., *Ecological imperialism: The biological expansion of Europe, 900–1900*, Cambridge, 1986

Cumberland, Richard, *The West Indian: a comedy*, London, 1771

Cundall, F. (ed.), *Lady Nugent's journal*, London, 1939

Dalzel, Archibald, *The history of Dahomey: An inland kingdom of Africa, 1793*; London, 1967

Dancer, Thomas, *A short dissertation on the Jamaica Bath waters*, Kingston, 1784

Darragh, J., 'The Catholic population of Scotland since the year 1680', *Innes Review*, 4 (1953), 49–59

Davis, Ralph, 'English foreign trade, 1700–1774', *Economic History Review*, 15, 2 (1962), 285–303

Davis, Ralph, *The rise of the Atlantic economies*, Ithaca, 1973

Devine, Thomas M., 'Glasgow colonial merchants and land, 1770–1815', in J. T. Ward and R. G. Wilson (eds), *Land and industry: The landed estate and the industrial revolution*, Newton Abbot, 1971

Devine, Thomas M., 'Transport problems of Glasgow–West India merchants in the American War of Independence, 1775–83', *Transport History*, 4, 3 (1971), 266–304

Devine, Thomas M., 'Sources of capital for the Glasgow tobacco trade, c. 1740–1780', *Business History*, 16, 2 (1974), 113–29

Devine, Thomas M., *The tobacco lords: A study of the tobacco merchants of Glasgow and their trading activities, c. 1740–1790*, Edinburgh, 1975

Devine, Thomas M., 'The colonial trades and industrial investment in Scotland, c. 1700–1815', *Economic History Review*, 29, 1 (1976), 1–13

Devine, Thomas M., 'An eighteenth-century business elite: Glasgow–West India merchants, c. 1750–1815', *Scottish Historical Review*, 57 (1978), 40–67

Devine, Thomas M., *The transformation of rural Scotland: Social change and the agrarian economy, 1600–1815*, Edinburgh, 1994

Devine, Thomas M., *Clanship to crofters' war: The social transformation of the Scottish Highlands*, Manchester, 1994

Devine, Thomas M., *Scottish Nation 1700–2000*, London, 1999

Devine, Thomas M., *Scotland's empire, 1600–1815*, London, 2003

Devine, Thomas M. (ed.), *A Scottish firm in Virginia, 1767–1777*, Edinburgh, 1984

Devine, Thomas M. (ed.), *Improvement and Enlightenment*, Edinburgh, 1989

BIBLIOGRAPHY

Devine, Thomas M. (ed.), *Scottish elites*, Edinburgh, 1994
Devine, T. M., and Jackson, G. (eds), *Glasgow*, vol. 1: *Beginnings to 1830*, Manchester, 1995
Devine, T. M., and Mitchison R. (eds), *People and society in Scotland*, vol. 1: *1760–1830*, Edinburgh, 1988
Devine, T. M., and Young, J. R. (eds), *Eighteenth-century Scotland: New perspectives*, East Linton, 1999
Dobson, David, *Scottish emigration to colonial America, 1607–1785*, Athens, GA, 1994
Dodgshon, R. A., *Land and society in early Scotland*, Oxford, 1981
Doig, A. et al., *William Cullen and the eighteenth-century medical world*, Edinburgh, 1993
Donald, Diana, *The age of caricature: Satirical prints in the reign of George III*, New Haven, 1996
Donaldson, Gordon, *The Scots overseas*, London, 1966
Donovan, R. K., 'Voices of distrust: The expression of anti-Catholic feeling in Scotland, 1778–81', *Innes Review*, 30 (1979), 62–76
Drescher, Seymour, *Econocide: British slavery in the age of abolition*, Pittsburgh, 1977
Dunn, Richard S., *Sugar and slaves: The rise of the planter class in the English West Indies, 1624–1713*, Chapel Hill, 1972
Dunn, Richard S., 'A tale of two plantations: Slave life at Mesopotamia in Jamaica and Mount Airy in Virginia', *William and Mary Quarterly*, 34, 1 (1977), 32–65
Durie, Alistair J., 'The markets for Scottish linen, 1730–1775', *Scottish Historical Review*, 52 (1973), 30–49
Durie, Alistair J., *The Scottish linen industry*, Edinburgh, 1979
Durie, Alistair J., *The British Linen Company, 1745–75*, Edinburgh, 1996
Dwyer, J. et al., *New perspectives on the politics and culture of early modern Scotland*, Edinburgh, 1982
Edwards, Bryan, *The history, civil and commercial, of the British colonies in the West Indies*, London, 1801, 1819
Eltis, David, *The rise of African slavery in the Americas*, Cambridge, 2000
Eltis, David et al., *The trans-Atlantic slave trade: A database on CD-ROM*, Cambridge, 1999
Evans, June, 'Africans/Caribbeans in Scotland: A socio-geographical study', PhD thesis, University of Edinburgh, 1996
Fagerstrom, Dalphy I., 'Scottish opinion and the American Revolution', *William and Mary Quarterly*, 11 (1954), 252–75
Farnie, Douglas A., 'The commercial empire of the Atlantic, 1607–1783', *Economic History Review*, 15, 2 (1962), 205–18
Ferguson, W., *Scotland, 1689 to the present*, Edinburgh, 1994
Feurtado, W. A., *Official and other personages of Jamaica, from 1655 to 1790*, Kingston, 1896
Flavell, Julie, ' "The school for modesty and humility": Colonial American youth in London and their parents, 1755–75', *Historical Journal*, 42, 2 (1999), 377–403

BIBLIOGRAPHY

Forbes, E., *An inaugural lecture on botany, considered as a science and a branch of medical education*, London, 1843
Foster, J., *Pedigree of the county families of Yorkshire*, 3 vols, London, 1874
Fraser, W., *Memoirs of the Maxwells of Pollock*, Edinburgh, 1863
Fraser-MacIntosh, Charles (ed.), *Letters of two centuries, chiefly connected with Inverness and the Highlands, from 1616 to 1815*, Inverness, 1890
Fry, Michael, *Patronage and principle*, Aberdeen, 1987
Fry, Michael, *The Dundas despotism*, Edinburgh, 1992
Fry, Michael, *Scottish empire*, East Linton, 2001
Fryer, Linda G., 'Robert Barclay of Ury and East New Jersey', *Northern Scotland*, 15 (1995), 1–17
Fryer, P., *Staying power: The history of black people in Britain*, London, 1987
Games, Alison, *Migration and the origins of the English Atlantic world*, Cambridge, MA, 1999
Geggus, David, 'Yellow fever in the 1790s: The British army in occupied St Domingue', *Medical History*, 23, 1 (1979), 38–58
Geyer-Kordesch, J., 'Comparative difficulties: Scottish medical education in the European context, c. 1690–1830', in V. Nutton and R. Porter (eds), *The history of medical education in Britain*, Amsterdam, 1995
Gibb, Andrew D., *Scottish empire*, London, 1937
Goodyear, J. D., 'The sugar connection: A new perspective on the history of yellow fever', *Bulletin of the History of Medicine*, 52, 1 (1978)
Gordon, Lord Adam, 'Journal of an officer who travelled in America and the West Indies in 1764 and 1765', in N. D. Meereness (ed.), *Travels in the American colonies*, New York, 1916
Gordon, J. F. S., *Glasgow: ancient and modern*, Glasgow, 1872
Gould, Eliga H., 'American independence and Britain's counter-revolution', *Past and Present*, 154 (1997), 107–141
Gould, Eliga H., 'A virtual nation: Greater Britain and the imperial legacy of the American Revolution', *American Historical Review*, 104, 2 (1999), 476–89
Gould, Eliga H., *The persistence of empire: British political culture in the era of the American Revolution*, Chapel Hill, 2000
Goveia, Elsa V., *Slave society in the British Leeward Islands at the end of the eighteenth century*, New Haven, 1965
Graham, I. C. C., *Colonists from Scotland: Emigration to North America, 1707–1783*, Ithaca, 1956
Grainger, J., *An essay on the more common West-India diseases; and remedies which that country itself produces*, London, 1764
Grant, A., and Stringer, K. J. (eds), *Uniting the kingdom? The making of British history*, London, 1995
Grant, F. J. (ed.), *Register of marriages in the city of Edinburgh*, Edinburgh, 1922
Gray, Malcolm, 'Scottish migration: The social impact of agrarian change in the rural lowlands, 1775–1875', *Perspectives in American History*, 7 (1973), 95–176

BIBLIOGRAPHY

Gray, Malcolm, *Scots on the move: Scottish migrants 1750–1914*, Edinburgh, 1990

Greene, Jack P., 'Changing identity in the British Caribbean: Barbados as a case study', in N. Canny and A. Pagden (eds), *Colonial identity in the Atlantic world, 1500–1800*, Princeton, 1987

Greene, Jack P., *Pursuits of happiness: The social development of early modern British colonies and the formation of American culture*, Chapel Hill and London, 1988

Greene, Jack P., 'The Jamaica privilege controversy, 1764–66: An episode in the process of constitutional definition in the early modern British Empire', *Journal of Imperial and Commonwealth History*, 22, 1 (1994), 15–63

Griffin, Patrick, *The people with no name: Ireland's Ulster Scots, America's Scots Irish, and the creation of a British Atlantic world, 1689–1764*, Princeton and Oxford, 2001

Griffiths, N. E. S., and Reid, J. G., 'New evidence on New Scotland, 1629', *William and Mary Quarterly*, 49, 3 (1992), 492–508

Grove, Richard H., *Green imperialism: Colonial expansion, tropical island edens and the origins of environmentalism, 1600–1800*, Cambridge 1995

Habermas, Jurgen, *The structural transformation of the public sphere*, London, 1989

Hall, Douglas (ed.), *In miserable slavery: Thomas Thistlewood in Jamaica, 1750–1786*, London, 1989

Hamilton, David, *The healers: A history of medicine in Scotland*, Edinburgh, 1981

Hamilton, Douglas J., 'Patronage and profit: Scottish networks in the British West Indies, c. 1763–1807', PhD thesis, University of Aberdeen, 1999

Hamilton, Douglas, 'Private enterprise and public service: Naval contracting in the Caribbean, 1720–50', *Journal for Maritime Research* (April 2004), www.jmr.nnm.ac.uk

Hamilton, H., 'The founding of the Glasgow Chamber of Commerce, 1783', *Scottish Journal of Political Economy*, 1 (1954), 33–48

Hancock, David, *Citizens of the world: London merchants and the integration of the British Atlantic community, 1735–1785*, Cambridge, 1995

Hancock, David, 'Commerce and conversation in the eighteenth-century Atlantic: The invention of Madeira wine', *Journal of Interdisciplinary History*, 39, 2 (1998), 197–219

Hancock, David, 'The British Atlantic world: coordination, complexity, and the emergence of an Atlantic market economy, 1651–1815', *Itinerario*, 23, 2 (1999), 107–26

Hargreaves, John D., *Aberdeenshire to Africa: Northeast Scots and British overseas expansion*, Aberdeen, 1981

Harlow, V., and Madden, F., *British colonial development, 1774–1834: Select documents*, Oxford, 1953

Harper, Marjory, *Emigration from north-east Scotland*, vol. 1: *Willing exiles*, Aberdeen, 1988

BIBLIOGRAPHY

Harris, Bob, "'American idols': Empire, war and the middling ranks in mid-eighteenth-century Britain', *Past and Present*, 150 (1996), 111–43

Henige, D. P. (ed.), *Colonial governors from the fifteenth century to the present*, Madison, 1970

Hibbert, Christopher, *King Mob: The story of Lord George Gordon and the riots of 1780*, London, 1958

Higman, Barry W., 'The West India "interest" in Parliament, 1807–1833', *Historical Studies*, 13, 1 (1967), 1–19

Higman, Barry W. (ed.), *Trade, government and society in Caribbean history, 1700–1920*, Kingston, 1983

Hobsbawm E., and Ranger, T. (eds), *The invention of tradition*, Cambridge, 1983

Hook, Andrew, *Scotland and America: A study of cultural relations, 1750–1835*, Glasgow and London, 1975

Hough, S. L., and Hough, P. R. O. (eds), *The Beinecke Lesser Antilles collection at Hamilton College, 1521–1860*, Gainesville, 1994

House of Assembly of Jamaica, *Proceedings of the Honourable House of Assembly of Jamaica in the sugar and slave trade*, London, 1793

Houston, R. A., 'The literacy myth? Illiteracy in Scotland, 1630–1760', *Past and Present*, 96 (1982), 81–102

Houston, R. A., and Whyte I. D. (eds), *Scottish society, 1500–1800*, Cambridge 1989

Hulme, P., and Whitehead, N. L. (eds), *Wild majesty: Encounters with Caribs from Columbus to the present day*, Oxford, 1992

Humboldt, Alexander von, *Personal narrative of travels to the equinoctial regions of America, during the years 1799–1804*, trans. T. Ross, London, 1852

Hunter, James, *The making of the crofting community*, Edinburgh, 1995

Hunter, P. W., *Purchasing identity in the Atlantic world: Massachusetts merchants 1670–1780*, Ithaca and London, 2001

Hyam, Ronald, 'Imperial interests and the Peace of Paris (1763)', in R. Hyam and G. Martin (eds), *Reappraisals in British imperial history*, London, 1975, 21–43

Inikori, J. E., *Africans and the industrial revolution in England: A study in international trade and development*, Cambridge, 2002

Inikori, J. E., and Engerman, S. L. (eds), *The Atlantic slave trade*, Durham, SC, 1992

Insh, George P., *Scottish colonial schemes, 1620–1686*, Glasgow, 1922

Israel, J. L., 'A conflict of empires: Spain and the Netherlands, 1618–1648', *Past and Present*, 76 (1977), 34–74

Jenkinson, J., *Scottish medical societies, 1731–1939: Their history and records*, Edinburgh, 1993

Judd, Gerrit P. (ed.), *Members of Parliament, 1734–1832*, New Haven, 1955

Karras, Alan L., 'The world of Alexander Johnston: The creolization of ambition, 1762–1787', *Historical Journal*, 30, 1 (1987), 53–76

Karras, Alan L., *Sojourners in the sun: Scottish migrants in Jamaica and the Chesapeake, 1740–1800*, Ithaca, 1992

BIBLIOGRAPHY

Karras, A. L., and McNeill, J. R. (eds), *Atlantic American societies: From Columbus through abolition, 1492–1888*, London and New York, 1992

Kidd, Colin, 'North Britishness and the nature of eighteenth-century patriotism', *Historical Journal*, 39, 2 (1996), 361–82

Kidd, Colin, 'The ideological significance of Robertson's *History of Scotland*', in S. J. Brown (ed.), *William Robertson and the expansion of empire*, Cambridge, 1997

Laidlaw, Zoë, 'Networks, patronage and information in governance: Britain, New South Wales and the Cape Colony, 1826–1843', DPhil thesis, University of Oxford, 2001

Landsman, Ned C., *Scotland and its first American colony, 1683–1765*, Princeton, 1985

Landsman, Ned C., *From colonials to provincials: American thought and culture, 1680–1760*, New York, 1998

Landsman, Ned C., 'Nation, migration and province in the first British Empire: Scotland and the Americas, 1600–1800', *American Historical Review*, 104, 2 (1999), 463–75

Landsman, Ned C. (ed.), *Nation and province in the first British Empire: Scotland and the Americas, 1600–1800*, Lewisburg, PA, and London, 2001

Latimer, J., *The history of the Society of Merchant Venturers of the city of Bristol*, 1903; New York, 1970

Law, Robin, 'The first Scottish Guinea company, 1634–39', *Scottish Historical Review*, 76, 2 (1997), 185–202

Lawrence-Archer, J. H., *Monumental inscriptions of the British West Indies*, London, 1875

Lawson, Philip, *The imperial challenge: Quebec and Britain in the age of the American Revolution*, Montreal, 1989

Lenman, Bruce P., *An economic history of modern Scotland 1660–1976*, London, 1977

Lenman, Bruce P., *Integration and Enlightenment: Scotland 1746–1832*, Edinburgh, 1981

Lillywhite, Bryant (ed.), *London coffee houses*, London, 1963

Long, Edward, *The history of Jamaica, or general survey of the antient and modern state of that island*, 1774; London, 1970

Macinnes, Allan I., 'A strategy for history: Inaugural lecture', *Aberdeen University Review*, 192 (1994), 349–60

Macinnes, Allan I., *Clanship, commerce and the House of Stuart, 1603–1788*, East Linton, 1996

Macinnes, Allan I., 'Scottish Gaeldom from clanship to commercial landlordism, c. 1600–c. 1850', in S. Foster, A. I. MacInnes and R. McInnes (eds), *Scottish power centres*, Glasgow, 1999

Macinnes, Allan I., Harper, M. D., and Fryer, L. G. (eds), *Scotland and the Americas: A documentary source book*, Edinburgh 2002

MacKay, J., *RB: A biography of Robert Burns*, Edinburgh, 1992

MacKenzie, John M., 'Essay and reflection: On Scotland and the empire', *International History Review*, 15, 4 (1993), 714–39

BIBLIOGRAPHY

MacKenzie, John M., *Empires of nature and the nature of empires: Imperialism, Scotland and the environment*, East Linton, 1997

MacKenzie, John M., 'Empire and national identities: The case of Scotland', *Transactions of the Royal Historical Society*, 6th series, 8 (1998), 215–31

Mackillop, A., and Murdoch S. (eds), *Military governors and imperial frontiers c. 1600–1800: A study of Scotland and empires*, Leiden, 2003

MacLaren, A. A., 'Patronage and professionalism: The 'forgotten middle class' 1760–1860', in D. McCrone et al. (eds), *The making of Scotland: Nation, culture and social change*, Edinburgh, 1989

MacLeod, R., and Lewis, M. (eds), *Disease, medicine and power: Perspectives on western medicine and the experience of European expansion*, London and New York, 1988

MacMillan, D. S., *Scotland and Australia 1788–1850: Emigration, commerce and investment*, Oxford, 1967

MacMillan, D. S., 'The 'new men' in action: Scottish mercantile and shipping operations in the North American colonies, 1760–1825', in D. S. MacMillan (ed.), *Canadian business history: Selected studies*, Toronto, 1972

Marshall, P., *Bristol and the abolition of slavery*, Bristol, 1975

Marshall, Peter J., 'Britain and the world in the eighteenth century, i: Reshaping the empire', *Transactions of the Royal Historical Society*, 6th series, 8 (1998), 1–18

Marshall, Peter J., 'Who cared about the Thirteen Colonies? Some evidence from philanthropy', *Journal of Imperial and Commonwealth History*, 27, 2 (1999), 52–67

Marshall, Peter J., 'Britain and the world in the eighteenth century, iv: The turning outwards of Britain', *Transactions of the Royal Historical Society*, 6th series, 11 (2001), 1–15

Marshall, Peter J. (ed.), *The Oxford history of the British Empire*, vol. 2: *The eighteenth century*, Oxford, 1998

Martin, R. M., *History of the West Indies, comprizing Jamaica, Honduras, Trinidad, Tobago, Grenada, the Bahamas and the Virgin Isles*, London, 1836

Matheson, D. L., 'Freemasonry in St Christopher's island 1739–1983', *Year Book of the Grand Lodge of Antient Free and Accepted Masons of Scotland* (1984), 78–80

Matthew, H. C. G., and Harrison, B. (eds), *Oxford dictionary of national biography*, Oxford, 2004

McCusker, J. J., and Morgan, K. (eds), *The early modern Atlantic economy*, Cambridge, 2001

McCusker, J. J., 'Weights and measures in the colonial sugar trade', *William and Mary Quarterly*, 30, 4 (1973), 599–624

McCusker, J. J., *Money and exchange in Europe and America, 1660–1775*, Chapel Hill, 1978

McCusker, J. J. (ed.), *Essays in the economic history of the Atlantic world*, London and New York, 1997

BIBLIOGRAPHY

McDonald, Roderick A. (ed.), *West Indies accounts: Essays on the history of the British Caribbean and the Atlantic economy in honour of Richard B. Sheridan*, Barbados, 1996

McDonald, Roderick A. (ed.), *Between slavery and freedom: Special Magistrate John Anderson's journal of St Vincent during the apprenticeship*, Kingston and Philadelphia, 2001

McFarlane, Anthony, *The British in the Americas 1480–1815*, London, 1994

McGrath, Patrick (ed.), *A Bristol miscellany*, Bristol, 1985

Meinig, D. W., *The shaping of America*, vol. 1: *Atlantic America*, New Haven, 1986

Minchinton, W. E. (ed.), *The trade of Bristol in the eighteenth century*, Bristol, 1957

Minchinton, W. E., *The port of Bristol in the eighteenth century*, Bristol, 1962

Minchinton, W. E., *Politics and the port of Bristol in the eighteenth century: The petitions of the Society of Merchant Venturers*, Bristol, 1963

Mintz, Sidney, *Sweetness and power: The place of sugar in modern history*, New York, 1985

Mitchell, B. R., and Deane, P. (ed.), *Abstract of British historical statistics*, Cambridge, 1962

Mitchison, Rosalind, *Agricultural Sir John: The life of Sir John Sinclair of Ulbster, 1754–1835*, London, 1962

Morgan, A., *The rise and progress of Scottish education*, Edinburgh and London, 1927

Morgan, Kenneth, *Bristol and the Atlantic trade in the eighteenth century*, Cambridge, 1993

Morton, A. G., *History of botanical science*, London, 1981

Morton, A. G., *John Hope, 1725–1786: Scottish botanist*, Edinburgh, 1986

Mosley, C. (ed.), *Burke's peerage and baronetage*, Crans, 1999

Mouser, Bruce L., 'Trade, coasters and conflict in the Rio Pongo from 1790–1808', *Journal of African History*, 14, 1 (1973), 45–64

Mowat, I. R. W., *Easter Ross 1750–1850: The double frontier*, Edinburgh, 1981

Munck, W. (ed.), *The roll of the Royal College of Physicians of London*, 2 vols, London, 1878

Munn, Charles W., *The Scottish provincial banking companies, 1747–1864*, Edinburgh, 1981

Munro, R. W., and Munro, J., *Tain through the centuries*, Tain, 1966

Murdoch, Alexander, *The people above: Politics and administration in mid-eighteenth-century Scotland*, Edinburgh, 1980

Murdoch, Alexander, 'Lord Bute, James Stuart MacKenzie and the government of Scotland', in K. Schweizer (ed.), *Lord Bute: Essays in re-interpretation*, Leicester, 1988, 117–46

Murdoch, Alexander, *British history 1660–1832: National identity and local culture*, Basingstoke, 1998

Murdoch, D. H., 'Land policy in the eighteenth-century British Empire: The sale of Crown lands in the Ceded Islands, 1763–1783', *Historical Journal*, 27, 3 (1984), 549–74

BIBLIOGRAPHY

Murdoch, Steve W., *Britain, Denmark-Norway and the House of Stuart, 1603–60*, East Linton, 2000
Namier, L., *The structure of politics at the accession of George III*, London, 1957
Namier, L., *Crossroads of power: Essays on eighteenth-century England*, London, 1962
Namier, L., and Brooke J. (eds), *The History of Parliament: The House of Commons, 1754–1790*, London, 1964
Nicolas, Armand, *Histoire de la Martinique, des Arawaks à 1848*, Paris and Montreal, 1996
Oliver, Vere L., *Caribbeana, being miscellaneous papers relating to the history, genealogy, topography and antiquities of the British West Indies*, 6 vols, London, 1909–19
Olson, Alison, G., 'The Board of Trade and London-American interest groups in the eighteenth century', *Journal of Imperial and Commonwealth History*, 8, 2 (1980), 33–50
O'Shaughnessy, Andrew J., 'The Stamp Act crisis in the British Caribbean', *William and Mary Quarterly*, 51, 2 (1994), 203–26
O'Shaughnessy, Andrew J., 'The formation of a commercial lobby: The West India interest, British colonial policy and the American Revolution', *Historical Journal*, 40, 1 (1997), 71–95
O'Shaughnessy, Andrew J., *An empire divided: The American Revolution and the British Caribbean*, Philadelphia, 2000
Pacquette, R. L., and Engerman, S. L. (eds), *The Lesser Antilles in the age of European expansion*, Gainesville, FL, 1996
Pares, Richard, *A West-India fortune*, London, 1950
Pares, Richard, 'The London sugar market, 1740–1769', *Economic History Review*, 9 (1956), 252–70
Pares, Richard, 'A London West India merchant house, 1740–69', in R. Pares and A. J. P. Taylor (eds), *Essays presented to Sir Lewis Namier*, London, 1956
Parker, Anthony W., *Scottish Highlanders in colonial Georgia: The recruitment, emigration and settlement at Darien, 1735–1748*, Athens, GA, 1997
Parry, J. H., 'The patent offices of the British West Indies', *English Historical Review*, 69 (1954), 200–25
Pearson, R., and Richardson, D., 'Business networking in the industrial revolution', *Economic History Review*, 54, 4 (2001), 657–79
Penson, Lillian M., 'The London West India interest in the eighteenth century', *English Historical Review*, 36 (1921), 373–92
Penson, Lillian M., *The colonial agents of the British West Indies: A study in colonial administration, mainly in the eighteenth century'*, 1924; London, 1971
Phillipson, Nicholas, 'The Scottish Enlightenment', in R. Porter and M. Teich (eds), *The enlightenment in national context*, Cambridge, 1981
Phillipson, N., and Mitchison R. (eds), *Scotland in the age of improvement*, Edinburgh, 1970
Pine, L. G. (ed.), *Burke's landed gentry*, London, 1952

BIBLIOGRAPHY

Pocock, J. G. A., 'British history: A plea for a new subject', *New Zealand Journal of History*, 8, 1 (1974), 3–21

Pocock, J. G. A., 'The limits and divisions of British history: In search of the unknown subject', *American Historical Review*, 87, 2 (1982), 311–36

Pocock, J. G. A., 'The new British history in Atlantic perspective: An Antipodean commentary', *American Historical Review*, 104, 2 (1999), 490–500

Pope, D. J., 'Shipping and trade in the port of Liverpool, 1783–1793', PhD thesis, University of Liverpool, 1970

Price, J. M., 'The rise of Glasgow in the Chesapeake tobacco trade, 1707–1775', *William and Mary Quarterly*, 11 (1954), 179–99

Price, J. M., *Capital and credit in British overseas trade: The view from the Chesapeake*, Cambridge, MA, 1980

Price, J. M., 'Buchanan & Simson, 1759–63: A different kind of Glasgow firm trading to the Chesapeake', *William and Mary Quarterly*, 40, 1 (1983), 3–41

Price, J. M., 'What did merchants do? Reflections on British overseas trade, 1660–1790', *Journal of Economic History*, 44, 2 (1989), 267–84

Price, R., and Price, S. (eds), *Stedman's Surinam: Life in an eighteenth-century slave society*, Baltimore, 1992

Quier, John, et al., *Letters and essays on the small pox and inoculation*, London and Edinburgh, 1778

Quintanilla, Mark, 'The world of Alexander Campbell: An eighteenth-century Grenadian planter', *Albion*, 35, 2 (2003), 229–56

Ragatz, L. J., 'Absentee landlordism in the British Caribbean, 1750–1833', *Journal of Agricultural History*, 5, 1 (1931), 7–24

Ragatz, L. J., *The fall of the planter class in the British Caribbean, 1763–1833*, 1928; New York, 1981

Rice, C. Duncan, 'Abolitionists and abolitionism in Aberdeen: A test case for the nineteenth-century abolition movement', *Northern Scotland*, 1, 1 (1972), 65–87

Richards, Eric, *A history of the Highland clearances*, London, 1985

Richardson, D., 'The slave trade, sugar and British economic growth, 1748–1776', *Journal of Interdisciplinary History*, 17, 4 (1987), 739–70

Riddell, Maria, *Voyages to the Madeira, and Leeward Caribbean islands*, Edinburgh and London, 1792

Robertson, John, *The Scottish Enlightenment and the militia issue*, Edinburgh, 1985

Robertson, M. L., 'Scottish commerce and the American War of Independence', *Economic History Review*, 9 (1956), 123–31

Roby, John, *Members of the assembly of Jamaica, from the institution of that branch of the legislature to the present time*, Montego Bay, 1831

Rocher, R., and Scorgie, M. E., 'A family empire: The Alexander Hamilton cousins, 1750–1830', *Journal of Imperial and Commonwealth History*, 23, 2 (1995), 189–210

Roger, G. C., et al. (eds), *The papers of Henry Laurens*, Columbia, SC, 1968–92

Rollo, John, *Observations on the means of preserving and restoring health in the West-Indies*, London, 1783

BIBLIOGRAPHY

Rosner, Lisa, *Medical education in the age of improvement*, Edinburgh, 1991

Rudé, George, 'The Gordon Riots: A study of the rioters and their victims', in G. Rudé, *Paris and London in the eighteenth century*, New York, 1971

Saville, Richard, *Bank of Scotland: A history 1695–1995*, Edinburgh, 1996

Schaw, Janet, *Journal of a lady of quality, being the narrative of a journey from Scotland to the West Indies, North Carolina and Portugal in the years 1774 to 1776*, ed. E. W. Andrews and C. M. Andrews, New Haven, 1923

Scott, H., *Fasti eccelsiae Scoticanae*, Edinburgh, 1928

Seal Coon, F., 'Scottish freemasonry in Jamaica', *Year Book of the Grand Lodge of Antient Free and Accepted Masons of Scotland* (1982), 100–3

Sedgwick, R. (ed.), *Letters of George III to Lord Bute, 1756–1766*, London, 1939

Seton, B. G., and Arnott, J. G., *The prisoners of the 45*, Edinburgh, 1928

Seymour, S., Daniels, S., and Watkins, C., 'Estate and empire: Sir George Cornewall's management of Moccas, Hertfordshire and La Taste, Grenada, 1771–1819', *Journal of Historical Geography*, 24, 3 (1998), 313–51

Shephard, Charles, *An historical account of the island of St Vincent*, London, 1831

Shepherd, Verene A., 'Pens and pen-keepers in a plantation society: Aspects of Jamaican economic and social history, 1740–1815', PhD thesis, University of Cambridge, 1988

Shepherd, Verene A. (ed.), *Slavery without sugar: Diversity in Caribbean society and economy since the seventeenth century*, Gainesville, FL, 2002

Sher, R. B., and Smitten, J. R. (eds), *Scotland and America in the age of the Enlightenment*, Edinburgh, 1990

Sheridan, Richard B., 'The commercial and financial organisation of the British slave trade, 1750–1807', *Economic History Review*, 11 (1958), 249–63

Sheridan, Richard B., 'The credit crisis of 1772 and the American colonies', *Journal of Economic History*, 20, 2 (1960), 161–86

Sheridan, Richard B., 'The rise of a colonial gentry: A case study of Antigua, 1730–1775', *Economic History Review*, 13, 3 (1961), 342–57

Sheridan, Richard B., 'The wealth of Jamaica in the eighteenth century', *Economic History Review*, 18, 2 (1965), 292–311

Sheridan, Richard B., *Sugar and slavery: An economic history of the British West Indies, 1623–1775*, Barbados, 1974

Sheridan, Richard B., 'The role of Scots in the economy and society of the West Indies', in V. Rubin and A. Tuden (eds), *Comparative perspectives on slavery in New World plantations*, New York, 1977

Sheridan, Richard B., *Doctors and slaves: A medical and demographic history of slavery in the British West Indies, 1680–1834*, Cambridge, 1985

Simmons, R. C., and Thomas, P. D. G. (eds), *Proceedings and debates of the British parliaments respecting North America, 1754–1783*, Millwood, NY, 1983

Simpson, Grant G. (ed.), *Scotland and Scandinavia, 800–1800*, Edinburgh, 1990

Simpson, Grant G. (ed.), *The Scottish soldier abroad, 1247–1967*, Edinburgh, 1992

Simpson, Grant G. (ed.), *Scotland and the Low Countries, 1124–1994*, East Linton, 1996

Sinclair, Sir John, *The statistical account of Scotland, 1791–1799*, ed. D. J. Withrington and I. R. Grant, Wakefield, 1975–83

Slaven, Anthony, *The development of the west of Scotland, 1750–1960*, London, 1975

Smith, S. D., '*Merchants and planters* revisited', *Economic History Review*, 15, 3 (2002), 434–65

Smith, Woodruff D., 'Complications of the commonplace: Tea, sugar and imperialism', *Journal of Interdisciplinary History*, 23, 2 (1992), 259–78

Smout, T. C., 'The early Scottish sugar houses, 1660–1720', *Economic History Review*, 14, 2 (1961), 240–53

Smout, T. C., 'Scottish landowners and economic growth, 1650–1850', *Scottish Journal of Political Economy*, 11 (1964), 218–34

Smout, T. C., *A history of the Scottish people 1560–1830*, London, 1969

Smout, T. C., Landsman, N. C., and Devine, T. M., 'Scottish migration in the seventeenth and eighteenth centuries', in N. Canny (ed.), *Europeans on the move: Studies in European migration 1500–1800*, Oxford, 1994

Sobel, Dava, *Longitude*, London, 1996

Sola-Corbacho, J. C., 'Family, *paisanaje*, and migration among Madrid's merchants (1750–1800)', *Journal of Family History*, 27, 1 (2002), 3–24

Solow, Barbara L. (ed.), *Slavery and the rise of the Atlantic system*, Cambridge, 1991

Stearns, R. P., 'Colonial fellows of the Royal Society of London, 1661–1778', *William and Mary Quarterly*, 3, 1 (1946), 208–68

Steele, Ian K., *The English Atlantic 1675–1740: An exploration of communication and community*, New York and Oxford, 1986

Stewart, J., *A view of the past and present state of the island of Jamaica*, 1823; New York, 1969

Stone, L. (ed.), *An imperial state at war*, London and New York, 1994

Strang, J., *Glasgow and its clubs, or glimpses of the condition, manners, characters and oddities of the city, during the past and present century*, London and Glasgow, 1856

Sumpter, E., *The British antidote to the Caledonian poison, consisting of the most satirical prints for the year 1762–3*, London, 1763

Sunter, Ronald M., *Patronage and politics in Scotland, 1707–1832*, Edinburgh, 1986

Taylor, C. (ed.), 'Journeys through the Caribbean', unpublished transcript, IHR

Thomas, P. D. G., *British politics and the Stamp Act crisis: The first phase on the American Revolution, 1763–67*, Oxford, 1975

Thomas, Robert P., 'The sugar colonies of the old empire: Profit or loss for Great Britain?', *Economic History Review*, 21, 1 (1968), 30–45

Thorne, R. G. (ed.), *The History of Parliament: The House of Commons, 1790–1820*, London, 1986

Thornton, A. P., *West India policy under the Restoration*, Oxford, 1956

Tilly, Charles, 'Transplanted networks', in V. Yans-McLaughlin (ed.), *Immigration reconsidered: History, sociology and politics*, New York and Oxford, 1990

BIBLIOGRAPHY

Timperley, L. A. (ed.), *A directory of landownership in Scotland, c. 1770*, Edinburgh, 1976

Turnbull, G., *Letters to a young planter, or observations on the management of a sugar plantation*, London, 1785

Vance, James, 'Constitutional radicalism in Scotland and Ireland in the age of the American Revolution, c. 1760–1789', PhD thesis, University of Aberdeen, 1998

Walvin, James, *Black ivory: A history of British slavery*, London, 1992

Walvin, James, *Fruits of empire: Exotic produce and British taste, 1660–1800*, Basingstoke, 1997

Ward, J. R., *West Indian slavery, 1750–1834: The process of amelioration*, Oxford, 1988

Ward, J. R., 'The industrial revolution and British imperialism, 1750–1850', *Economic History Review*, 47, 1 (1994), 44–65

Watson, Charles B. B. (ed.), *Register of Edinburgh apprentices, 1666–1755*, Edinburgh, 1929

Watson, M., 'The British West Indian legislatures in the seventeenth and eighteenth centuries: An historiographical introduction', in P. Lawson (ed.), *Parliament and the Atlantic empire*, Edinburgh 1995

Watts, Sheldon, *Epidemics and history: Disease, power and imperialism*, New Haven, 1997

Williams, Eric, *Capitalism and slavery*, Chapel Hill, 1945

Williamson, John, *Medical and miscellaneous observations, relative to the West India islands*, Edinburgh, 1817

Wilson, Kathleen, 'Inventing revolution: 1688 and eighteenth-century popular politics', *Journal of British Studies*, 28 (1989), 349–86

Wilson, Kathleen, *The sense of the people: Politics, culture and imperialism in England, 1715–1785*, Cambridge, 1995

Withers, Charles W. J., 'Improvement and Enlightenment: Agriculture and natural history in the work of the Rev. John Walker (1731–1801)', in P. Jones (ed.), *Philosophy and science in the Scottish Enlightenment*, Edinburgh, 1988

Wood, Marguerite (ed.), *Register of Edinburgh apprentices, 1756–1800*, Edinburgh, 1963

Wood, P. B., *The Aberdeen Enlightenment: The arts curriculum in the eighteenth century*, Aberdeen, 1993

Wright, W., 'Description and use of the cabbage-bark tree of Jamaica', *Philosophical Transactions of the Royal Society*, 67 (December 1777), 507–11

Wright, W., 'Description of the Jesuits bark tree', *Philosophical Transactions of the Royal Society*. 67 (December 1777), 504–6

Young, William, *Considerations which may tend to promote the settlement of our new West-India colonies, by encouraging individuals to embark on the undertaking*, London, 1764

Zacek, Natalie, A., 'Sex, sexuality, and social control in the eighteenth-century Leeward Islands', in M. D. Smith (ed.), *Sex and sexuality in colonial America, 1492–1800*, New York, 1998

Zuckerman, Michael, 'The fabrication of identity in early America', *William and Mary Quarterly*, 34, 2 (1977), 183–214

INDEX

Aberdeen 3, 16, 23
absenteeism 38, 40, 62, 72–8, 90, 161, 209
academies 19, 204–9
 see also education
Act of Union (1707) 2, 3, 4, 19, 28, 93
Africa 1, 89, 100, 130, 186
Akers & Houstoun 87
Alexander Houstoun & Co. 45, 71, 84–8, 93–7, 101–5, 106, 182–5, 198, 204, 215, 217
American Revolution 159–62, 165, 221
Anderson, Alexander 132, 133
Anderson & Sutor 36
anti-abolition campaign 186–90
anti-Catholicism 153–9, 165, 221
 in Scotland 158–9
Antigua 3, 5, 24, 41, 48, 60, 69, 91, 113–14, 123, 126, 196
Argyll 56, 197–8, 200, 202
 Community in Jamaica 4, 55, 143–4
 Ilay Campbell, Third Duke of 19, 20, 215
 John Campbell, Second Duke of 19, 56
assemblies 141, 142
 privileges of 149–50, 151–3
 Scots in 143–65
Atwood, Thomas 34, 46

Baillie
 Alexander, of Dochfour 66, 89, 195
 Evan, of Dochfour 67, 71, 76, 90–2, 96, 98, 100, 106, 178–80, 182–5, 188, 199–200, 204, 213–14
 family 84, 88–93, 98, 178, 199, 222
 George 88, 96, 98–9, 106, 182–5
 James 1, 4, 41, 66, 67, 71, 88–9, 96, 98, 100, 105, 106, 156, 180–1, 182–5, 189, 206, 214–15
 James Evan 92, 201–2
 Peter 92, 178–80, 199–200
Balcarres, Alexander Lindsay, Sixth Earl of 37, 176
Bance Island 99, 188, 190
banks 85, 99, 105, 184–5, 198
Banks, Joseph 130–1, 134
Barbados 2, 3, 35, 44, 91, 152

Barclay
 George, of Cairness 57, 196
 James, of Cairness 57, 61, 112
Bath 195, 214
Beggars' Bennison 49
Bellefield estate, Demerara 71, 73
Belmont estate, Grenada 67, 78
Bequia 69, 147
Berbice 69, 92, 104, 131, 208
black people in Scotland 47, 209–10
book-keepers 18, 35, 40
botanic gardens 131–4
botany 129
Boyd, Benfield & Co. 104–5
Boyd, Walter 104
Brisbane, William, of Ayr 36, 70
Bristol 21, 67, 77, 91, 98, 178–80, 186, 187, 195, 200
 Scots in 212–14
British Guiana Association 92, 201
British Linen Company 15
Britishness 141, 153, 157, 158, 159–62, 165
Buchanan & Simpson 99–100
Burns, Robert 1
Bute, John Stuart, Third Earl of 20, 21, 170–1

Cameron, Archibald, of Fassfern 35
Campbell
 Alexander 38, 68, 90, 92, 152, 156, 164, 180–1, 215
 family 143
 John, Colonel 56, 61, 143–4
Campbell v. *Hall* 152–3, 160, 162
capital 28, 89, 98, 104, 105
Caribs 32, 33, 37, 162–4
Carolina 3, 4
 North 24
 South 48, 90
Carriacou 69, 98, 203, 204
Catholics 72, 141, 158–9
Ceded Islands *see* Windward Islands
Chesapeake 4, 94–5, 104
Chisholm, Dr Colin 71, 74, 119, 122, 126, 127, 128, 213–14

[245]

INDEX

Church of Scotland 48–9
clanship 5–6, 25–7, 55, 56
Clark, Dr James 117, 127, 128
clubs 95, 174, 187, 202
coal 16, 203
coffee 35
commission system 93, 96
convoys 103
cotton
  manufacturing 15, 98, 105, 203–4
  production 35
  trade 15, 98–9, 203–4
councils 141
  role of 142
  Scots in 143–65
Coutts, Thomas 173, 215
Crawfurd & Co. 104
credit 35, 95, 96, 101–3, 104, 105, 106, 221
Cruikshank, Patrick, of Stracathro 177–8, 191
Curaçao 3
Cuthbert, Lewis 115, 206

Dalzel, Archibald 187–8
Dalzell
  Frances 45
  Gibson 45
Dancer, Thomas 119, 127, 128, 132
Darien scheme 3, 4, 11, 55
debt 66, 102, 103, 104, 126, 182–5
Demerara 40, 69, 70, 71, 72, 93, 208
disease
  in the Caribbean 18, 47, 112, 119, 121–2, 127, 129
  in Scotland 17–18
Dochfour estate, Inverness 66, 199–200
doctors 18, 35, 112–35, 210, 223
  see also medicine
Dominica 2, 33, 41, 43, 44, 62, 53–6, 69, 100, 101, 118, 120, 121, 124, 129–30, 144, 146–9
Douglas, Admiral Sir James 36, 70
Dundas, Henry 19, 106, 153, 159, 163–4, 171–7, 178, 179, 180–1, 182–5, 190, 215, 222

East India Company 20, 181
East New Jersey 3
Edinburgh 1, 113, 158, 174, 175
education
  in the Caribbean 42–3
  in Scotland 18–19, 204–11
Edwards, Bryan 39, 141
Elder, Alexander 65, 67

Elgin 64–5, 71
Elphinstone, Dr William 59, 144
Evan Baillie & Co. *see* Baillie, Evan

Fedon's Rebellion 38–9, 74–6, 115
Fife, James Duff, Second Earl of 171, 176
Fillan, Dr Andrew 47, 117, 118, 120, 122, 123, 124
fishing 15, 89
Fitzmaurice, Ulysses 155–7
Florida 69
  East 57, 69, 170, 197
  West 74, 170
Fortrose 179–80, 208–9
Fraser, Alexander 67, 200
free people of colour 32, 36, 163
French in the Caribbean 33, 34, 37, 38, 40, 62, 72, 88, 153–6, 163–4, 175
French Revolution 162–4, 221
Frontier estate, Jamaica 76
Fullerton, Dr Alexander 114, 117, 121, 144
Fyffe, David 59, 61

George III 20, 162
George Baillie & Co. *see* Baillie, George, of Dochfour
Georgia 4, 48
ginger 35
Glasgow 4, 11, 15, 76, 77, 84, 87, 93–6, 96–8, 100, 101, 158, 186, 187, 203
Gordon
  Charles, of Buthlaw 58, 59–60, 73, 118
  James Brebner 69
  John, of Buthlaw 57
Governors 4, 142, 143, 151, 154, 162–3
  Scots as 173–7, 190
Graham
  family, of Airth 58, 199
  Robert 57, 151
Grainger, James 118, 121, 127, 133
Grant
  Sir Alexander, of Dalvey 57–8, 69, 114, 188, 215
  Sir Archibald, of Monymusk 14, 57–8, 69, 114, 197
  Francis 57–8, 59, 73, 144
  James, of Ballindalloch, General 57–8, 69, 170, 190
  James, of Bught 179, 200
  Sir James, of Grant 58, 61, 197
  John 60, 61, 67, 73, 144, 197
  Lewis 58
  Thomas 36, 70
  Dr Walter 114

INDEX

Grant, Oswald & Co. 99, 188
Greenock 1, 15, 23, 24, 25, 61, 100, 203
Grenada 1, 33, 36, 40, 62, 66–9, 71, 72, 74–6, 89–91, 96, 98, 100, 103, 105, 106, 115, 122, 129, 143, 144, 152–3, 153–9, 163–4, 173–5, 204

Hampden estate, Jamaica 37–8, 58, 76–7
Hermitage estate, Grenada 66, 67, 89
Highlands 13, 17, 20, 22, 25, 27, 56, 67, 199–201
Hogarth, William 20–1
Holland *see* Netherlands
Home
  George 68, 115, 123, 174–5, 184
  Ninian 38, 67, 68, 91, 153, 159, 163–4, 173–5, 203
Hope & Co. 88, 104, 106
Hope estate, Jamaica 47
House of Commons 21, 141, 182, 197
  Scots in 21–2, 183–4, 212
House of Lords 141
Houstoun
  Alexander Jun. 87–8, 90
  family 199
Houstoun & Paterson 87–8, 101, 102

improvement 12–14, 133, 196–200, 205
indigo 35, 69
industry 14–16, 28
  investment in 202–4, 222
Inglis
  George 40, 71, 73–4, 96, 98–9, 200, 203, 213–14
  Hugh 73–4, 96, 214
insurance 73, 86, 92, 102
Inverness 1, 88, 178–80, 196, 204–7
Irvine, Dr Charles 60, 87, 126

Jacobites 12, 20, 59, 154, 160
Jamaica 1, 2, 3, 4, 15, 23, 24, 33, 34, 37, 41, 42, 47, 48, 49, 55–61, 64, 73, 76–8, 86, 94, 100, 101, 112, 114, 116–17, 119, 120, 124–6, 128, 131, 132, 143–4, 149, 197
James Baillie & Co. *see* Baillie, James
J. E. Baillie, Fraser & Co. 92
Johnston, Dr Alexander 44, 48, 60, 67, 114–15, 116–17, 120–1, 122, 123, 124–5, 126, 208
Johnstone
  Alexander, of Westerhall 74, 184
  family, of Westerhall 74
  George, of Westerhall 74, 170
  see also Pulteney, William Johnstone

Jones, William 23, 39, 46
J. Petrie, Campbell & Co. 75–6, 96

King's College, Aberdeen 117, 126
  see also universities
Kingston, Jamaica 57, 86, 114
Kingstown, St Vincent 37, 64
kinship 5, 26–7, 68, 78, 116, 117, 173, 191, 209, 221
Knight v. *Wedderburn* 99, 189

Lambert, Blair & Co. 104
landownership
  in Jamaica 44
  in Scotland 196, 196–202, 222
  in the Windward Islands 62–4
Lascelles family, earls of Harewood 115, 198
Laurens, Henry 90, 100
Leith 23, 100
linen 15
Liston, Lady Henrietta 23, 41
Liverpool 21, 76, 98, 186, 187, 212
loans 59, 75, 182–5
lobbying 21, 169, 180–5, 191
London 76, 77, 96–8, 100, 104, 212
  Scots in 169, 214–15
Long, Edward 5, 42, 45, 55, 118, 119, 120, 127, 129, 132, 141, 144, 209
Lowlands 13, 18, 27
loyalists 70, 160–1
Lucky Hill estate, Jamaica 45, 72

McDowall
  James 187, 203, 204
  William, Colonel 45, 85, 94, 199
  William II, of Garthland 199
  William III, of Castlesemple 104, 183–5, 187, 198, 199, 203, 204
McGlashan, Dr Duncan 59, 114
MacKenzie, Kenneth Francis 38, 71, 164
Malcolm
  Donald, of Poltalloch 188
  Neil, of Poltalloch 197–8
Marischal College, Aberdeen 114, 117
  see also universities
Maroons 32, 37
marriage 26, 27, 45, 58, 90, 91, 92
Martinique 71, 91, 103
Masonic lodges 49
Maxwell
  Sir James, of Pollok 3
  Thomas 2–3
medicine 18

INDEX

medical societies 116, 117
  regulation of 118–20
  see also doctors
Melville, Robert, General 62, 64, 131–2, 146–9, 154–9, 165, 170, 203
merchants 4, 6, 45, 84–107
Mesopotamia estate, Jamaica 47
migration 22–5, 55–6
Milliken
  family 199
  James I 45, 85
  James II 94
miscegenation 32, 40, 46–8
  see also black people in Scotland
Montserrat 3
Mony Musk estate, Jamaica 45
mortality 40
Munro, Sir Alexander 179–80
Murray, James 112

Netherlands 3, 16, 70, 88, 104, 106
Nevis 3, 33, 84, 89, 91, 96, 101, 195
New York 4, 48
North America 22, 24, 25, 33, 35, 48, 49, 87, 101
Northbrook estate, Demerara 71, 98
Northern Infirmary, Inverness 67, 204
Nova Scotia 1, 2, 48
Nugent, Lady Maria 34, 45

Oswald, Richard 45, 188, 215

Paraclete estate, Grenada 68, 92
Paterson
  Fergus 87–8
  John 86–7
Paul, Robert 87, 104
Pelham, Henry 19
pharmacies 121, 122, 123
Philadelphia 48, 129
Pinney family 92
Pitt, William the Younger 106, 172, 176, 183
plantations 35, 55–78
  see also individual estates
political patronage 169–91
population growth 15, 16–17, 56
Port Antonio, Jamaica 1
Port Glasgow 23, 203
Pringle, Walter 64, 146, 148
professional contacts 116–17
Pulteney, Sir William Johnstone 74–5, 183–4
  see also Johnstone

Quebec 154, 170
Quier, Dr John 119, 123

racial hierarchies 23
Riddell, Maria 23
riots 150, 156–7, 158, 160
Rollo, John 127
Rose, Alexander 71
Roseau, Dominica 34, 44, 47, 63–4, 101, 117, 121, 124
Royal College of Physicians of Edinburgh 116, 117, 128, 134
Royal College of Physicians of London 116

St Andrew's Society of Philadelphia 48, 49
St Croix 44, 71, 98, 203
St Domingue 38, 103, 162–3
St Eustatius 43, 71, 88, 89, 90, 104
St George's, Grenada 38, 91
St John's, Antigua 41, 44, 171
St Kitts 4, 33, 45, 47, 49, 84, 87, 89, 94, 100, 150
St Lucia 2, 71
St Vincent 1, 33, 37, 43, 49, 62, 63–6, 69, 71, 87, 91, 96, 102–4, 105, 106, 144, 151–2, 164
satire 20, 21, 161
Schaw, Janet 4, 23, 39, 46, 49, 171, 209
Scots Magazine 33, 69, 157
Scottish Guinea Company 1–2
Scottophobia 20, 147, 216
Shand, John 48
Shetland 24
Simond & Hankey 75, 184
Sinclair, Brebner & Co. 85, 215
Sinclair, Sir John, of Ulbster 115
slaves 18, 32, 33, 35, 36, 43, 46, 70, 74, 76–8, 105, 112, 113, 121, 123, 129–30, 131, 143, 161, 222
  compensation for 201
  health of 123–4, 125
  revolts by 34, 37–9, 106, 162–4
slave trade 89–90, 99–101
  abolition of 76, 77, 180, 181, 185–90
Sloane, Sir Hans 127, 130
smallpox inoculation 17–18, 123
Smith, William 48
social rank 40–2
Spanish Town, Jamaica 41, 206
Stamp Act 150–1
  repeal of 171
Stephenson, Dr William 115, 122–4
Stewart, John 120

INDEX

Stirling
  Charles 58, 187
  James, of Keir 37–8, 76
  John, of Keir 76
  Robert, of Keir 76
  Thomas 58
store system 87, 94, 102
sugar
  consumption 17, 98
  monopoly 181
  prices 35, 89, 96–8
  production in Scotland 203
  trade 15, 35, 46, 89, 91, 93–8

tacksmen 12
Tacky's Rebellion 37
Tain 208–9
Thirteen Colonies *see* North America
Thistlewood, Thomas 36, 131
Thornton, Baillie & Campbell 91
tobacco
  lords 27, 84, 94–5
  trade 15, 94–5, 187, 202
Tobago 33, 34, 43, 49, 62, 63–6, 69, 87, 103–4, 144, 162, 175–6, 183, 189–90
Toussaint Louverture 38
Troup, Dr Jonathon 40, 43, 47, 117, 118, 120, 121–2, 129, 130–1, 163
Tullideph, Dr Walter 60, 113–14, 122, 126, 130, 196
Turnbull, William 113–14
Turner, Coll 87, 95
Turner & Co. 104
Turner & Paul 87, 101–2, 104

universities
  Aberdeen 116 *see also* King's College, Aberdeen; Marischal College, Aberdeen
  Edinburgh 116, 134–5, 216
  Glasgow 116, 134

St Andrews 116
  in Scotland 18, 112, 135, 205, 210–11
urbanisation 14–16

Virginia 100, 130
Virgin Islands 100

Walpole, Robert 19
Waltham estate, Grenada 68, 74–5, 78, 115–16, 122–4, 184
wars
  of American Independence (1776–83) 33–4, 69–70, 76, 91, 101–3, 162–3
  Anglo-Dutch War (1664–67) 2
  French Revolutionary and Napoleonic (1793–1815) 33–4, 70, 103, 105, 175, 200
  Seven Years War (1756–63) 20, 62, 91, 190
Wedderburn, John 59
Weilburg estate, Demerara 36, 70
Weir, John 64, 146–8
Westerhall estate, Grenada 74–6, 96, 97, 122, 184
white women 32, 43–8
Wilkes, John 20, 156
Williamson, Dr John 115, 119, 121, 125, 127, 133
Windward Islands 23, 24, 33, 34, 62–9, 72, 84, 115, 146, 221
  see also Dominica; Grenada; St Vincent; Tobago
Witherspoon, John 48, 161
Worthy Park estate, Jamaica 119, 123
Wright, Dr William 117, 128, 131, 134

Young, family of Delaford 65–6, 69
  Sir William, First Baronet 37, 66, 69, 146–9, 162
  Sir William, Second Baronet 66, 132–3, 189

EU authorised representative for GPSR:
Easy Access System Europe, Mustamäe tee 50,
10621 Tallinn, Estonia
gpsr.requests@easproject.com